Your Lie in April volume 9 is a work of fiction. Names, characters, places, and incidents are the products of the author's imagination or are used fictitiously. Any resemblance to actual events, locales, or persons, living or dead, is entirely coincidental.

A Kodansha Comics Trade Paperback Original

Published in the United States by Kodansha Comics, an imprint of Kodansha USA Publishing, LLC, New York.

Publication rights for this English edition arranged through Kodansha Ltd, Tokyo.

ISBN 978-1-63236-179-0

Special thanks:
Akinori Osawa, Rieko Ikeda, and Kaori Yamazaki

Printed in the United States of America.

www.kodanshacomics.com

9 8 7 6 5 4 3 2 1
Translation: Alethea and Athena Nibley
Lettering: Paige Pumphrey
Editing: Paul Starr
Kodansha Comics edition cover design by Phil Balsman

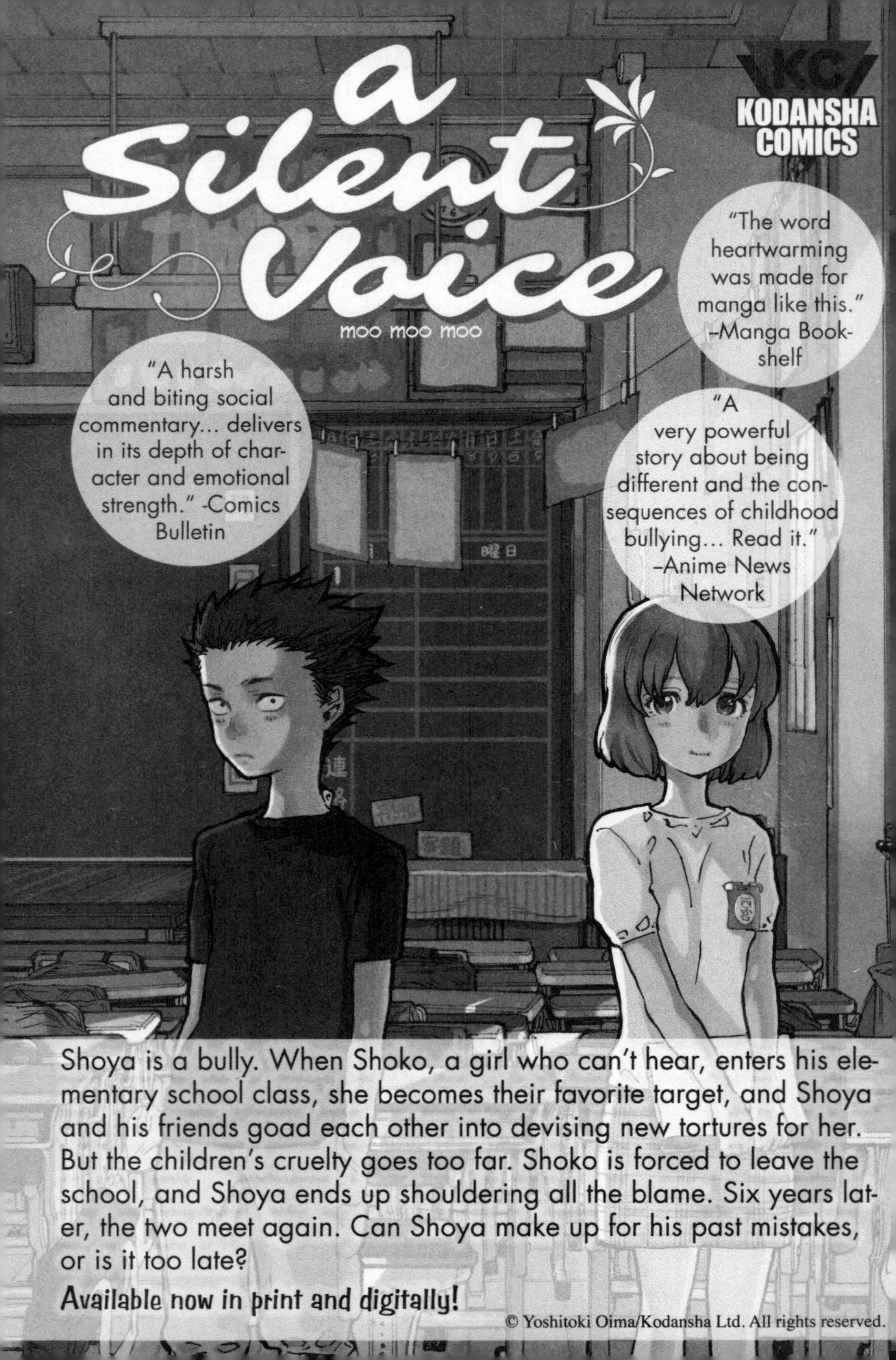
KC
KODANSHA COMICS
a Silent Voice
moo moo moo
"A harsh and biting social commentary... delivers in its depth of character and emotional strength." -Comics Bulletin
"The word heartwarming was made for manga like this." –Manga Bookshelf
"A very powerful story about being different and the consequences of childhood bullying… Read it." –Anime News Network
Shoya is a bully. When Shoko, a girl who can't hear, enters his elementary school class, she becomes their favorite target, and Shoya and his friends goad each other into devising new tortures for her. But the children's cruelty goes too far. Shoko is forced to leave the school, and Shoya ends up shouldering all the blame. Six years later, the two meet again. Can Shoya make up for his past mistakes, or is it too late?
Available now in print and digitally!
© Yoshitoki Oima/Kodansha Ltd. All rights reserved.

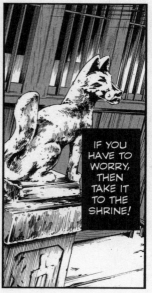

IF YOU HAVE TO WORRY, THEN TAKE IT TO THE SHRINE!

Take it to the shrine, page 124

Specifically, Nagi tells her brother to take all his worries to *O-Inari-san* (Inari), a Japanese deity associated with foxes (hence the image of a fox statue). As has been suggested in the story, she and her brother used to spend a lot of time at Shinto shrines together, so it's reasonable that she would think of the shrine as a place for him to take his concerns.

Taiyaki, page 173

Taiyaki is a kind of cake made with pancake or waffle batter, and stuffed with any kind of filling you can think of, most commonly red bean paste, although of course there are some fillings that are likely to be avoided, such as *natto*—fermented soy beans. The cake is baked *(yaki)* in the shape of a kind of fish (sea bream, or *tai*), hence the name.

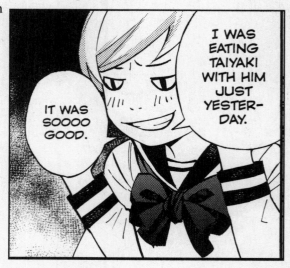

I WAS EATING TAIYAKI WITH HIM JUST YESTER-DAY.
IT WAS SOOOO GOOD.

Going for the lolicon vote, page 65

The Japanese word "lolicon" derives from the term "Lolita complex," and refers to a type of female character whose appeal—sexual or otherwise—is in her youth, cuteness, and innocent charm. The term also refers to fans of such characters, which is how the passer-by in this scene is using it.

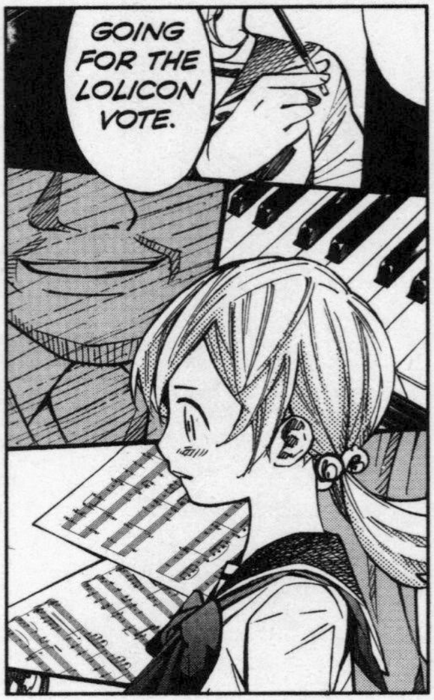
GOING FOR THE LOLICON VOTE.

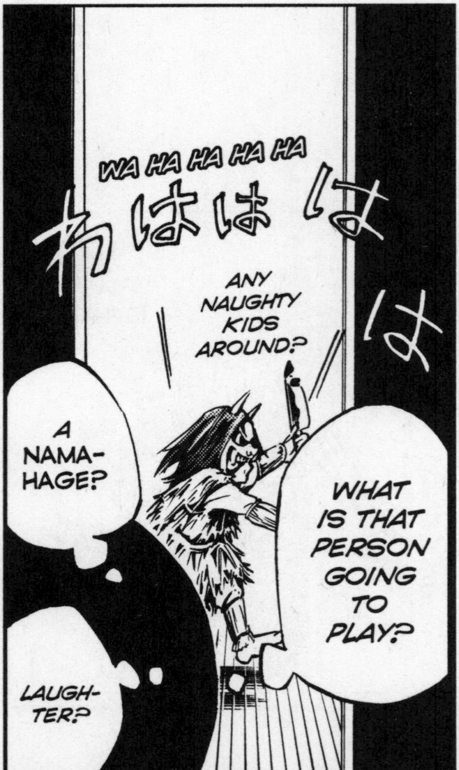
WA HA HA HA HA
わはははは
ANY NAUGHTY KIDS AROUND?
WHAT IS THAT PERSON GOING TO PLAY?
A NAMA-HAGE?
LAUGH-TER?

Any naughty kids around?, page 80

This festival musician is dressed as a *namahage*—a scary demon that goes around the city of Oga at New Year's, scaring new members of the community, such as children, into being good. They barge into houses demanding to know, "Any naughty kids around?" This is supposedly so they can punish them. The family intervenes on behalf of the children, gives the *namahage* some hospitality (food and liquor), and sends him on his way.

❀Kaori Miyazono

A quirky violinist. She failed to show up at the gala concert because of her hospitalization.

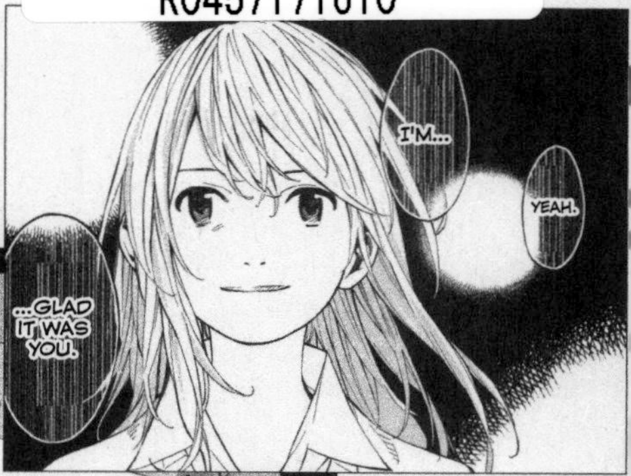
I'M...
YEAH.
...GLAD IT WAS YOU.

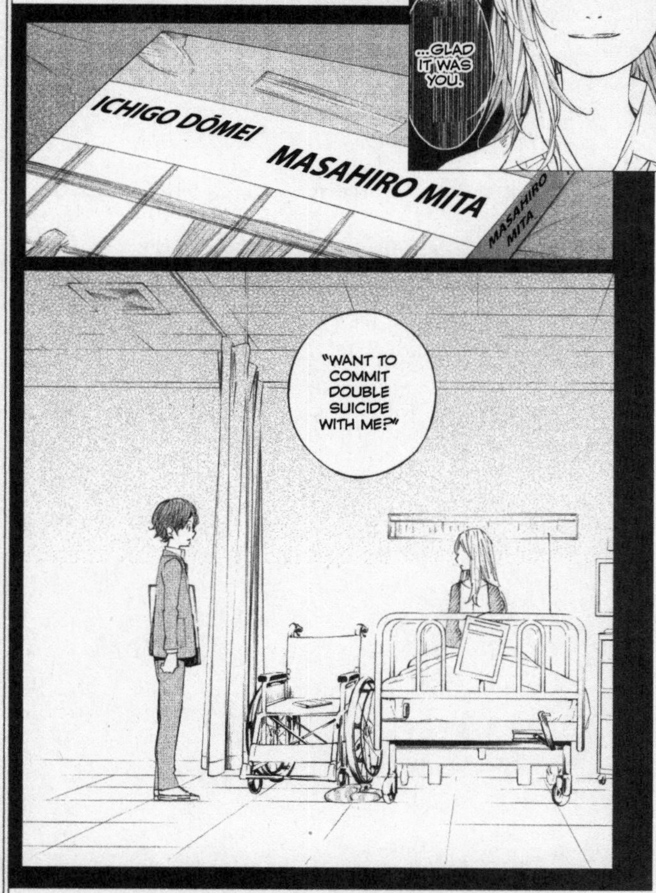
ICHIGO DŌMEI
MASAHIRO MITA
MASAHIRO MITA
"WANT TO COMMIT DOUBLE SUICIDE WITH ME?"

Meanwhile, Kaori having failed to appear at the gala concert, was once again in a hospital bed.... Although a new term started, she had not been back to school, and her behavior was more erratic than ever. Kōsei was pained to see what happened to his mother now happening to Kaori. And then she asked him, "Want to commit double suicide with me?"

contents

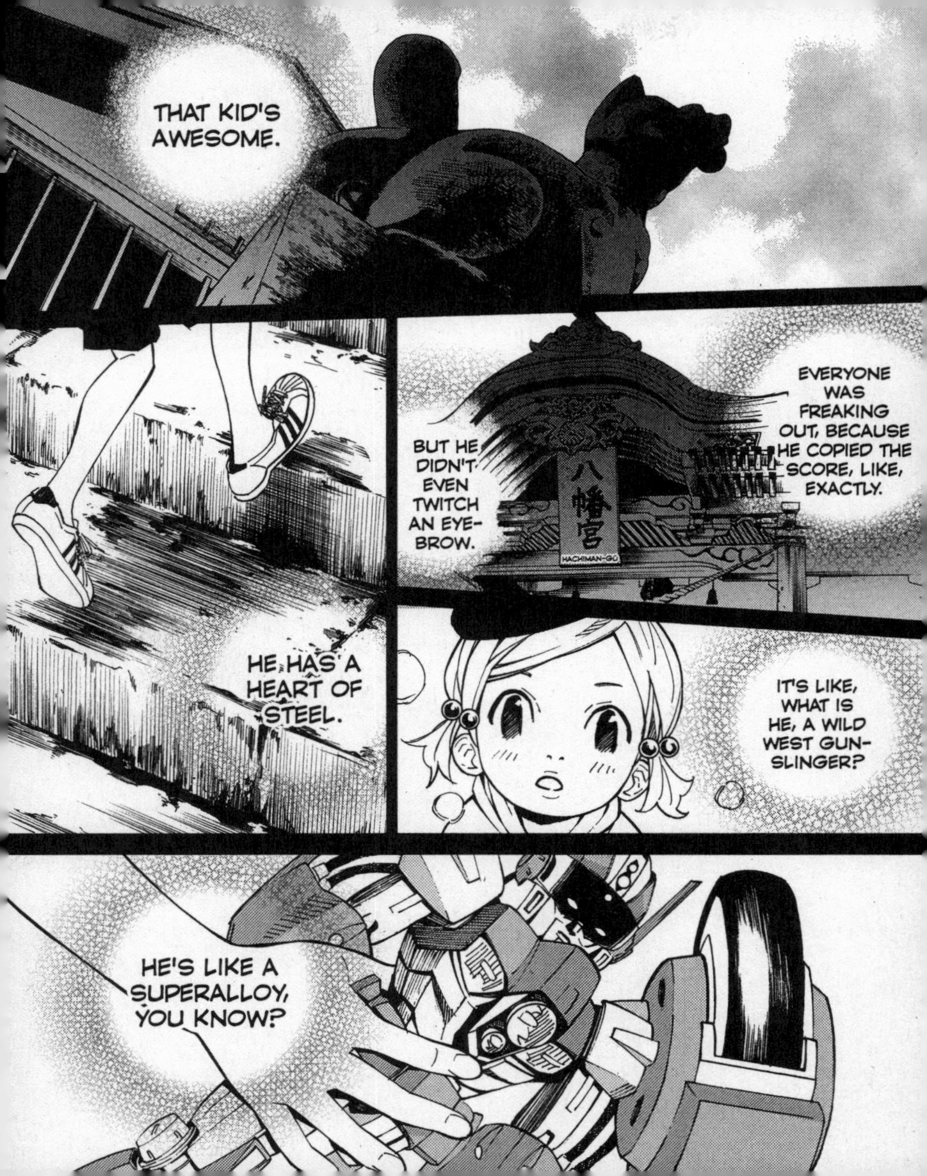
THAT KID'S AWESOME.
EVERYONE WAS FREAKING OUT, BECAUSE HE COPIED THE SCORE, LIKE, EXACTLY.
BUT HE DIDN'T EVEN TWITCH AN EYE-BROW.
八幡宮
HACHIMAN-GU
IT'S LIKE, WHAT IS HE, A WILD WEST GUN-SLINGER?
HE HAS A HEART OF STEEL.
HE'S LIKE A SUPERALLOY, YOU KNOW?

Chapter 33: Twilight

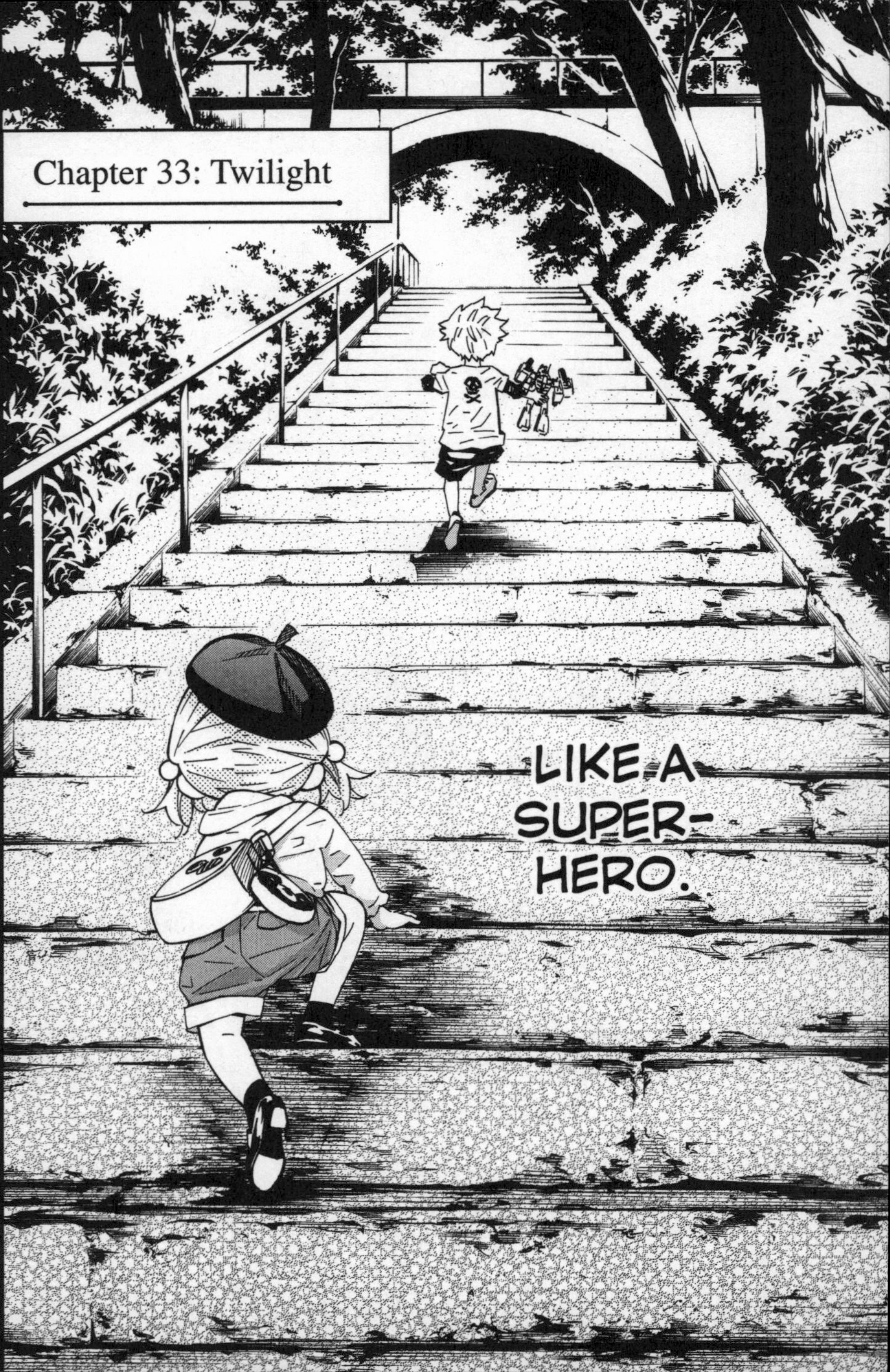
LIKE A SUPER-HERO.

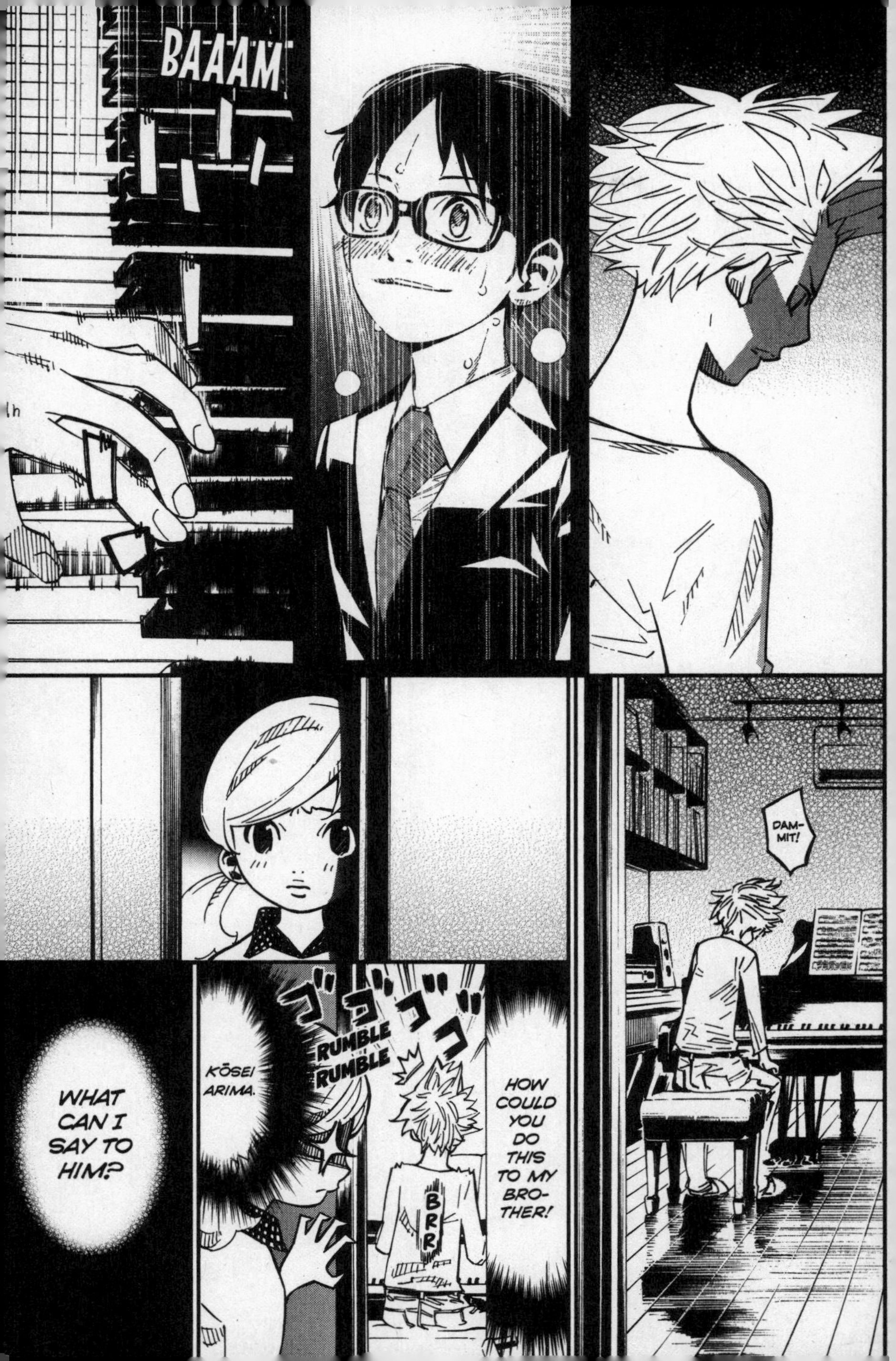

BAAAM
DAM-MIT!
RUMBLE RUMBLE
KŌSEI ARIMA.
HOW COULD YOU DO THIS TO MY BRO-THER!
BRR
WHAT CAN I SAY TO HIM?

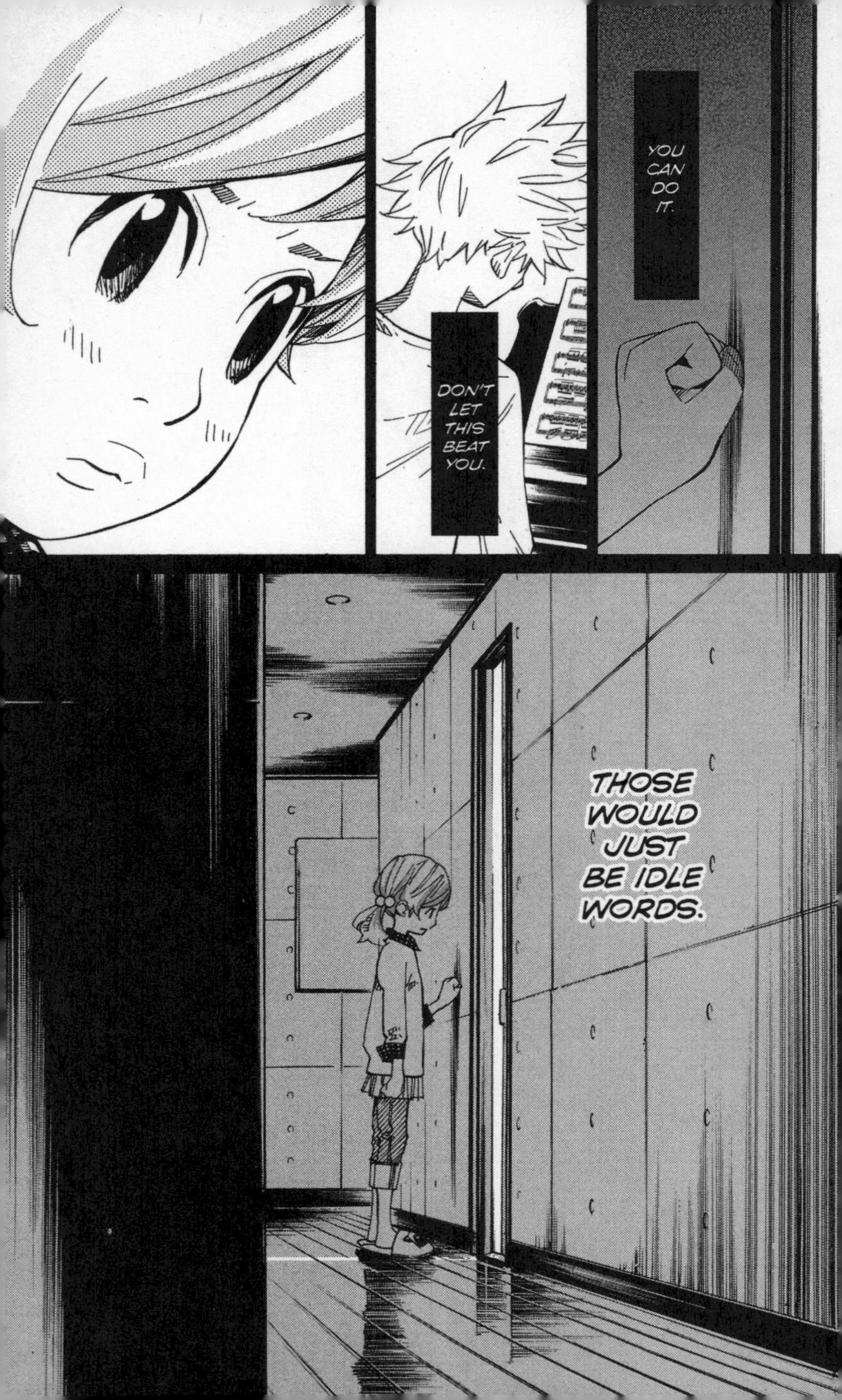
YOU CAN DO IT.
DON'T LET THIS BEAT YOU.
THOSE WOULD JUST BE IDLE WORDS.

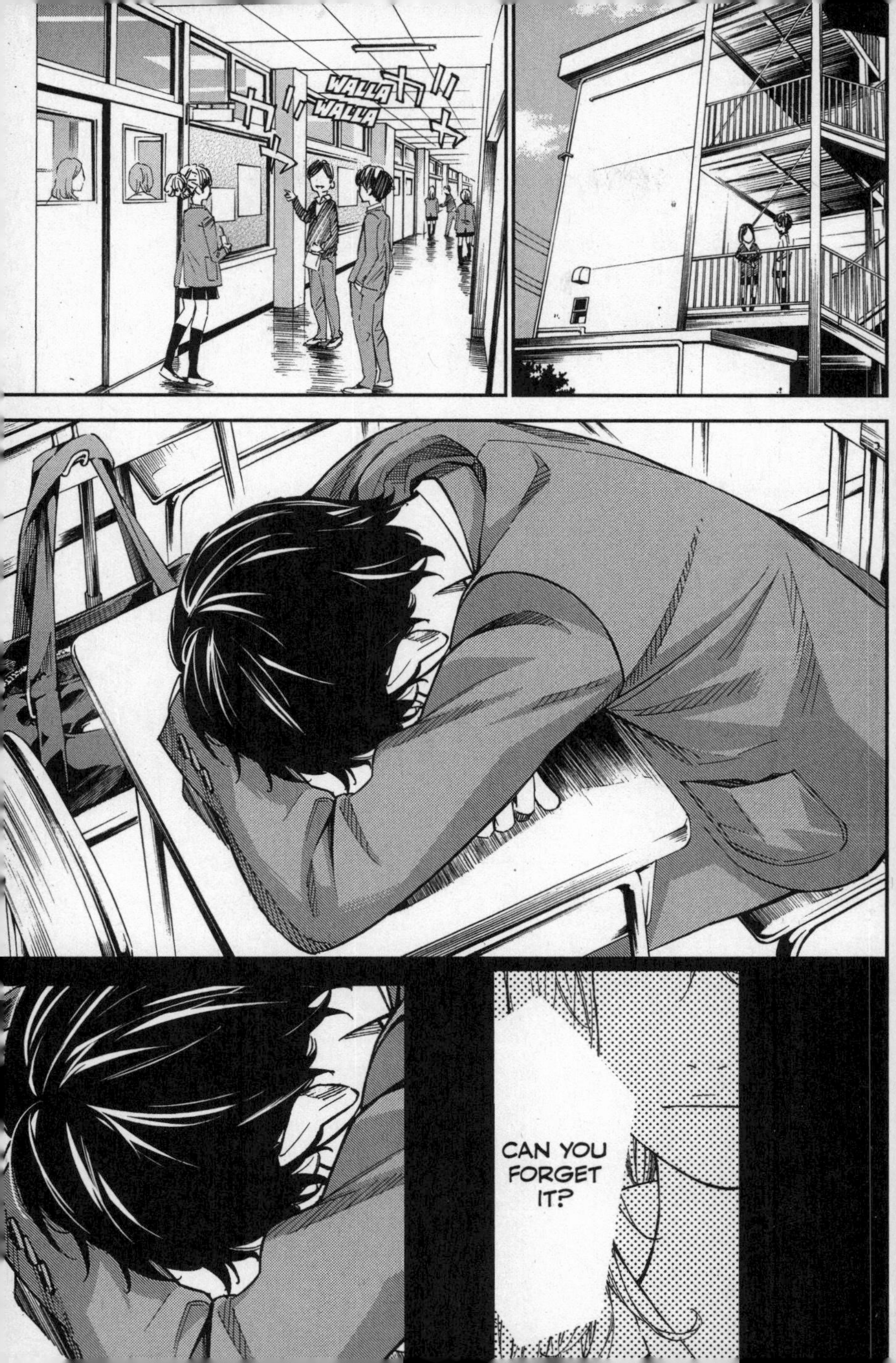
WALLA WALLA
CAN YOU FORGET IT?

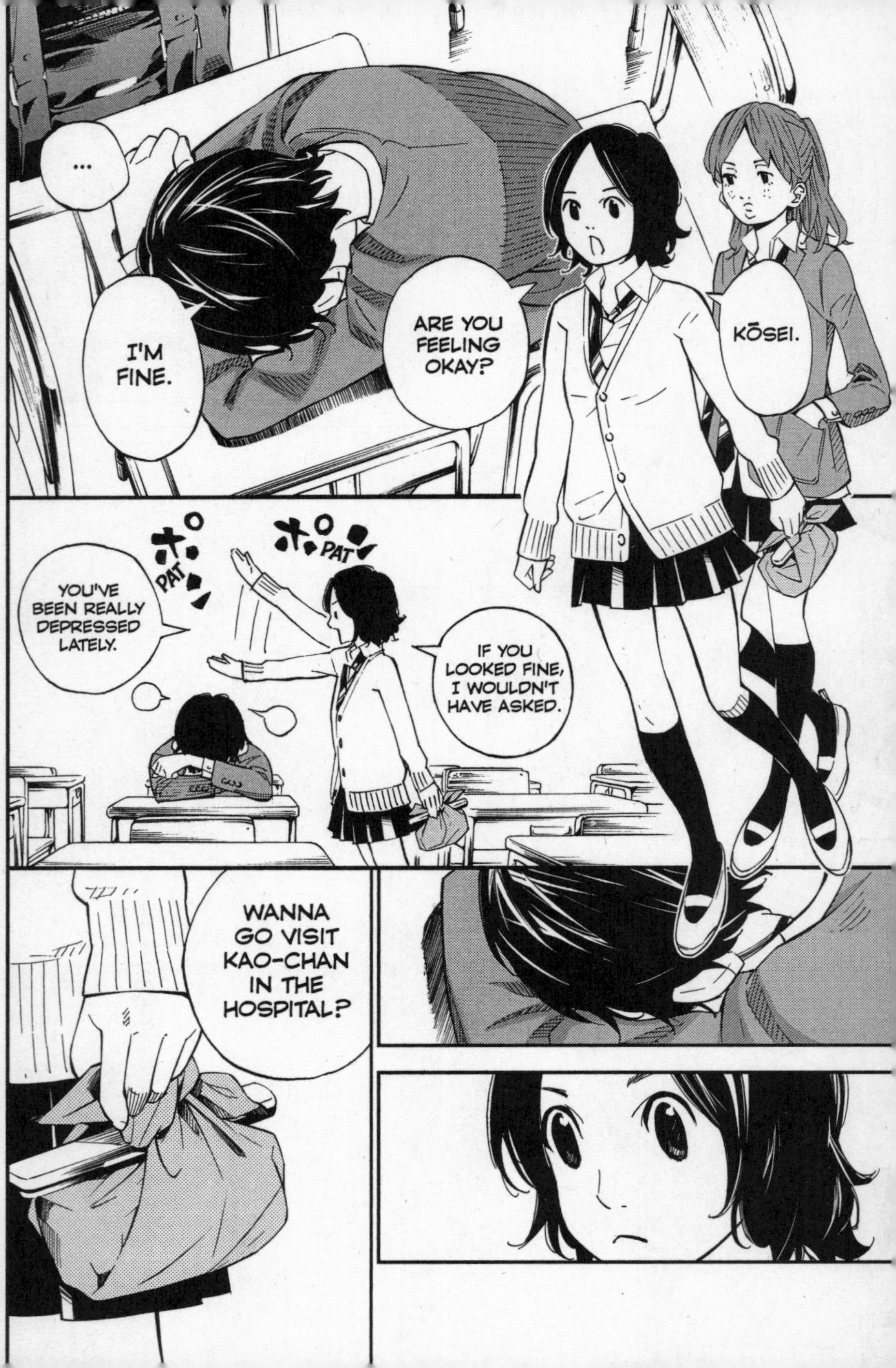
KŌSEI.
ARE YOU FEELING OKAY?
...
I'M FINE.
IF YOU LOOKED FINE, I WOULDN'T HAVE ASKED.
PAT PAT
YOU'VE BEEN REALLY DEPRESSED LATELY.
WANNA GO VISIT KAO-CHAN IN THE HOSPITAL?

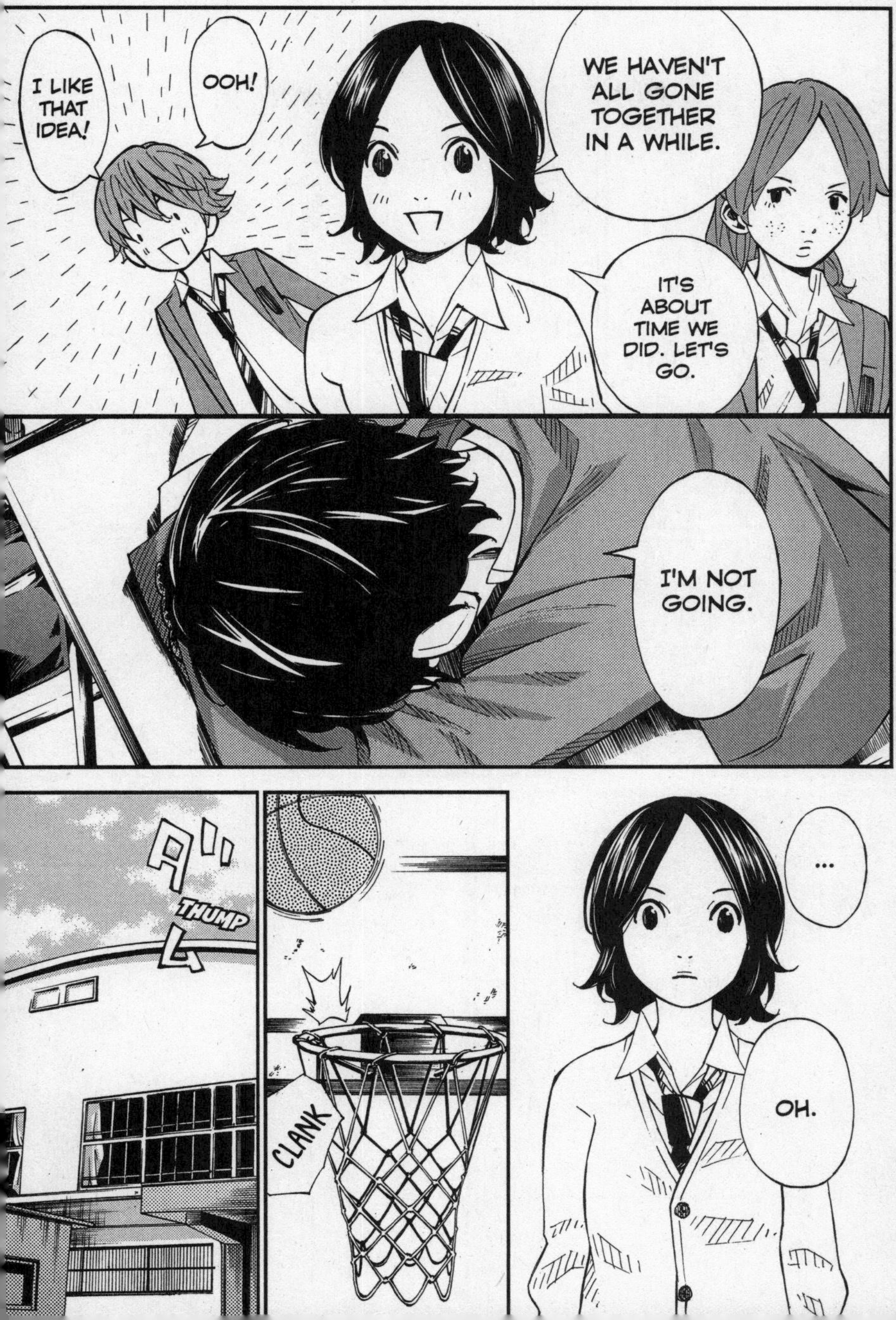
WE HAVEN'T ALL GONE TOGETHER IN A WHILE.
IT'S ABOUT TIME WE DID. LET'S GO.
OOH!
I LIKE THAT IDEA!
I'M NOT GOING.
...
OH.
CLANK
THUMP

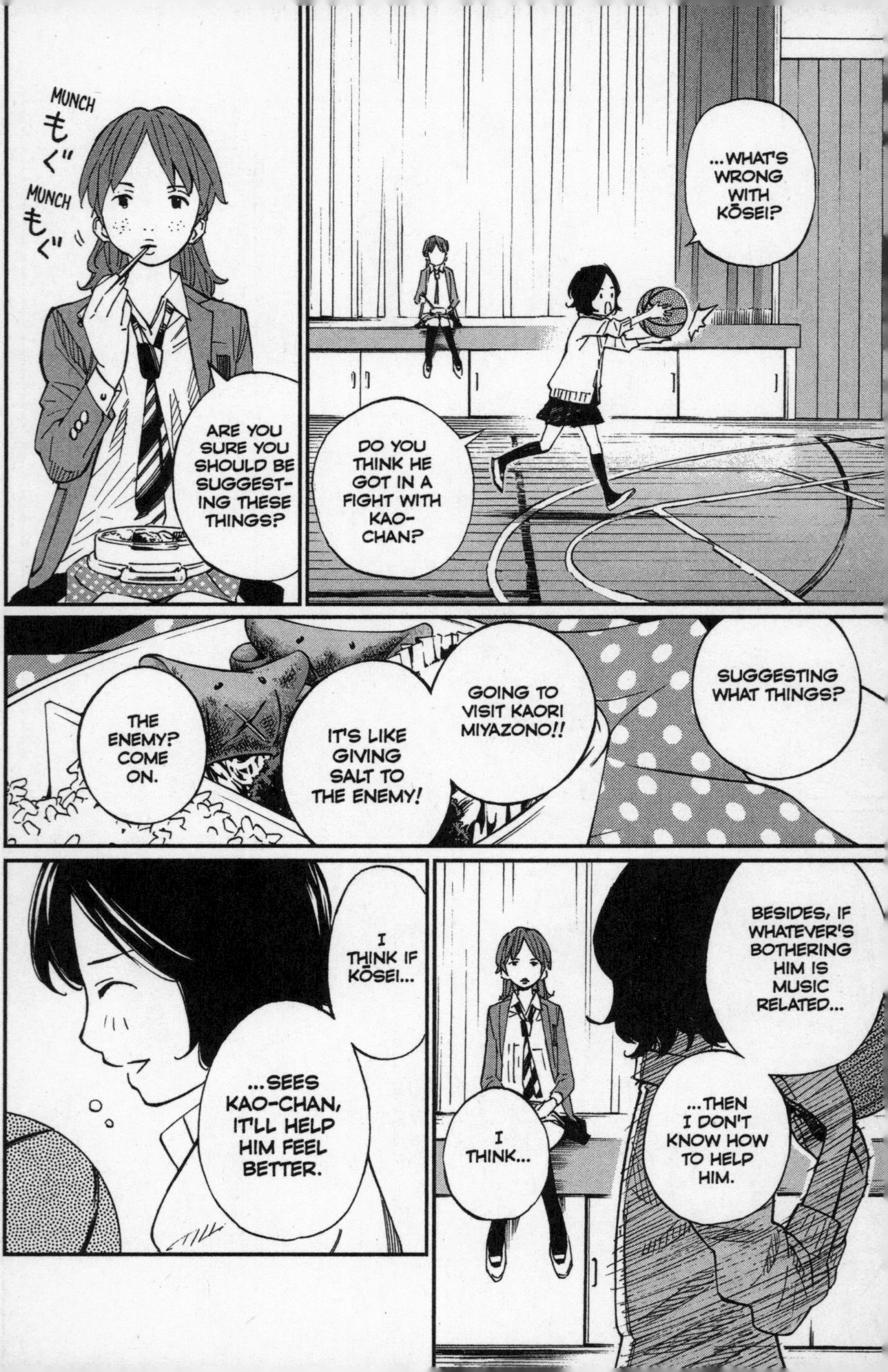
...WHAT'S WRONG WITH KŌSEI?
DO YOU THINK HE GOT IN A FIGHT WITH KAO-CHAN?
MUNCH もぐ
MUNCH もぐ
ARE YOU SURE YOU SHOULD BE SUGGEST-ING THESE THINGS?
SUGGESTING WHAT THINGS?
GOING TO VISIT KAORI MIYAZONO!!
IT'S LIKE GIVING SALT TO THE ENEMY!
THE ENEMY? COME ON.
BESIDES, IF WHATEVER'S BOTHERING HIM IS MUSIC RELATED...
...THEN I DON'T KNOW HOW TO HELP HIM.
I THINK...
I THINK IF KŌSEI...
...SEES KAO-CHAN, IT'LL HELP HIM FEEL BETTER.

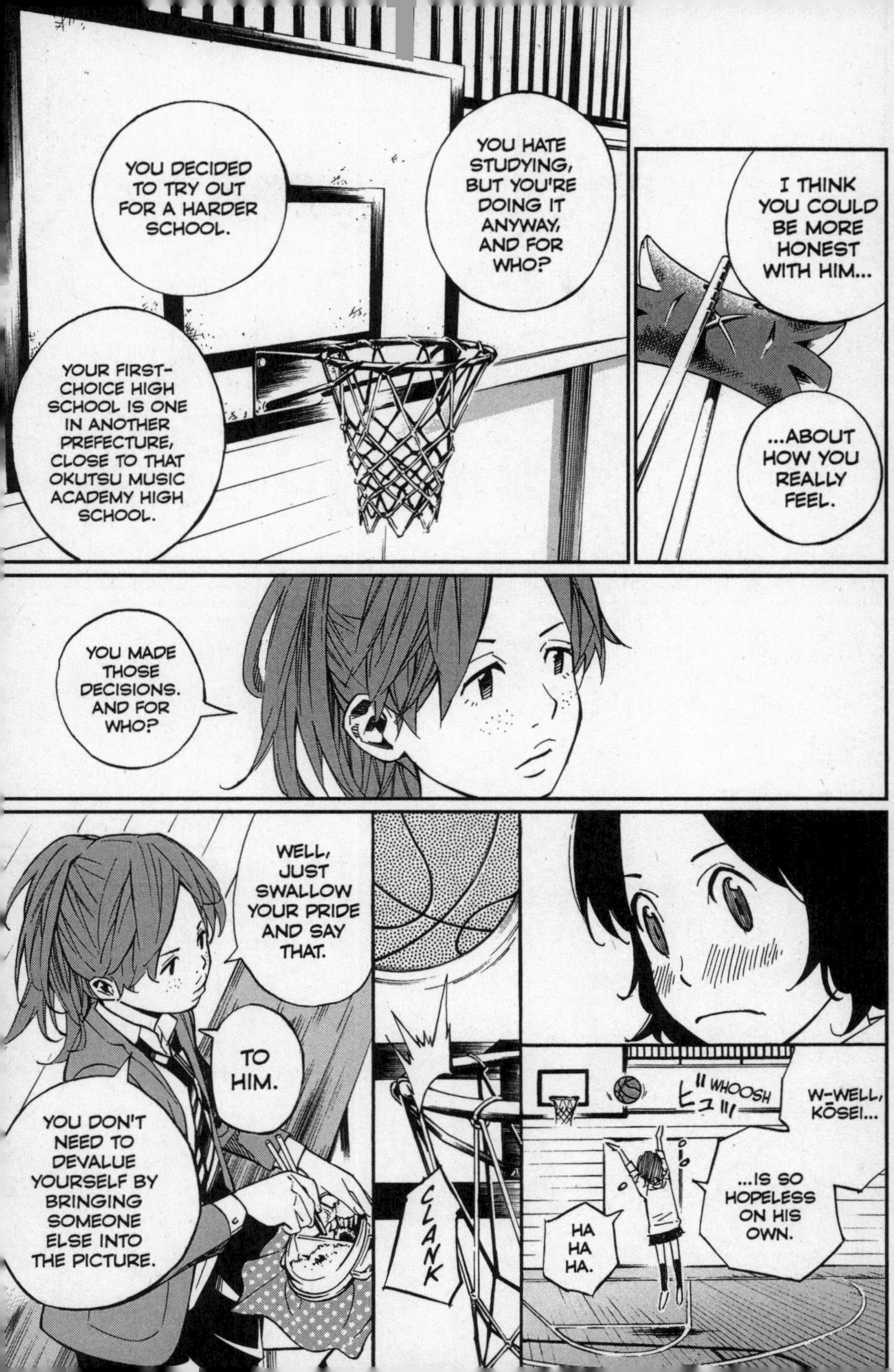
I THINK YOU COULD BE MORE HONEST WITH HIM...
...ABOUT HOW YOU REALLY FEEL.
YOU HATE STUDYING, BUT YOU'RE DOING IT ANYWAY, AND FOR WHO?
YOU DECIDED TO TRY OUT FOR A HARDER SCHOOL.
YOUR FIRST-CHOICE HIGH SCHOOL IS ONE IN ANOTHER PREFECTURE, CLOSE TO THAT OKUTSU MUSIC ACADEMY HIGH SCHOOL.
YOU MADE THOSE DECISIONS. AND FOR WHO?
W-WELL, KŌSEI...
ヒュ WHOOSH
...IS SO HOPELESS ON HIS OWN.
HA HA HA.
CLANK
WELL, JUST SWALLOW YOUR PRIDE AND SAY THAT.
TO HIM.
YOU DON'T NEED TO DEVALUE YOURSELF BY BRINGING SOMEONE ELSE INTO THE PICTURE.

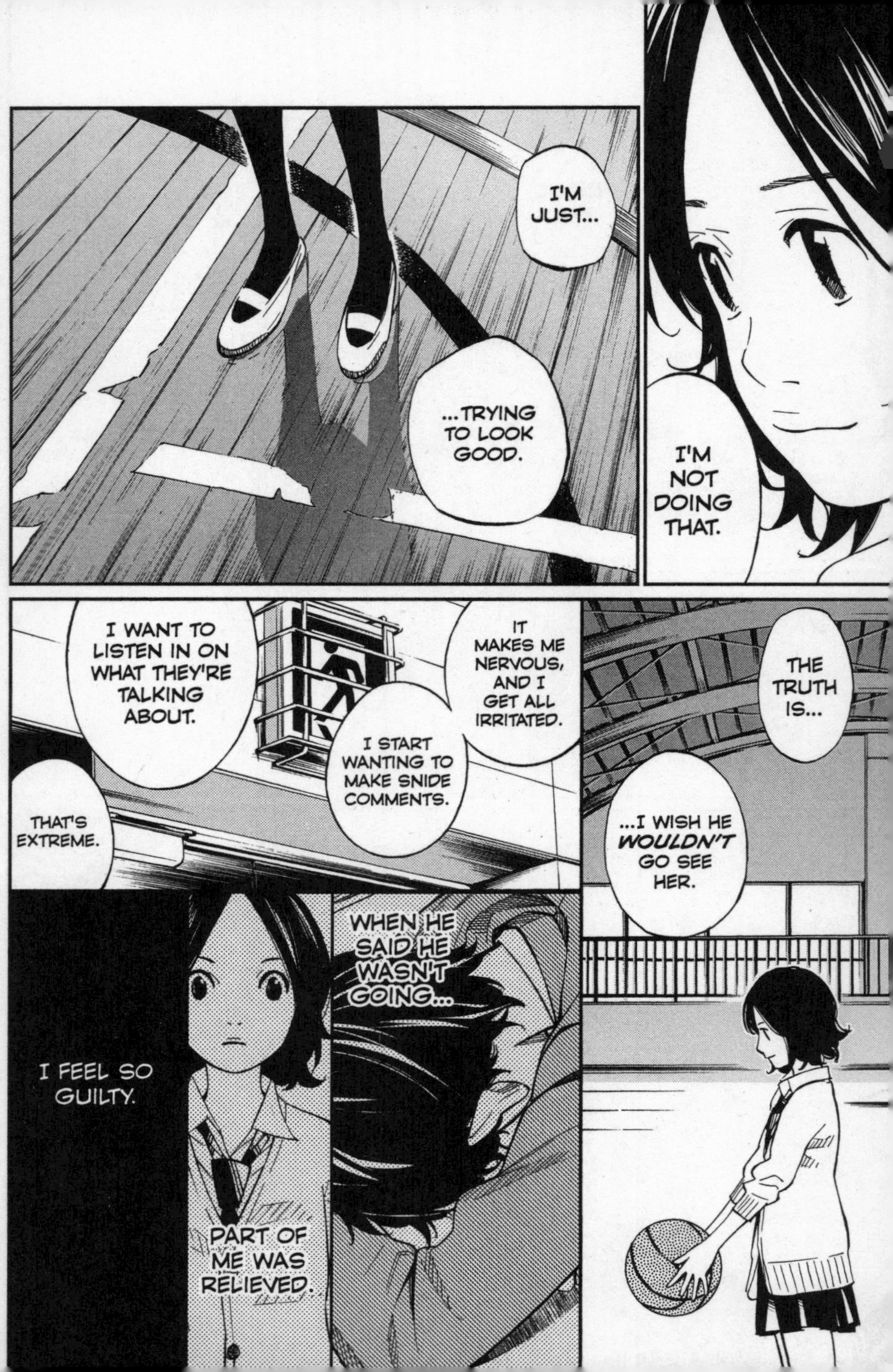
I'M NOT DOING THAT.
I'M JUST...
...TRYING TO LOOK GOOD.
THE TRUTH IS...
...I WISH HE *WOULDN'T* GO SEE HER.
IT MAKES ME NERVOUS, AND I GET ALL IRRITATED.
I WANT TO LISTEN IN ON WHAT THEY'RE TALKING ABOUT.
I START WANTING TO MAKE SNIDE COMMENTS.
THAT'S EXTREME.
WHEN HE SAID HE WASN'T GOING...
PART OF ME WAS RELIEVED.
I FEEL SO GUILTY.

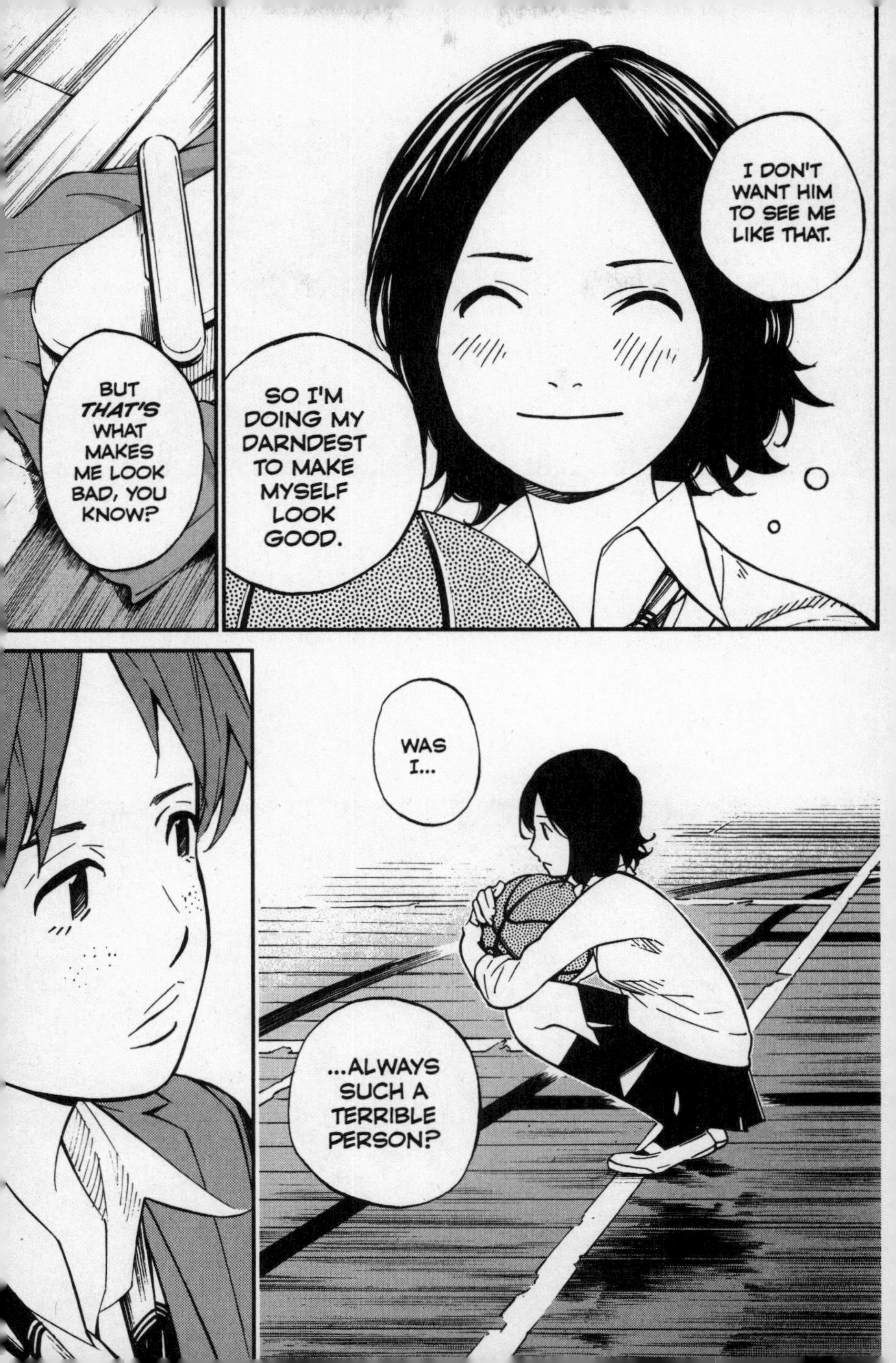
I DON'T WANT HIM TO SEE ME LIKE THAT.
SO I'M DOING MY DARNDEST TO MAKE MYSELF LOOK GOOD.
BUT *THAT'S* WHAT MAKES ME LOOK BAD, YOU KNOW?
WAS I...
...ALWAYS SUCH A TERRIBLE PERSON?

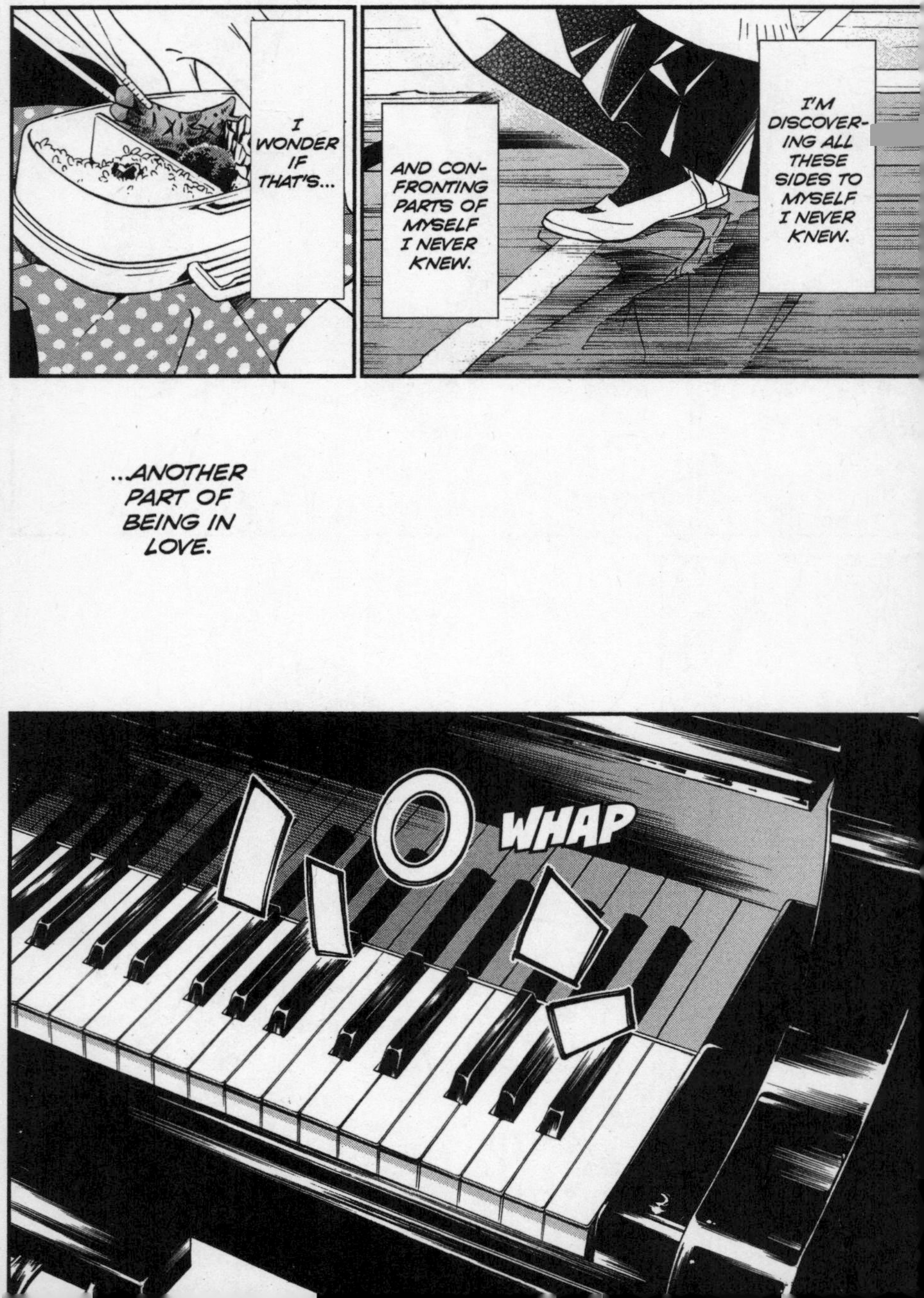
I'M DISCOVERING ALL THESE SIDES TO MYSELF I NEVER KNEW.
AND CONFRONTING PARTS OF MYSELF I NEVER KNEW.
I WONDER IF THAT'S...
...ANOTHER PART OF BEING IN LOVE.
WHAP

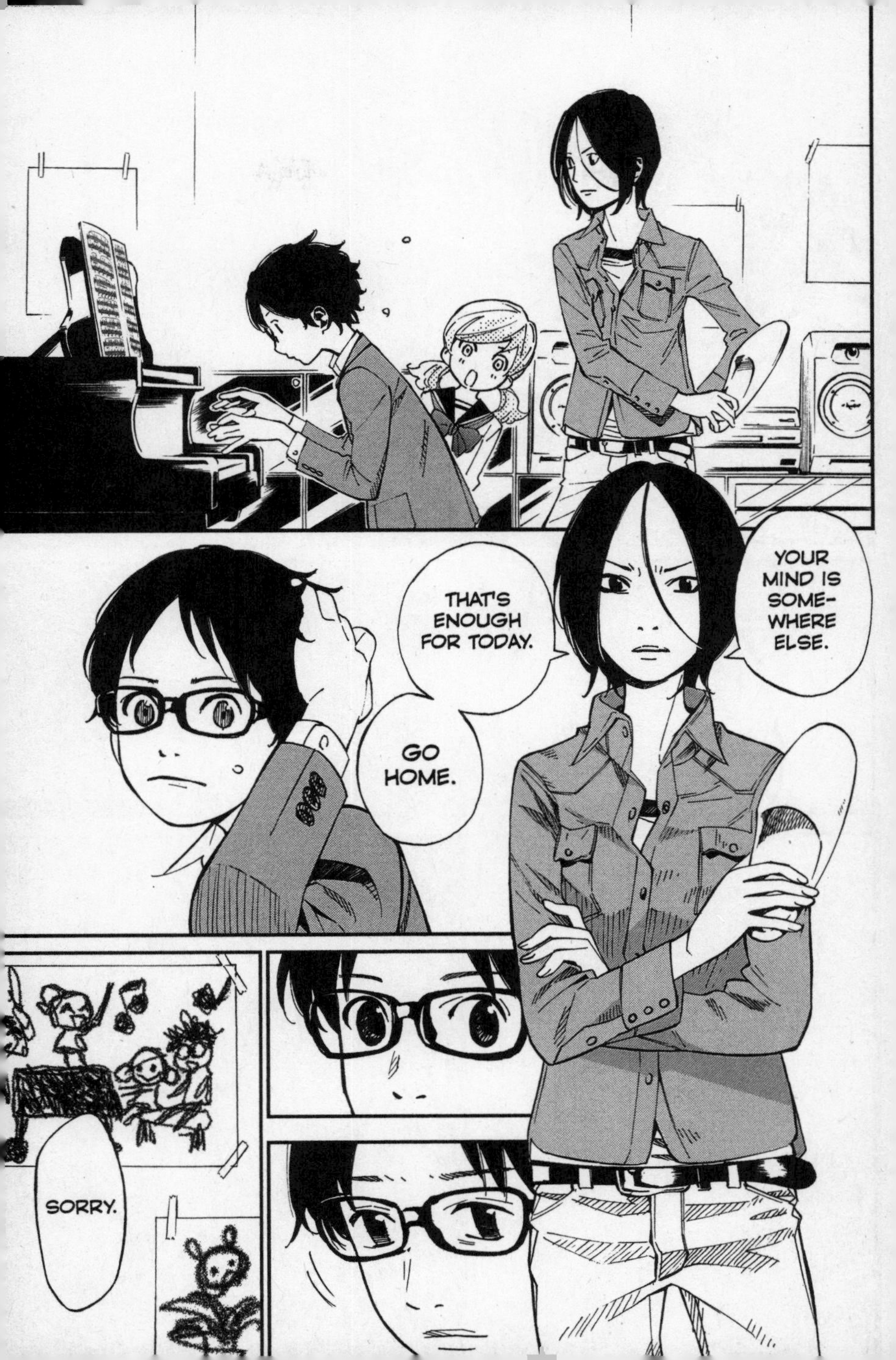
YOUR MIND IS SOMEWHERE ELSE.
THAT'S ENOUGH FOR TODAY.
GO HOME.
SORRY.

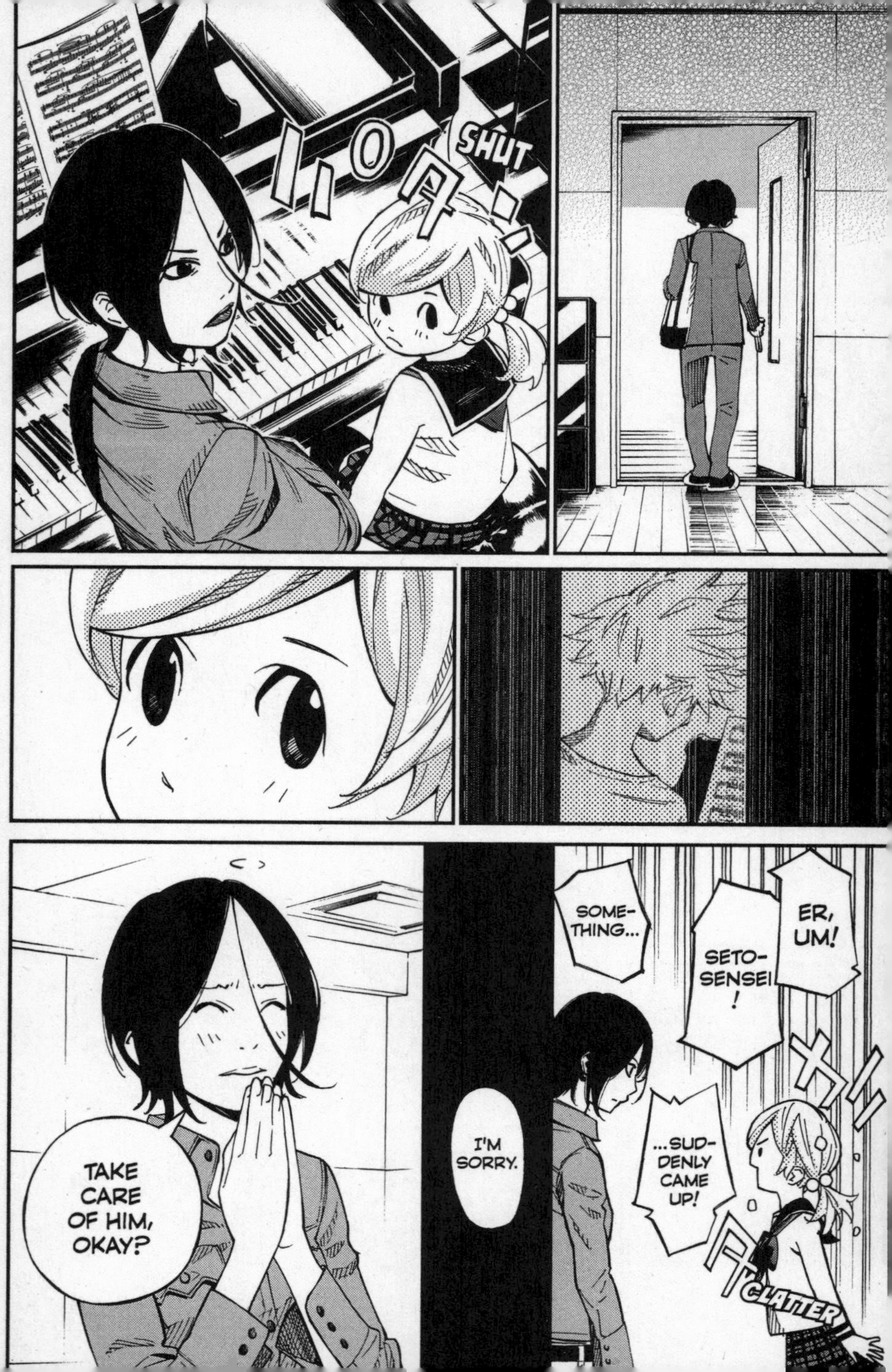
SHUT
ER, UM!
SETO-SENSEI!
SOME-THING...
...SUD-DENLY CAME UP!
CLATTER
I'M SORRY.
TAKE CARE OF HIM, OKAY?

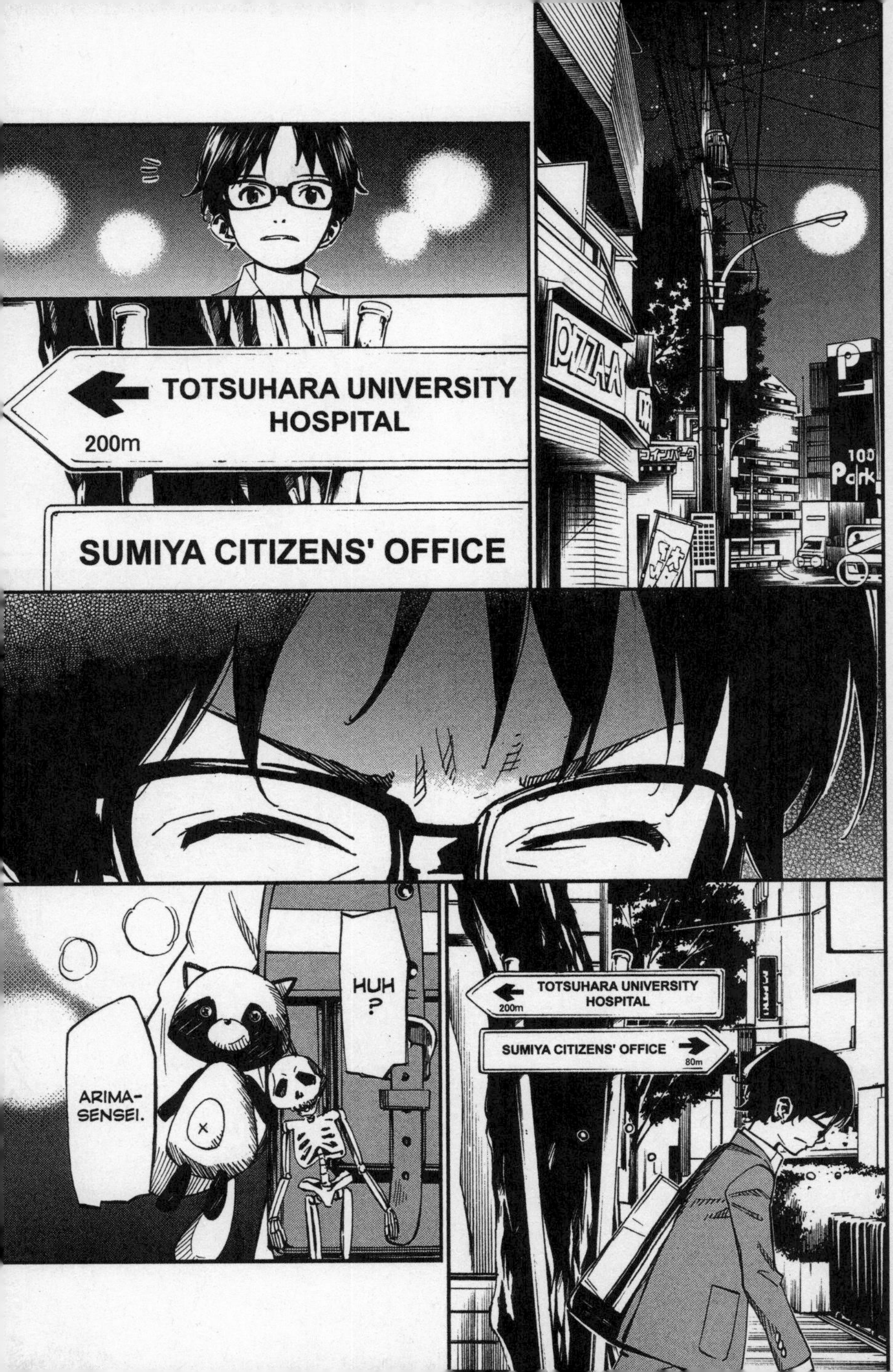
TOTSUHARA UNIVERSITY HOSPITAL
200m
SUMIYA CITIZENS' OFFICE
TOTSUHARA UNIVERSITY HOSPITAL
200m
SUMIYA CITIZENS' OFFICE
80m
HUH ?
ARIMA-SENSEI.

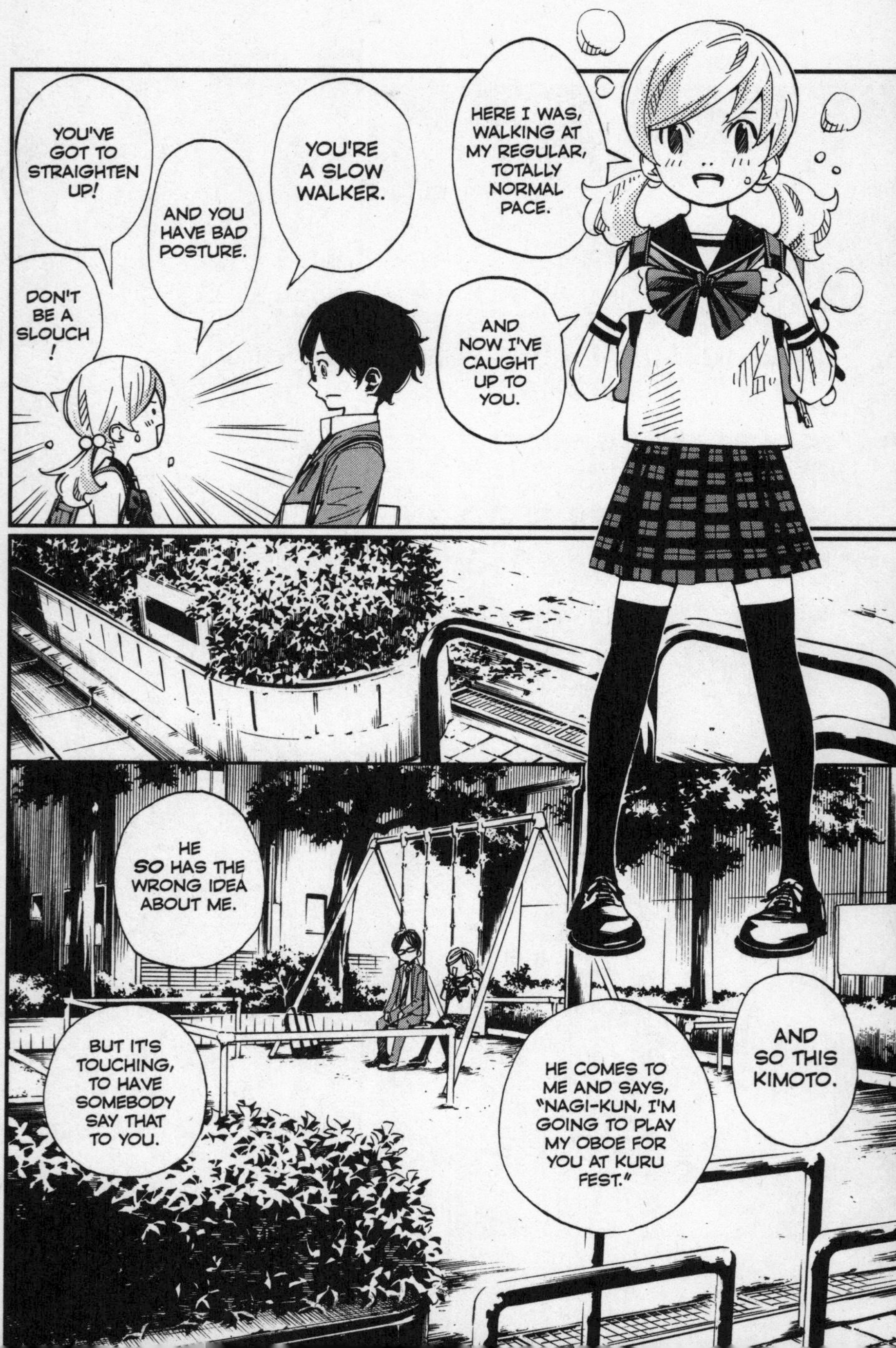
HERE I WAS, WALKING AT MY REGULAR, TOTALLY NORMAL PACE.
AND NOW I'VE CAUGHT UP TO YOU.
YOU'RE A SLOW WALKER.
AND YOU HAVE BAD POSTURE.
YOU'VE GOT TO STRAIGHTEN UP!
DON'T BE A SLOUCH!
AND SO THIS KIMOTO.
HE COMES TO ME AND SAYS, "NAGI-KUN, I'M GOING TO PLAY MY OBOE FOR YOU AT KURU FEST."
HE SO HAS THE WRONG IDEA ABOUT ME.
BUT IT'S TOUCHING, TO HAVE SOMEBODY SAY THAT TO YOU.

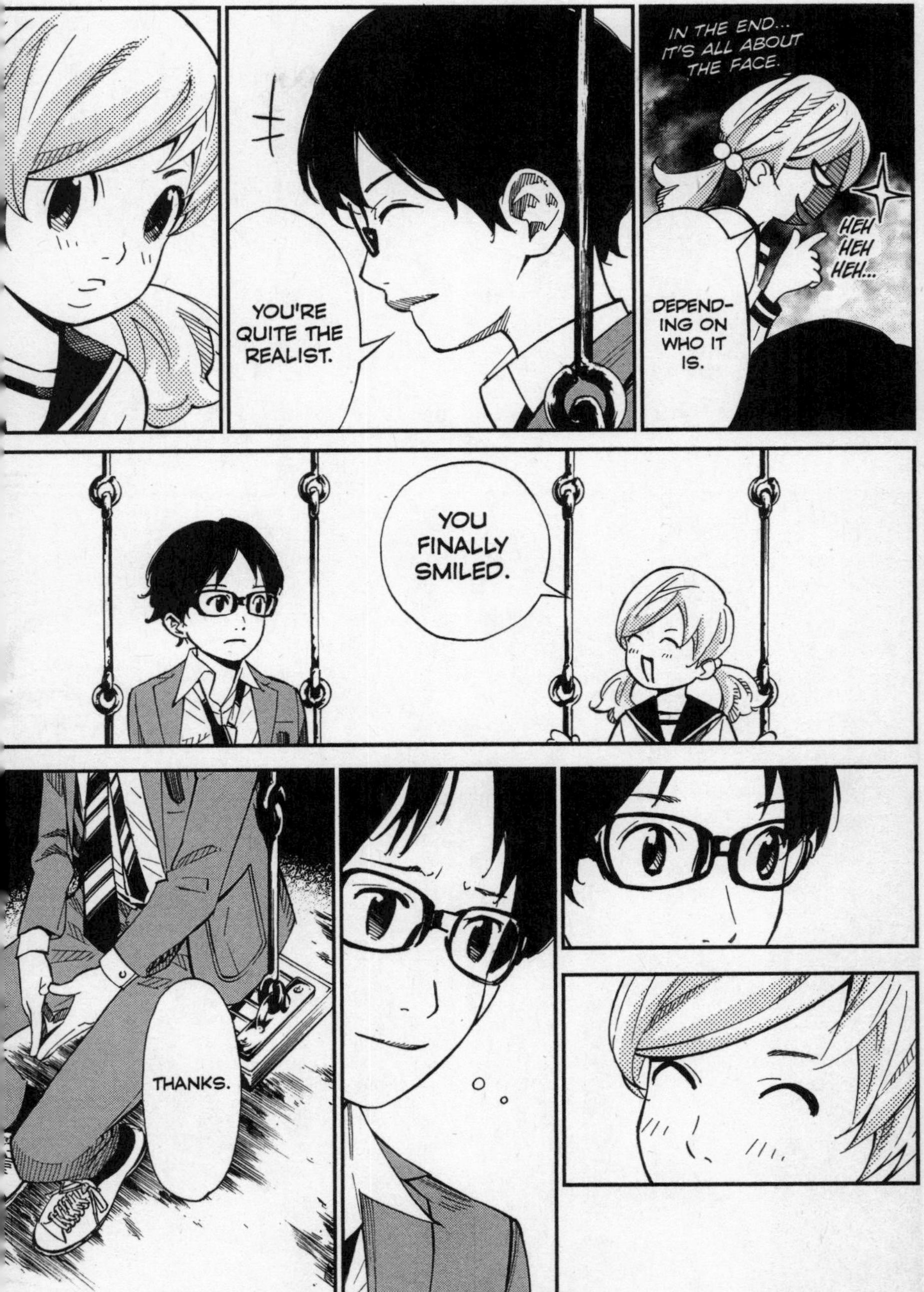
IN THE END... IT'S ALL ABOUT THE FACE.
HEH HEH HEH...
DEPENDING ON WHO IT IS.
YOU'RE QUITE THE REALIST.
YOU FINALLY SMILED.
THANKS.

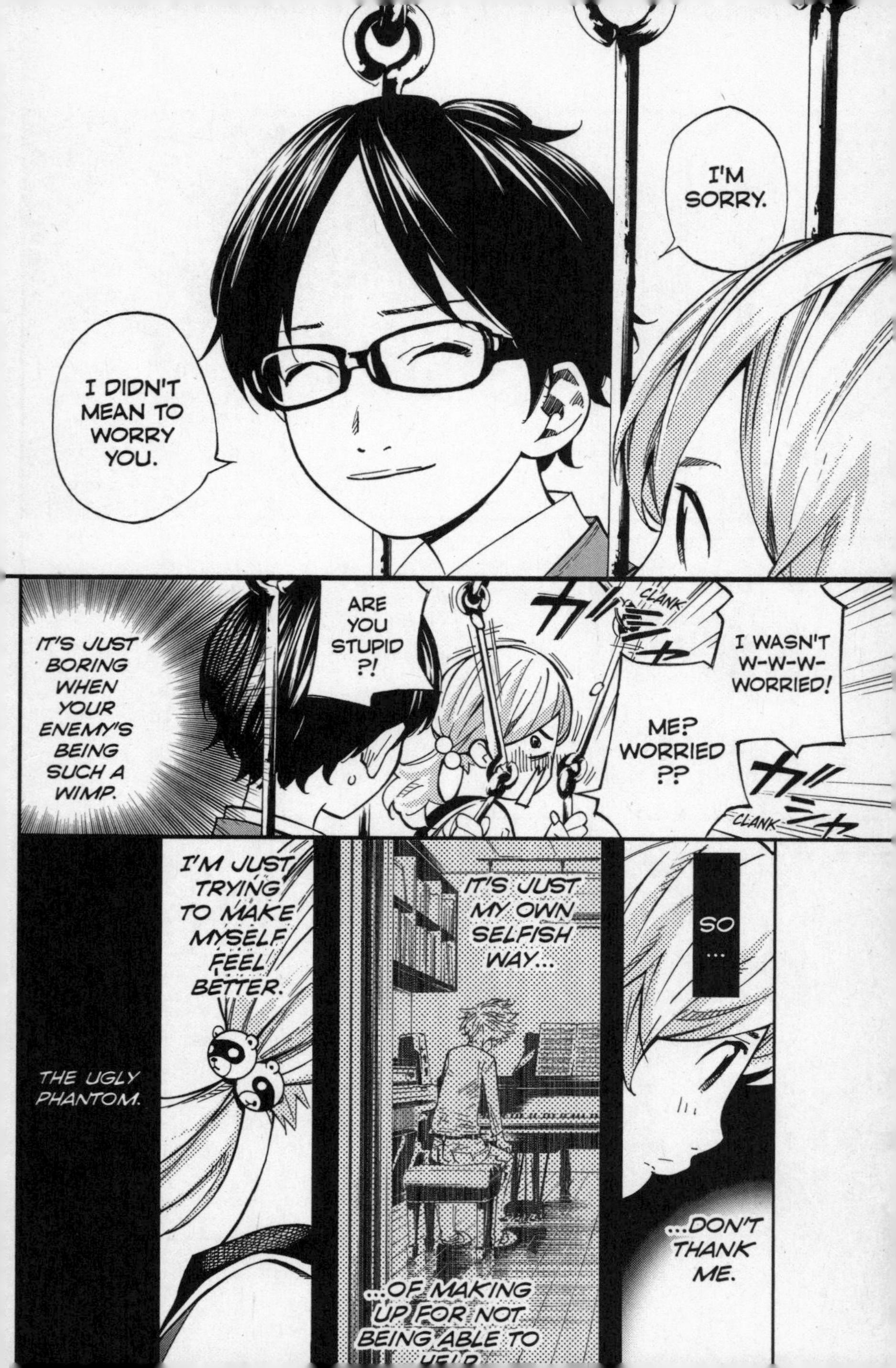
I'M SORRY.
I DIDN'T MEAN TO WORRY YOU.
CLANK
I WASN'T W-W-W-WORRIED!
ME? WORRIED??
CLANK
ARE YOU STUPID?!
IT'S JUST BORING WHEN YOUR ENEMY'S BEING SUCH A WIMP.
SO...
...DON'T THANK ME.
IT'S JUST MY OWN SELFISH WAY...
...OF MAKING UP FOR NOT BEING ABLE TO
I'M JUST TRYING TO MAKE MYSELF FEEL BETTER.
THE UGLY PHANTOM.

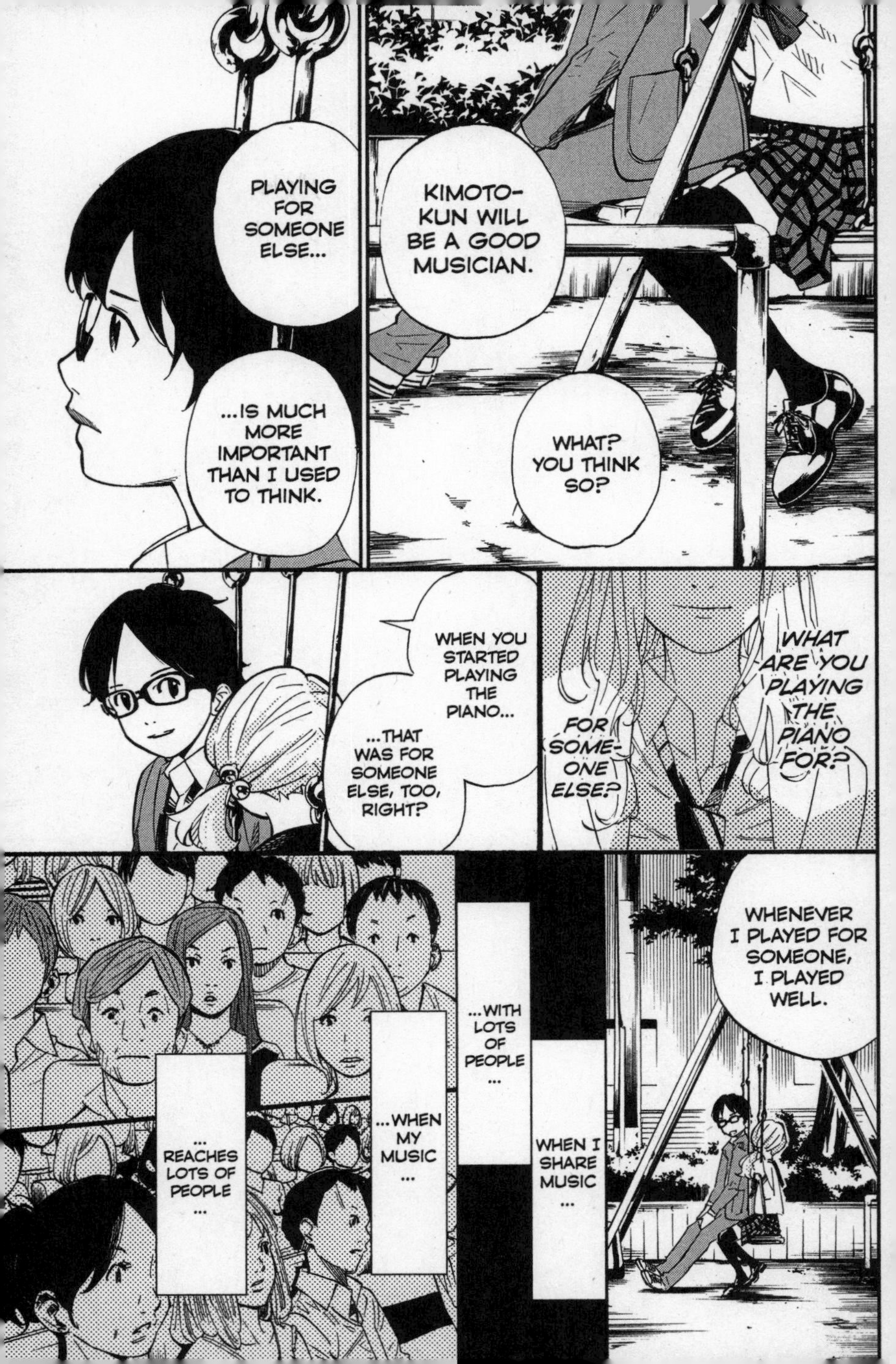
KIMOTO-KUN WILL BE A GOOD MUSICIAN.
WHAT? YOU THINK SO?
PLAYING FOR SOMEONE ELSE...
...IS MUCH MORE IMPORTANT THAN I USED TO THINK.
WHAT ARE YOU PLAYING THE PIANO FOR?
FOR SOMEONE ELSE?
WHEN YOU STARTED PLAYING THE PIANO...
...THAT WAS FOR SOMEONE ELSE, TOO, RIGHT?
WHENEVER I PLAYED FOR SOMEONE, I PLAYED WELL.
WHEN I SHARE MUSIC...
...WITH LOTS OF PEOPLE...
...WHEN MY MUSIC...
...REACHES LOTS OF PEOPLE...

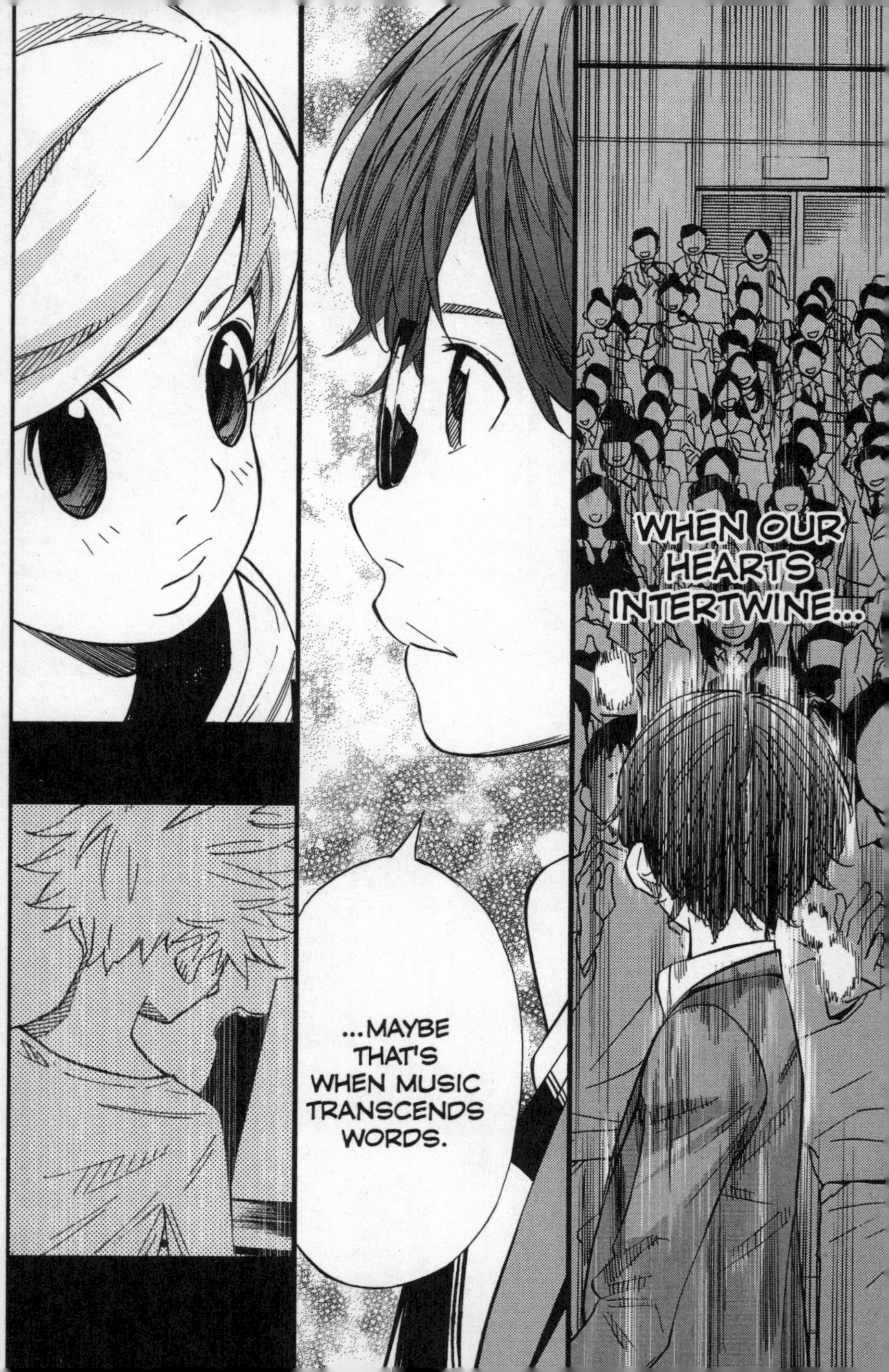
WHEN OUR HEARTS INTERTWINE...
...MAYBE THAT'S WHEN MUSIC TRANSCENDS WORDS.

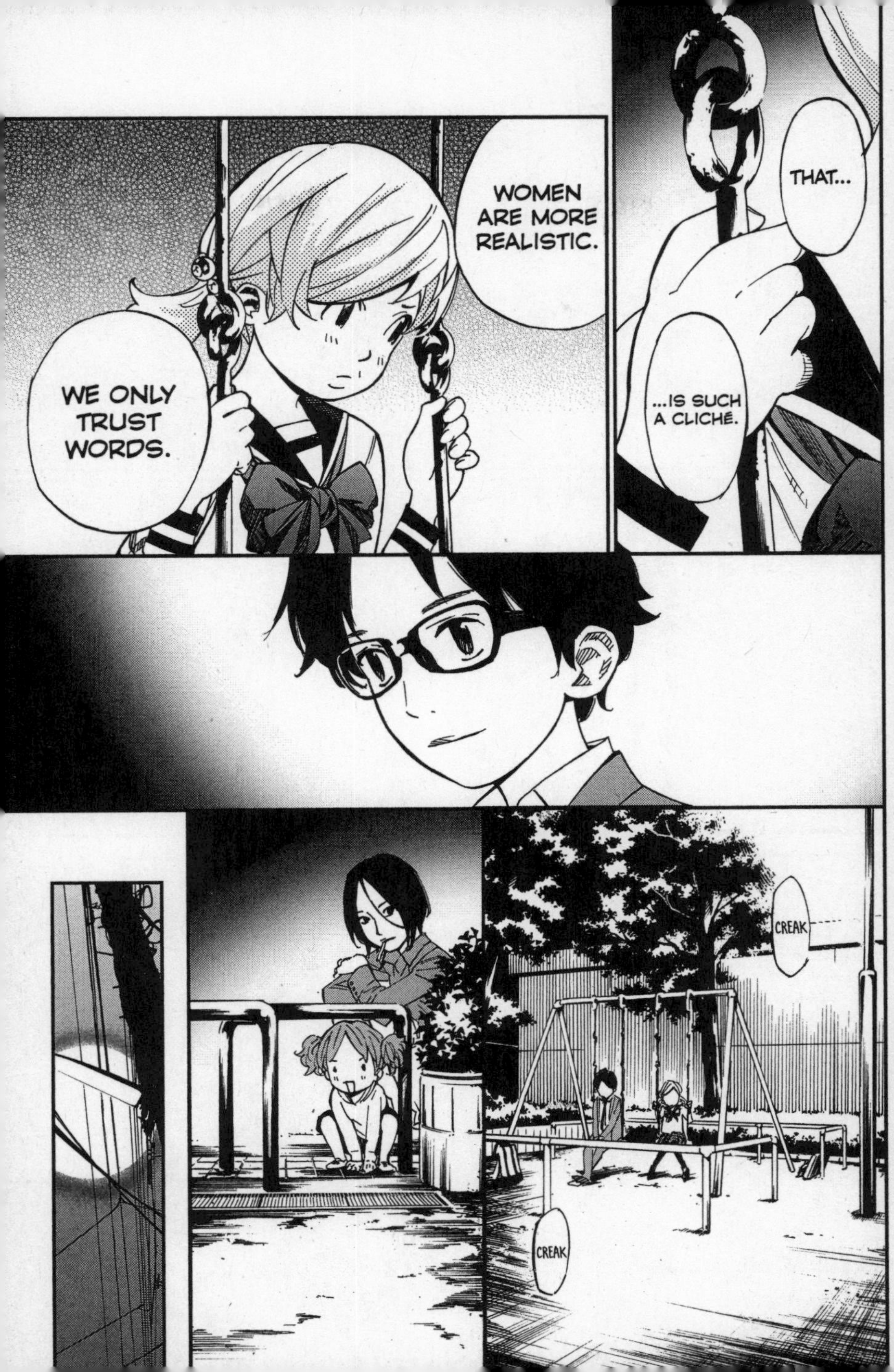
THAT...
...IS SUCH A CLICHÉ.
WOMEN ARE MORE REALISTIC.
WE ONLY TRUST WORDS.
CREAK
CREAK

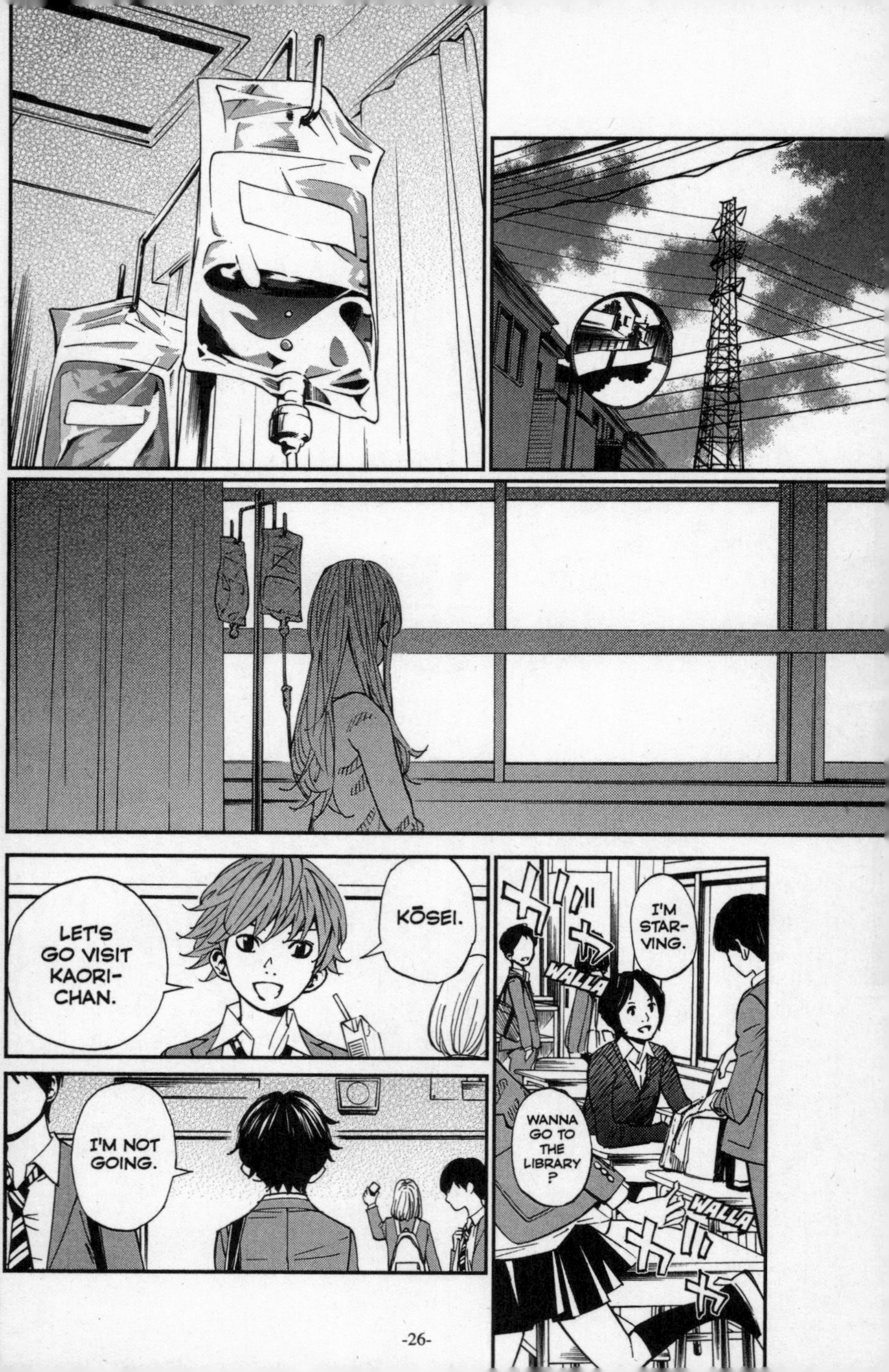
I'M STARVING.
WALLA
WANNA GO TO THE LIBRARY?
WALLA
KŌSEI.
LET'S GO VISIT KAORI-CHAN.
I'M NOT GOING.

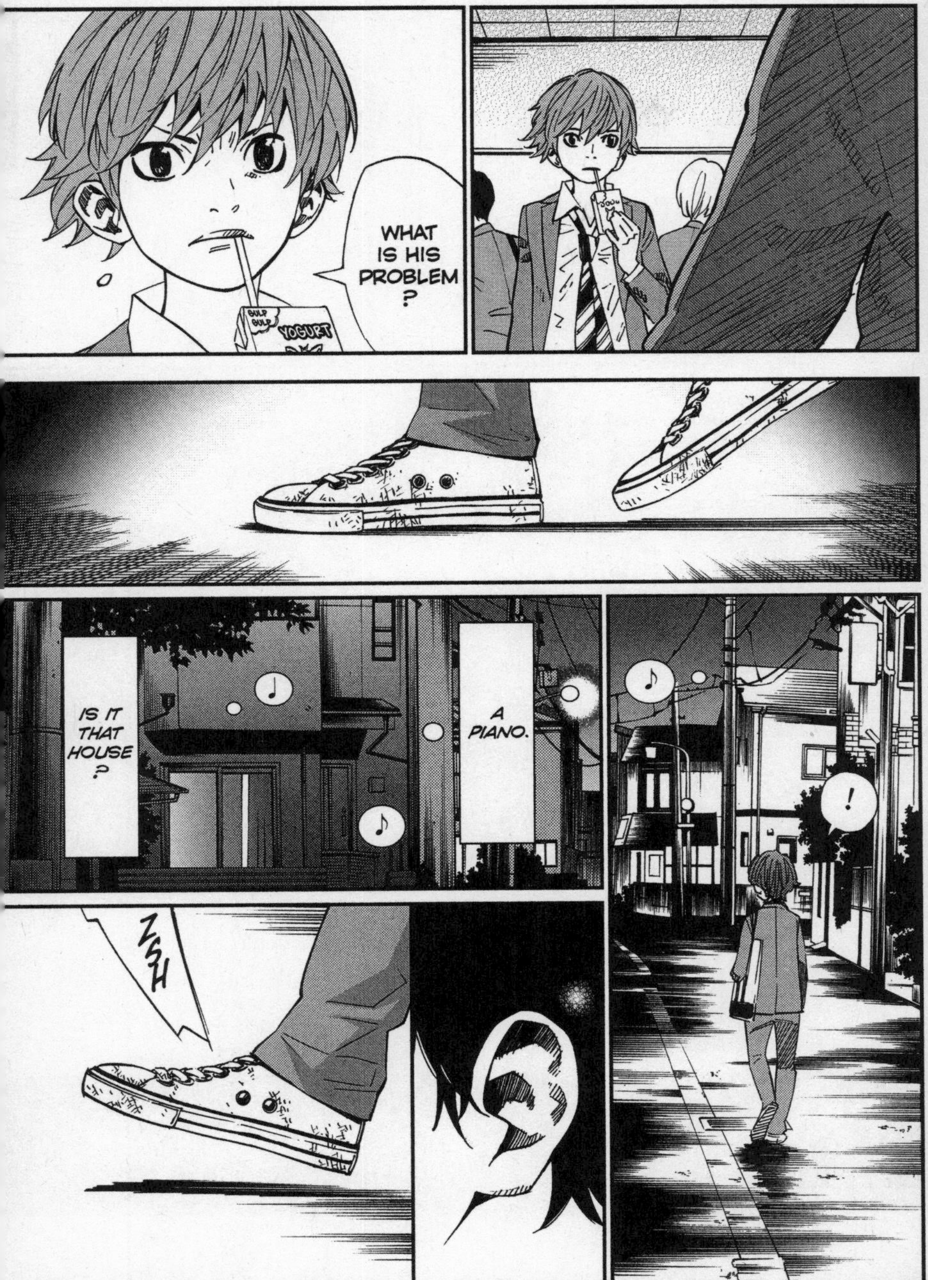
WHAT IS HIS PROBLEM?
GULP GULP
YOGURT
!
A PIANO.
IS IT THAT HOUSE?
ZSH

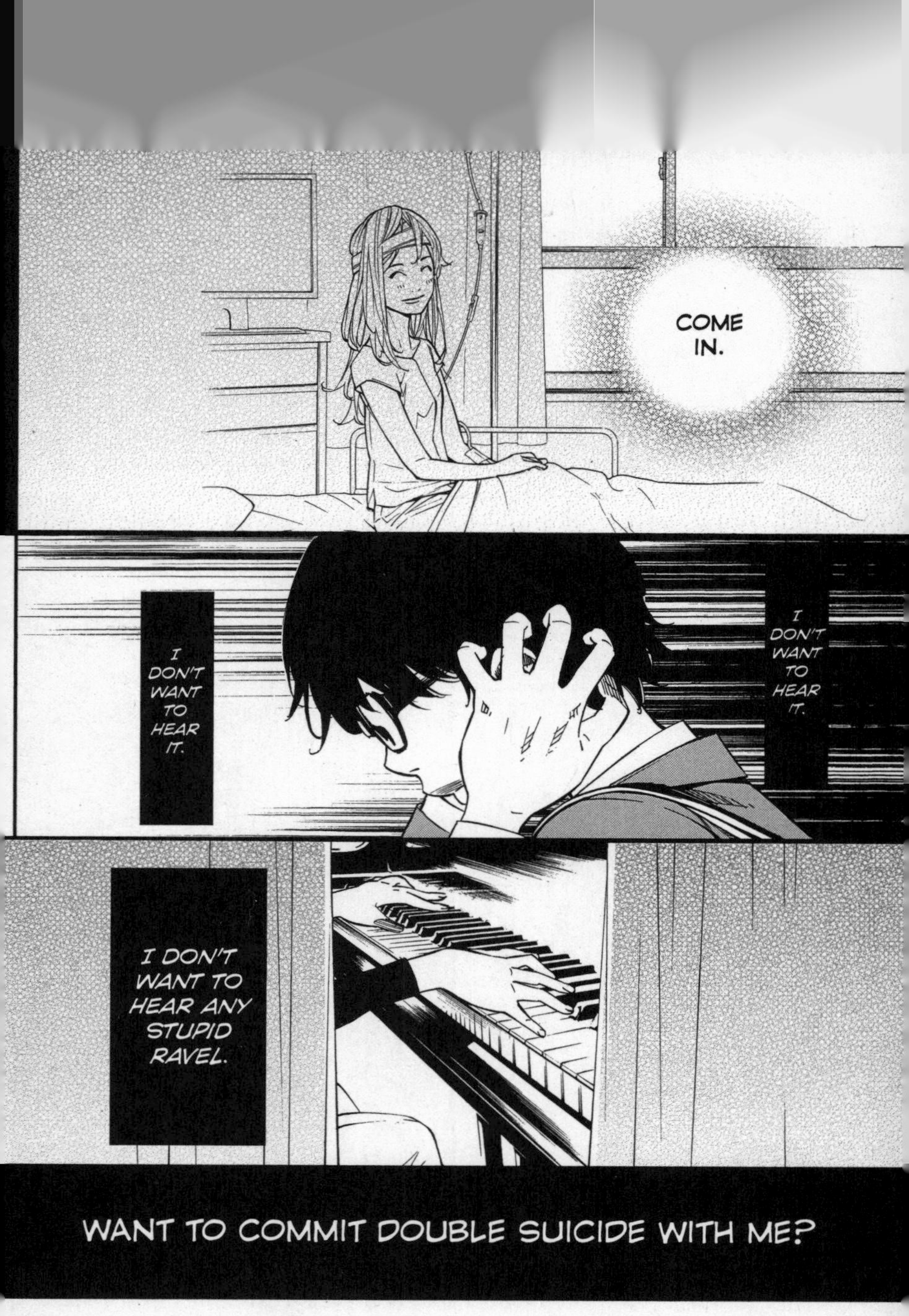
COME IN.
I DON'T WANT TO HEAR IT.
I DON'T WANT TO HEAR IT.
I DON'T WANT TO HEAR ANY STUPID RAVEL.
WANT TO COMMIT DOUBLE SUICIDE WITH ME?

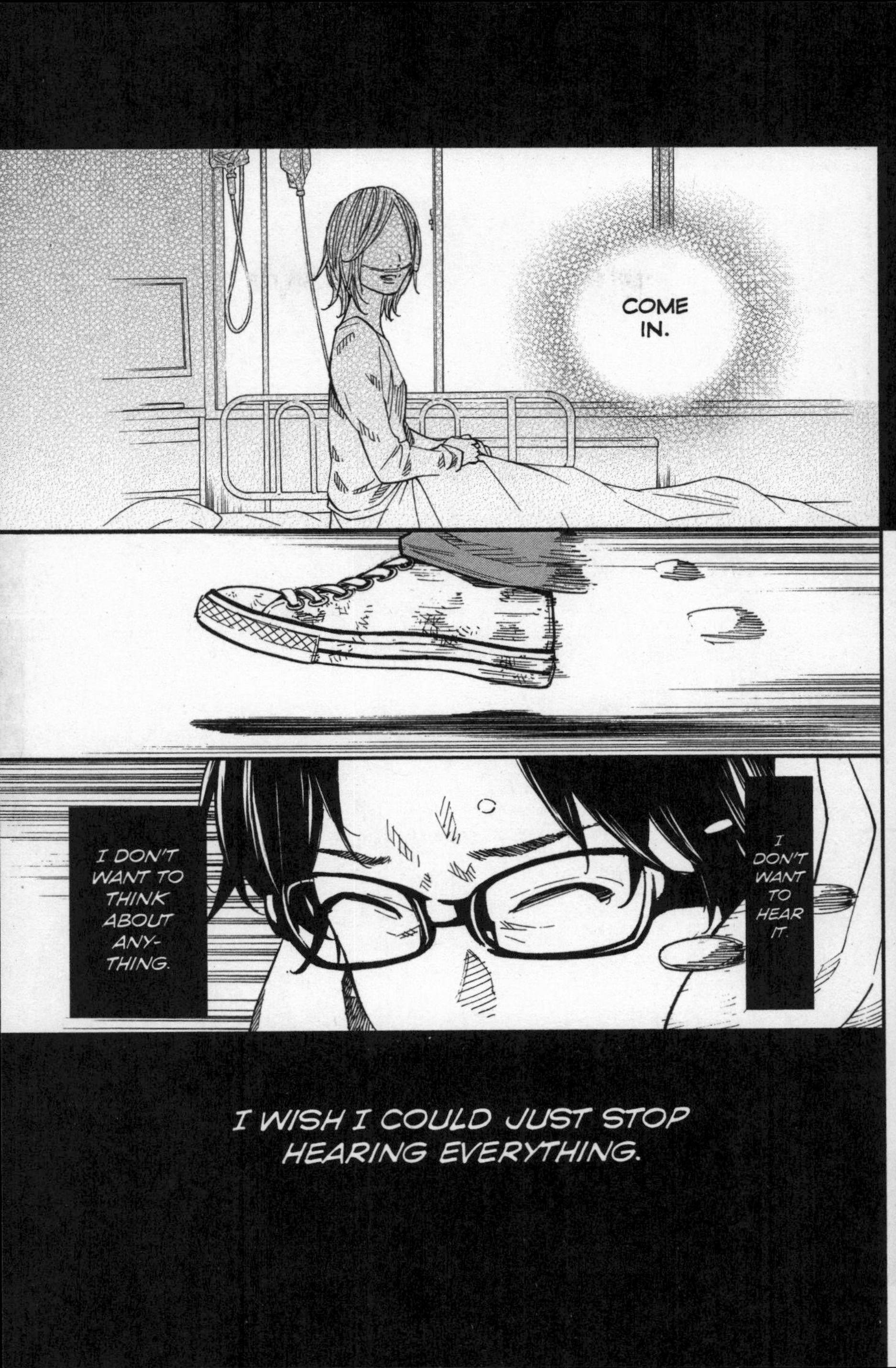
COME IN.
I DON'T WANT TO HEAR IT.
I DON'T WANT TO THINK ABOUT ANYTHING.
I WISH I COULD JUST STOP HEARING EVERYTHING.

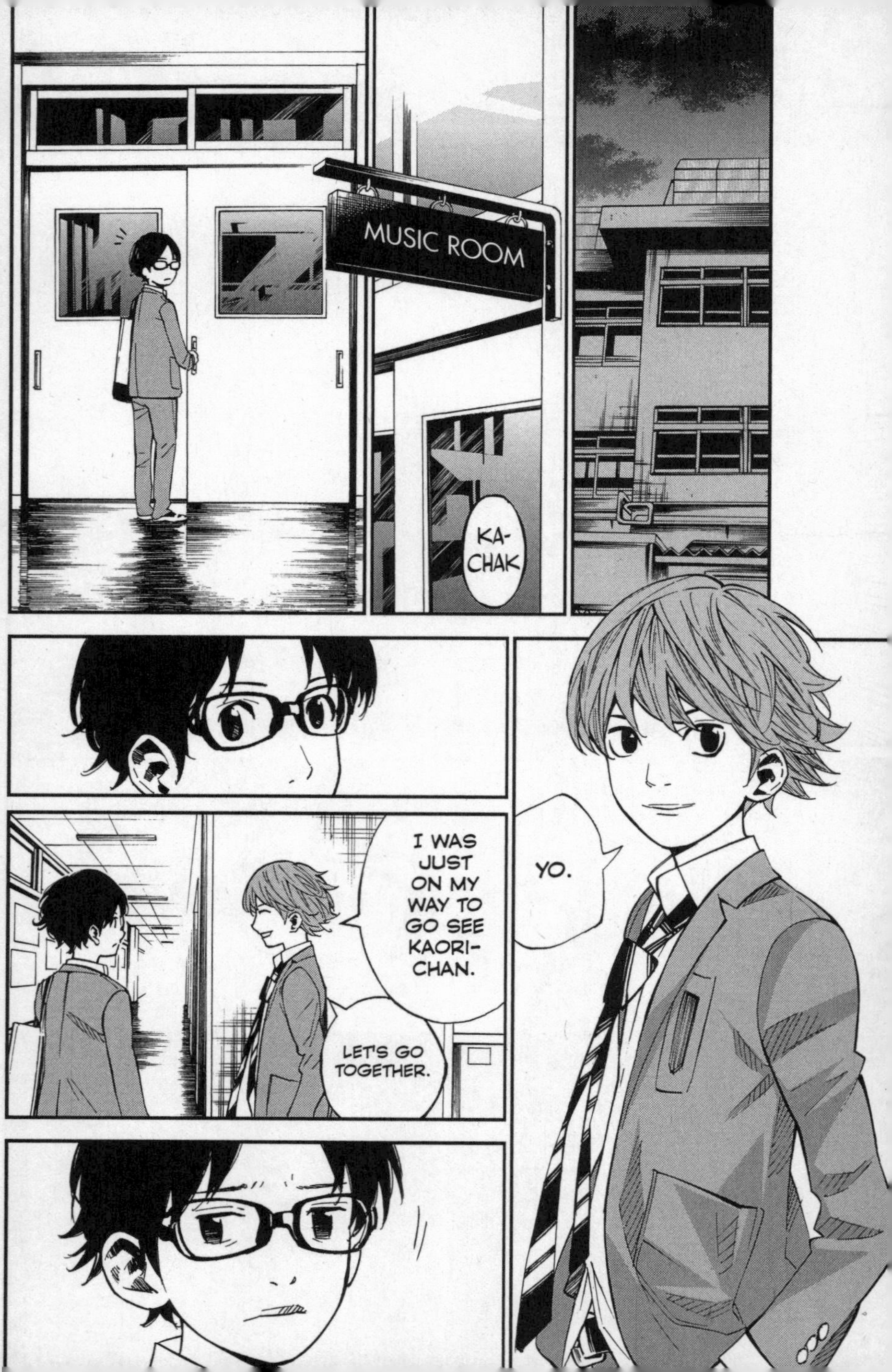
MUSIC ROOM
KA-CHAK
YO.
I WAS JUST ON MY WAY TO GO SEE KAORI-CHAN.
LET'S GO TOGETHER.

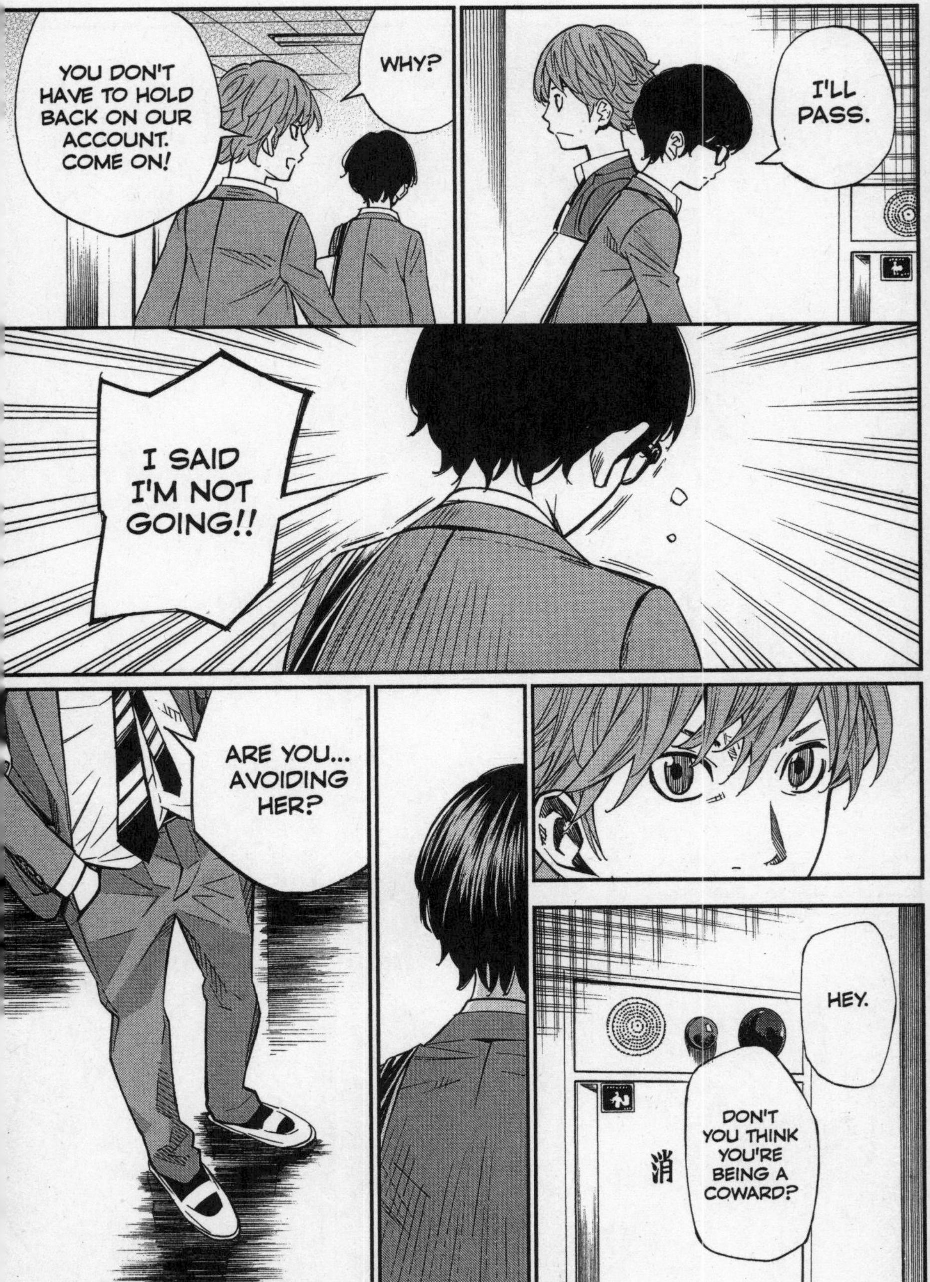
I'LL PASS.
WHY?
YOU DON'T HAVE TO HOLD BACK ON OUR ACCOUNT. COME ON!
I SAID I'M NOT GOING!!
HEY.
DON'T YOU THINK YOU'RE BEING A COWARD?
消
ARE YOU... AVOIDING HER?

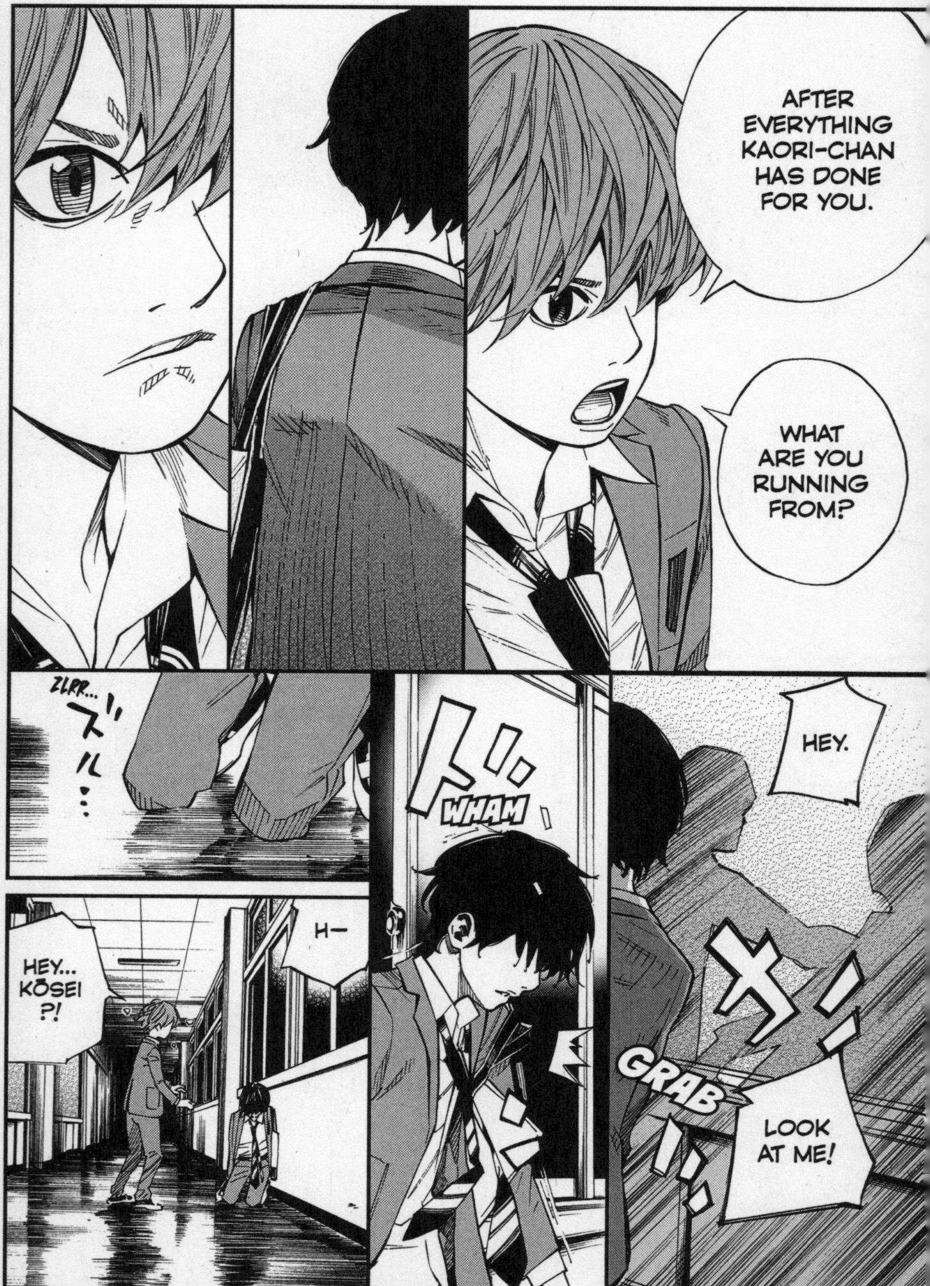
AFTER EVERYTHING KAORI-CHAN HAS DONE FOR YOU.
WHAT ARE YOU RUNNING FROM?
HEY.
GRAB
LOOK AT ME!
WHAM
ZLRR...
ズル…
H-
HEY... KŌSEI ?!

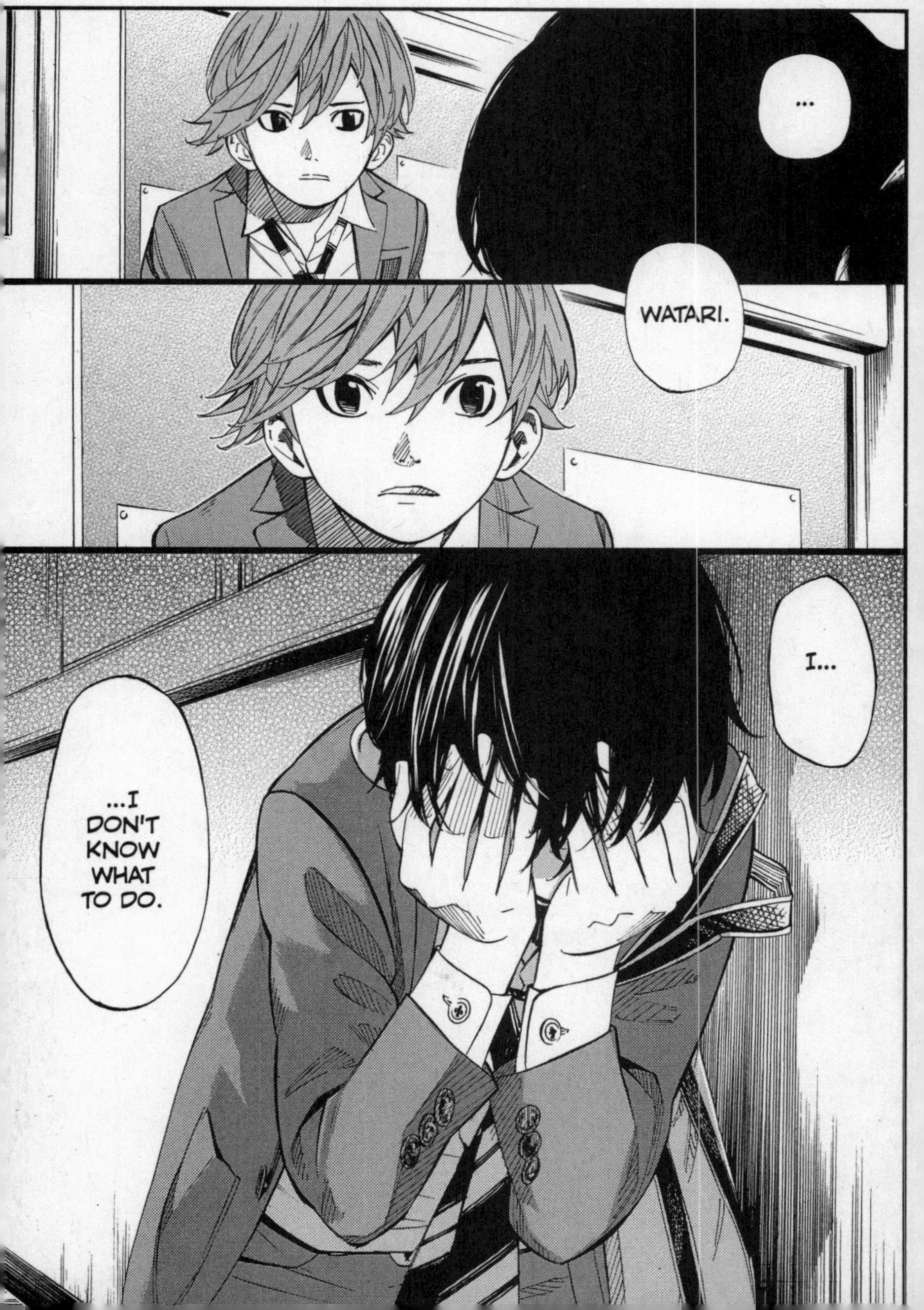
...
WATARI.
I...
...I DON'T KNOW WHAT TO DO.

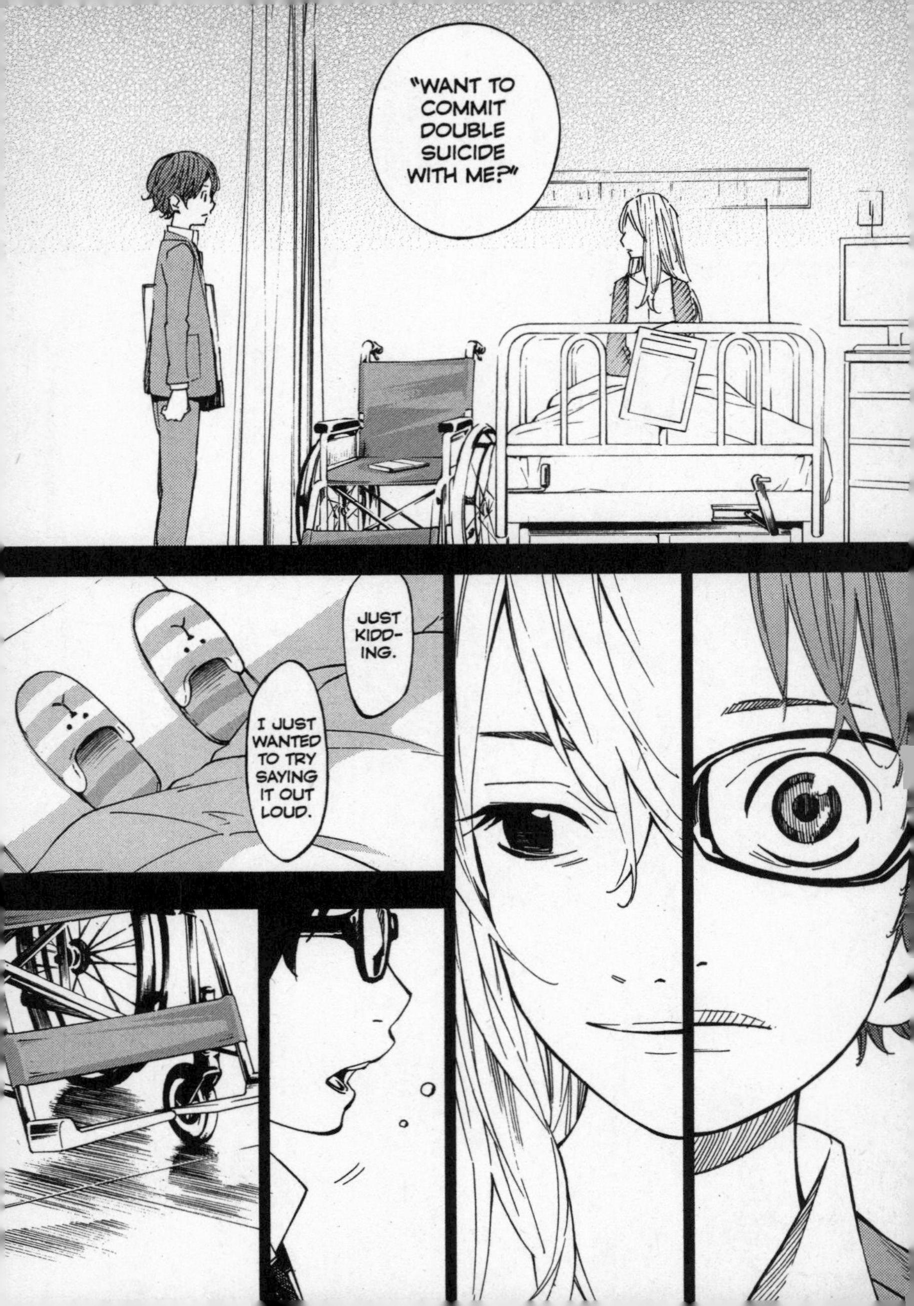
"WANT TO COMMIT DOUBLE SUICIDE WITH ME?"
JUST KIDD-ING.
I JUST WANTED TO TRY SAYING IT OUT LOUD.

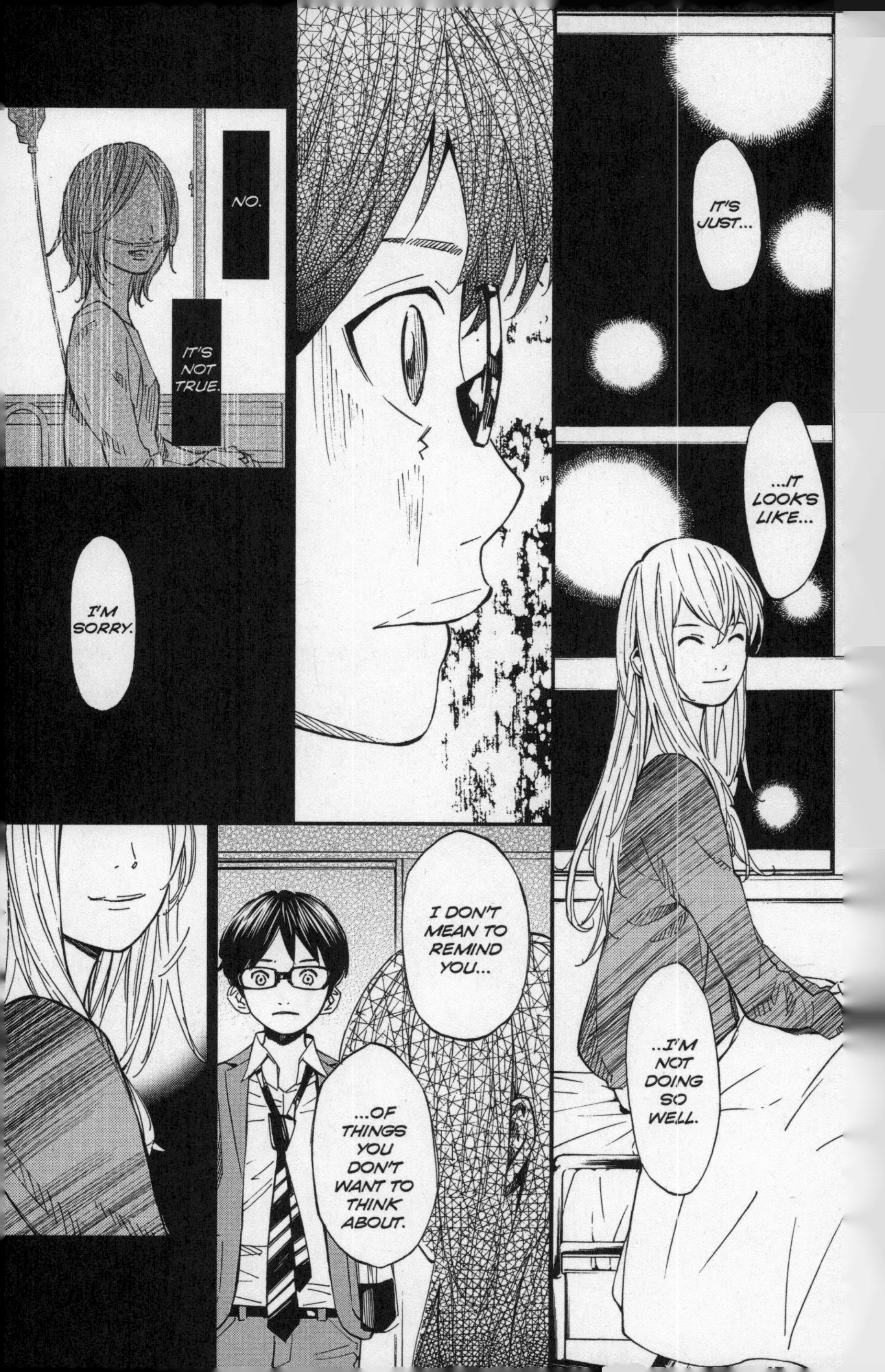
IT'S JUST...
...IT LOOKS LIKE...
...I'M NOT DOING SO WELL.
NO.
IT'S NOT TRUE.
I'M SORRY.
I DON'T MEAN TO REMIND YOU...
...OF THINGS YOU DON'T WANT TO THINK ABOUT.

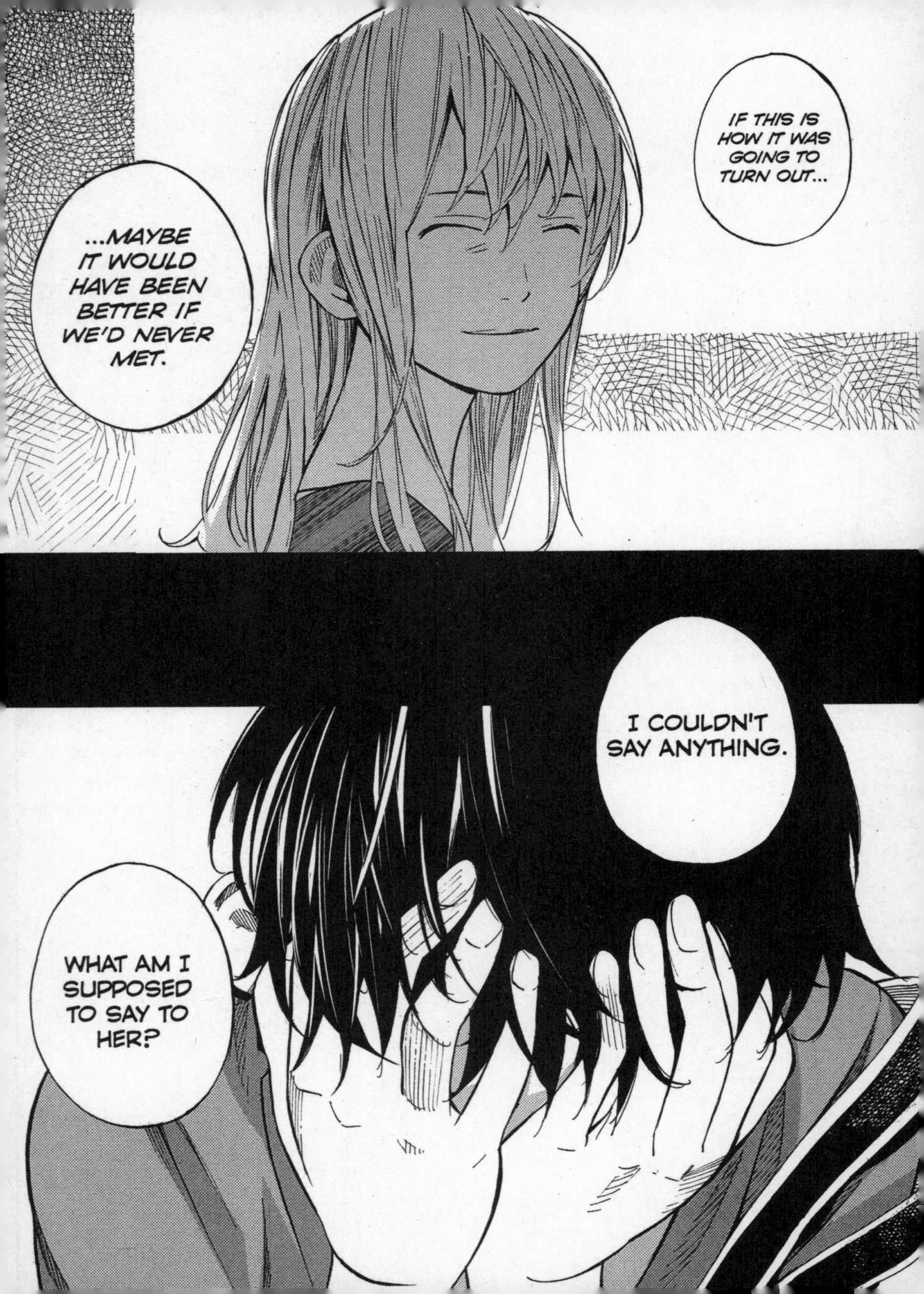
IF THIS IS HOW IT WAS GOING TO TURN OUT...
...MAYBE IT WOULD HAVE BEEN BETTER IF WE'D NEVER MET.
I COULDN'T SAY ANYTHING.
WHAT AM I SUPPOSED TO SAY TO HER?

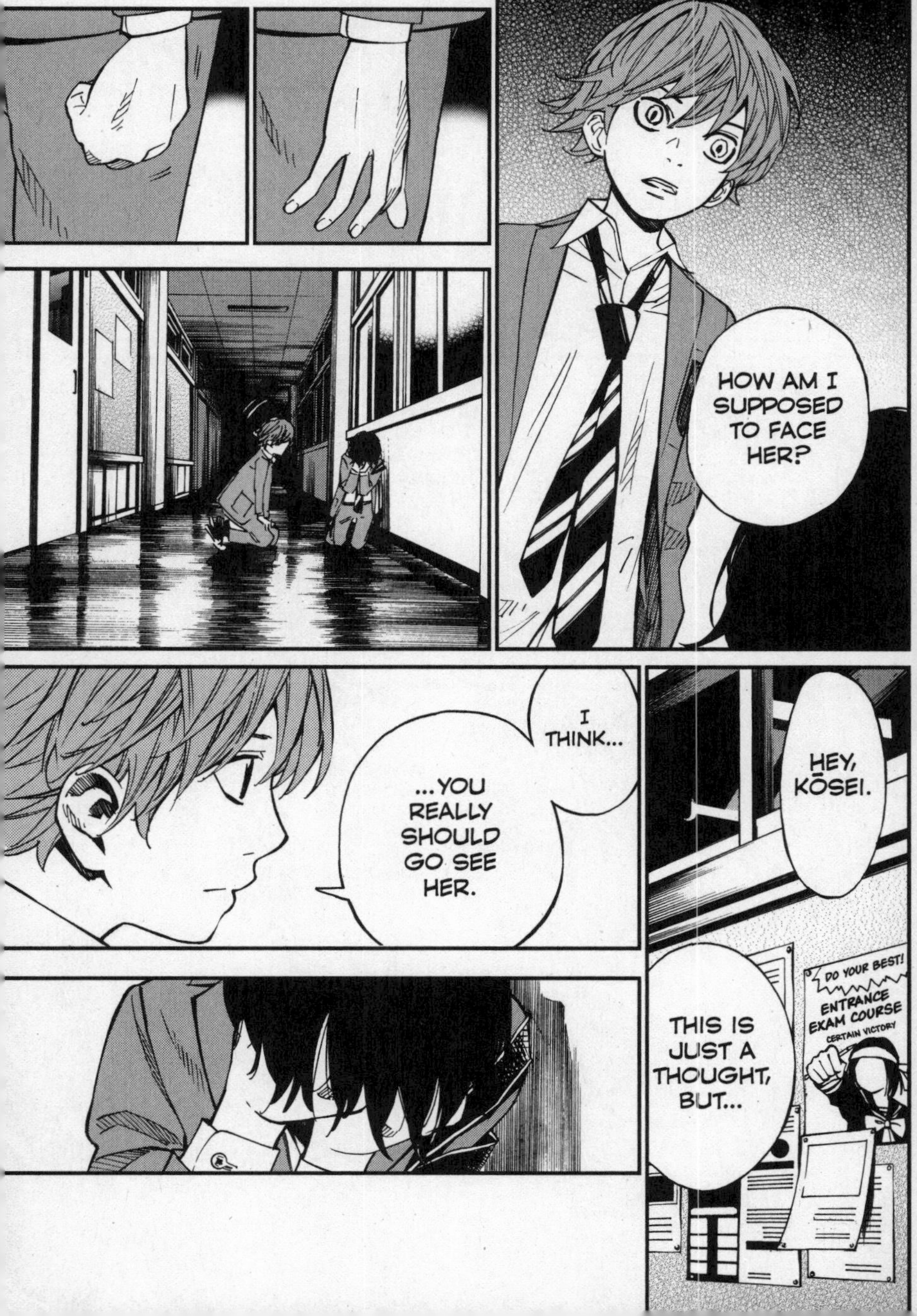
HOW AM I SUPPOSED TO FACE HER?
HEY, KŌSEI.
THIS IS JUST A THOUGHT, BUT...
DO YOUR BEST!
ENTRANCE EXAM COURSE
CERTAIN VICTORY
I THINK...
...YOU REALLY SHOULD GO SEE HER.

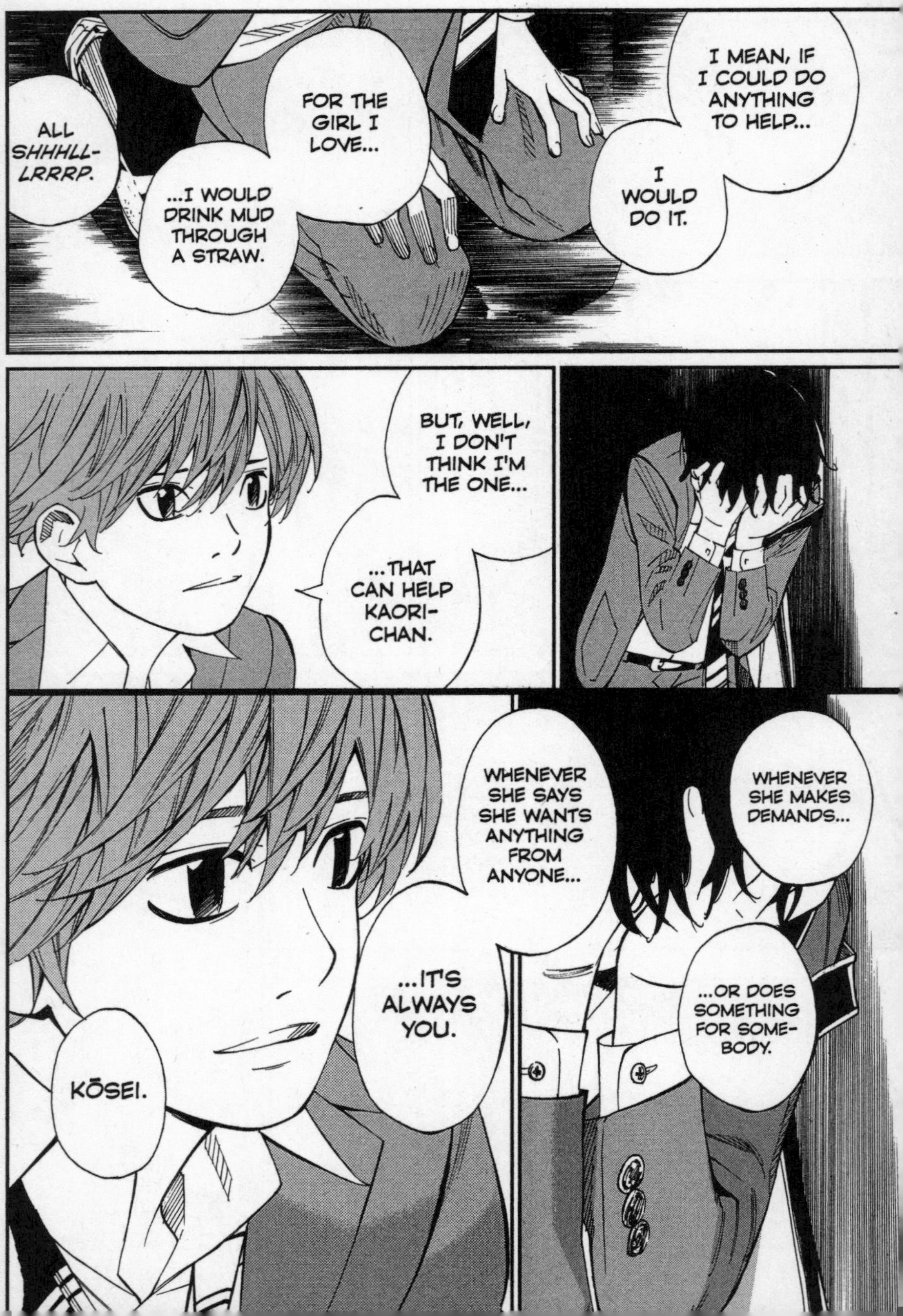
I MEAN, IF I COULD DO ANYTHING TO HELP...
I WOULD DO IT.
FOR THE GIRL I LOVE...
...I WOULD DRINK MUD THROUGH A STRAW.
ALL SHHHLL-LRRRP.
BUT, WELL, I DON'T THINK I'M THE ONE...
...THAT CAN HELP KAORI-CHAN.
WHENEVER SHE MAKES DEMANDS...
...OR DOES SOMETHING FOR SOME-BODY.
WHENEVER SHE SAYS SHE WANTS ANYTHING FROM ANYONE...
...IT'S ALWAYS YOU.
KŌSEI.

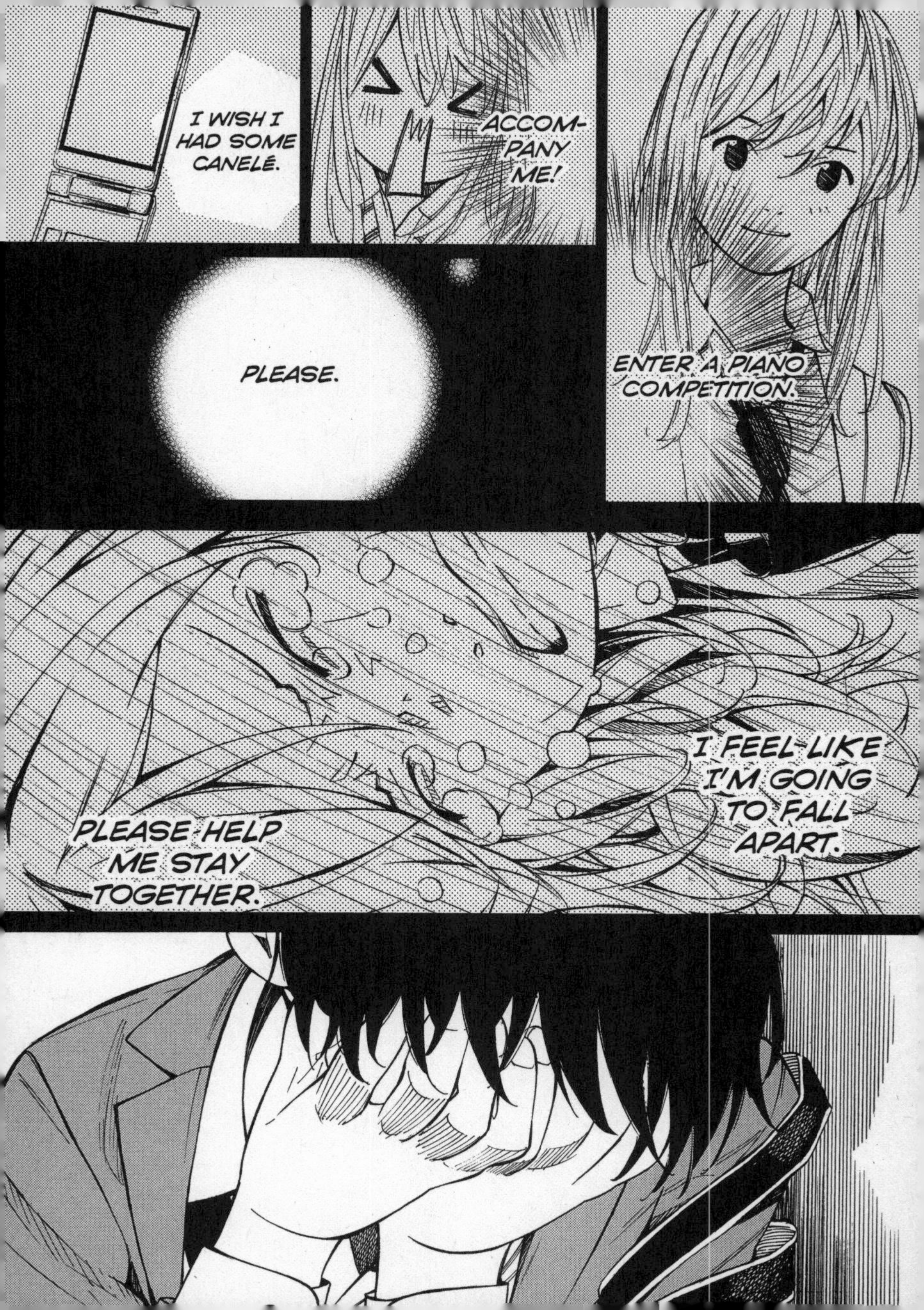
ENTER A PIANO COMPETITION.
ACCOM-PANY ME!
I WISH I HAD SOME CANELÉ.
PLEASE.
I FEEL LIKE I'M GOING TO FALL APART.
PLEASE HELP ME STAY TOGETHER.

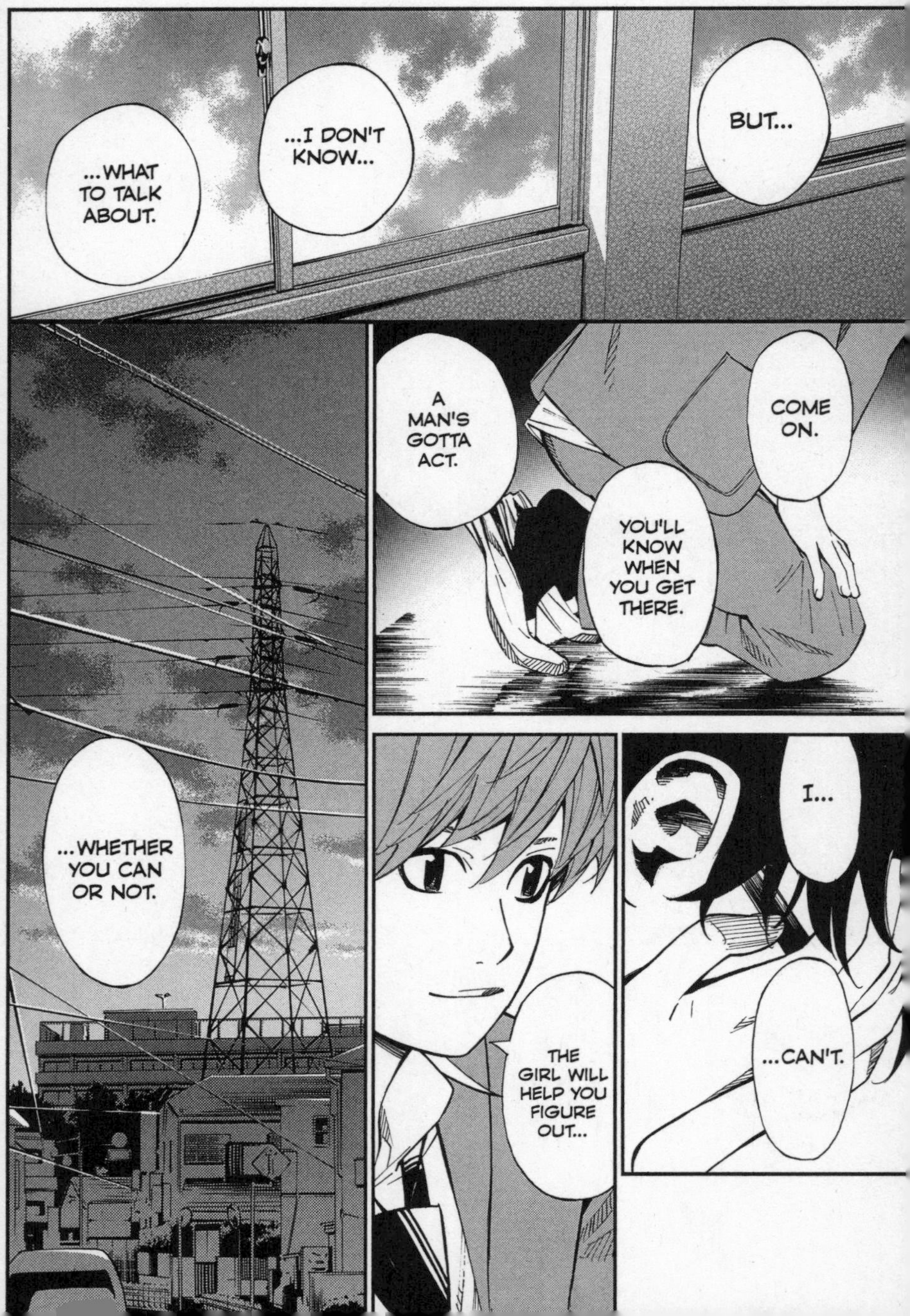
BUT...
...I DON'T KNOW...
...WHAT TO TALK ABOUT.
COME ON.
A MAN'S GOTTA ACT.
YOU'LL KNOW WHEN YOU GET THERE.
I...
...CAN'T.
THE GIRL WILL HELP YOU FIGURE OUT...
...WHETHER YOU CAN OR NOT.

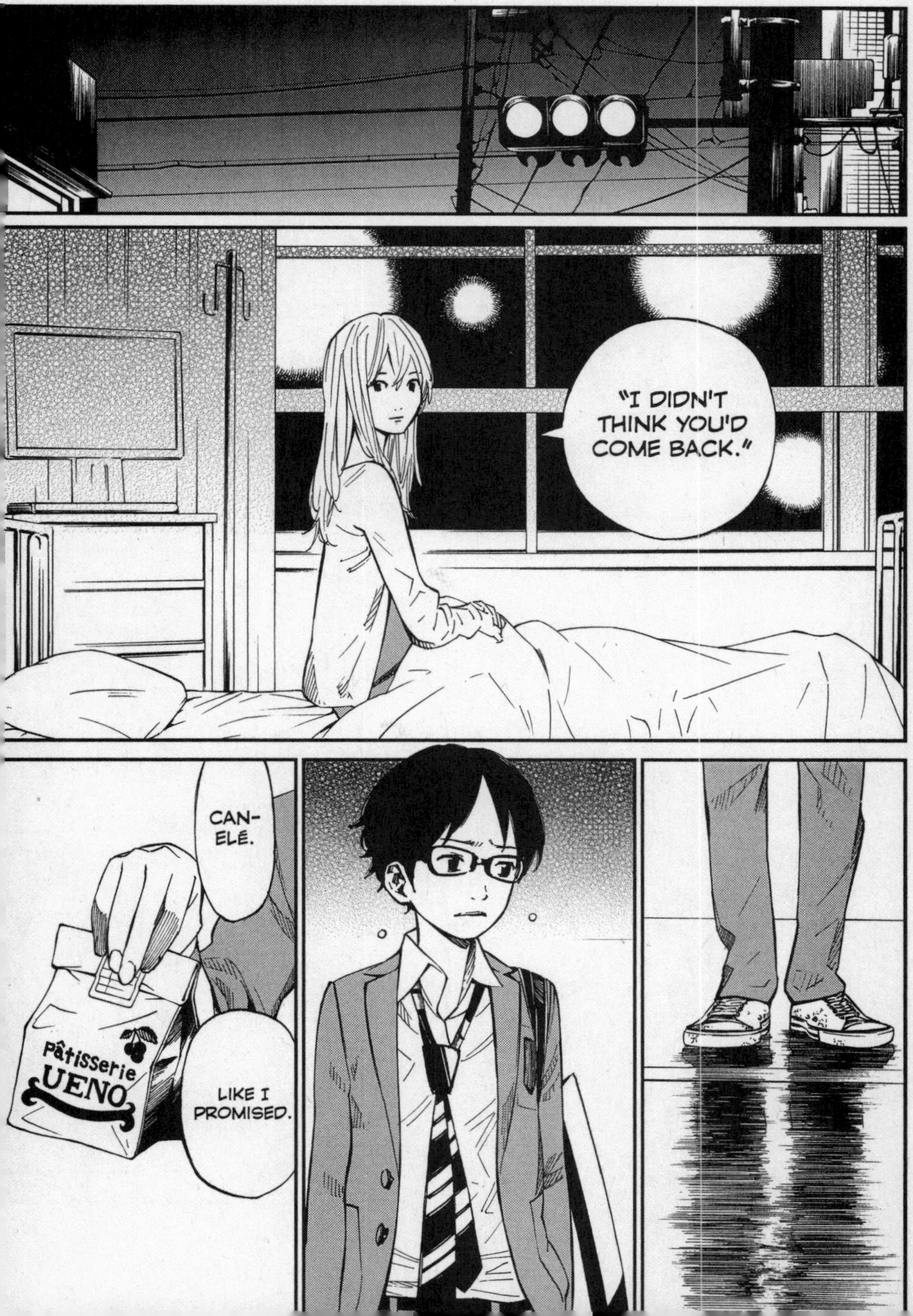
"I DIDN'T THINK YOU'D COME BACK."
CAN-ELÉ.
pâtisserie UENO
LIKE I PROMISED.

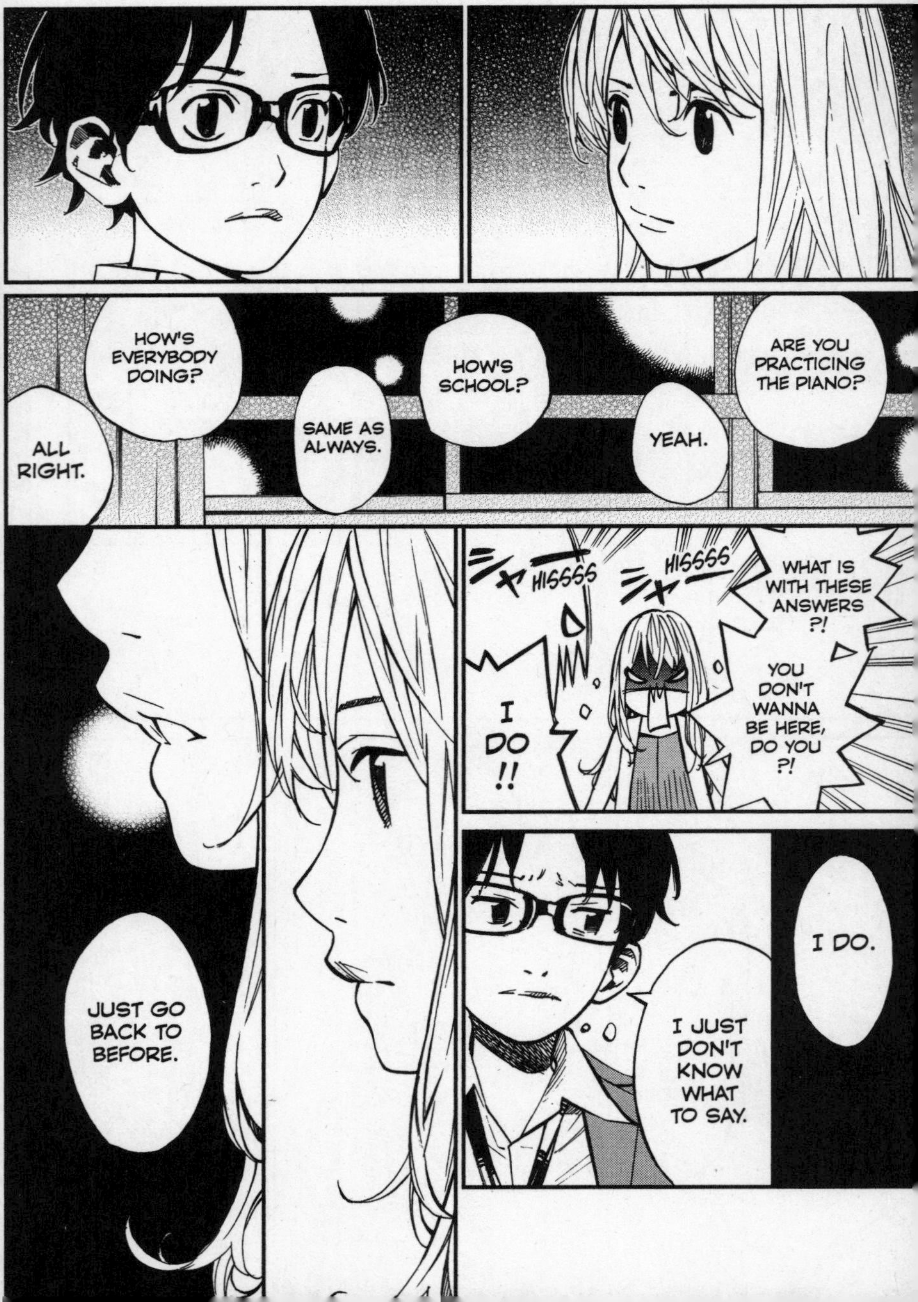
ARE YOU PRACTICING THE PIANO?
YEAH.
HOW'S SCHOOL?
SAME AS ALWAYS.
HOW'S EVERYBODY DOING?
ALL RIGHT.
シャー HISSSS
シャー HISSSS
WHAT IS WITH THESE ANSWERS?!
YOU DON'T WANNA BE HERE, DO YOU?!
I DO!!
I DO.
I JUST DON'T KNOW WHAT TO SAY.
JUST GO BACK TO BEFORE.

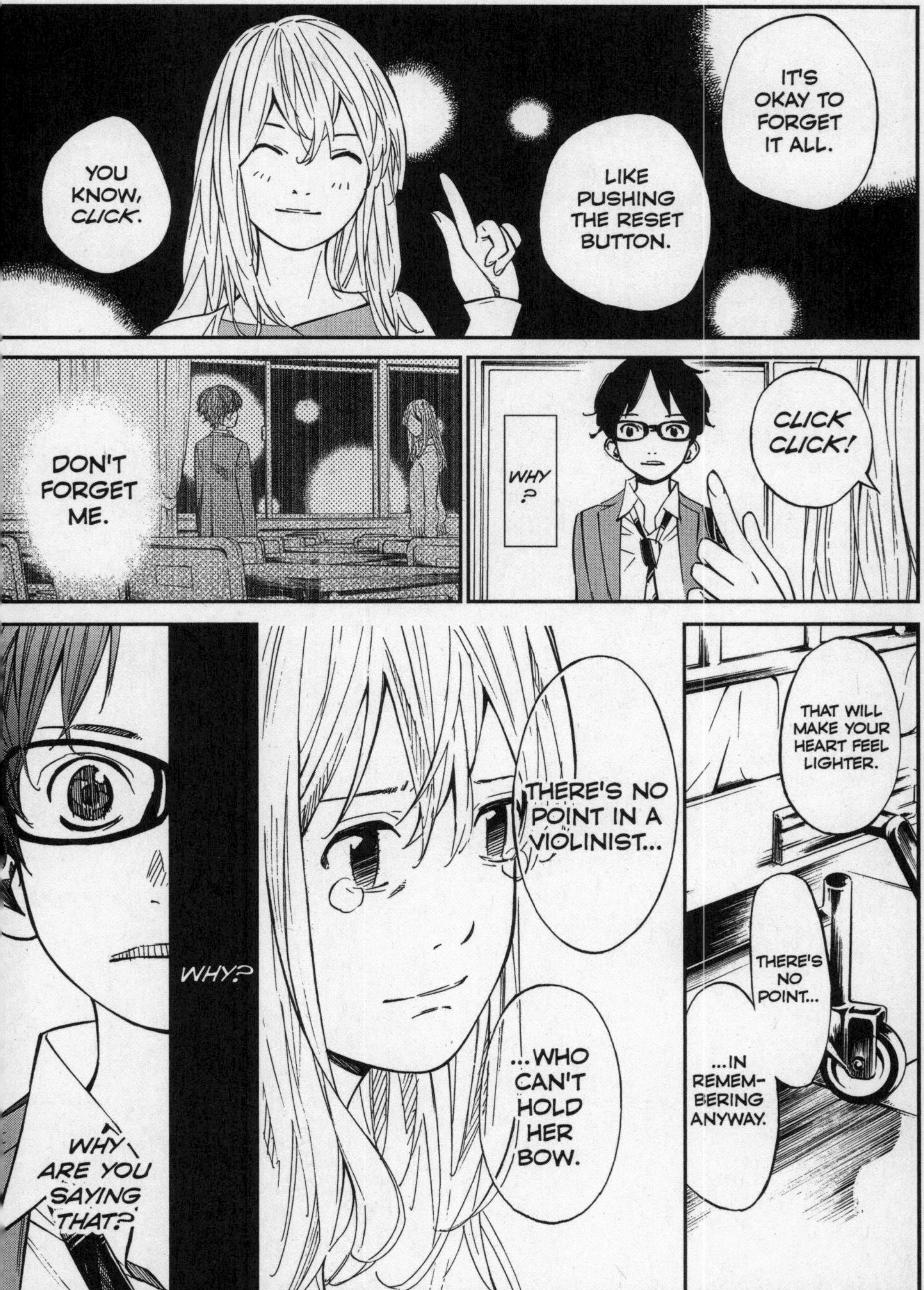
IT'S OKAY TO FORGET IT ALL.
LIKE PUSHING THE RESET BUTTON.
YOU KNOW, CLICK.
CLICK CLICK!
WHY?
DON'T FORGET ME.
THAT WILL MAKE YOUR HEART FEEL LIGHTER.
THERE'S NO POINT...
...IN REMEM-BERING ANYWAY.
THERE'S NO POINT IN A VIOLINIST...
...WHO CAN'T HOLD HER BOW.
WHY?
WHY ARE YOU SAYING THAT?

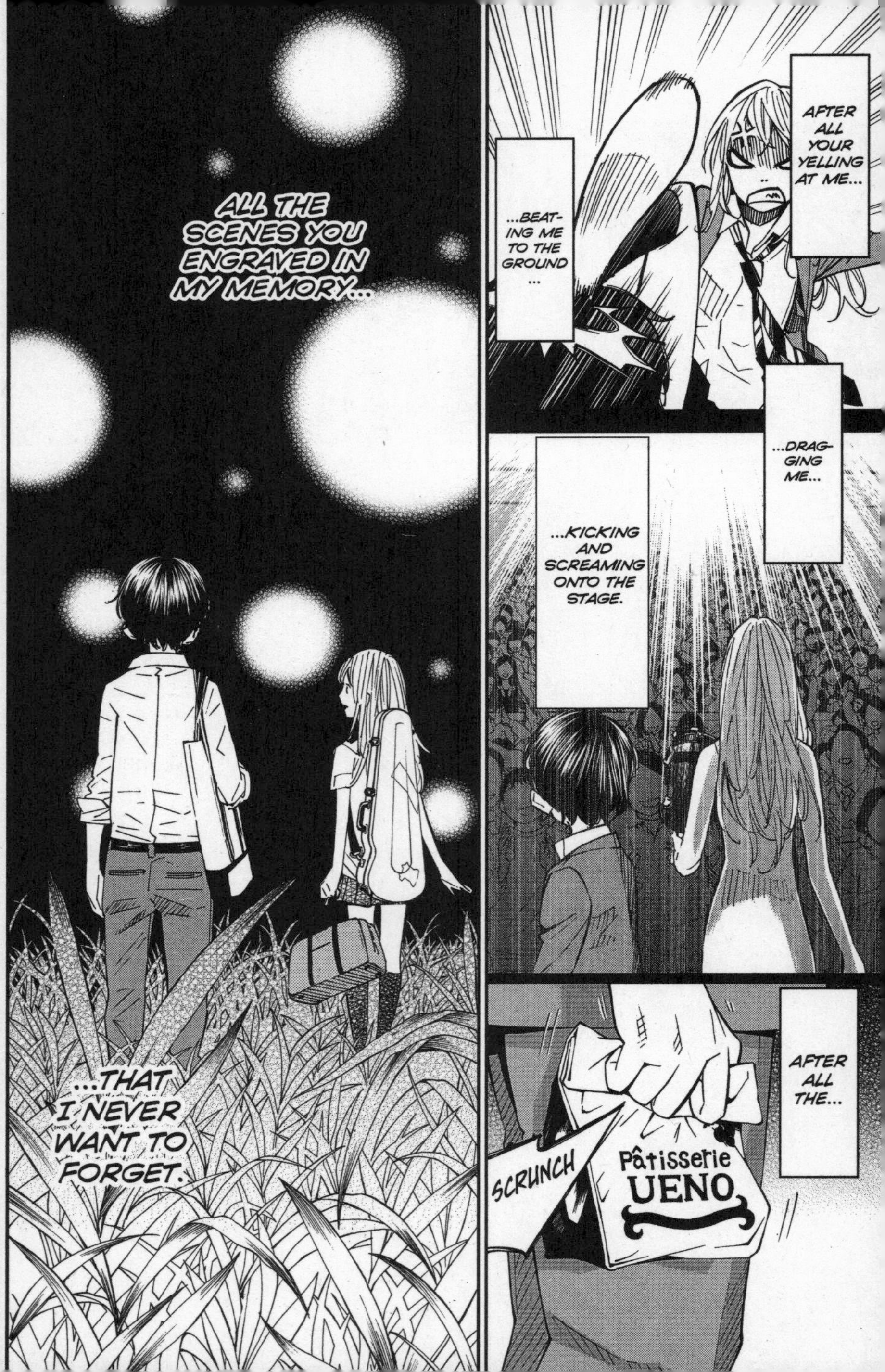
AFTER ALL YOUR YELLING AT ME...
...BEATING ME TO THE GROUND...
...DRAGGING ME...
...KICKING AND SCREAMING ONTO THE STAGE.
AFTER ALL THE...
Pâtisserie UENO
SCRUNCH
ALL THE SCENES YOU ENGRAVED IN MY MEMORY...
...THAT I NEVER WANT TO FORGET.

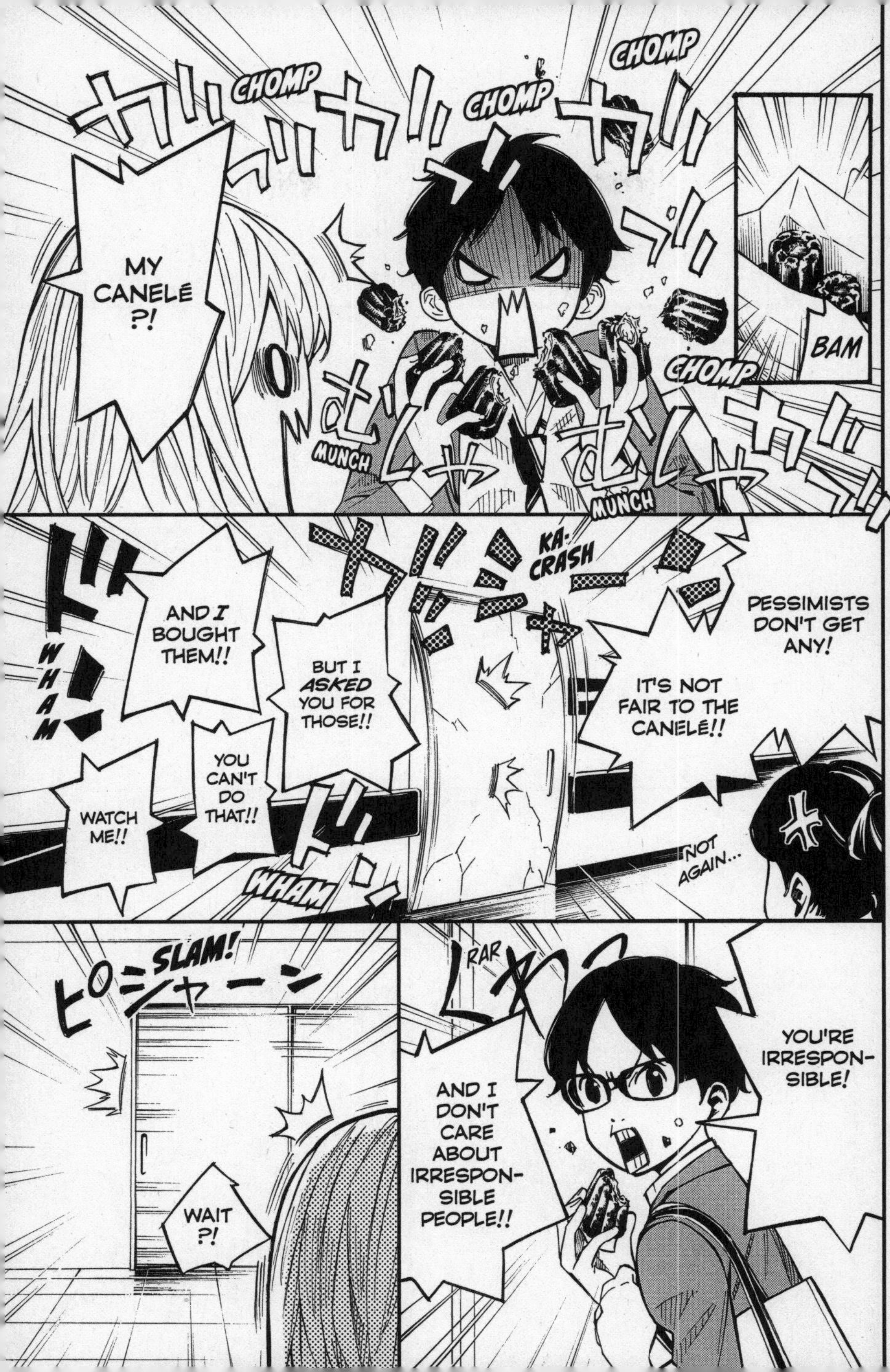
BAM
CHOMP
CHOMP
CHOMP
MY CANELÉ ?!
CHOMP
MUNCH
MUNCH
PESSIMISTS DON'T GET ANY!
IT'S NOT FAIR TO THE CANELÉ!!
NOT AGAIN...
KA-CRASH
BUT I *ASKED* YOU FOR THOSE!!
AND *I* BOUGHT THEM!!
YOU CAN'T DO THAT!!
WHAM
WATCH ME!!
WHAM
RAR
YOU'RE IRRESPON-SIBLE!
AND I DON'T CARE ABOUT IRRESPON-SIBLE PEOPLE!!
SLAM!
WAIT ?!

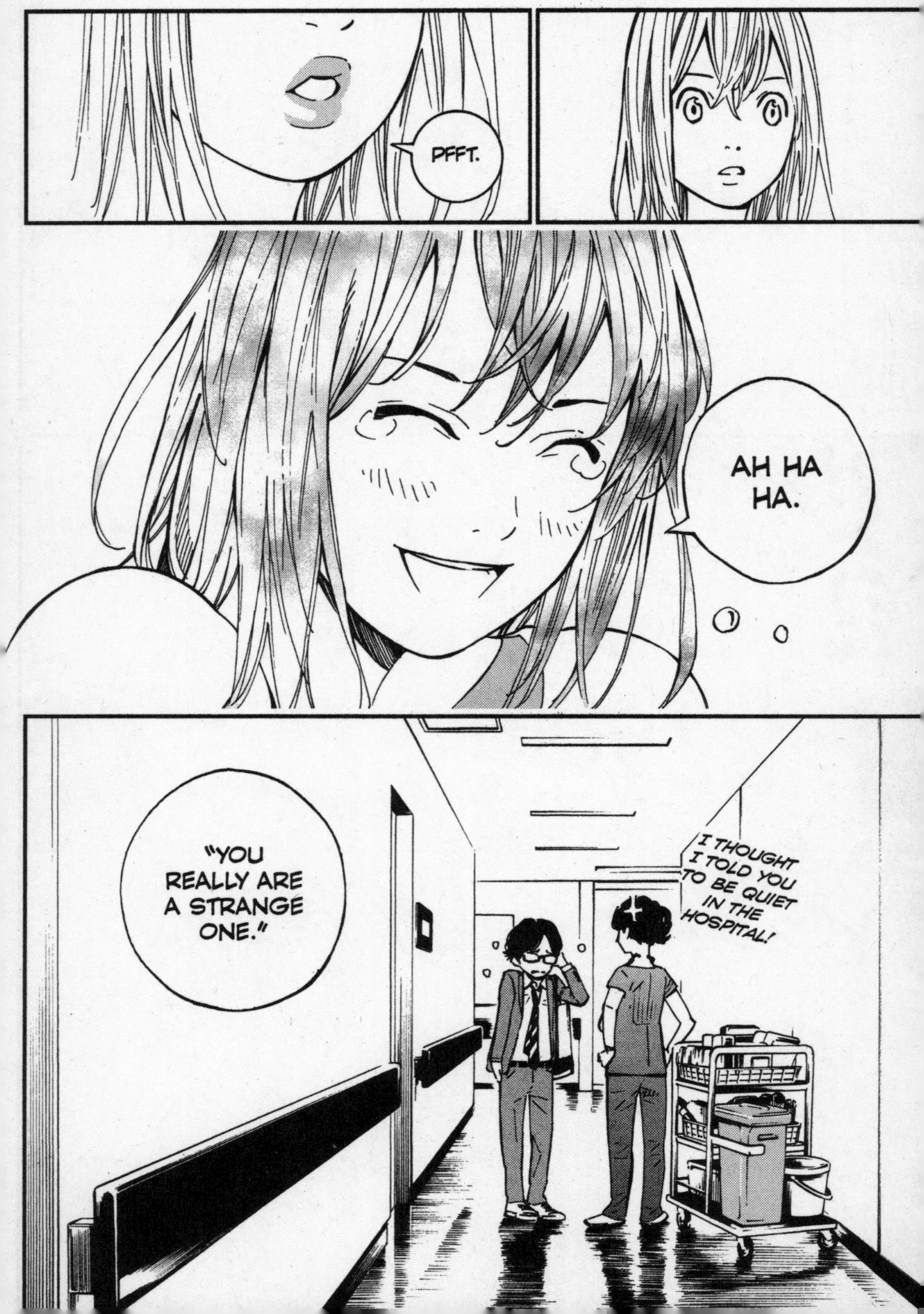
PFFT.
AH HA HA.
I THOUGHT I TOLD YOU TO BE QUIET IN THE HOSPITAL!
"YOU REALLY ARE A STRANGE ONE."

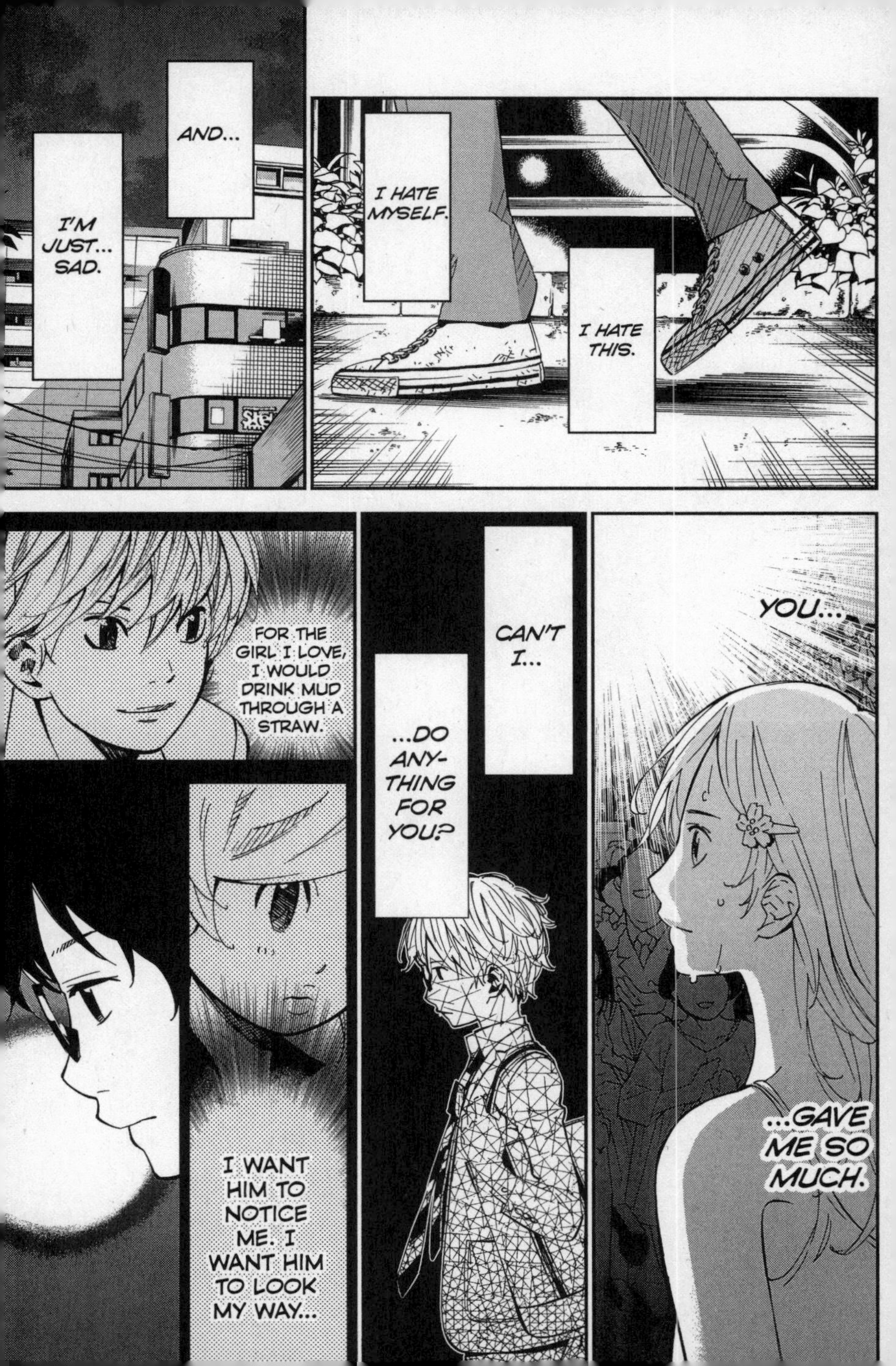
I HATE MYSELF.
I HATE THIS.
AND...
I'M JUST... SAD.
YOU...
...GAVE ME SO MUCH.
CAN'T I...
...DO ANYTHING FOR YOU?
FOR THE GIRL I LOVE, I WOULD DRINK MUD THROUGH A STRAW.
I WANT HIM TO NOTICE ME. I WANT HIM TO LOOK MY WAY...

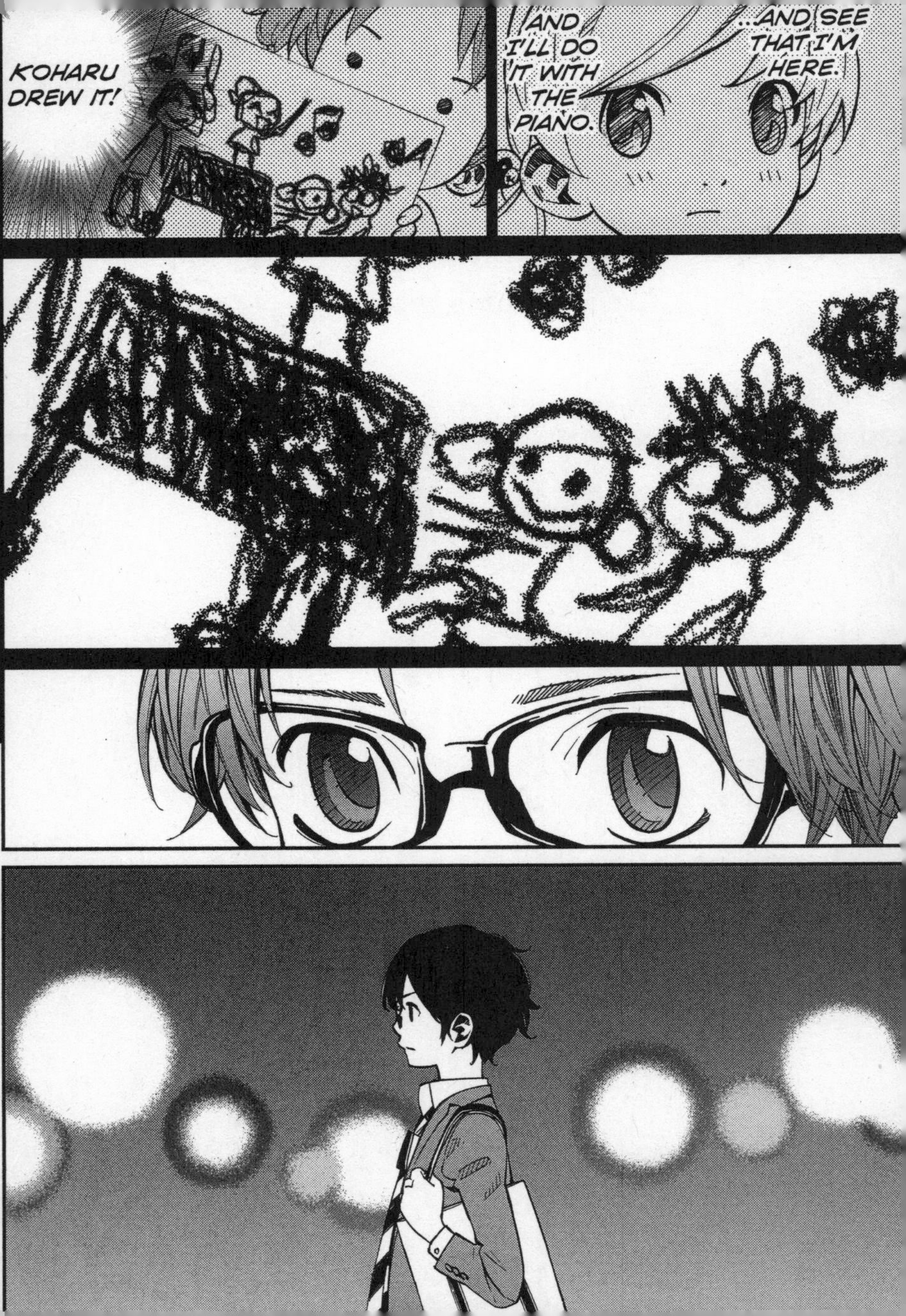
AND I'LL DO IT WITH THE PIANO.
...AND SEE THAT I'M HERE.
KOHARU DREW IT!

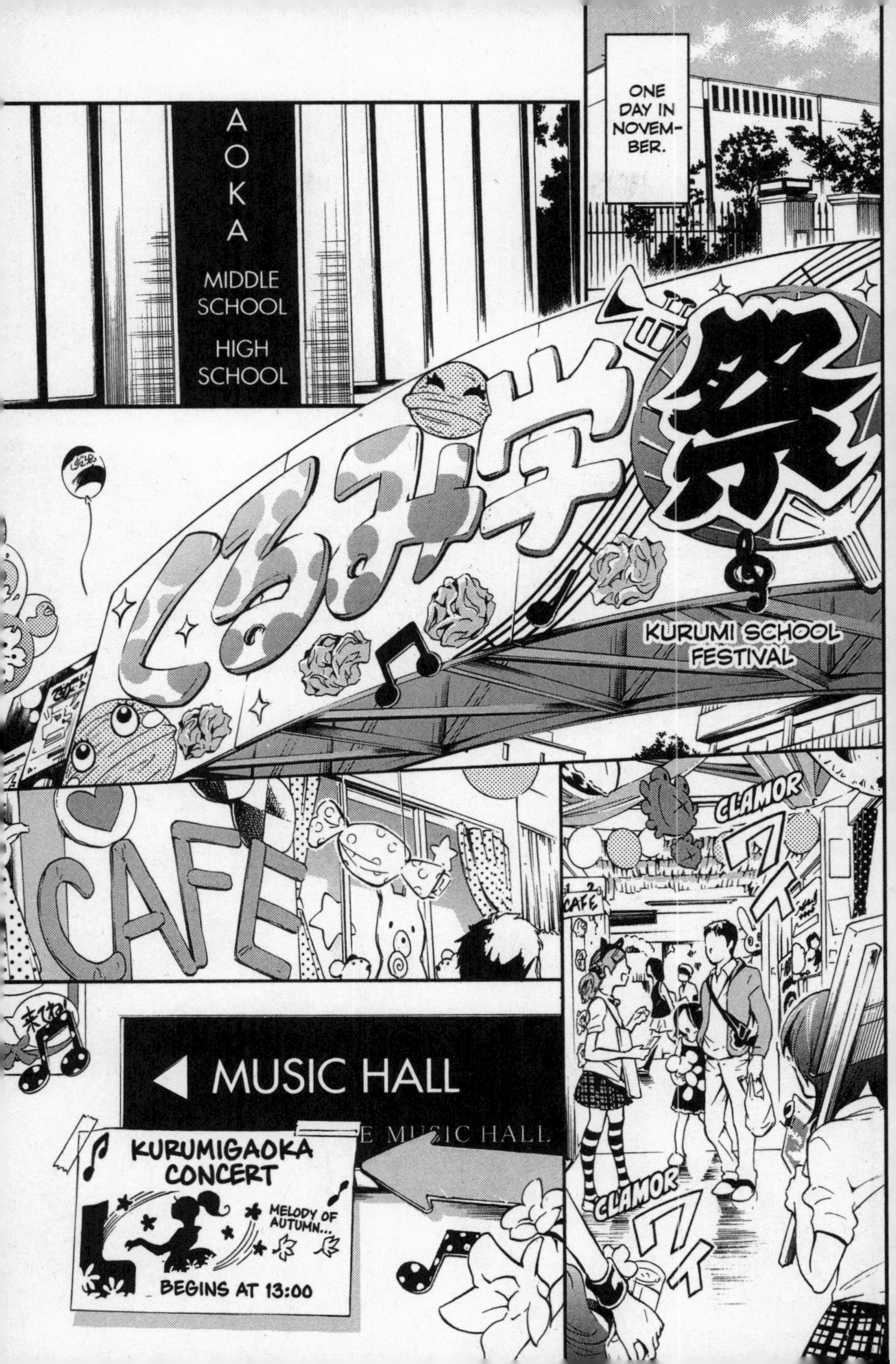
ONE DAY IN NOVEM-BER.
A O K A
MIDDLE SCHOOL
HIGH SCHOOL
KURUMI SCHOOL FESTIVAL
CLAMOR
CLAMOR
CAFE
CAFE
◀ MUSIC HALL
KURUMIGAOKA CONCERT
MELODY OF AUTUMN...
BEGINS AT 13:00

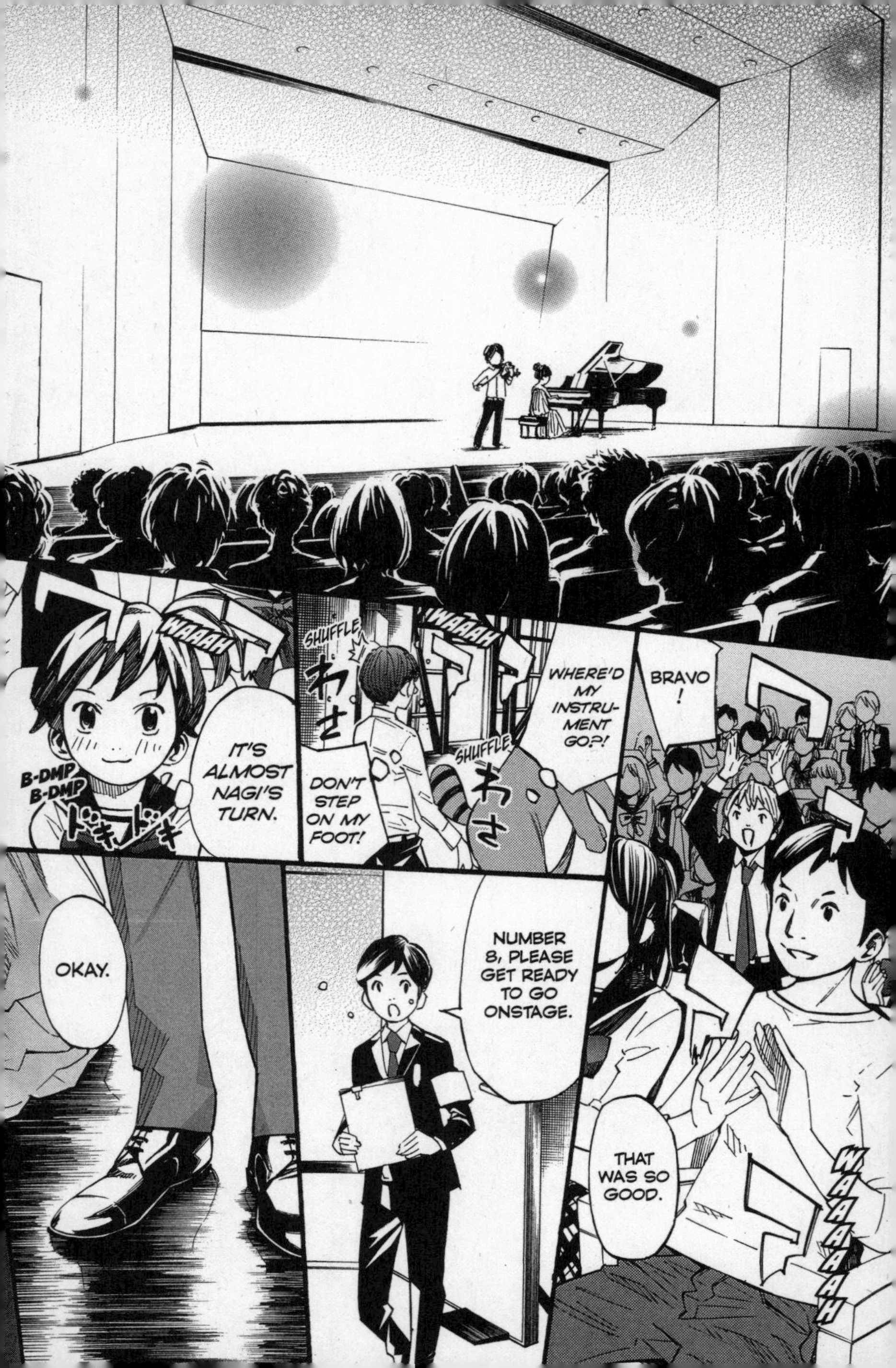
BRAVO!
THAT WAS SO GOOD.
WAAAAAAH
WAAAH
WHERE'D MY INSTRU-MENT GO?!
SHUFFLE
わさ
SHUFFLE
わさ
DON'T STEP ON MY FOOT!
WAAAH
IT'S ALMOST NAGI'S TURN.
B-DMP B-DMP
ドキドキ
NUMBER 8, PLEASE GET READY TO GO ONSTAGE.
OKAY.

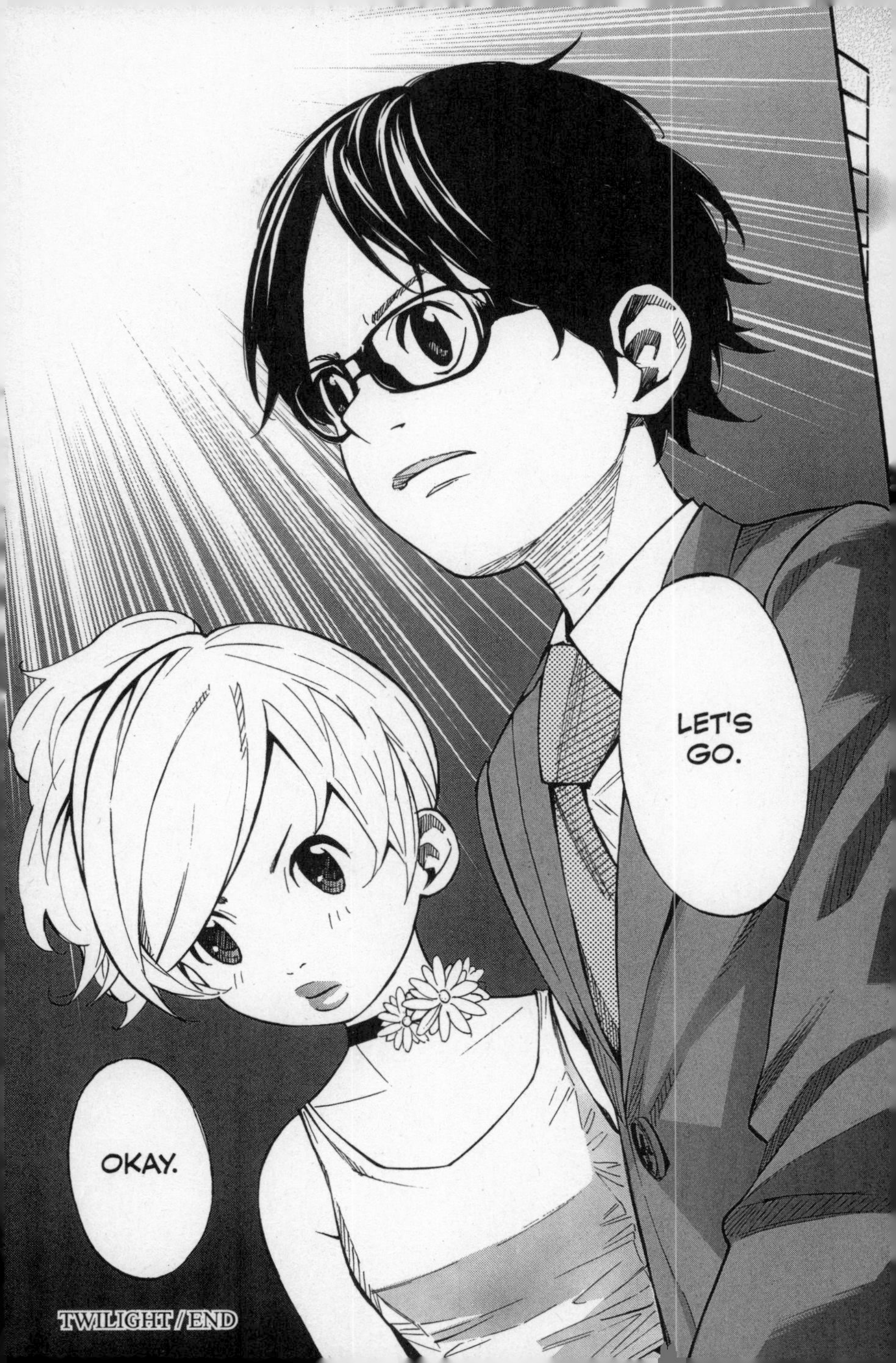
LET'S GO.
OKAY.
TWILIGHT / END

Your Lie in April

I met the girl under full-bloomed cherry blossoms, and my fate has begun to change.

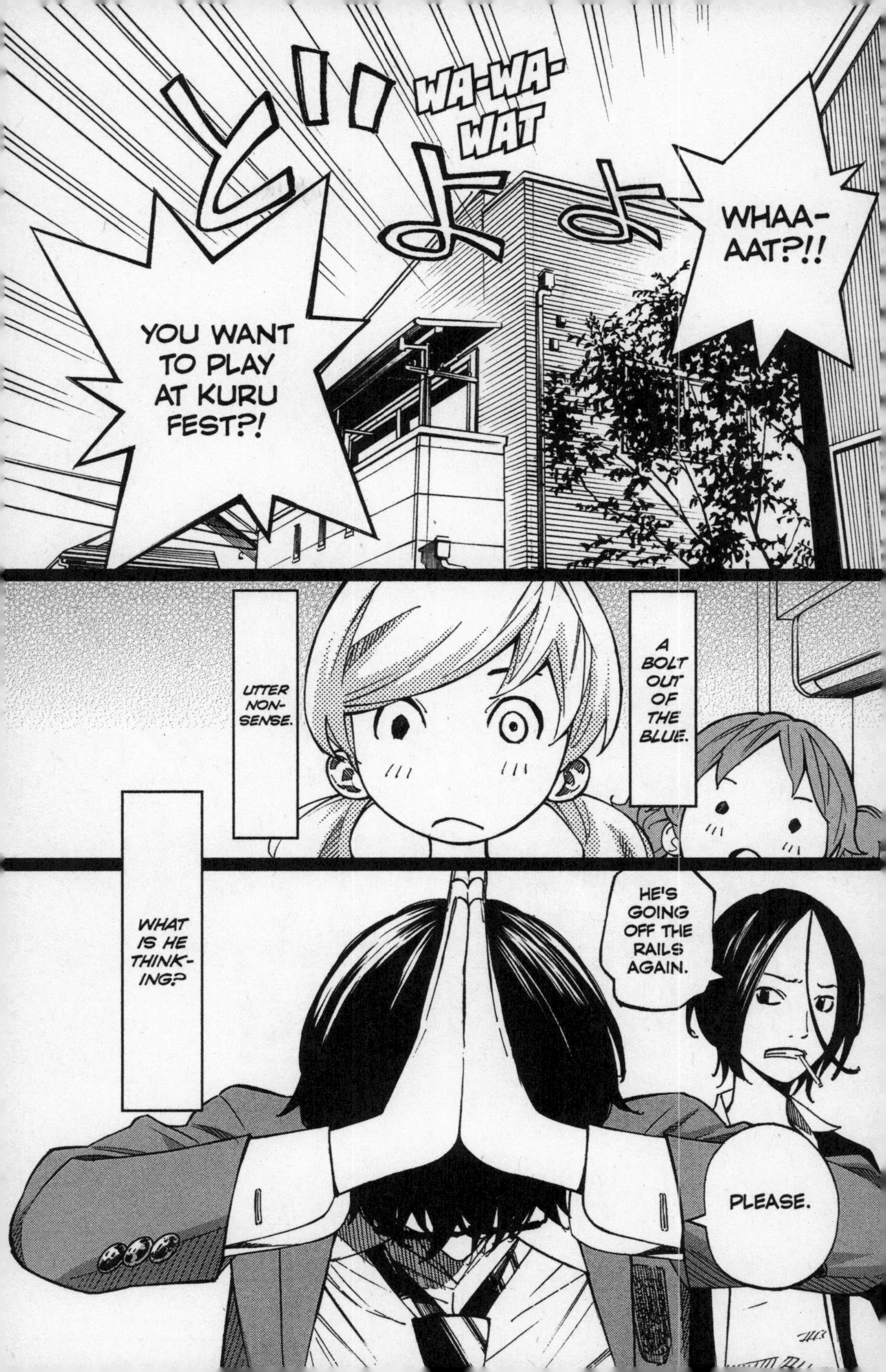
どよよ
WA-WA-WAT
WHAAA-AAT?!!
YOU WANT TO PLAY AT KURU FEST?!
A BOLT OUT OF THE BLUE.
UTTER NON-SENSE.
HE'S GOING OFF THE RAILS AGAIN.
WHAT IS HE THINK-ING?
PLEASE.

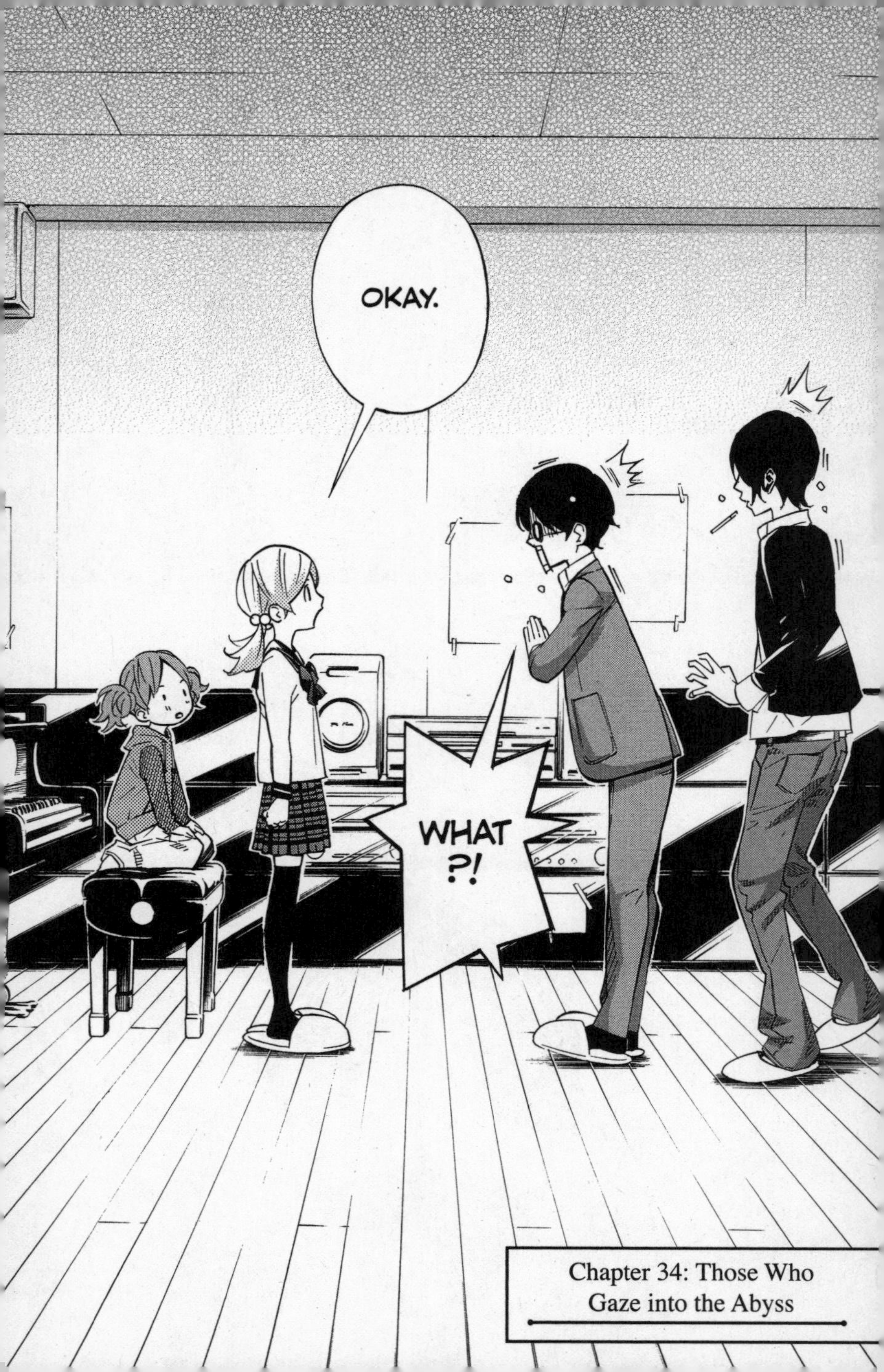
OKAY.
WHAT ?!

Chapter 34: Those Who Gaze into the Abyss

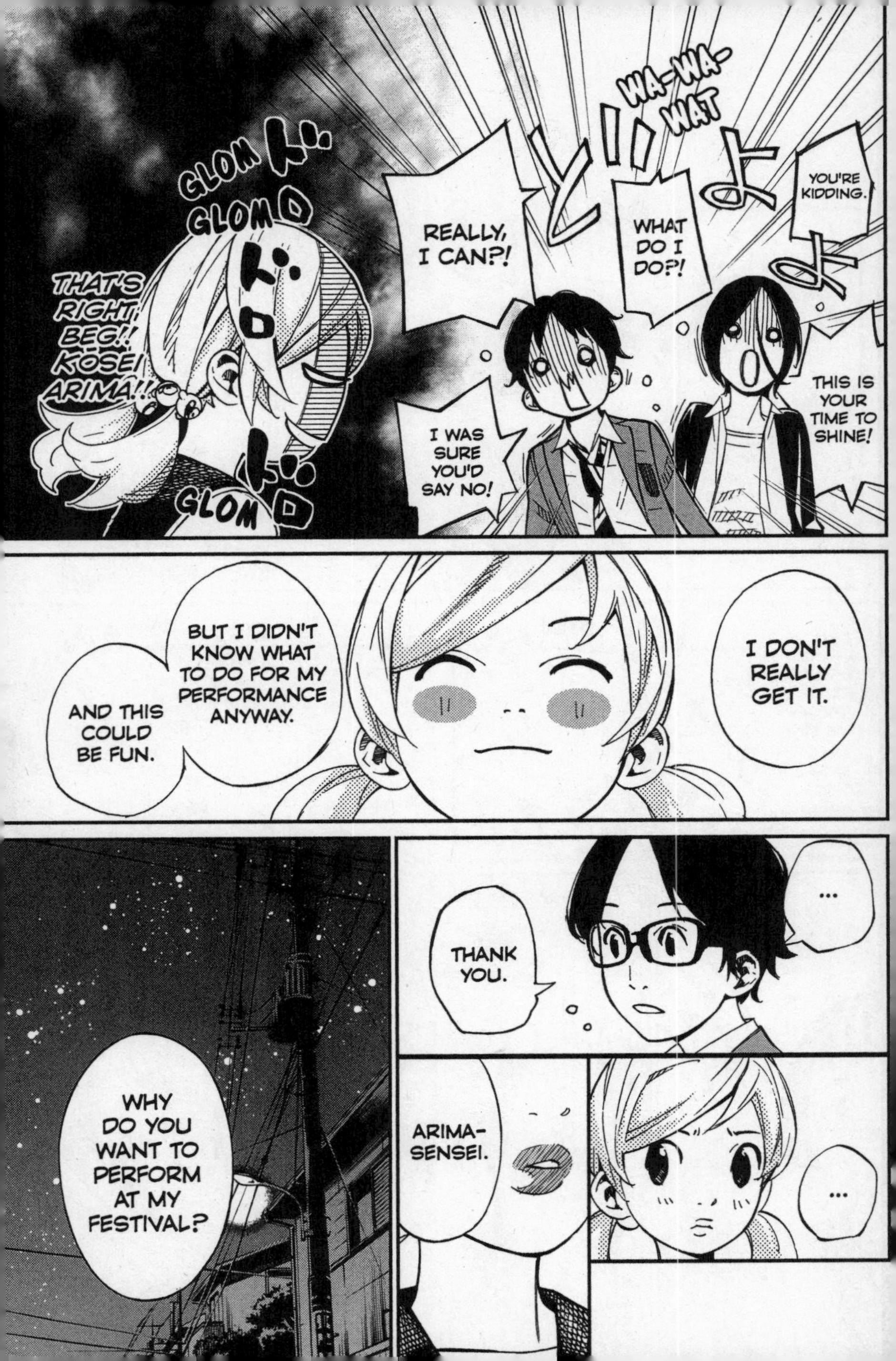
WA-WA-WAT
YOU'RE KIDDING.
WHAT DO I DO?!
REALLY, I CAN?!
THIS IS YOUR TIME TO SHINE!
I WAS SURE YOU'D SAY NO!
GLOM GLOM
THAT'S RIGHT BEG!! KŌSEI ARIMA!!
GLOM
I DON'T REALLY GET IT.
BUT I DIDN'T KNOW WHAT TO DO FOR MY PERFORMANCE ANYWAY.
AND THIS COULD BE FUN.
...
THANK YOU.
...
ARIMA-SENSEI.
WHY DO YOU WANT TO PERFORM AT MY FESTIVAL?

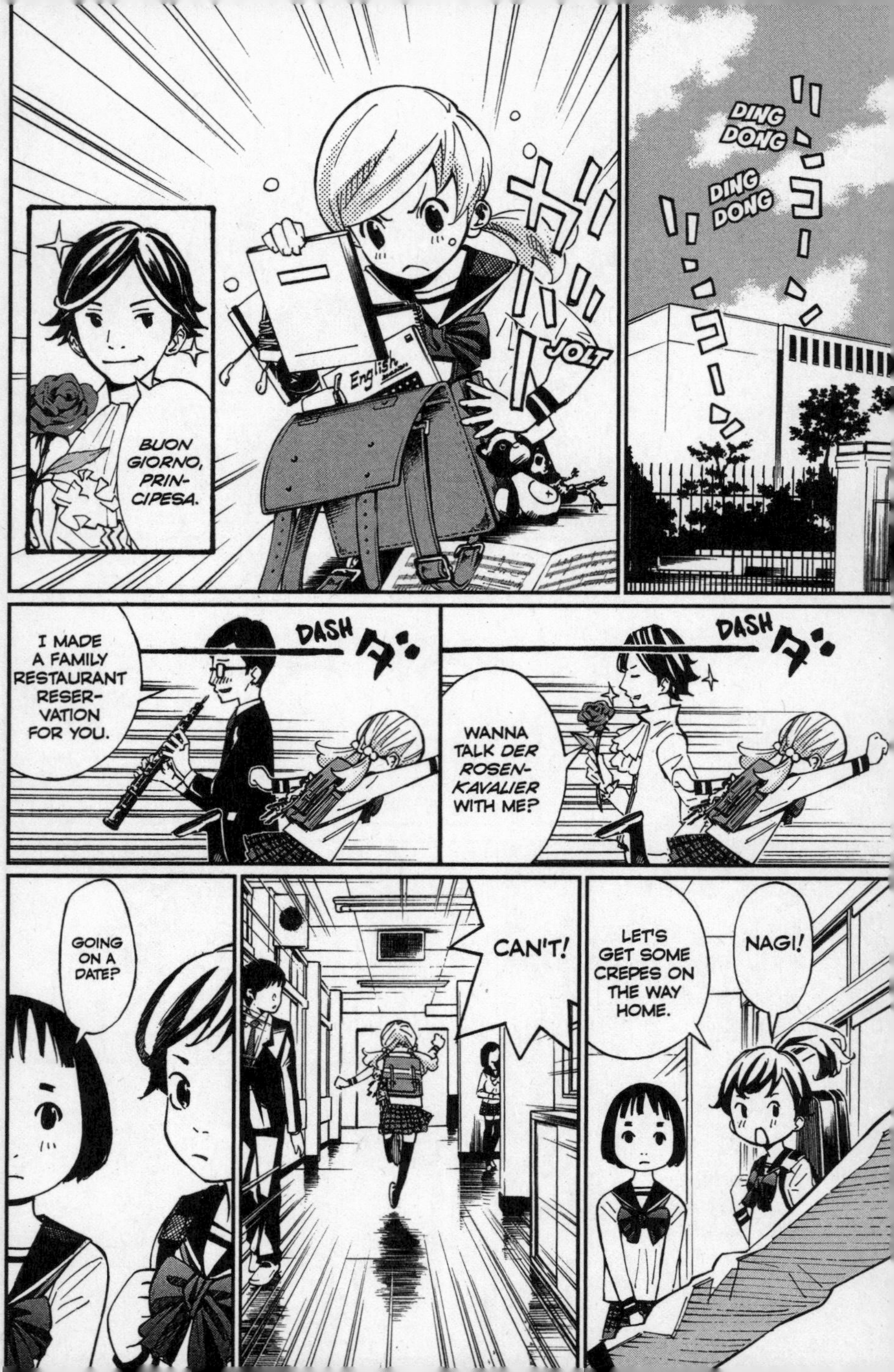
DING DONG
DING DONG
JOLT
English
BUON GIORNO, PRIN-CIPESA.
DASH
WANNA TALK DER ROSEN-KAVALIER WITH ME?
DASH
I MADE A FAMILY RESTAURANT RESER-VATION FOR YOU.
NAGI!
LET'S GET SOME CREPES ON THE WAY HOME.
CAN'T!
GOING ON A DATE?

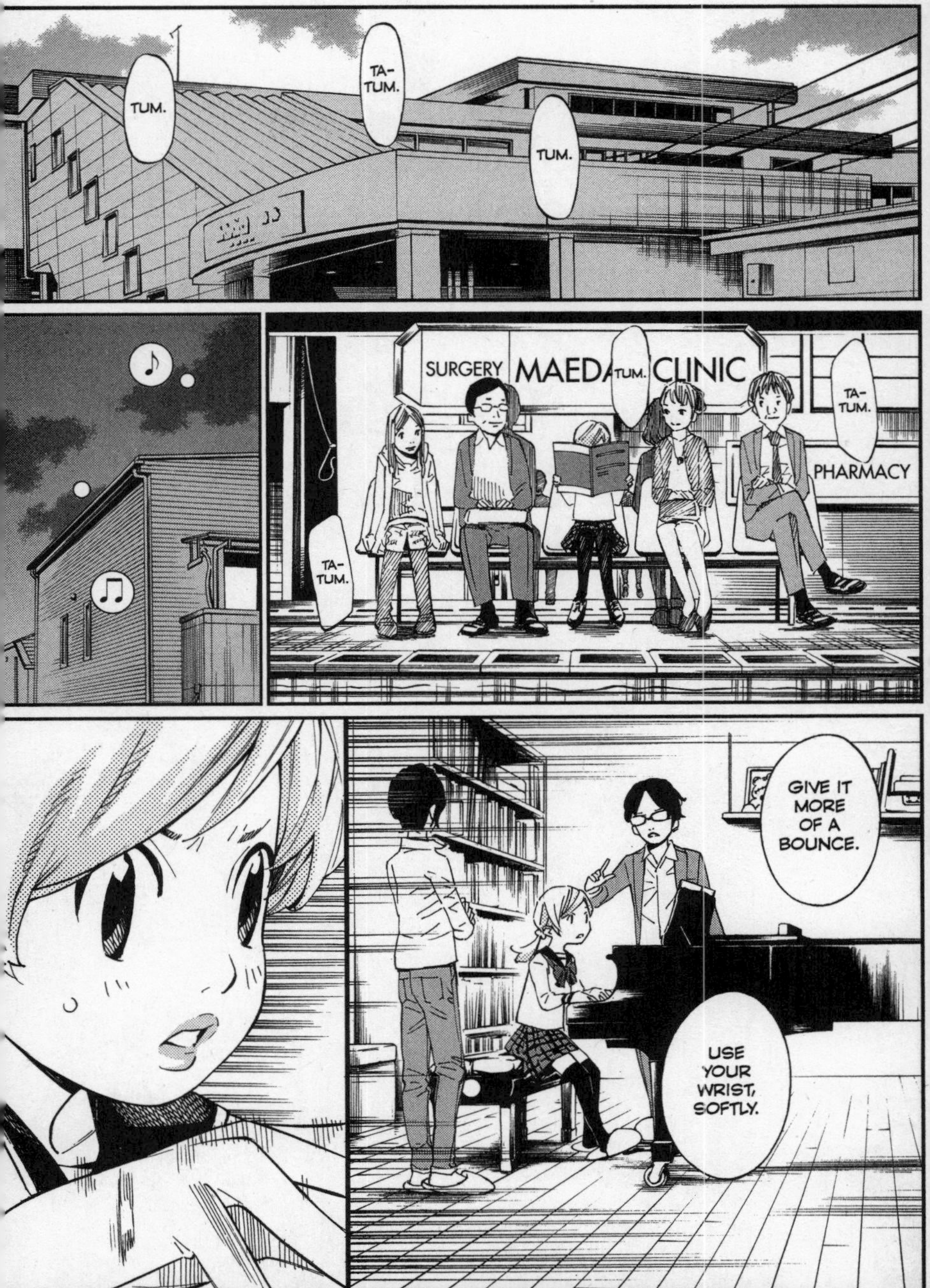
TUM.
TA-TUM.
TUM.
TA-TUM.
PHARMACY
SURGERY MAEDA CLINIC
TUM.
TA-TUM.
GIVE IT MORE OF A BOUNCE.
USE YOUR WRIST, SOFTLY.

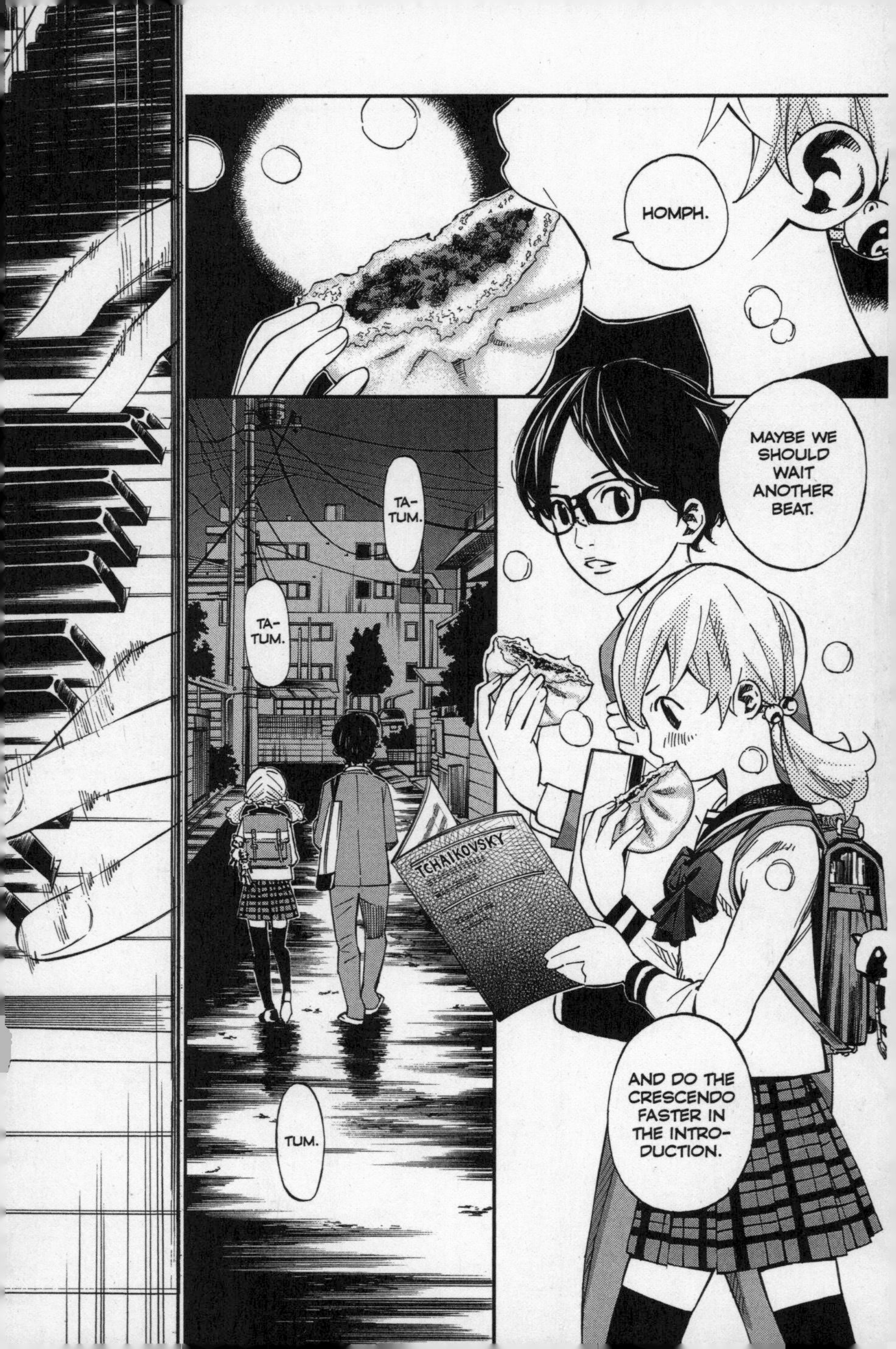
HOMPH.
MAYBE WE SHOULD WAIT ANOTHER BEAT.
TCHAIKOVSKY
AND DO THE CRESCENDO FASTER IN THE INTRO-DUCTION.
TA-TUM.
TA-TUM.
TUM.

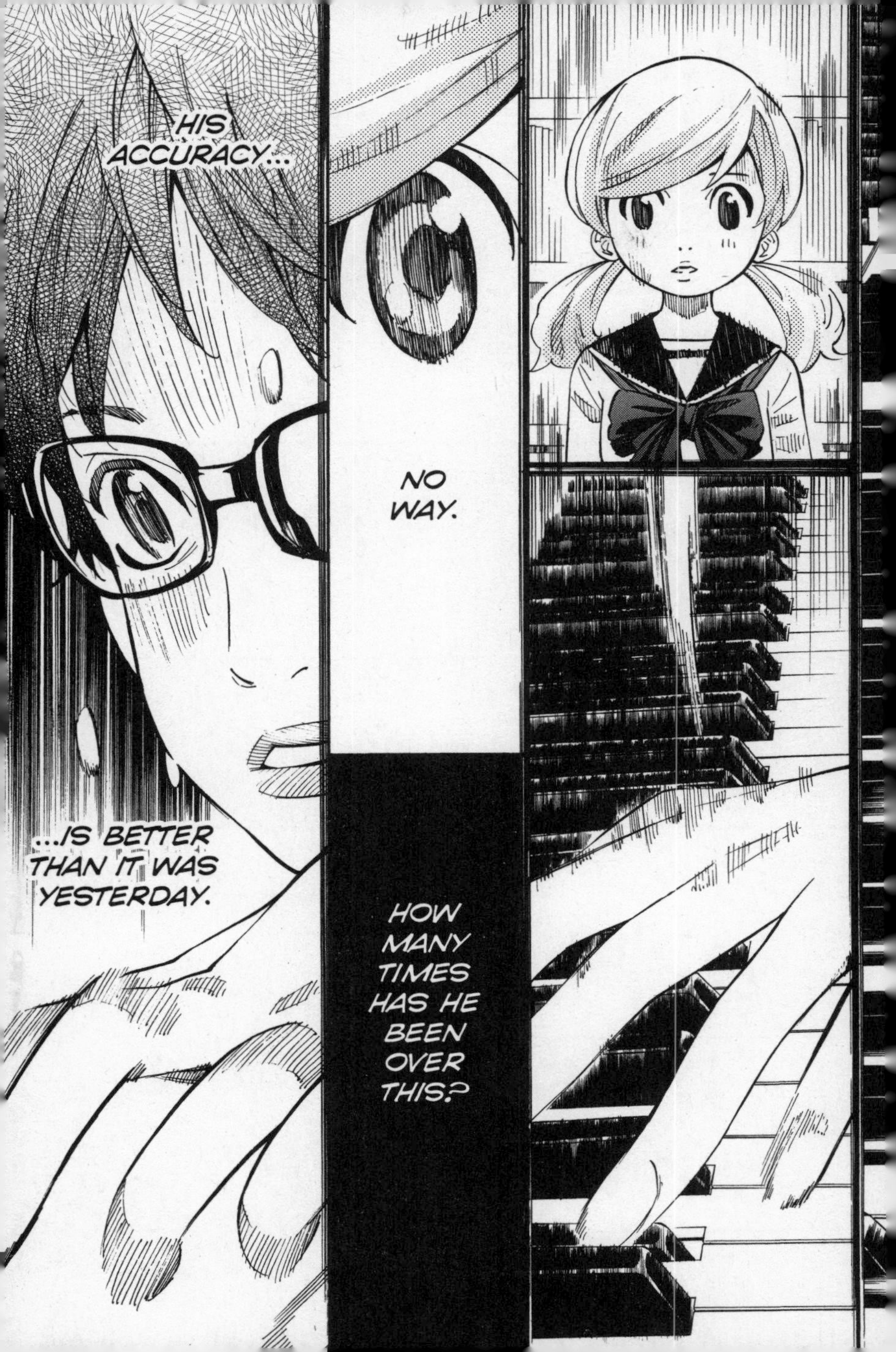
NO WAY.
HOW MANY TIMES HAS HE BEEN OVER THIS?
HIS ACCURACY...
...IS BETTER THAN IT WAS YESTERDAY.

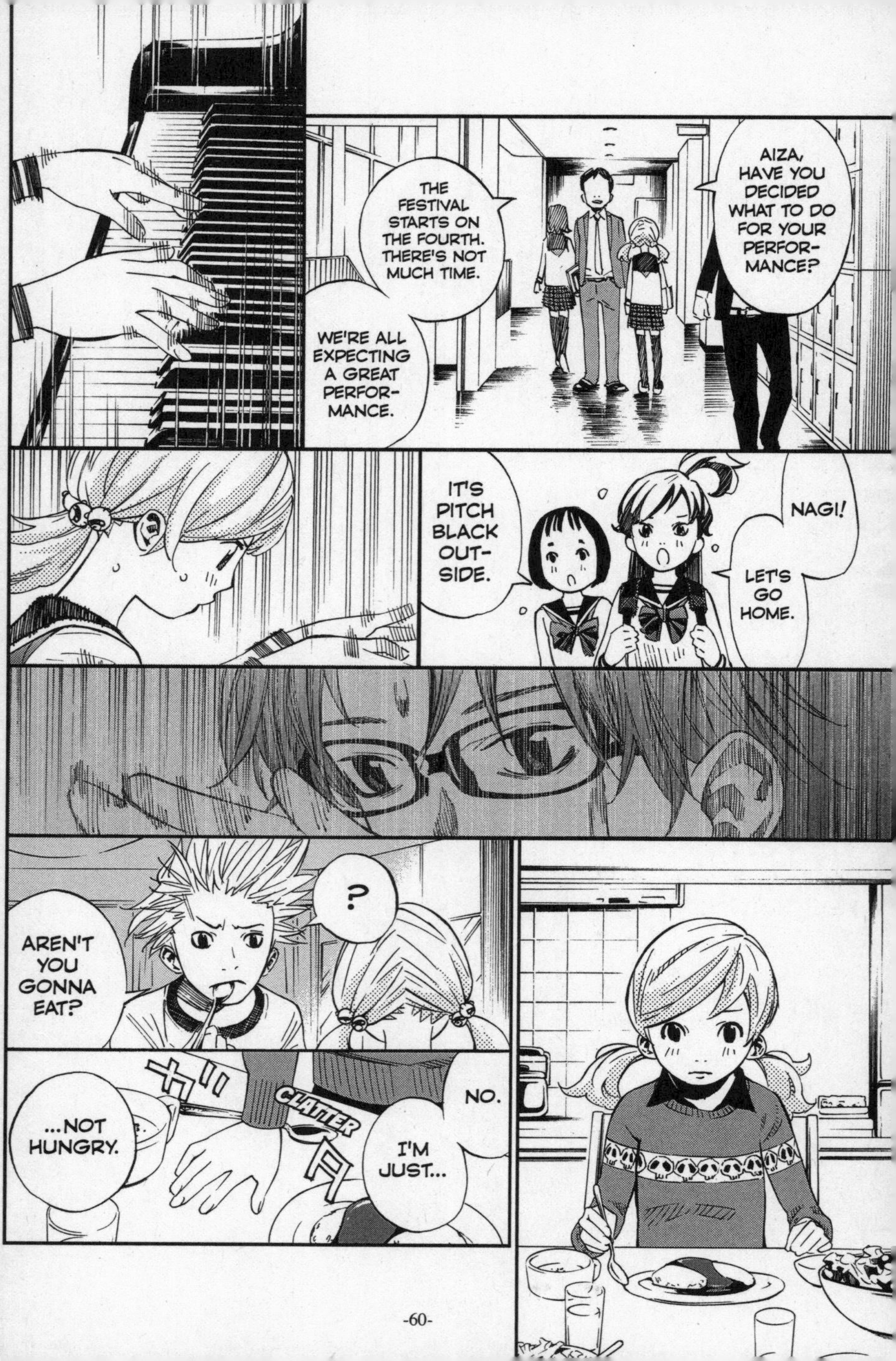
AIZA, HAVE YOU DECIDED WHAT TO DO FOR YOUR PERFORMANCE?
THE FESTIVAL STARTS ON THE FOURTH. THERE'S NOT MUCH TIME.
WE'RE ALL EXPECTING A GREAT PERFORMANCE.
NAGI!
LET'S GO HOME.
IT'S PITCH BLACK OUTSIDE.
?
AREN'T YOU GONNA EAT?
NO.
CLATTER
I'M JUST...
...NOT HUNGRY.

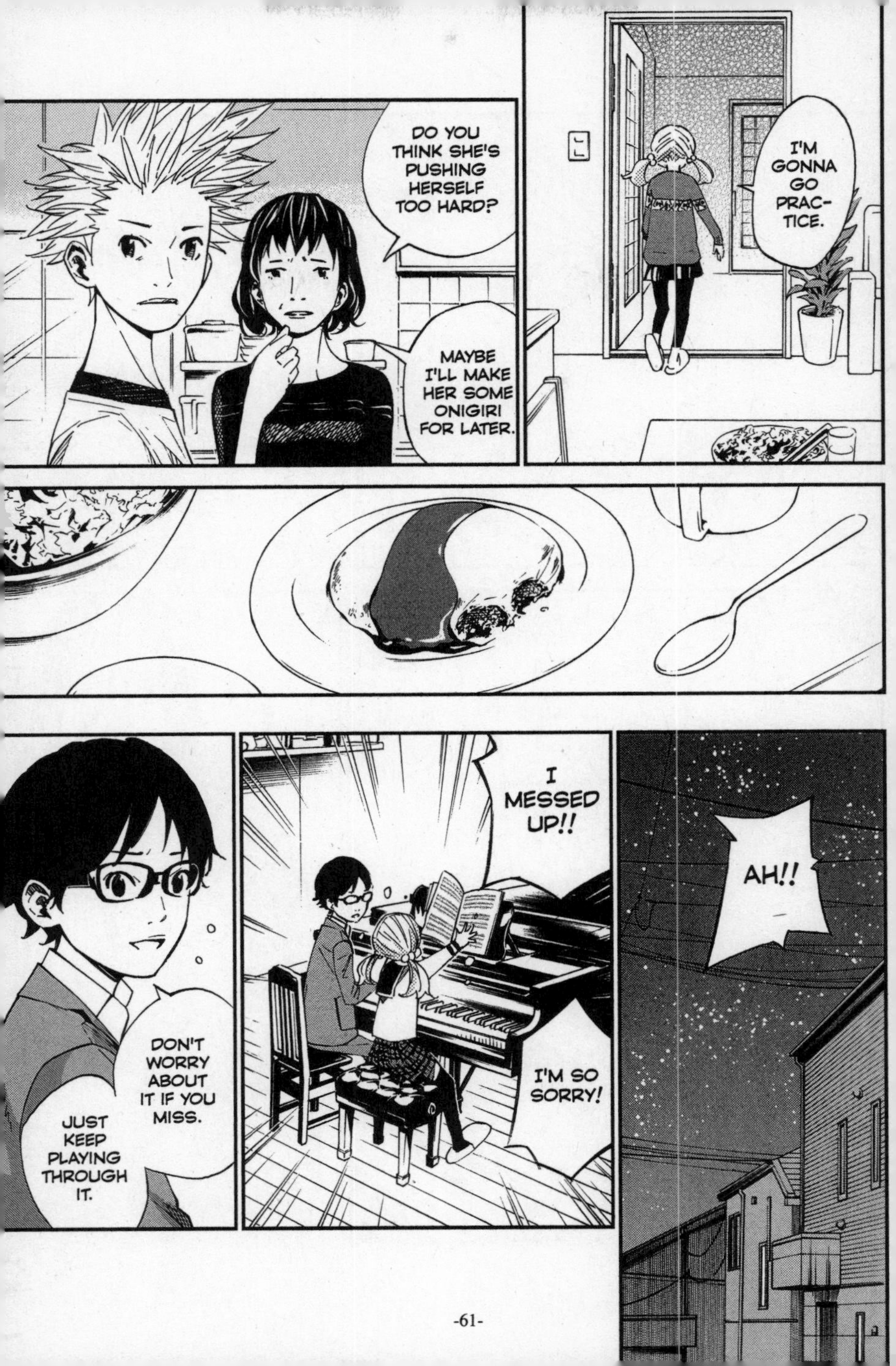
I'M GONNA GO PRAC-TICE.
DO YOU THINK SHE'S PUSHING HERSELF TOO HARD?
MAYBE I'LL MAKE HER SOME ONIGIRI FOR LATER.
AH!!
I MESSED UP!!
I'M SO SORRY!
DON'T WORRY ABOUT IT IF YOU MISS.
JUST KEEP PLAYING THROUGH IT.

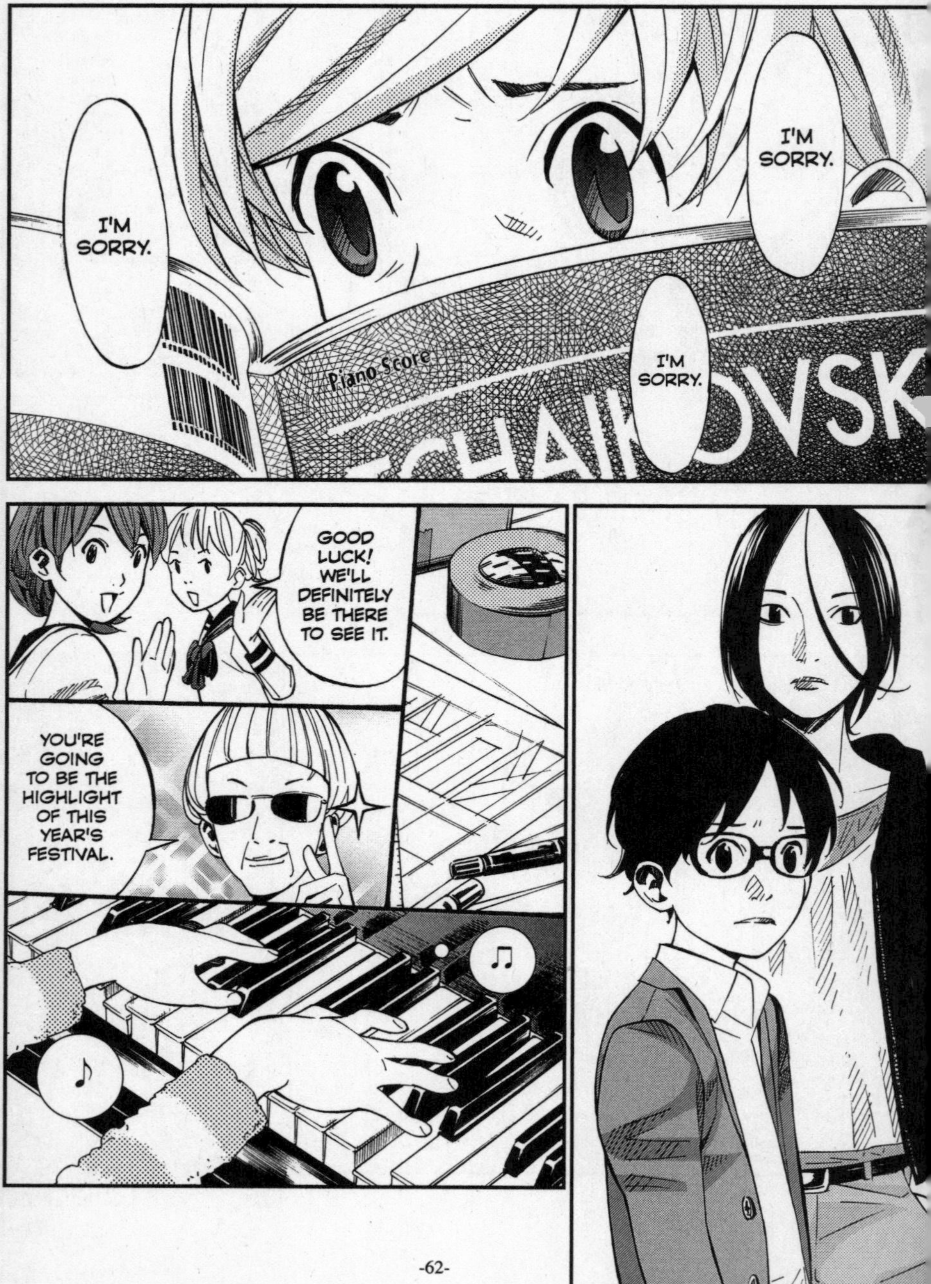
I'M SORRY.
I'M SORRY.
I'M SORRY.
Piano Score
GOOD LUCK! WE'LL DEFINITELY BE THERE TO SEE IT.
YOU'RE GOING TO BE THE HIGHLIGHT OF THIS YEAR'S FESTIVAL.

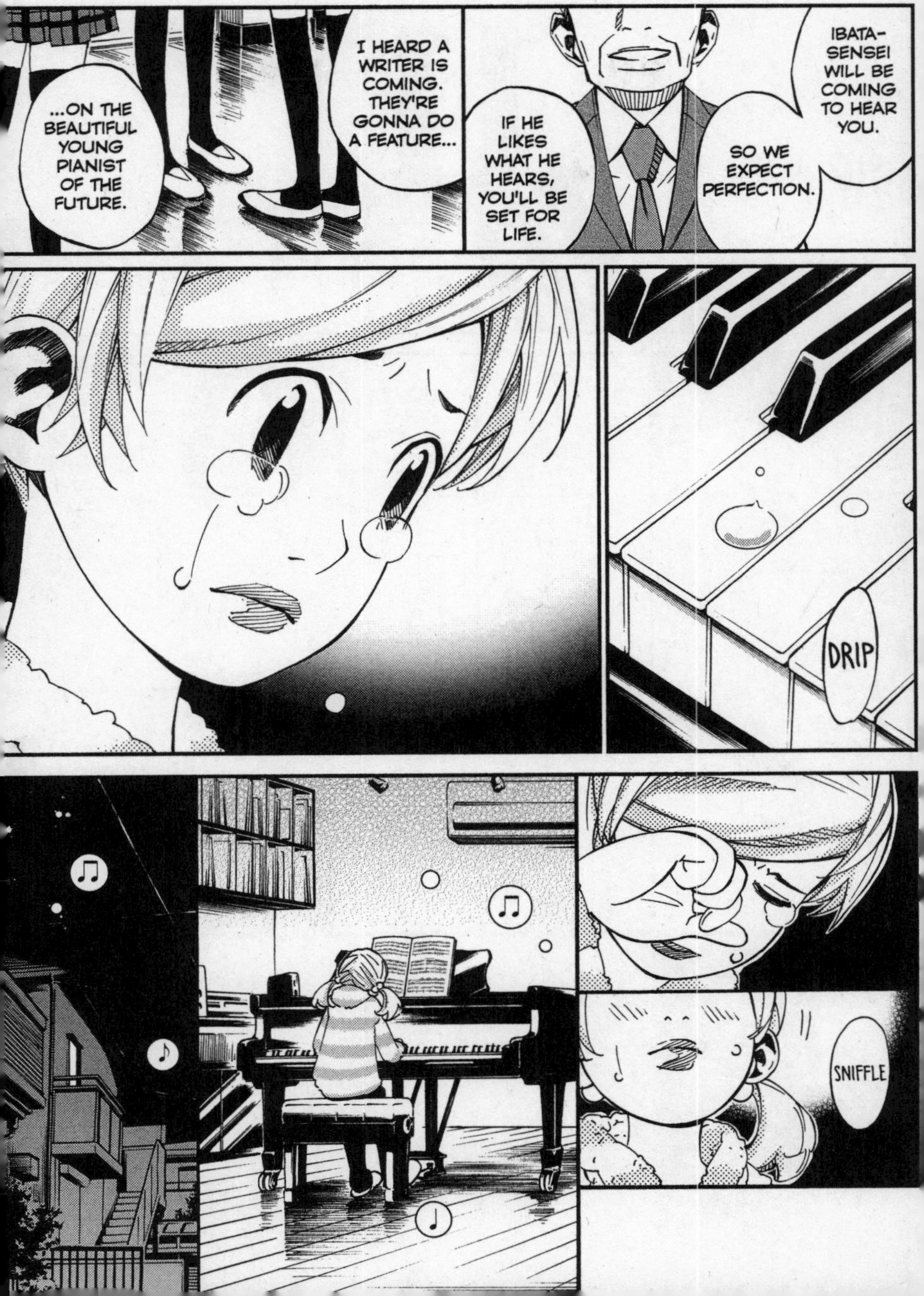
IBATA-SENSEI WILL BE COMING TO HEAR YOU.
SO WE EXPECT PERFECTION.
IF HE LIKES WHAT HE HEARS, YOU'LL BE SET FOR LIFE.
I HEARD A WRITER IS COMING. THEY'RE GONNA DO A FEATURE...
...ON THE BEAUTIFUL YOUNG PIANIST OF THE FUTURE.
DRIP
SNIFFLE

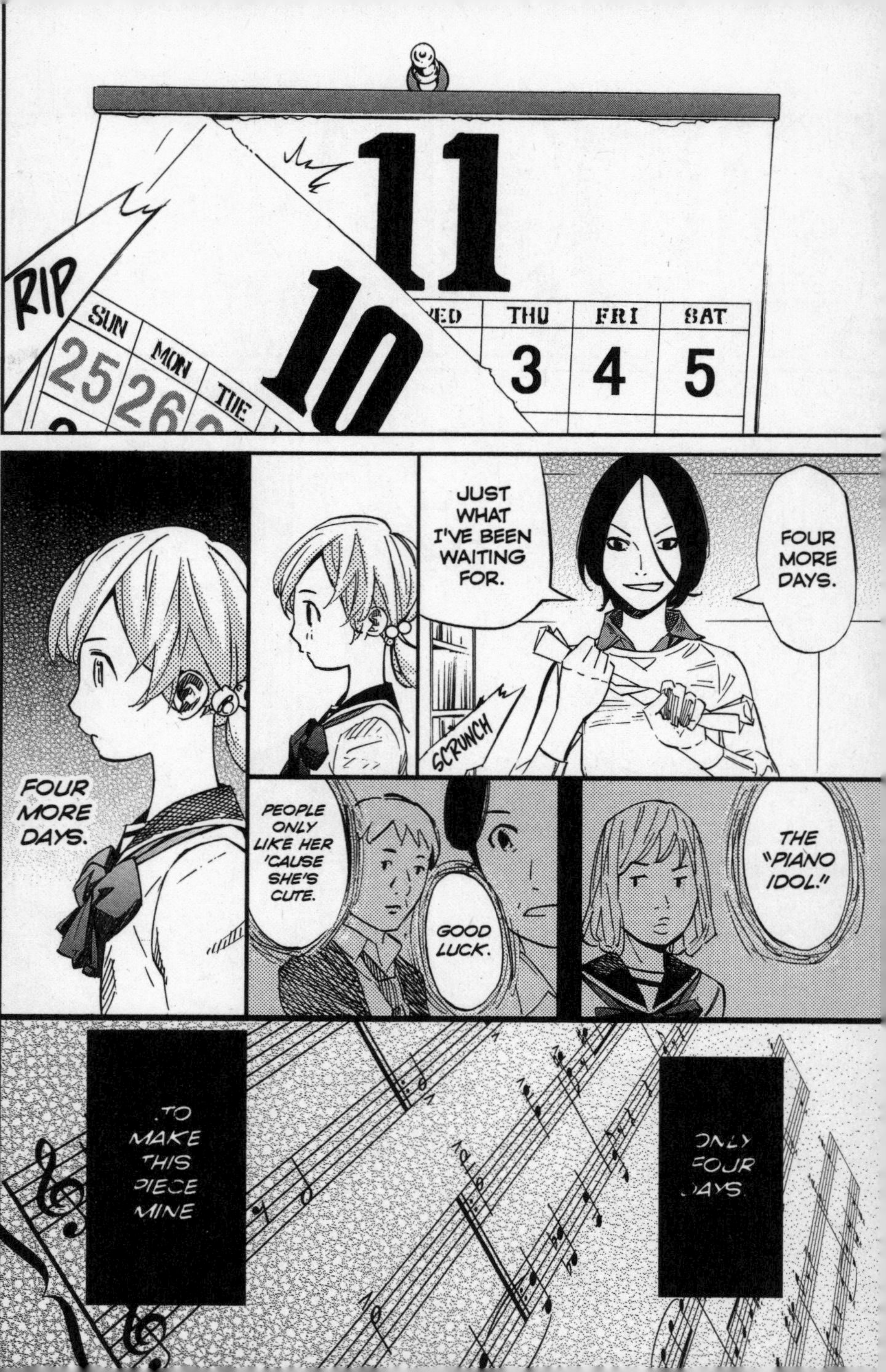

11
10
RIP
SUN
MON
TUE
WED
THU
FRI
SAT
25
26
3
4
5
FOUR MORE DAYS.
JUST WHAT I'VE BEEN WAITING FOR.
SCRUNCH
THE "PIANO IDOL."
PEOPLE ONLY LIKE HER 'CAUSE SHE'S CUTE.
GOOD LUCK.
FOUR MORE DAYS.
ONLY FOUR DAYS.
...TO MAKE THIS PIECE MINE

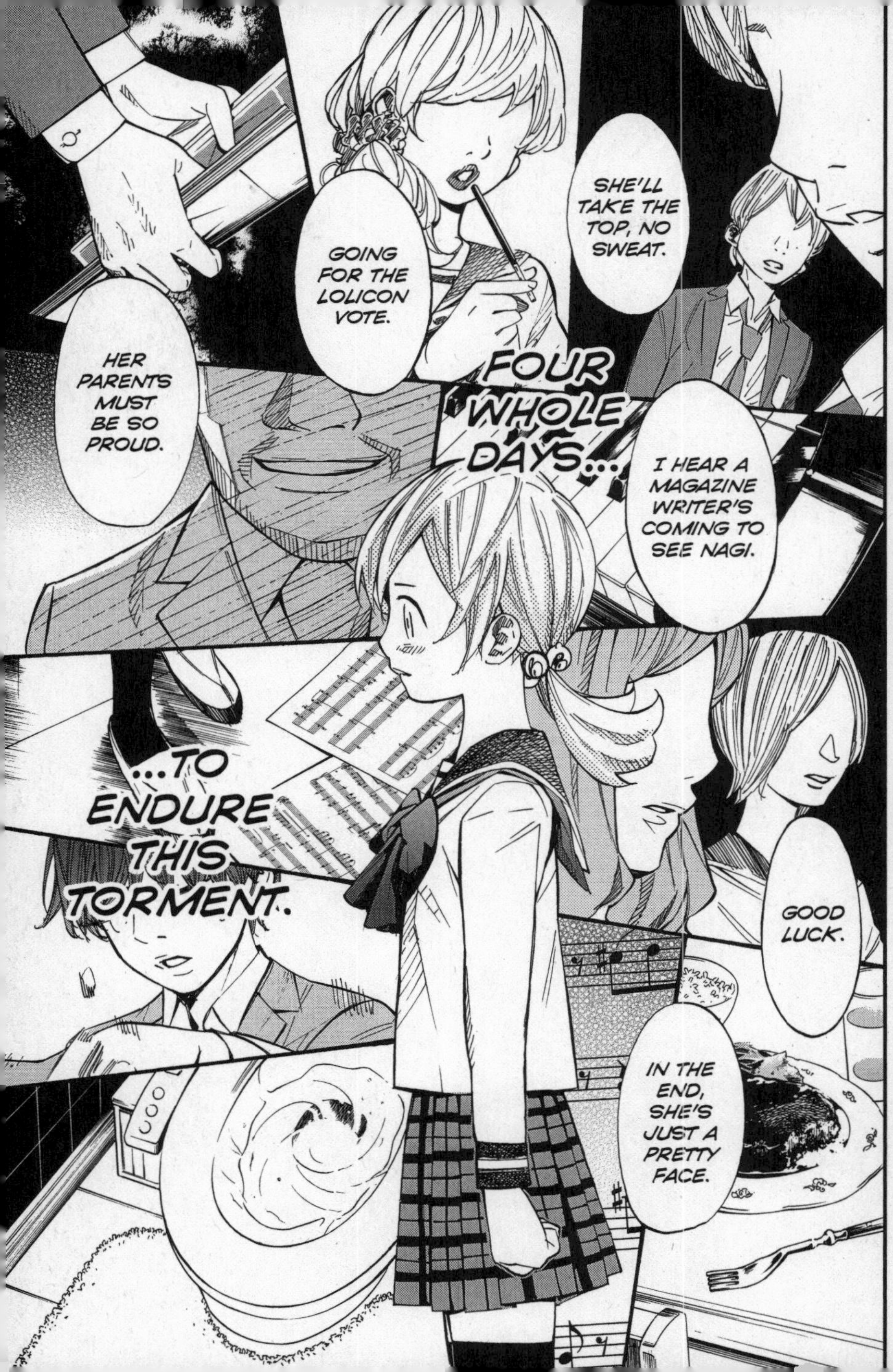
SHE'LL TAKE THE TOP, NO SWEAT.
GOING FOR THE LOLICON VOTE.
HER PARENTS MUST BE SO PROUD.
I HEAR A MAGAZINE WRITER'S COMING TO SEE NAGI.
FOUR WHOLE DAYS...
GOOD LUCK.
IN THE END, SHE'S JUST A PRETTY FACE.
...TO ENDURE THIS TORMENT.

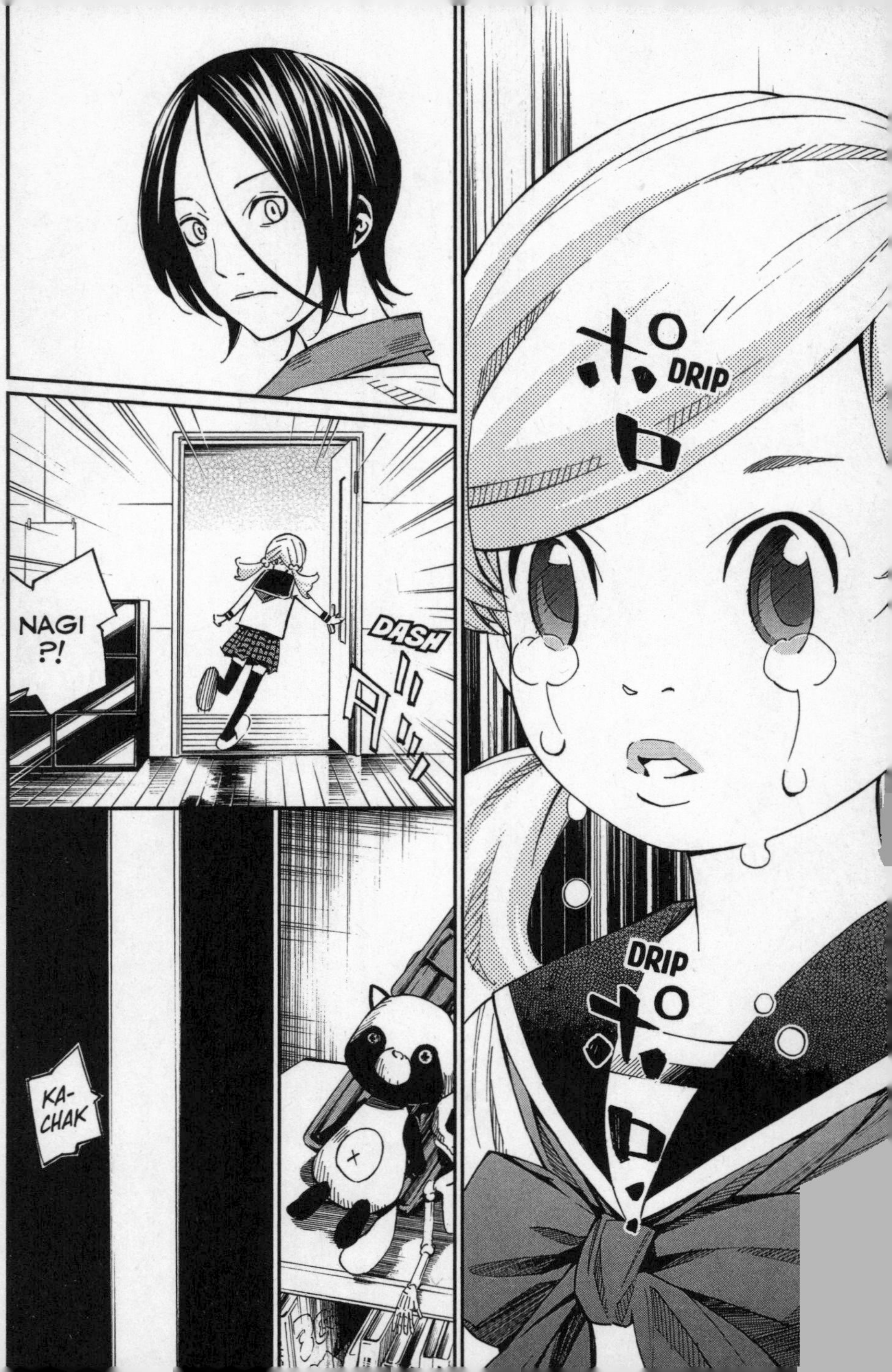
ポロ
DRIP
DRIP
ポロ
NAGI ?!
DASH
ダッ
KA-CHAK

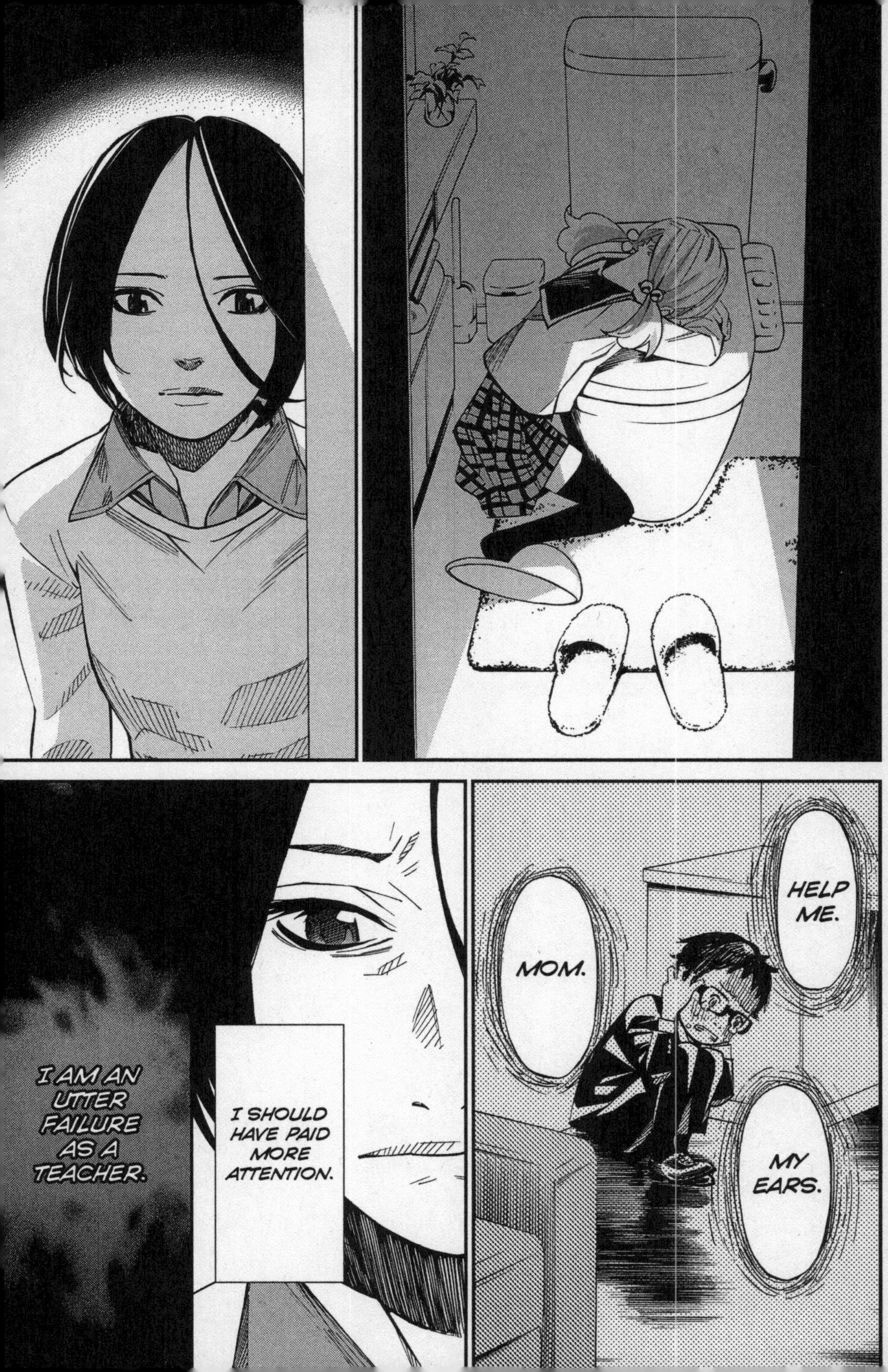
HELP ME.
MOM.
MY EARS.
I SHOULD HAVE PAID MORE ATTENTION.
I AM AN UTTER FAILURE AS A TEACHER.

THE SAME THING...
...IS ABOUT TO HAPPEN AGAIN.
NAGI.
...
I'M...
...SCARED.
IT'S JUST A LITTLE FESTIVAL ENTERTAINMENT.
IT'S NOWHERE NEAR AS IMPORTANT AS A COMPETITION.
THIS HAS NEVER HAPPENED BEFORE.
I'M SCARED— SO SCARED I CAN'T STAND IT.
ALL THE ATTENTION...
ALL THE SLANDER...
I'VE NEVER...
...BEEN SO AFRAID TO BE JUDGED BY OTHER PEOPLE.

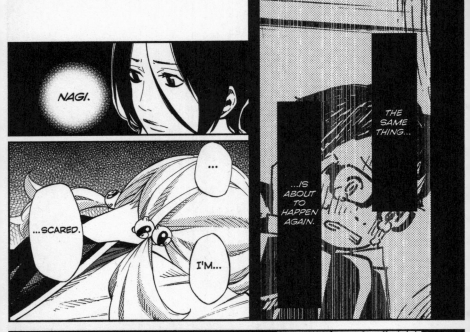

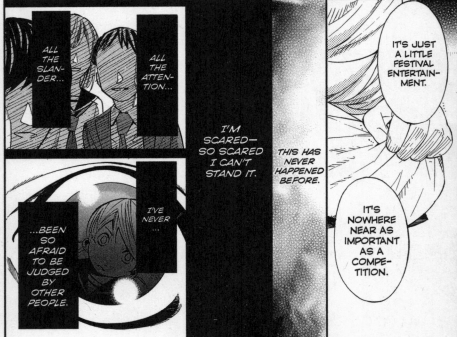

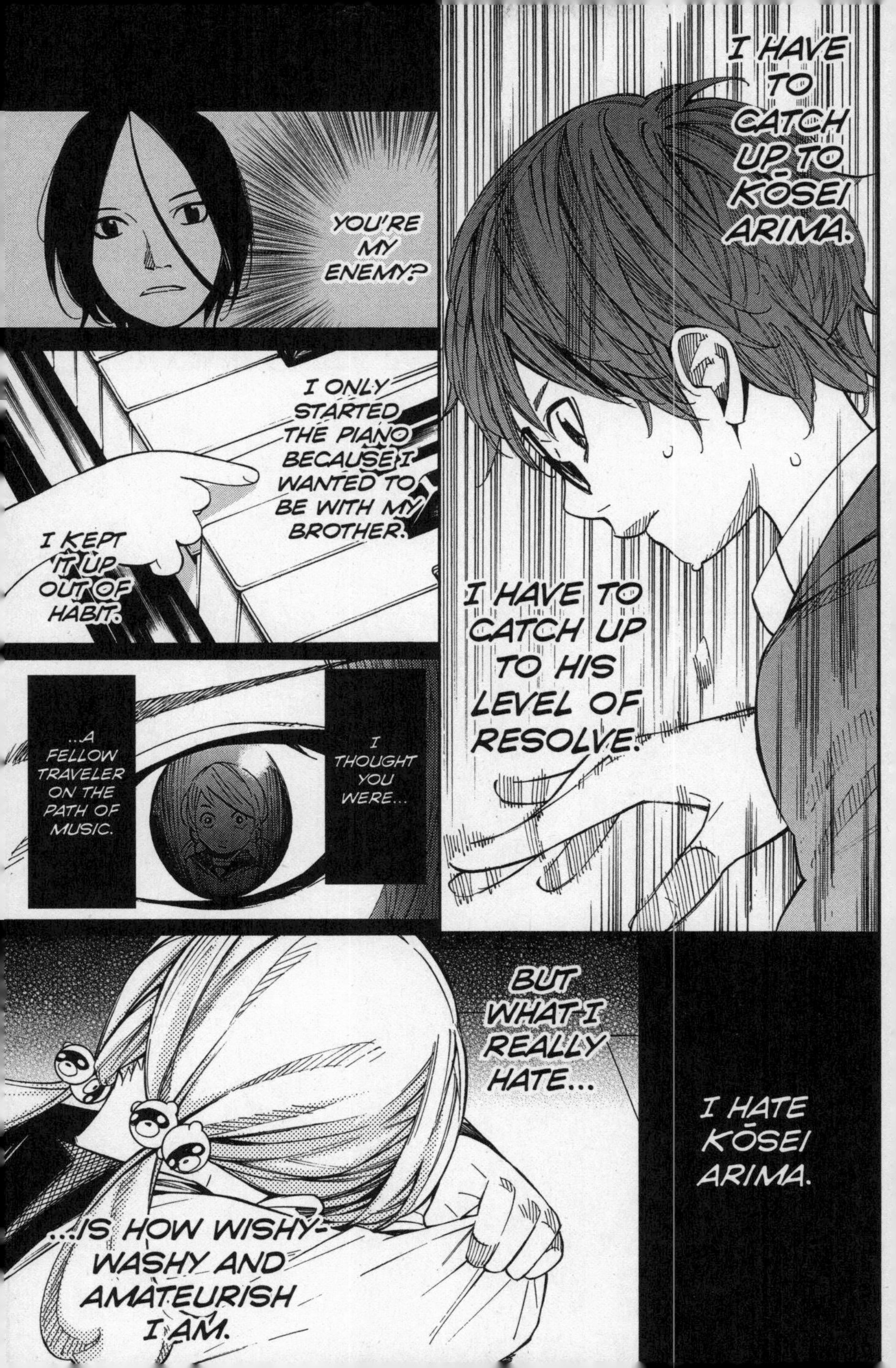
I HAVE TO CATCH UP TO KŌSEI ARIMA.
I HAVE TO CATCH UP TO HIS LEVEL OF RESOLVE.
YOU'RE MY ENEMY?
I ONLY STARTED THE PIANO BECAUSE I WANTED TO BE WITH MY BROTHER.
I KEPT IT UP OUT OF HABIT.
I THOUGHT YOU WERE...
...A FELLOW TRAVELER ON THE PATH OF MUSIC.
I HATE KŌSEI ARIMA.
BUT WHAT I REALLY HATE...
...IS HOW WISHY-WASHY AND AMATEURISH I AM.

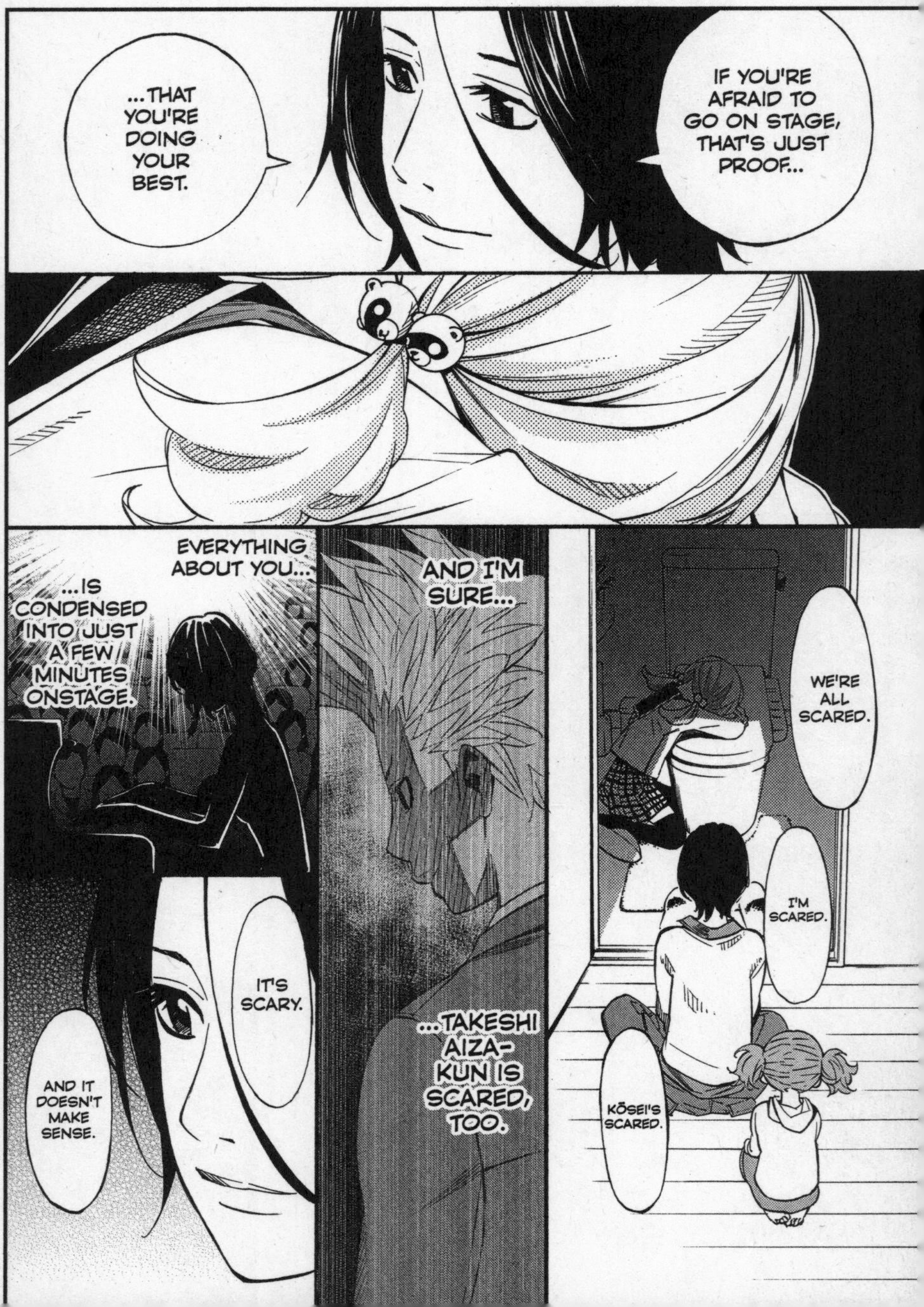
IF YOU'RE AFRAID TO GO ON STAGE, THAT'S JUST PROOF...
...THAT YOU'RE DOING YOUR BEST.
WE'RE ALL SCARED.
I'M SCARED.
KŌSEI'S SCARED.
AND I'M SURE...
...TAKESHI AIZA-KUN IS SCARED, TOO.
EVERYTHING ABOUT YOU...
...IS CONDENSED INTO JUST A FEW MINUTES ONSTAGE.
IT'S SCARY.
AND IT DOESN'T MAKE SENSE.

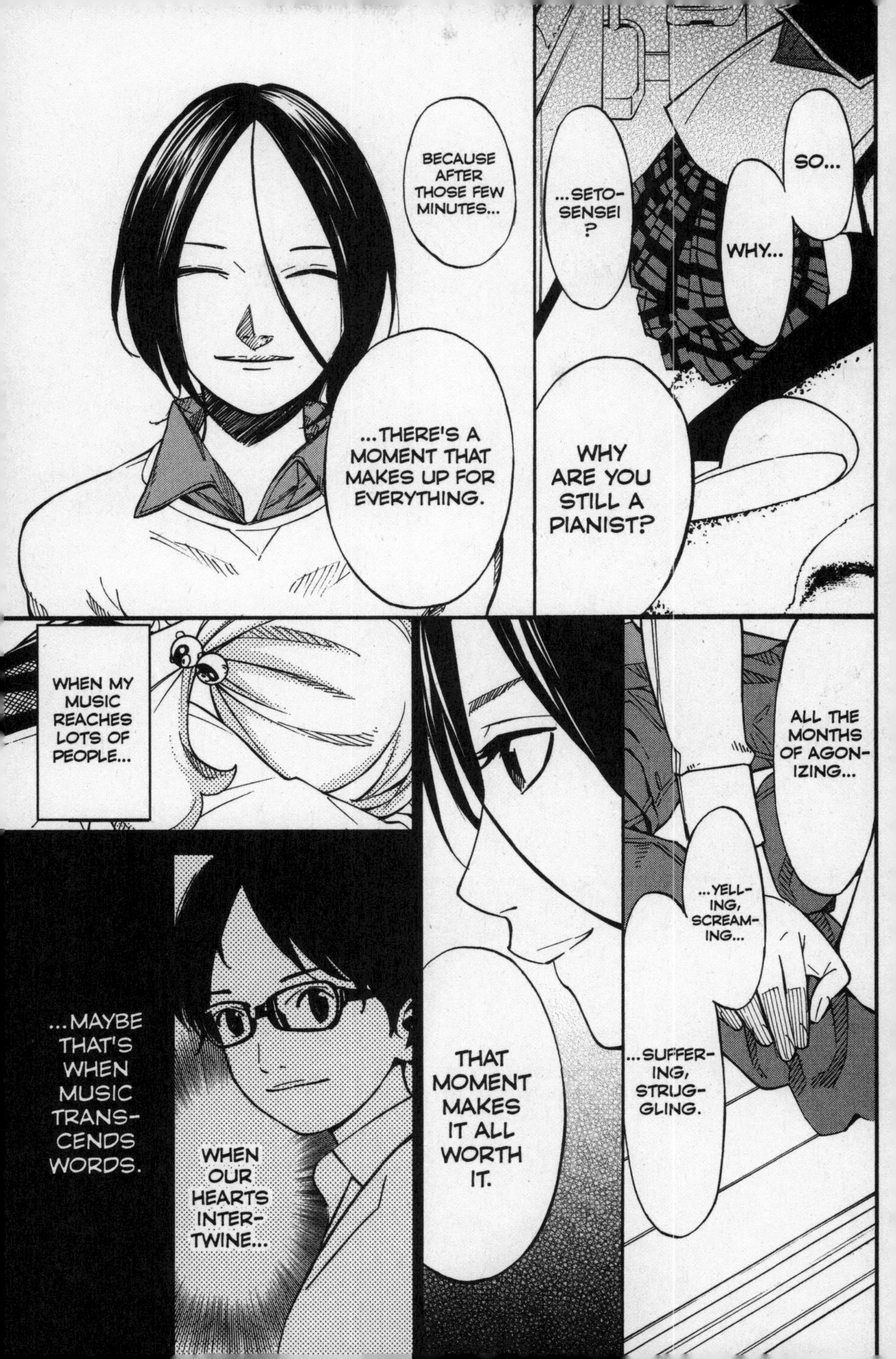
SO...
WHY...
...SETO-SENSEI?
WHY ARE YOU STILL A PIANIST?
BECAUSE AFTER THOSE FEW MINUTES...
...THERE'S A MOMENT THAT MAKES UP FOR EVERYTHING.
ALL THE MONTHS OF AGONIZING...
...YELLING, SCREAMING...
...SUFFERING, STRUGGLING.
THAT MOMENT MAKES IT ALL WORTH IT.
WHEN MY MUSIC REACHES LOTS OF PEOPLE...
WHEN OUR HEARTS INTERTWINE...
...MAYBE THAT'S WHEN MUSIC TRANSCENDS WORDS.

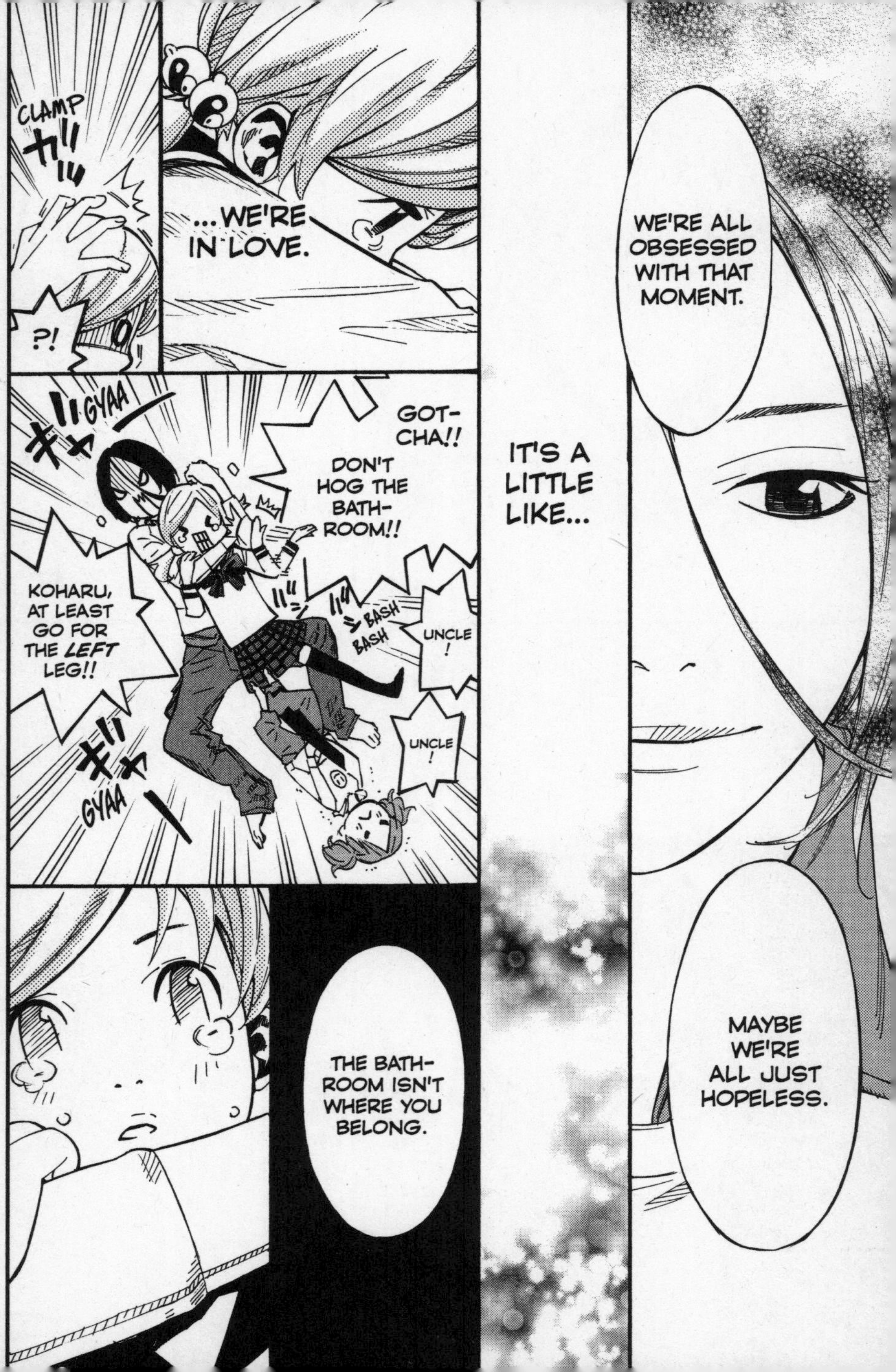
WE'RE ALL OBSESSED WITH THAT MOMENT.
MAYBE WE'RE ALL JUST HOPELESS.
IT'S A LITTLE LIKE...
...WE'RE IN LOVE.
CLAMP
?!
GOT-CHA!!
DON'T HOG THE BATH-ROOM!!
GYAA
KOHARU, AT LEAST GO FOR THE *LEFT* LEG!!
BASH BASH
UNCLE!
UNCLE!
GYAA
THE BATH-ROOM ISN'T WHERE YOU BELONG.

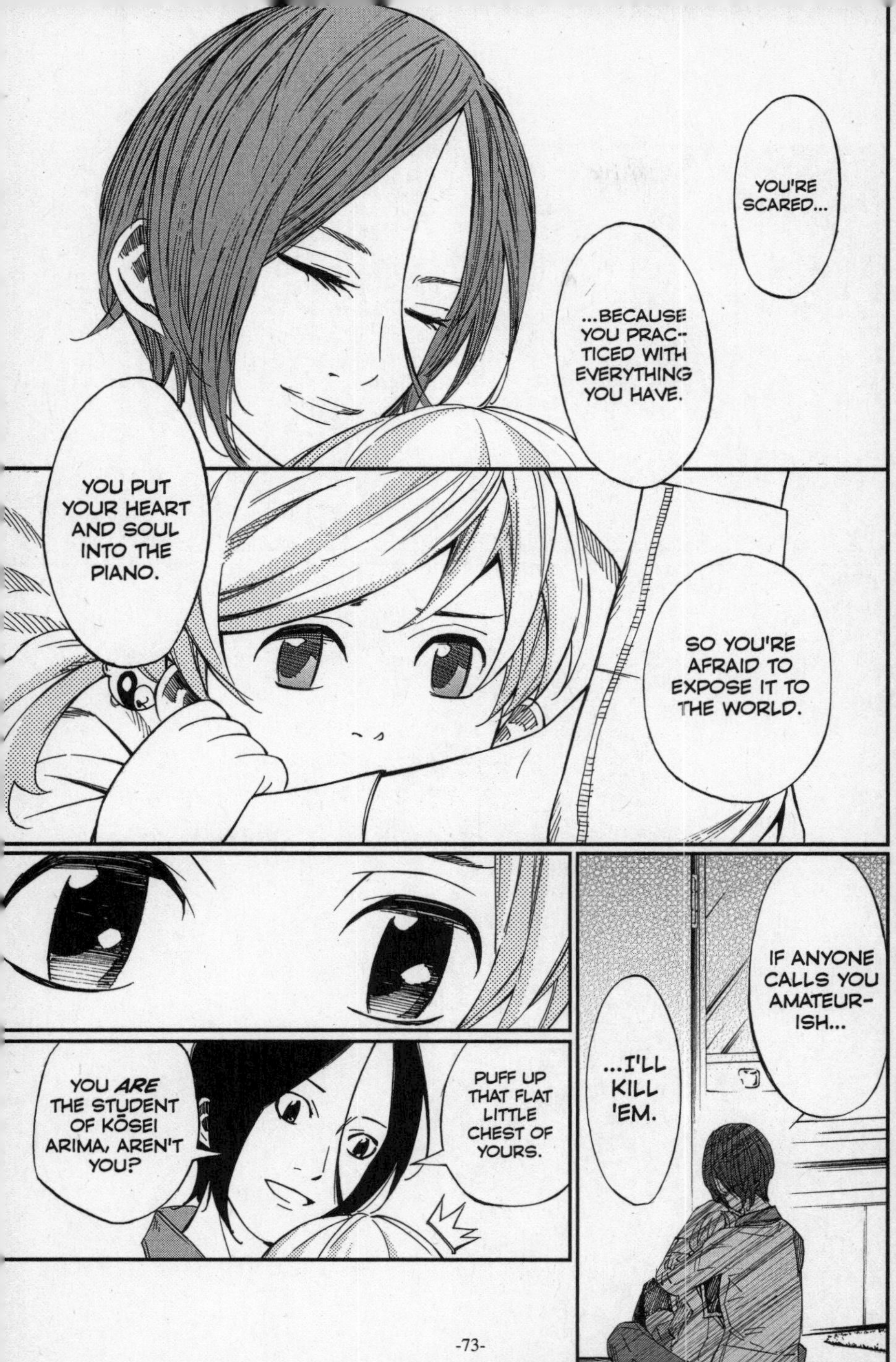
YOU'RE SCARED...
...BECAUSE YOU PRAC-TICED WITH EVERYTHING YOU HAVE.
YOU PUT YOUR HEART AND SOUL INTO THE PIANO.
SO YOU'RE AFRAID TO EXPOSE IT TO THE WORLD.
IF ANYONE CALLS YOU AMATEUR-ISH...
...I'LL KILL 'EM.
PUFF UP THAT FLAT LITTLE CHEST OF YOURS.
YOU *ARE* THE STUDENT OF KŌSEI ARIMA, AREN'T YOU?

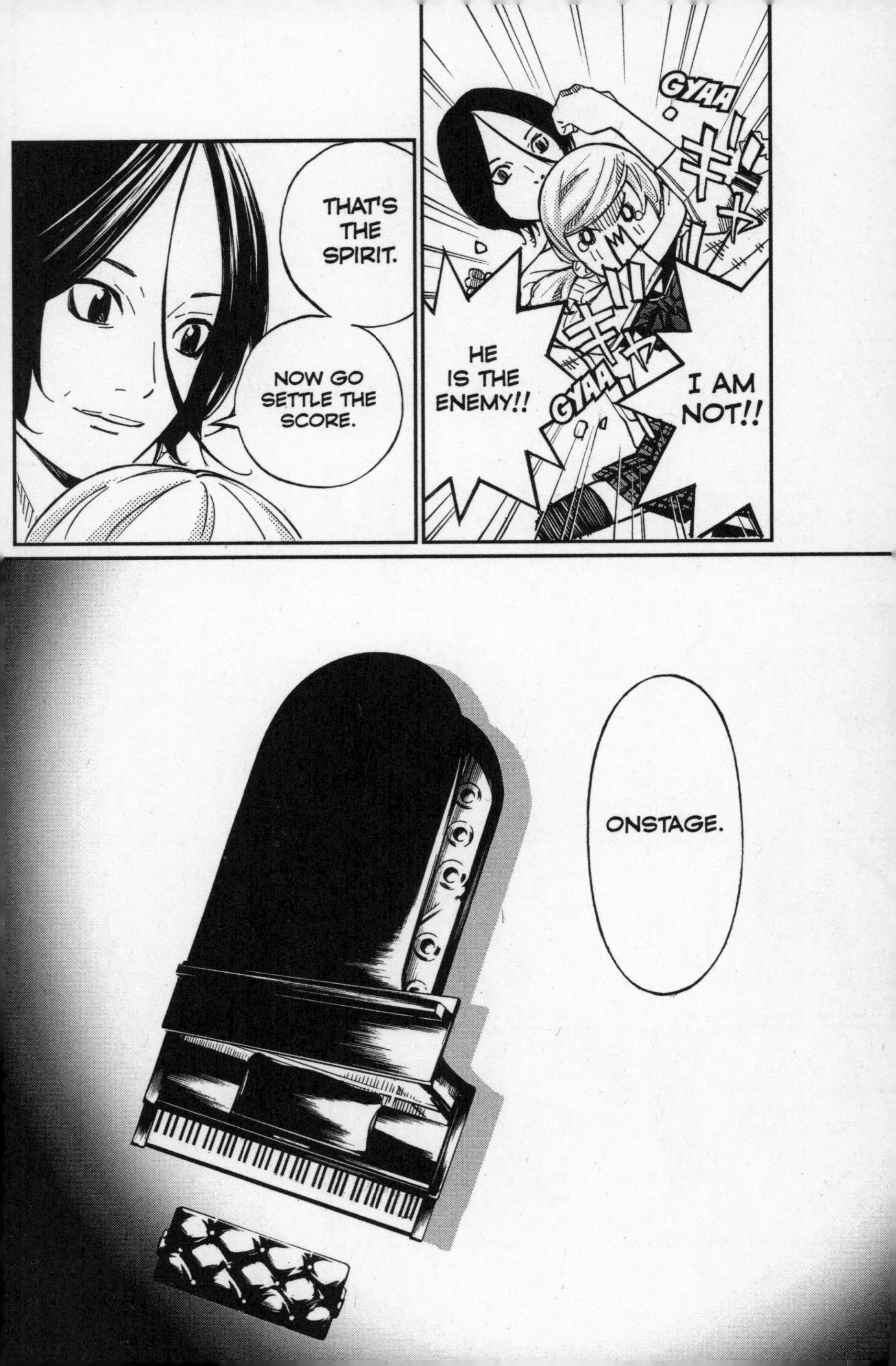
GYAA
I AM NOT!!
HE IS THE ENEMY!!
GYAA
THAT'S THE SPIRIT.
NOW GO SETTLE THE SCORE.
ONSTAGE.

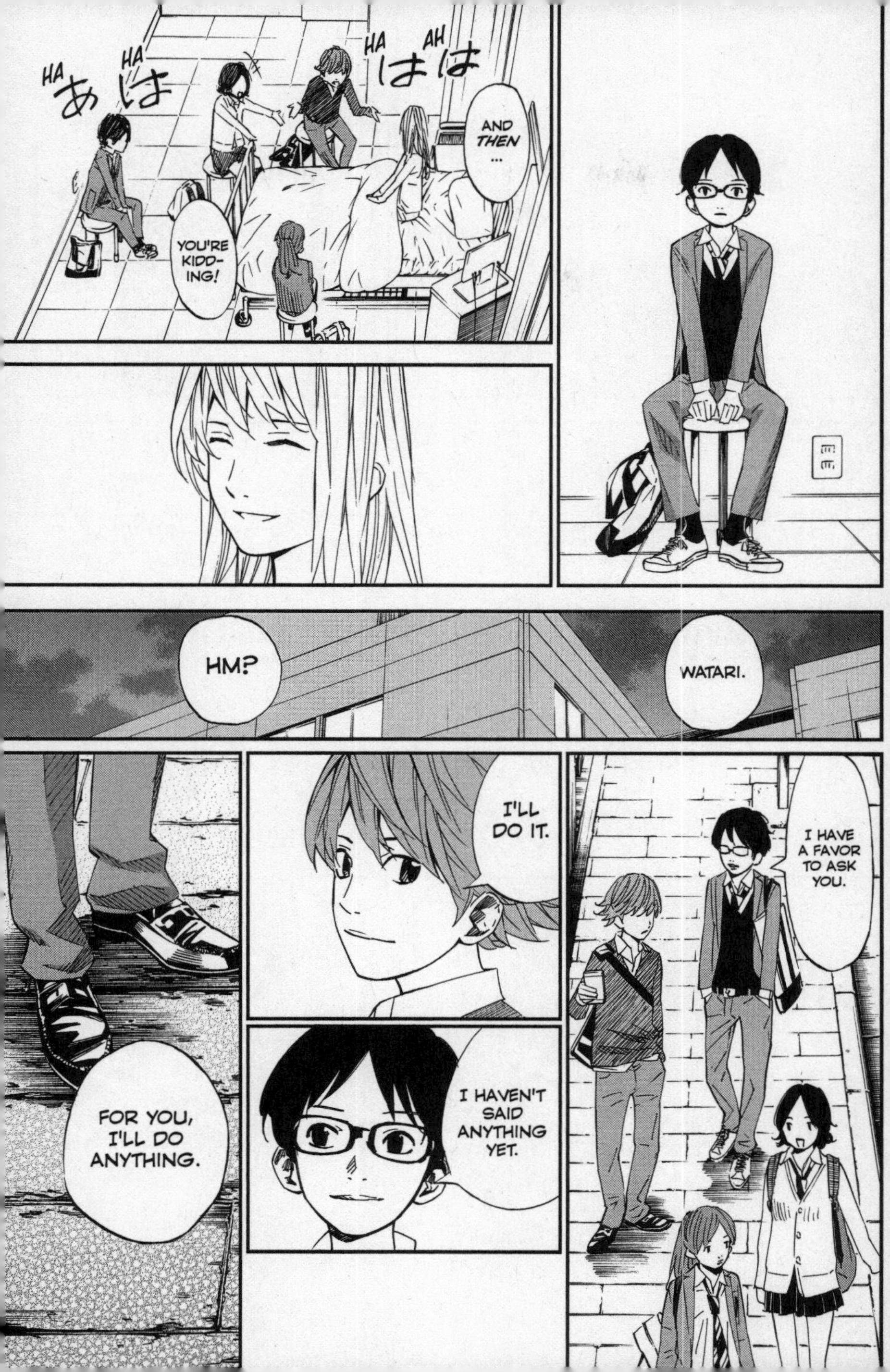
HA AH
はは
AND THEN ...
HA HA
あは
YOU'RE KIDD-ING!
WATARI.
HM?
I HAVE A FAVOR TO ASK YOU.
I'LL DO IT.
I HAVEN'T SAID ANYTHING YET.
FOR YOU, I'LL DO ANYTHING.

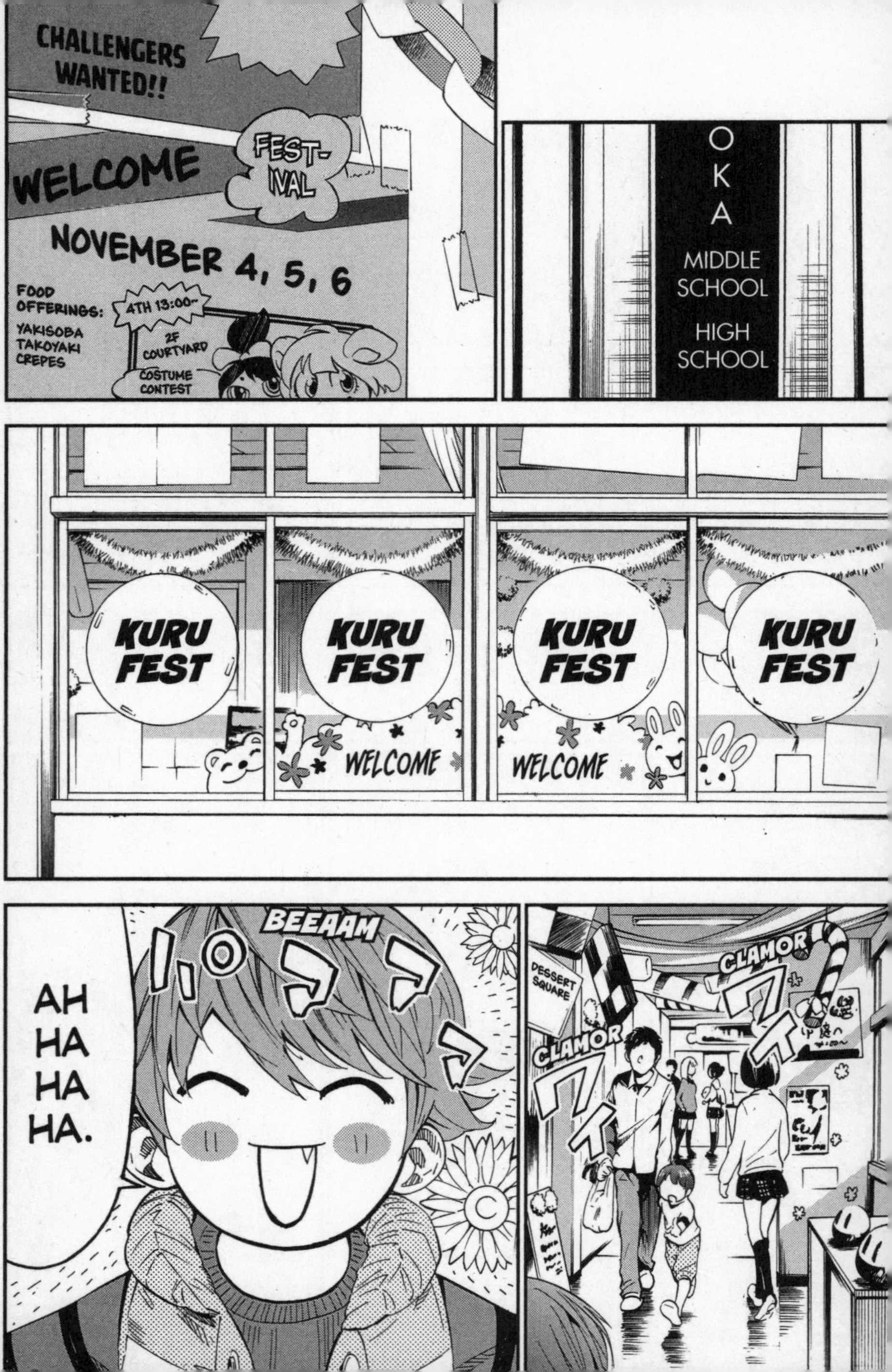

OKA
MIDDLE SCHOOL
HIGH SCHOOL
CHALLENGERS WANTED!!
WELCOME
FEST-IVAL
NOVEMBER 4, 5, 6
FOOD OFFERINGS:
YAKISOBA
TAKOYAKI
CREPES
4TH 13:00~
2F COURTYARD
COSTUME CONTEST
KURU FEST
KURU FEST
KURU FEST
KURU FEST
WELCOME
WELCOME
CLAMOR
CLAMOR
DESSERT SQUARE
BEEAAM
AH HA HA HA.

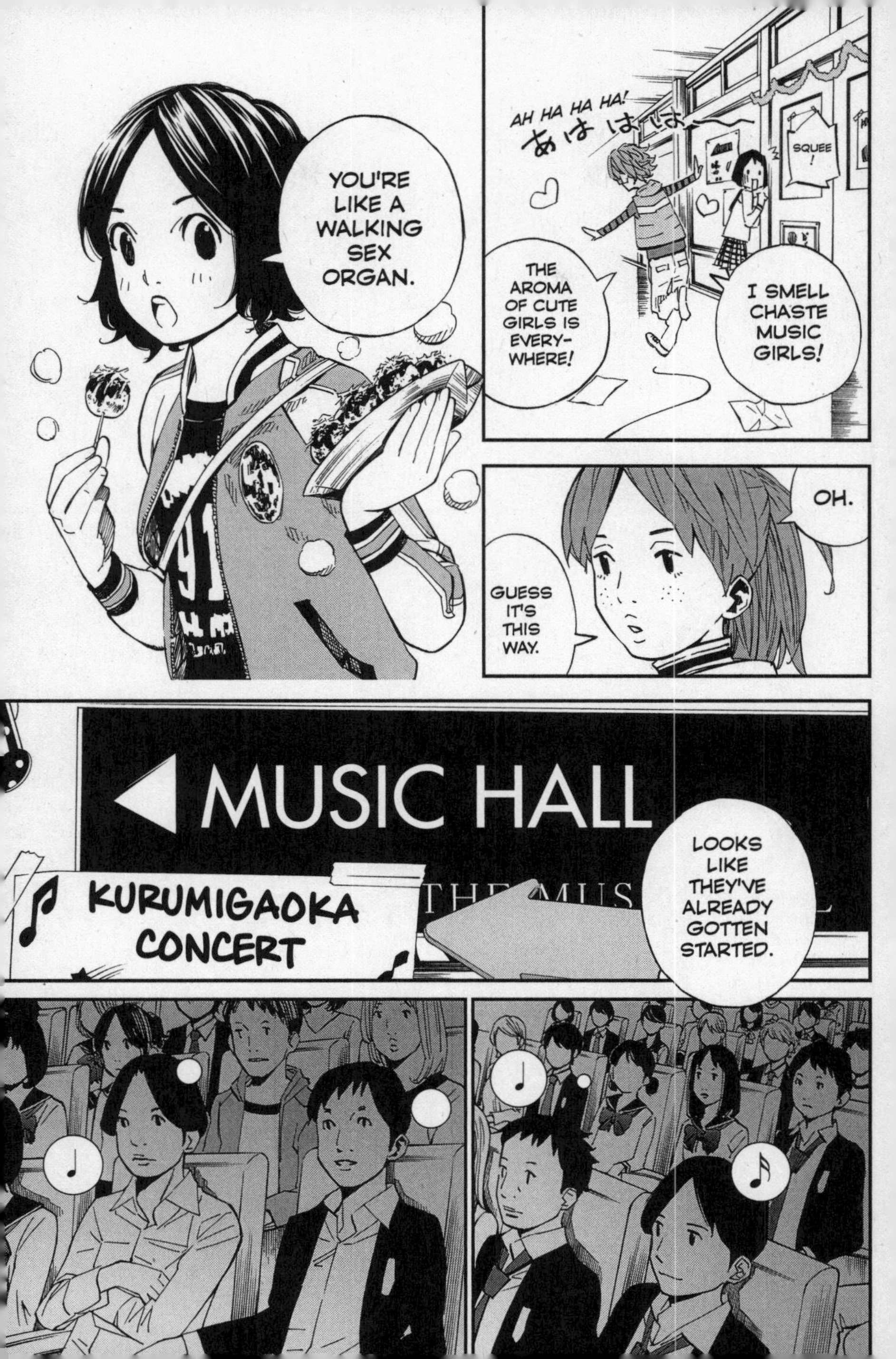
SQUEE!
AH HA HA HA!
I SMELL CHASTE MUSIC GIRLS!
THE AROMA OF CUTE GIRLS IS EVERY-WHERE!
OH.
GUESS IT'S THIS WAY.
YOU'RE LIKE A WALKING SEX ORGAN.
LOOKS LIKE THEY'VE ALREADY GOTTEN STARTED.
MUSIC HALL
KURUMIGAOKA CONCERT

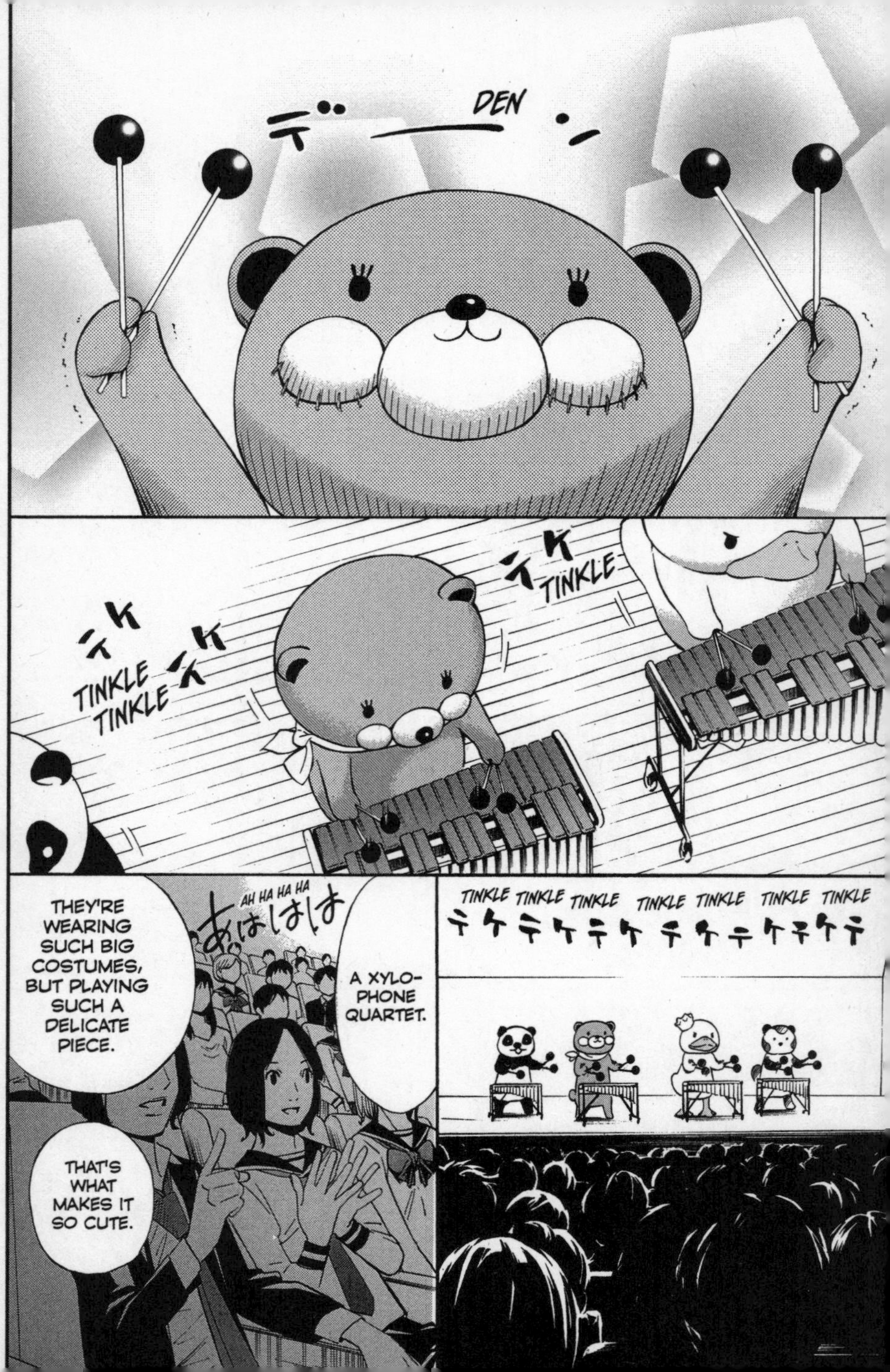
DEN
TINKLE
TINKLE
TINKLE
TINKLE TINKLE TINKLE TINKLE TINKLE TINKLE TINKLE
A XYLO-PHONE QUARTET.
AH HA HA HA
THEY'RE WEARING SUCH BIG COSTUMES, BUT PLAYING SUCH A DELICATE PIECE.
THAT'S WHAT MAKES IT SO CUTE.

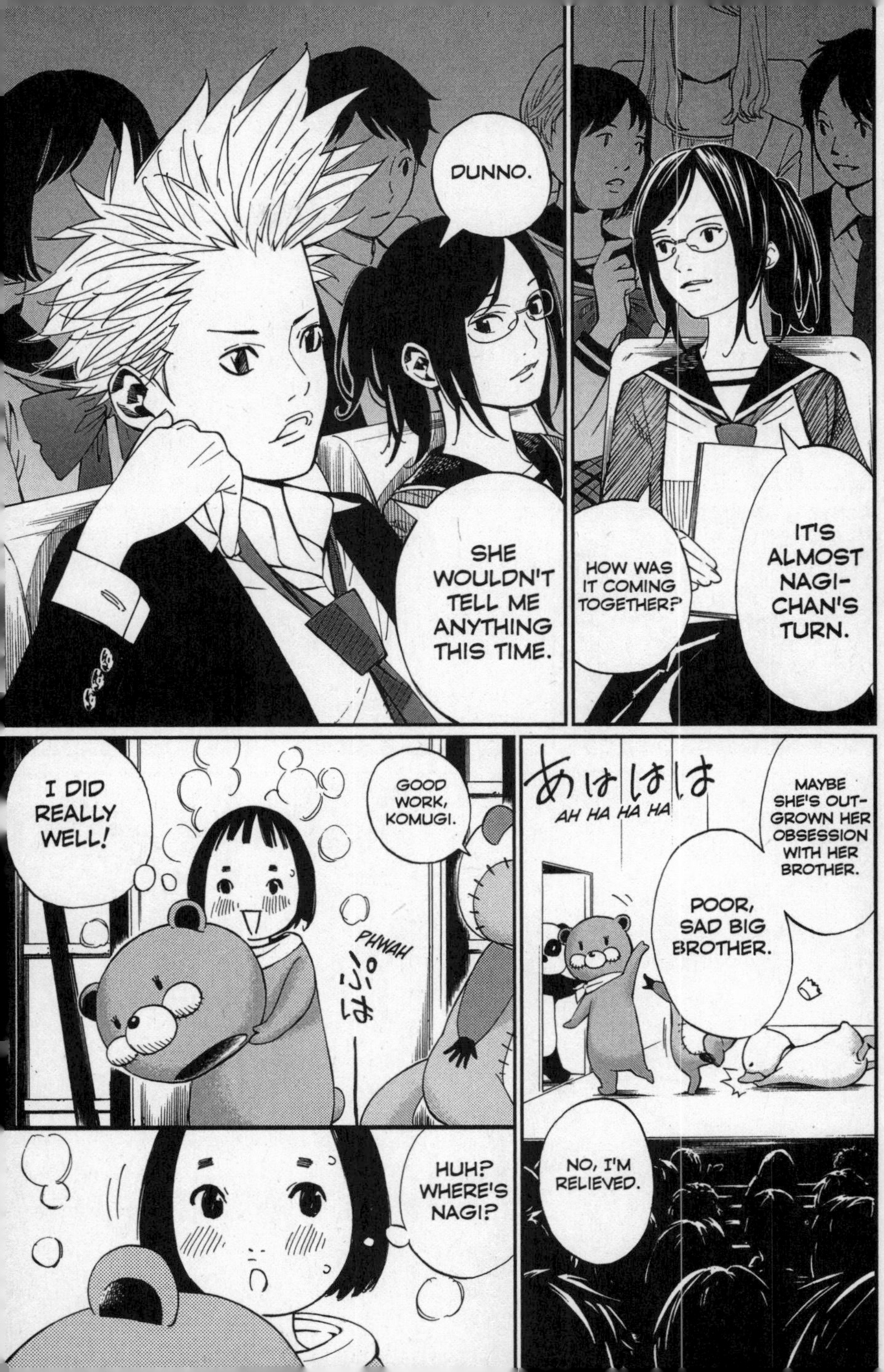
IT'S ALMOST NAGI-CHAN'S TURN.
HOW WAS IT COMING TOGETHER?
DUNNO.
SHE WOULDN'T TELL ME ANYTHING THIS TIME.
あははは
AH HA HA HA
MAYBE SHE'S OUT-GROWN HER OBSESSION WITH HER BROTHER.
POOR, SAD BIG BROTHER.
GOOD WORK, KOMUGI.
I DID REALLY WELL!
ぷは
PHWAH
NO, I'M RELIEVED.
HUH? WHERE'S NAGI?

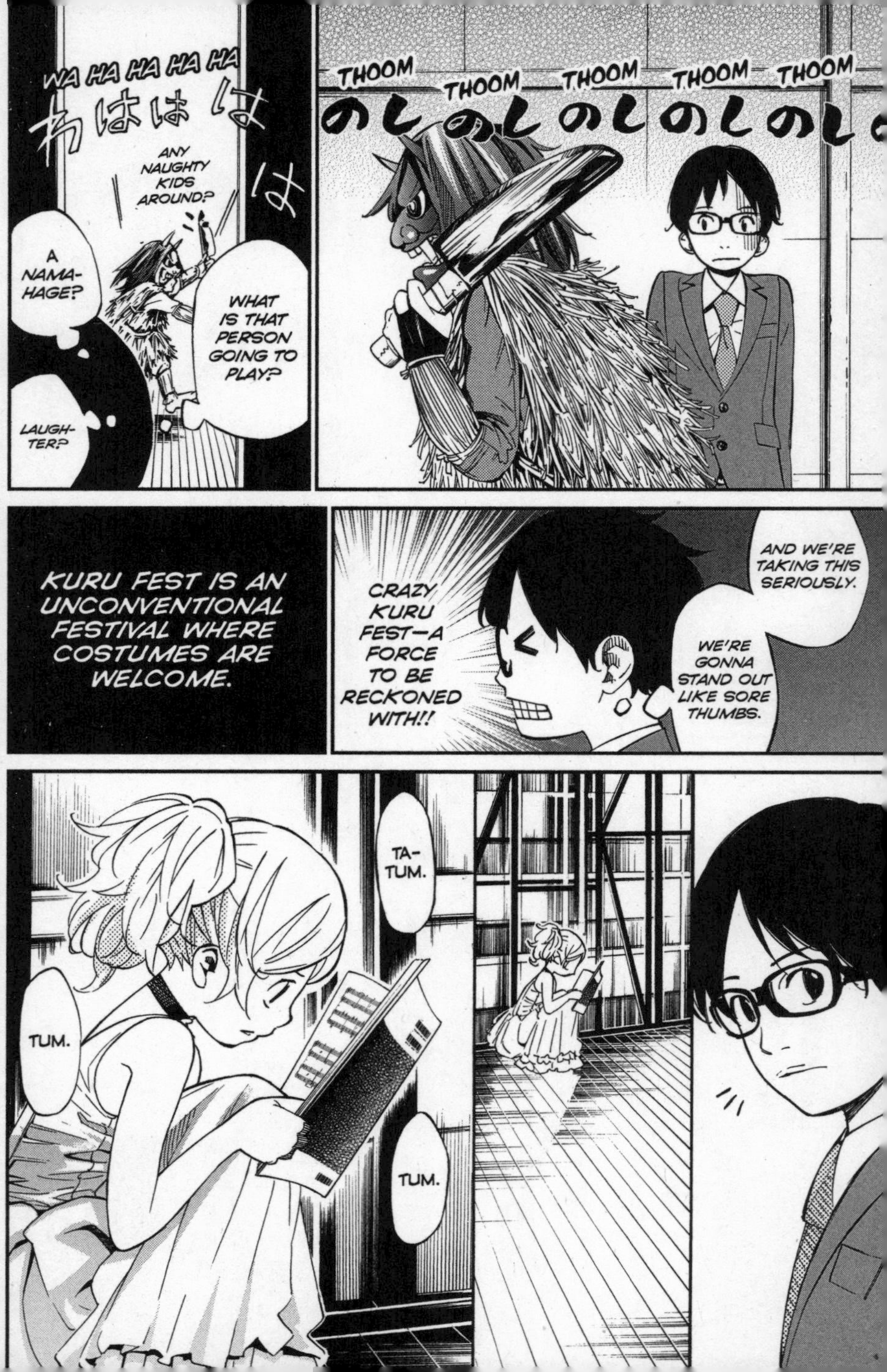
THOOM THOOM THOOM THOOM THOOM
のしのしのしのしの
WA HA HA HA HA
わははは は
ANY NAUGHTY KIDS AROUND?
WHAT IS THAT PERSON GOING TO PLAY?
A NAMA-HAGE?
LAUGHTER?
AND WE'RE TAKING THIS SERIOUSLY.
WE'RE GONNA STAND OUT LIKE SORE THUMBS.
CRAZY KURU FEST—A FORCE TO BE RECKONED WITH!!
KURU FEST IS AN UNCONVENTIONAL FESTIVAL WHERE COSTUMES ARE WELCOME.
TA-TUM.
TUM.
TUM.

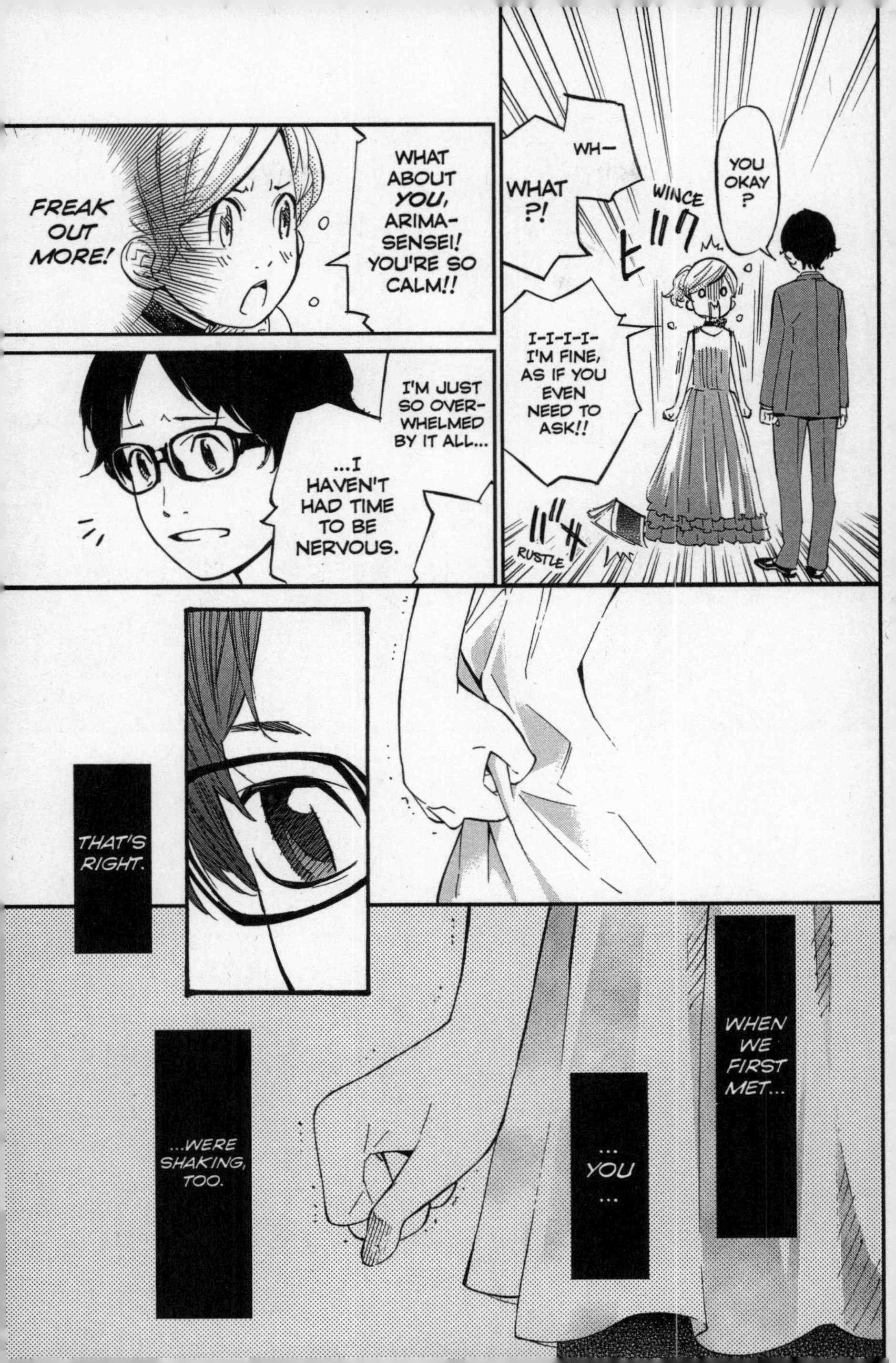
YOU OKAY?
WINCE
WH— WHAT?!
I-I-I-I-I'M FINE, AS IF YOU EVEN NEED TO ASK!!
RUSTLE
WHAT ABOUT YOU, ARIMA-SENSEI! YOU'RE SO CALM!!
FREAK OUT MORE!
I'M JUST SO OVER-WHELMED BY IT ALL...
...I HAVEN'T HAD TIME TO BE NERVOUS.
THAT'S RIGHT.
WHEN WE FIRST MET...
...YOU...
...WERE SHAKING, TOO.

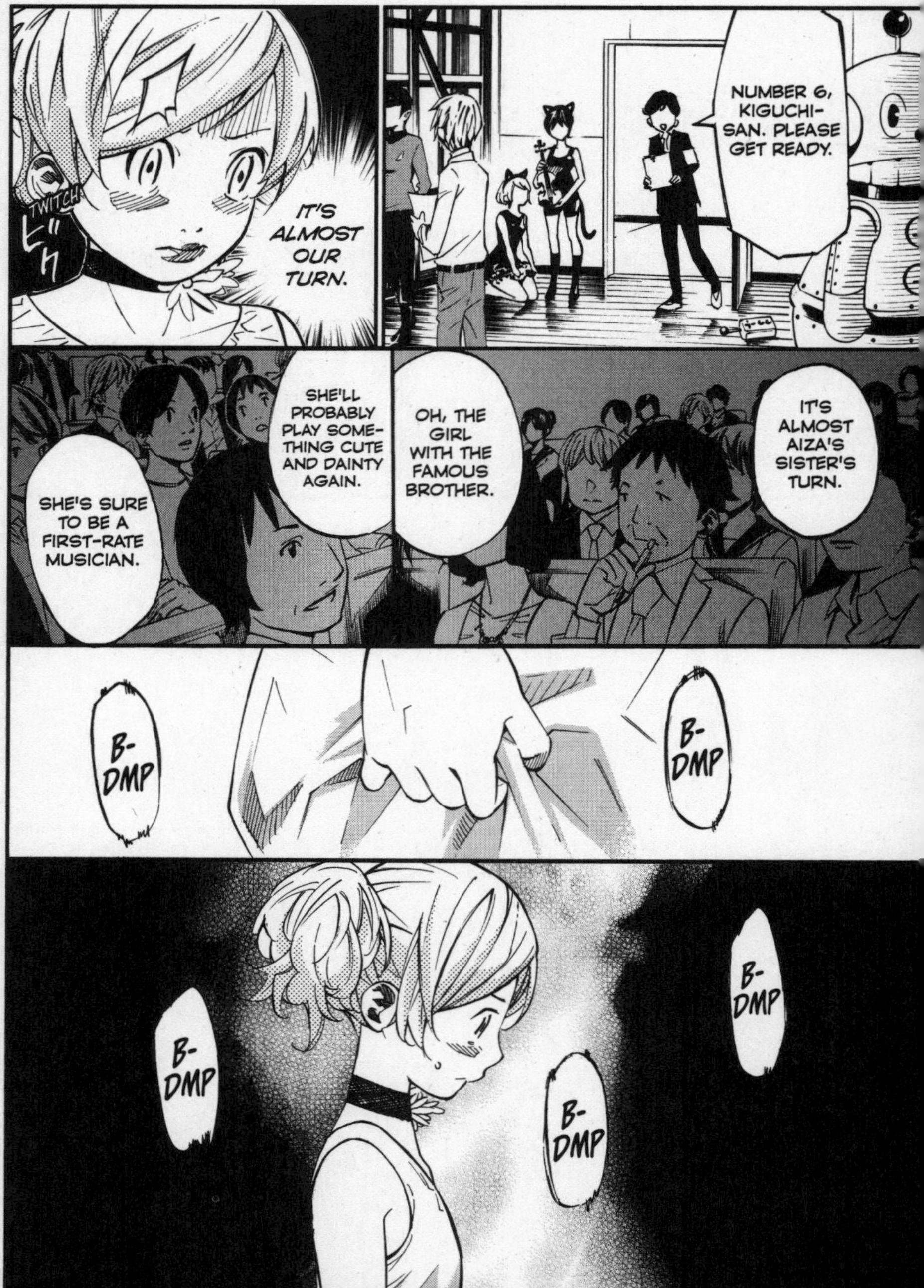
NUMBER 6, KIGUCHI-SAN. PLEASE GET READY.
IT'S ALMOST OUR TURN.
TWITCH
ビク
IT'S ALMOST AIZA'S SISTER'S TURN.
OH, THE GIRL WITH THE FAMOUS BROTHER.
SHE'LL PROBABLY PLAY SOME-THING CUTE AND DAINTY AGAIN.
SHE'S SURE TO BE A FIRST-RATE MUSICIAN.
B-DMP
B-DMP
B-DMP
B-DMP
B-DMP

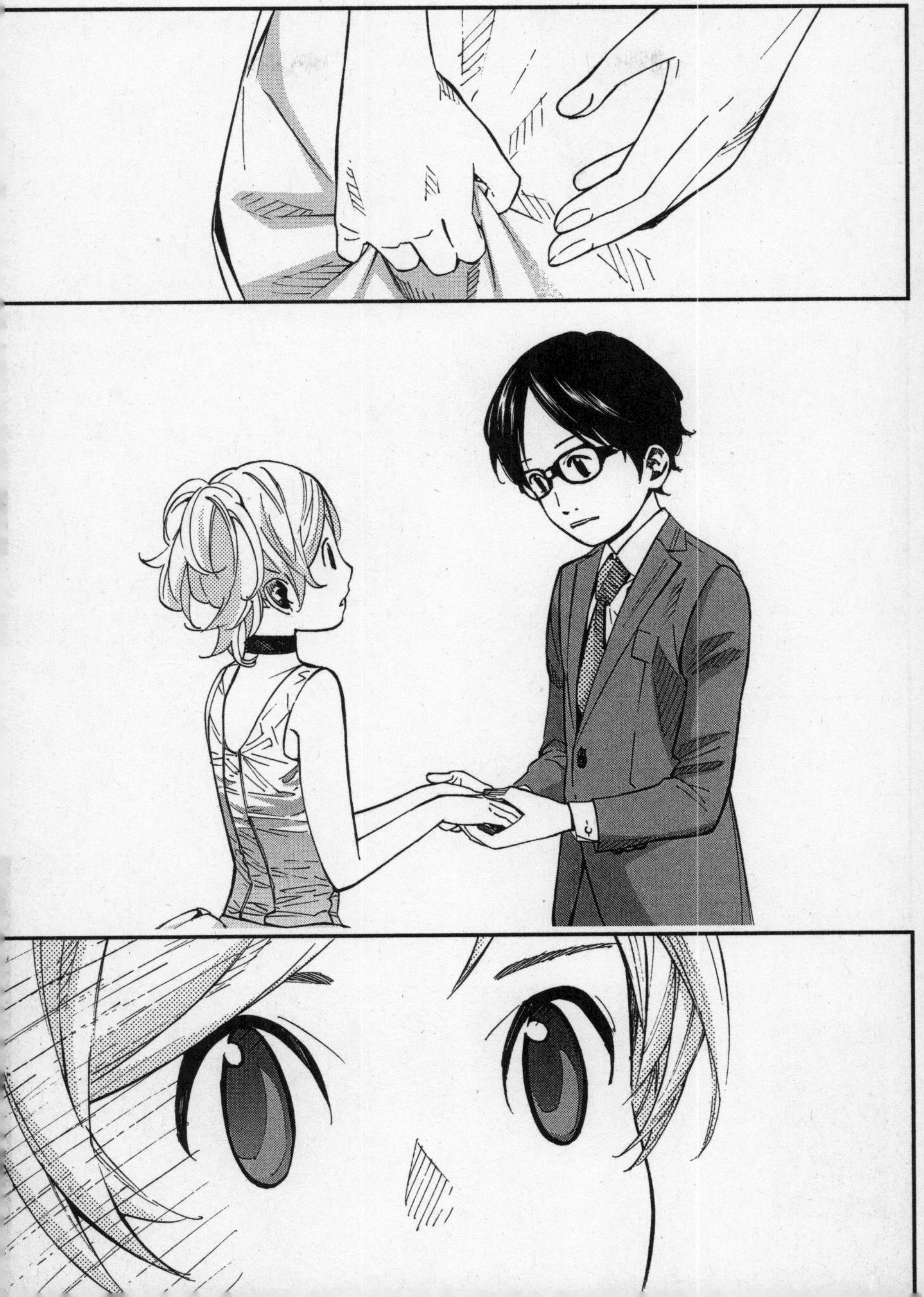

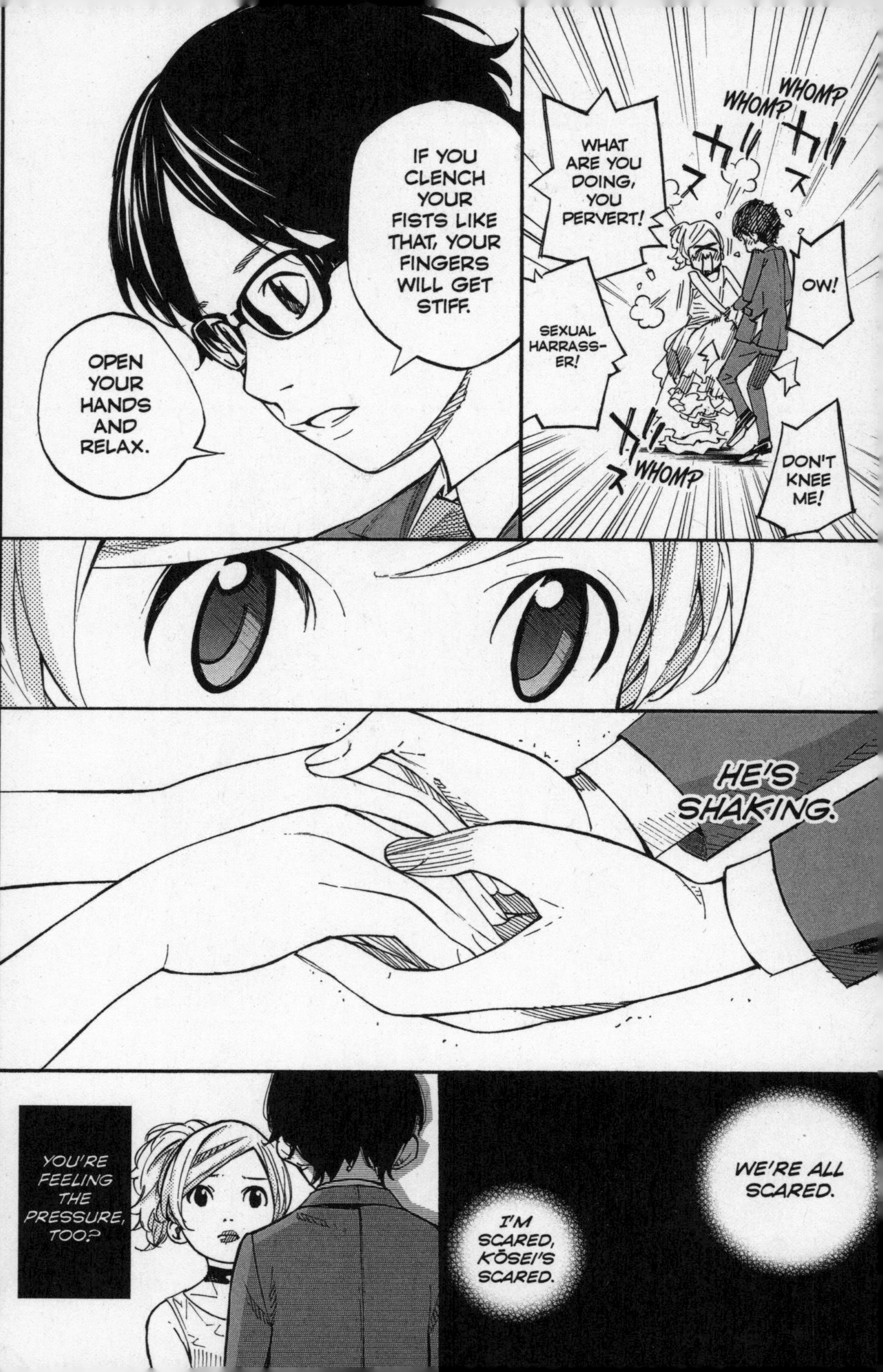
WHOMP
WHOMP
WHAT ARE YOU DOING, YOU PERVERT!
OW!
SEXUAL HARRASS-ER!
DON'T KNEE ME!
WHOMP
IF YOU CLENCH YOUR FISTS LIKE THAT, YOUR FINGERS WILL GET STIFF.
OPEN YOUR HANDS AND RELAX.
HE'S SHAKING.
WE'RE ALL SCARED.
I'M SCARED, KŌSEI'S SCARED.
YOU'RE FEELING THE PRESSURE, TOO?

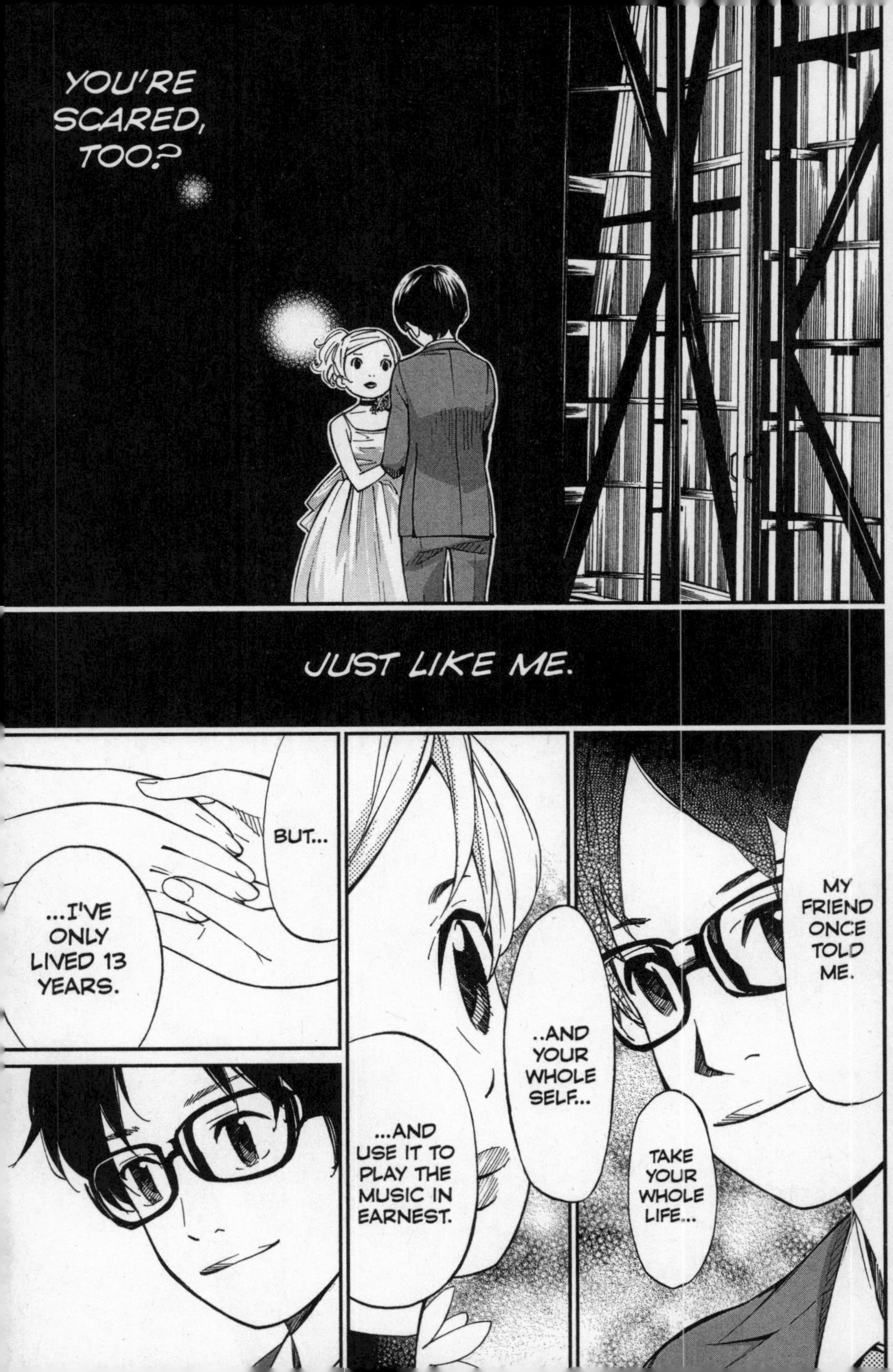
YOU'RE SCARED, TOO?
JUST LIKE ME.
MY FRIEND ONCE TOLD ME.
TAKE YOUR WHOLE LIFE...
..AND YOUR WHOLE SELF...
...AND USE IT TO PLAY THE MUSIC IN EARNEST.
BUT...
...I'VE ONLY LIVED 13 YEARS.

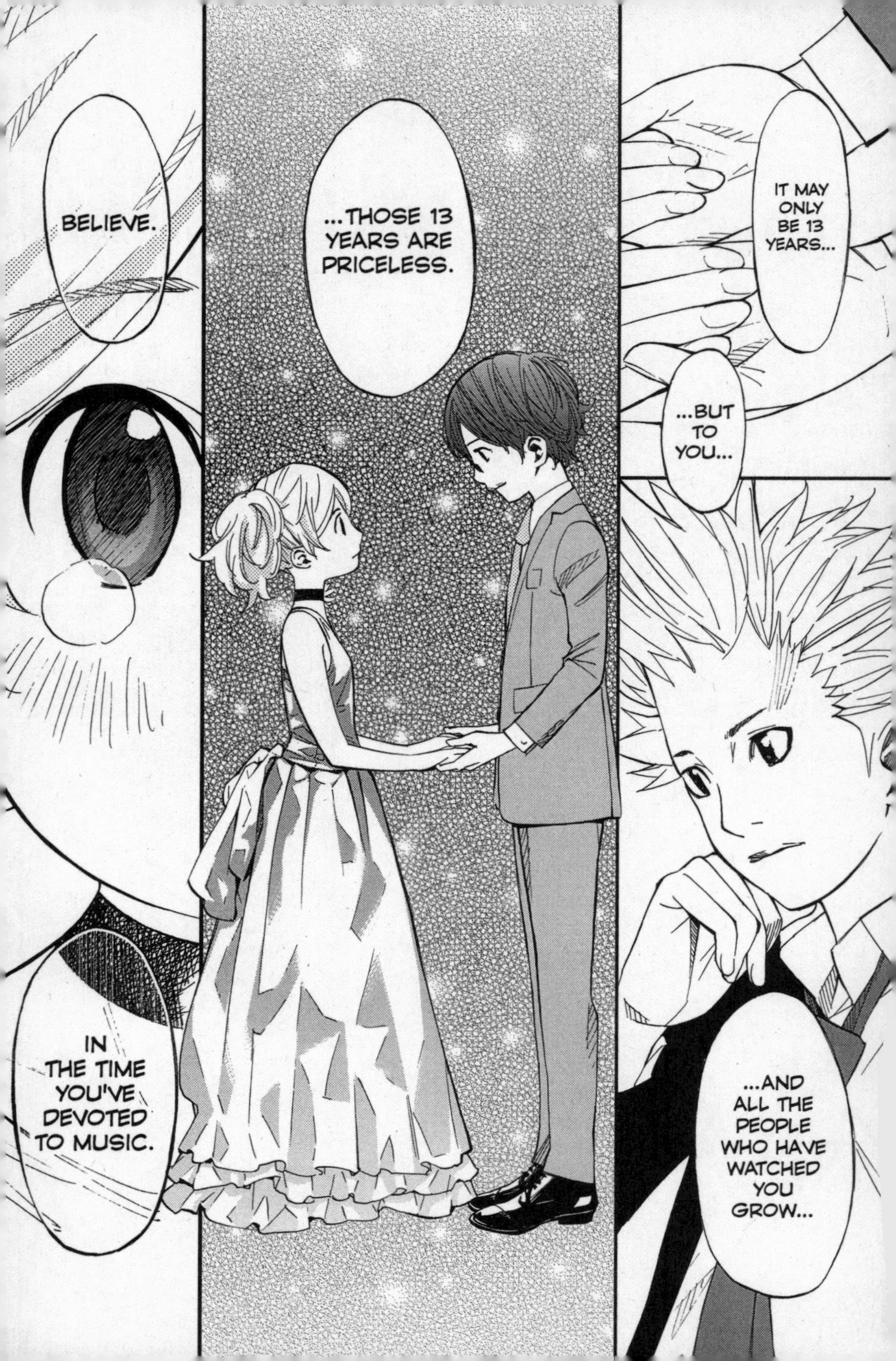
IT MAY ONLY BE 13 YEARS...
...BUT TO YOU...
...AND ALL THE PEOPLE WHO HAVE WATCHED YOU GROW...
...THOSE 13 YEARS ARE PRICELESS.
BELIEVE.
IN THE TIME YOU'VE DEVOTED TO MUSIC.

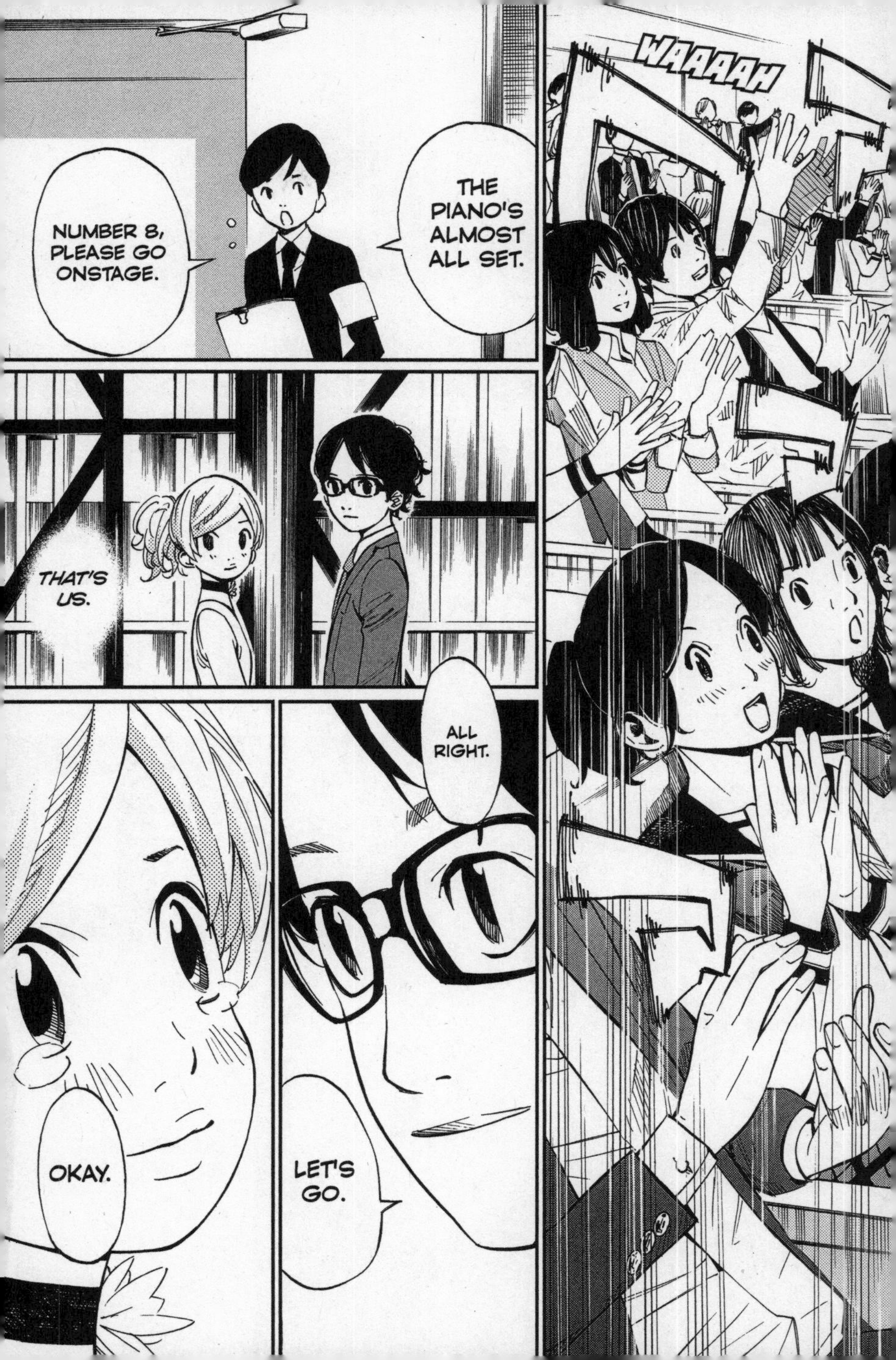

WAAAAH
THE PIANO'S ALMOST ALL SET.
NUMBER 8, PLEASE GO ONSTAGE.
THAT'S US.
ALL RIGHT.
LET'S GO.
OKAY.

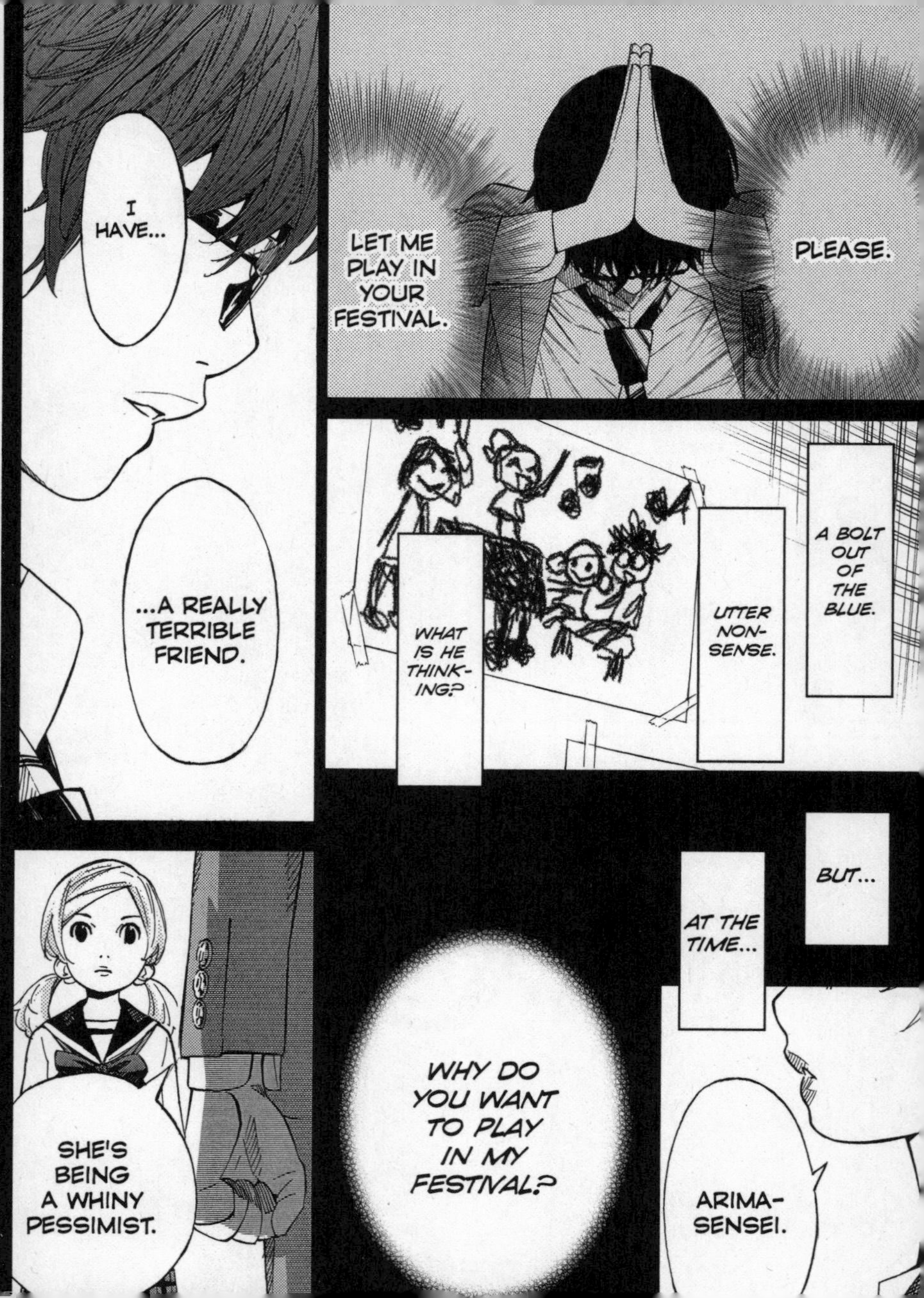
PLEASE.
LET ME PLAY IN YOUR FESTIVAL.
A BOLT OUT OF THE BLUE.
UTTER NONSENSE.
WHAT IS HE THINKING?
I HAVE...
...A REALLY TERRIBLE FRIEND.
BUT...
AT THE TIME...
ARIMA-SENSEI.
WHY DO YOU WANT TO PLAY IN MY FESTIVAL?
SHE'S BEING A WHINY PESSIMIST.

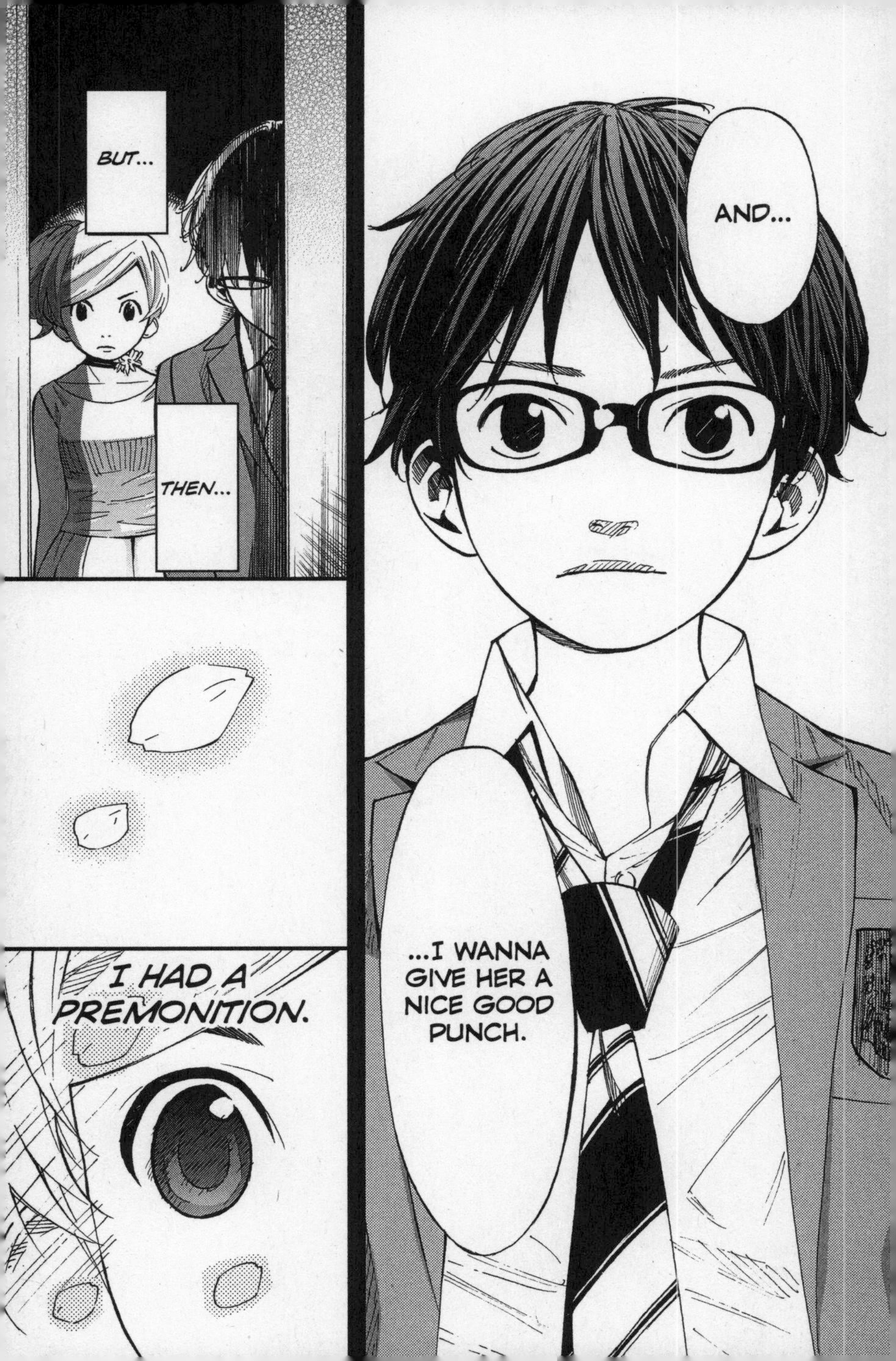
AND...
...I WANNA GIVE HER A NICE GOOD PUNCH.
BUT...
THEN...
I HAD A PREMONITION.

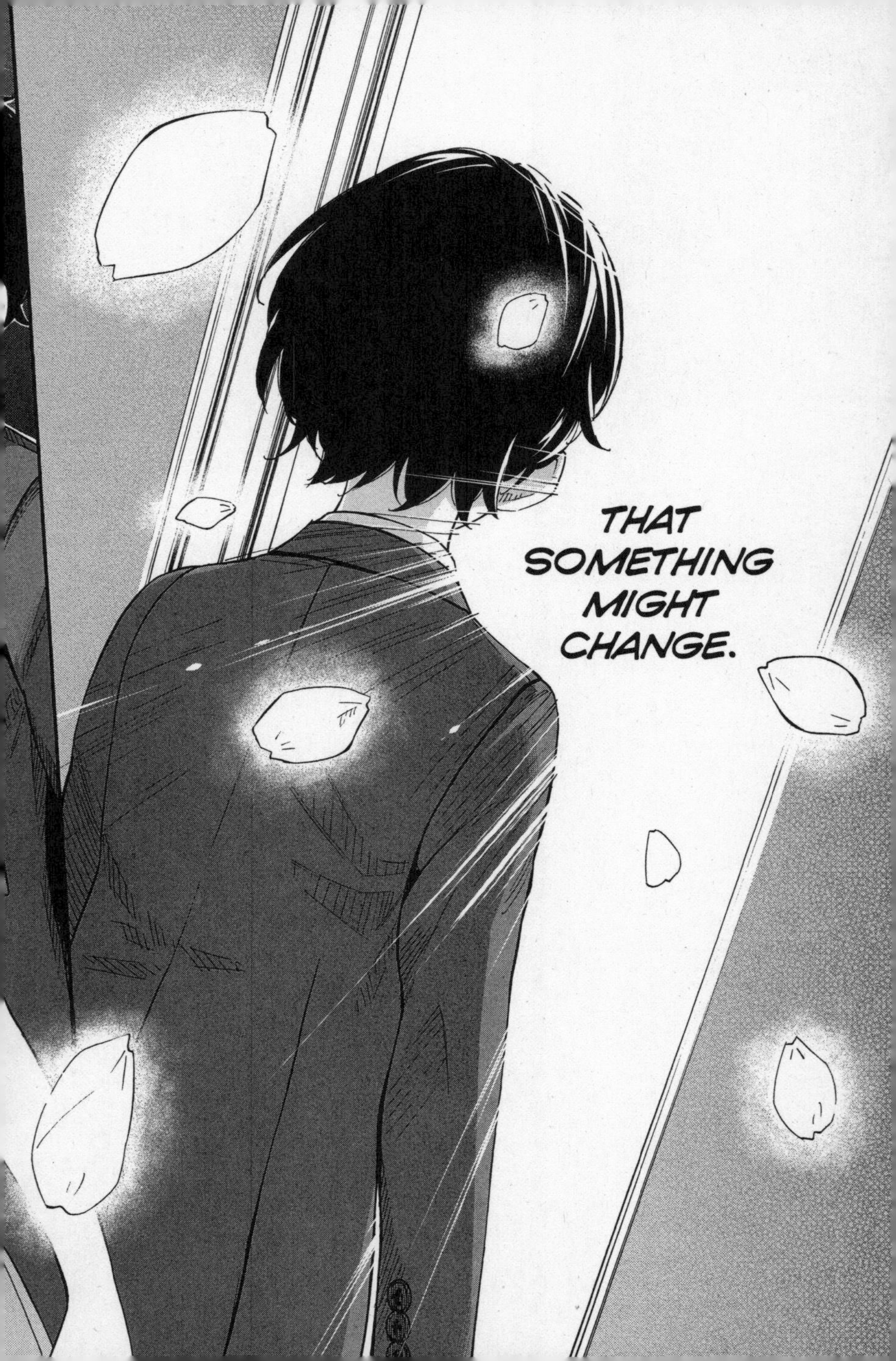
THAT SOMETHING MIGHT CHANGE.

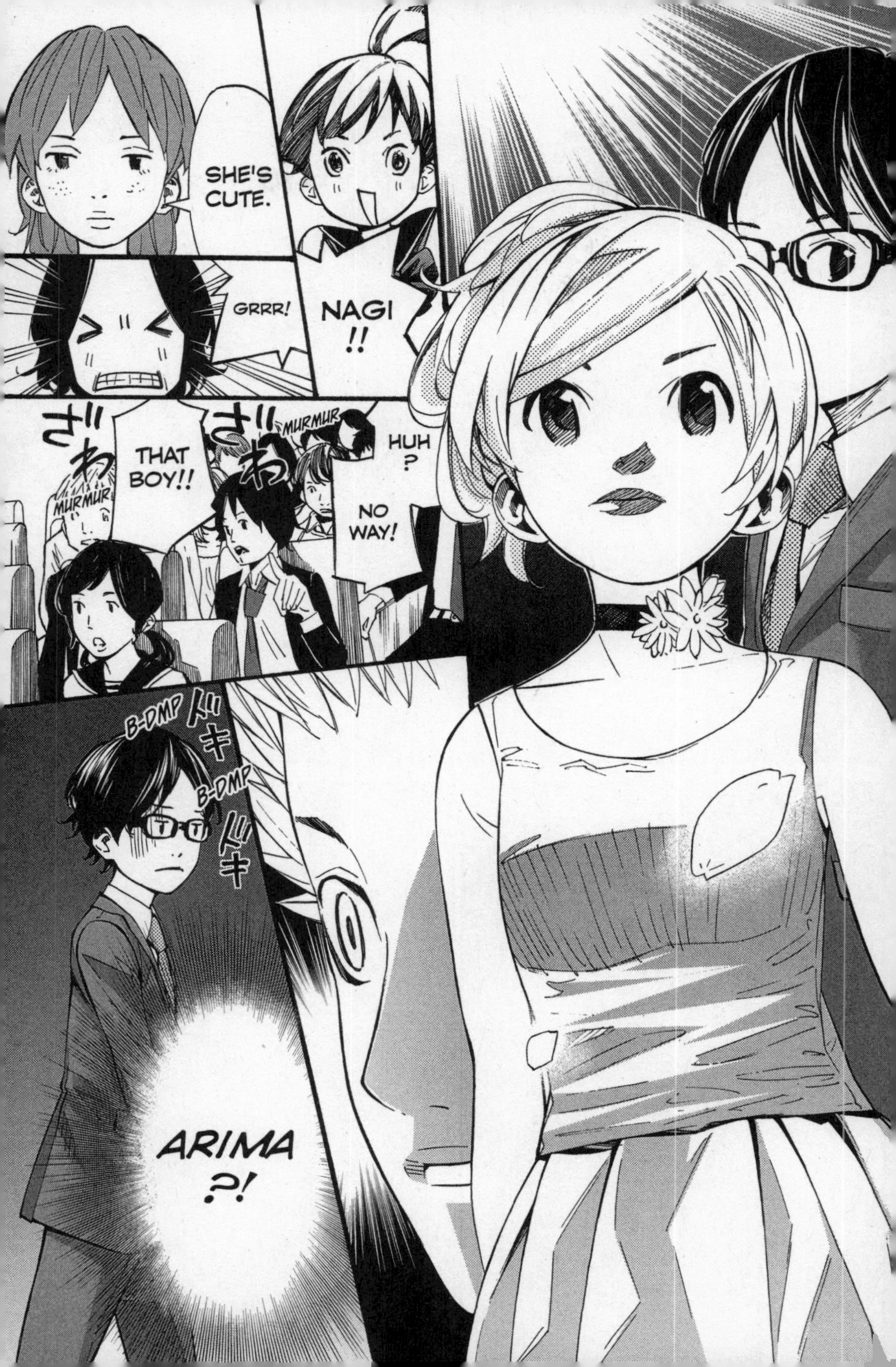
SHE'S CUTE.
NAGI !!
GRRR!
HUH ?
MURMUR
ざわ
NO WAY!
THAT BOY!!
ざわ
MURMUR
B-DMP ドキ
B-DMP ドキ
ARIMA ?!

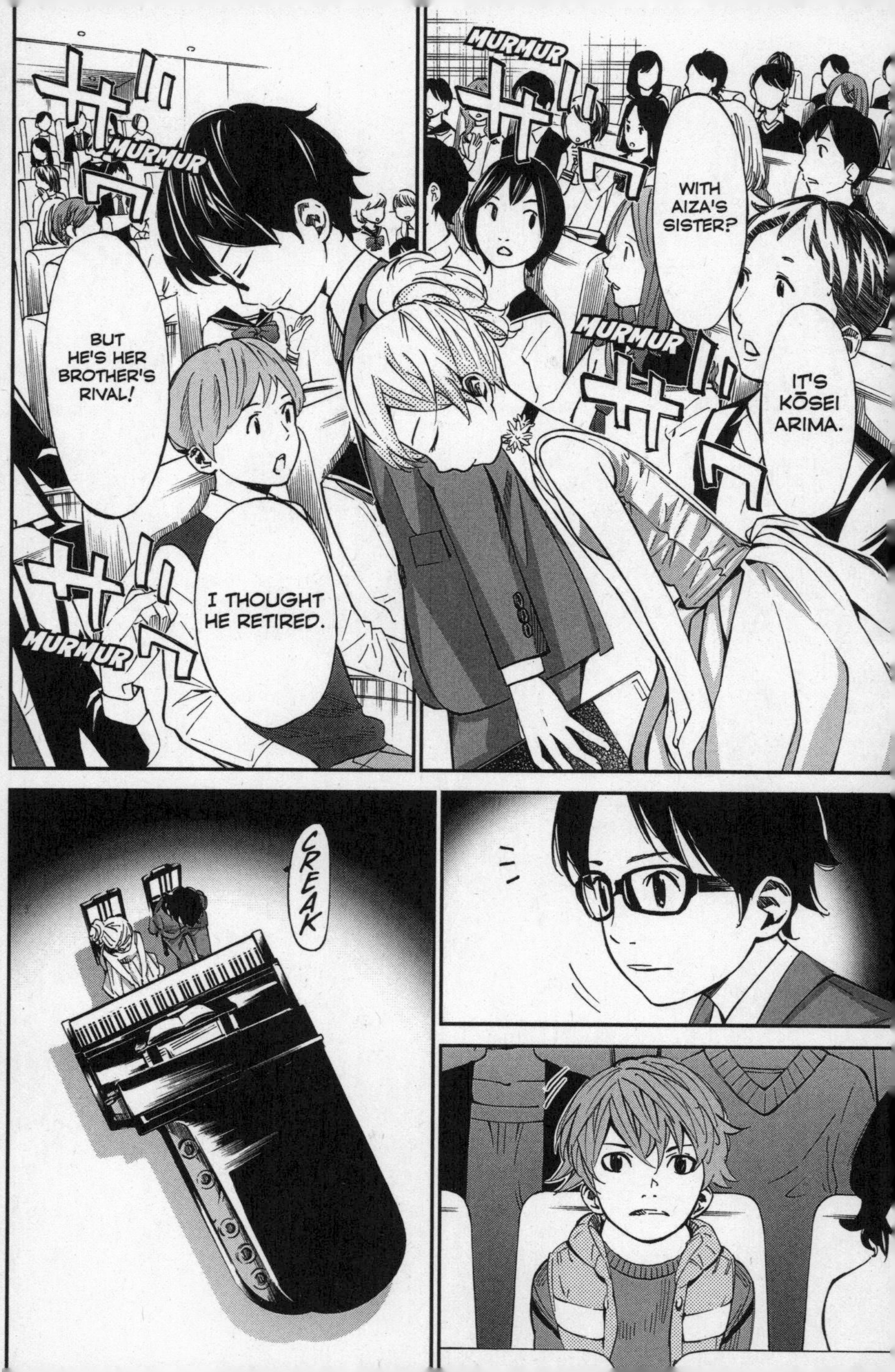
MURMUR
WITH AIZA'S SISTER?
MURMUR
IT'S KŌSEI ARIMA.
MURMUR
BUT HE'S HER BROTHER'S RIVAL!
I THOUGHT HE RETIRED.
MURMUR
CREAK

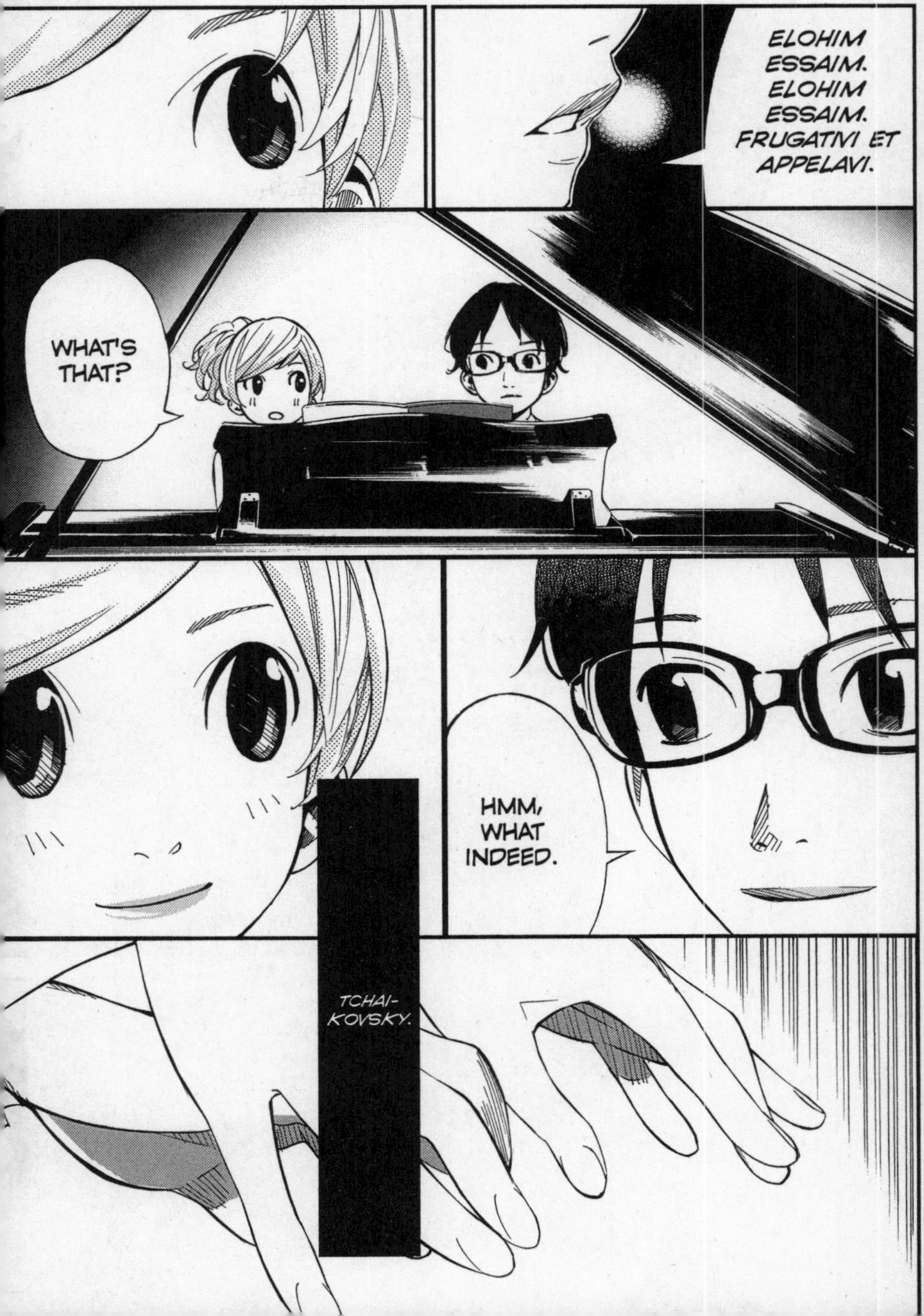
ELOHIM ESSAIM. ELOHIM ESSAIM. FRUGATIVI ET APPELAVI.
WHAT'S THAT?
HMM, WHAT INDEED.
TCHAI-KOVSKY.

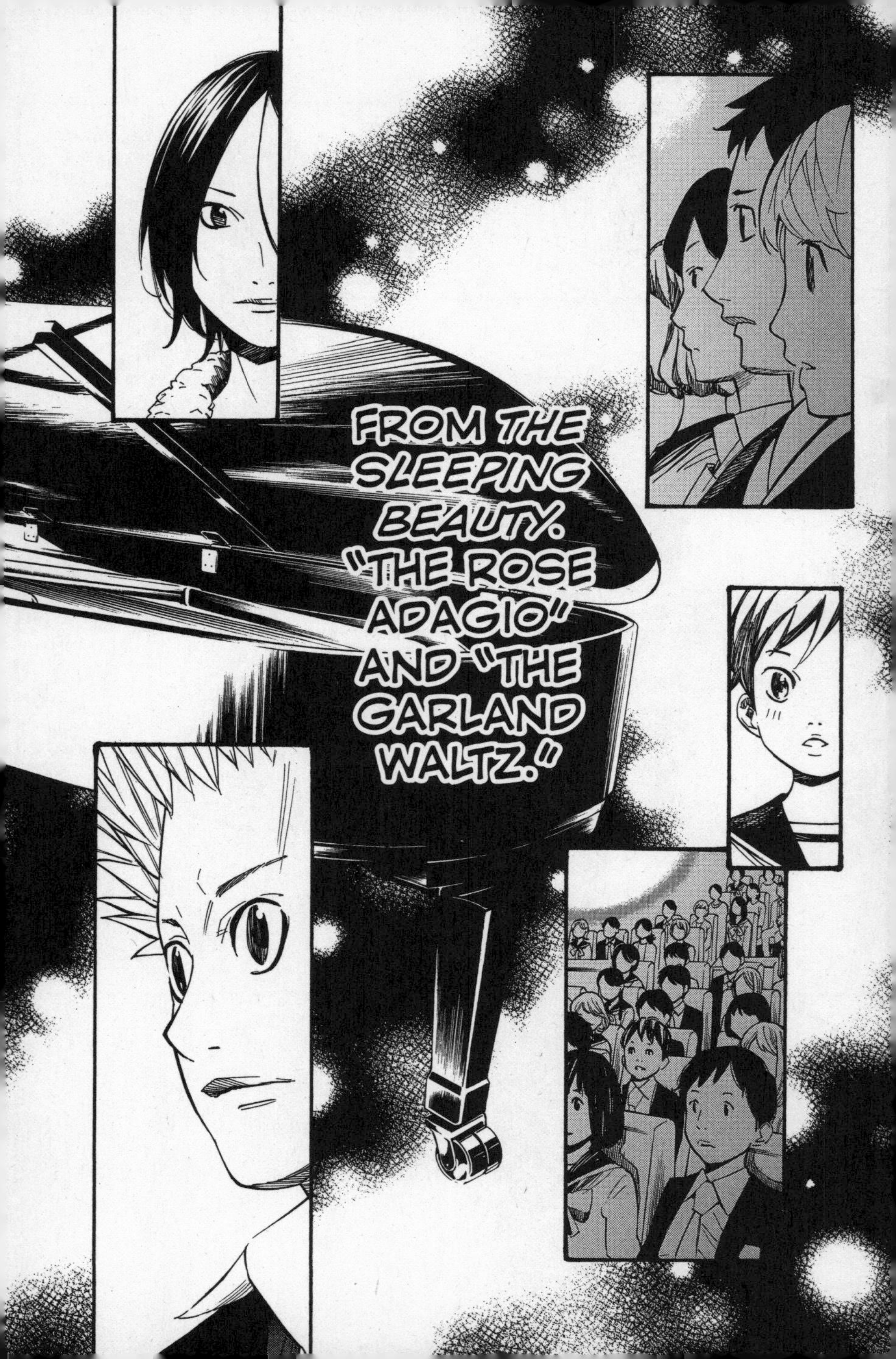
FROM THE SLEEPING BEAUTY. "THE ROSE ADAGIO" AND "THE GARLAND WALTZ."

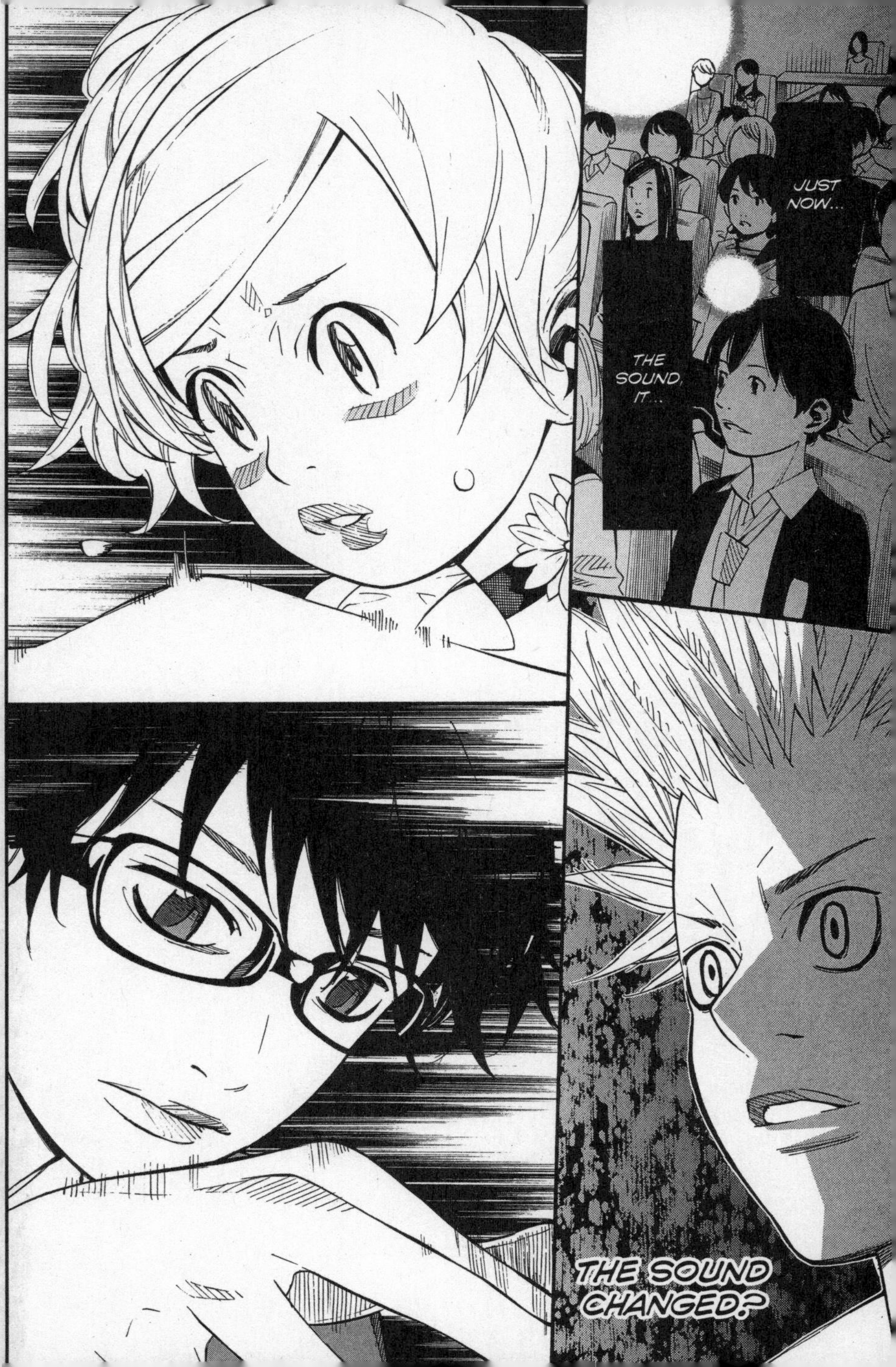
JUST NOW...
THE SOUND, IT...
THE SOUND CHANGED?

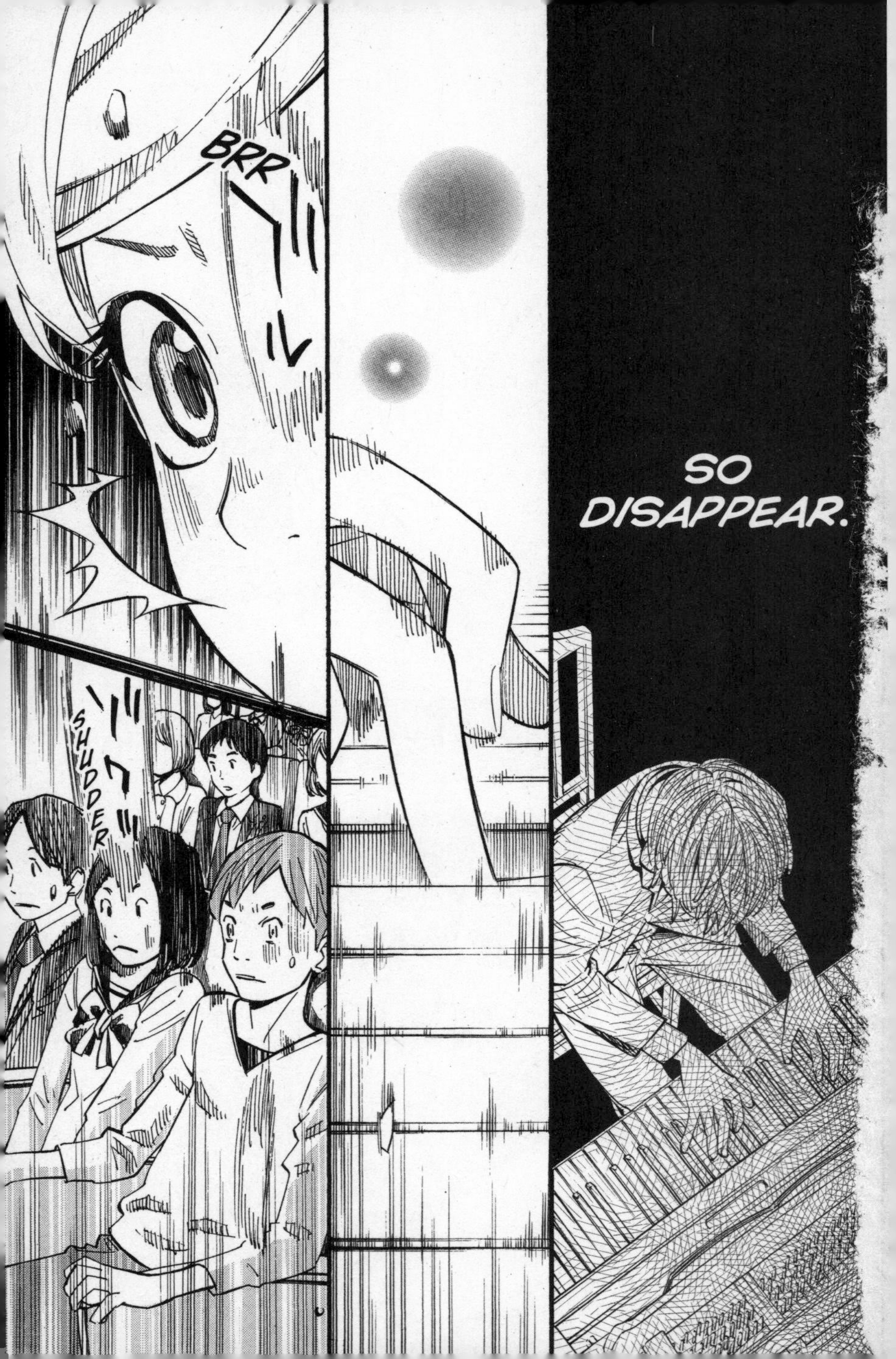
SO DISAPPEAR.
BRR
SHUDDER

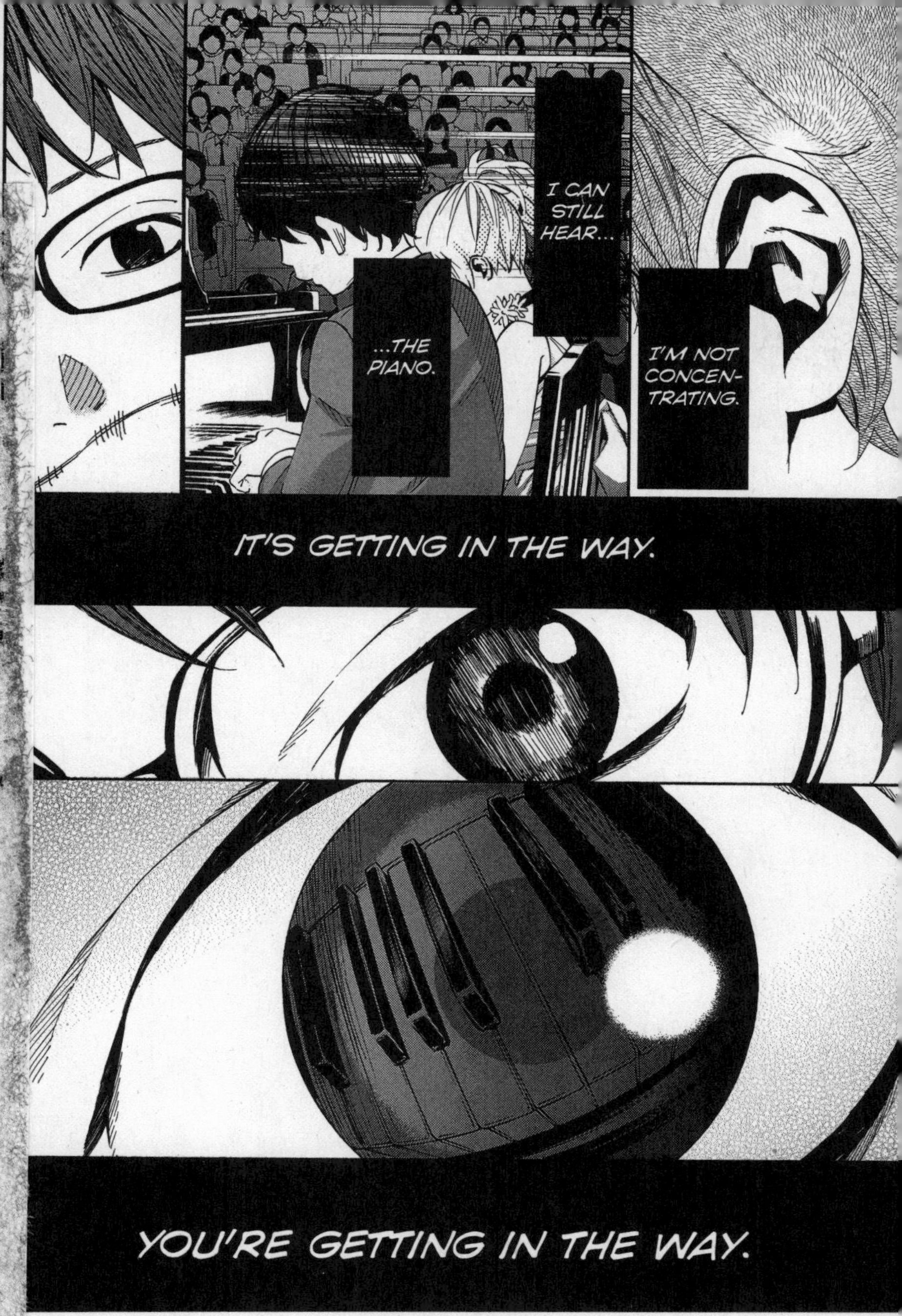
I'M NOT CONCENTRATING.
I CAN STILL HEAR...
...THE PIANO.
IT'S GETTING IN THE WAY.
YOU'RE GETTING IN THE WAY.

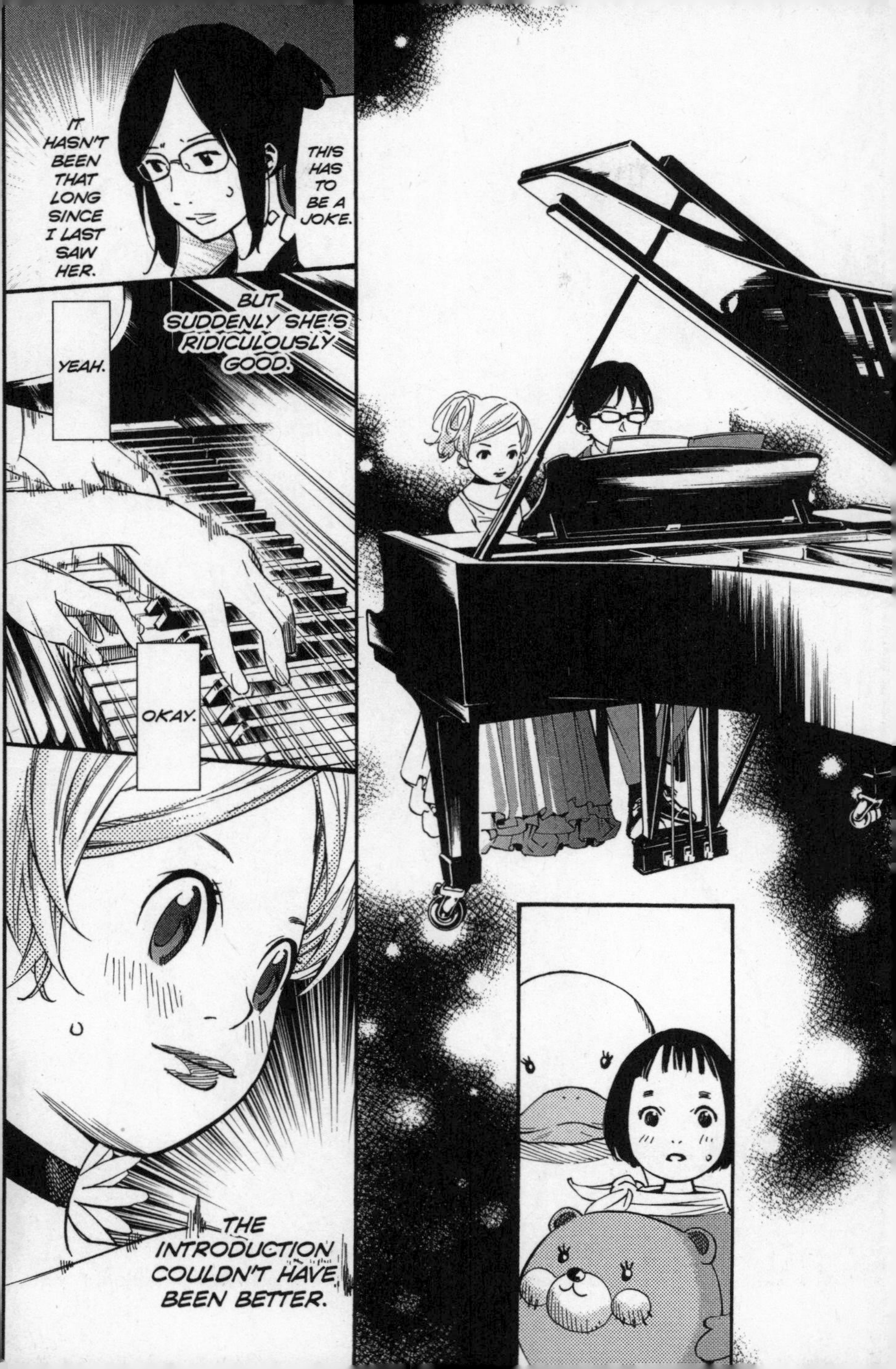
THIS HAS TO BE A JOKE.
IT HASN'T BEEN THAT LONG SINCE I LAST SAW HER.
BUT SUDDENLY SHE'S RIDICULOUSLY GOOD.
YEAH.
OKAY.
THE INTRODUCTION COULDN'T HAVE BEEN BETTER.

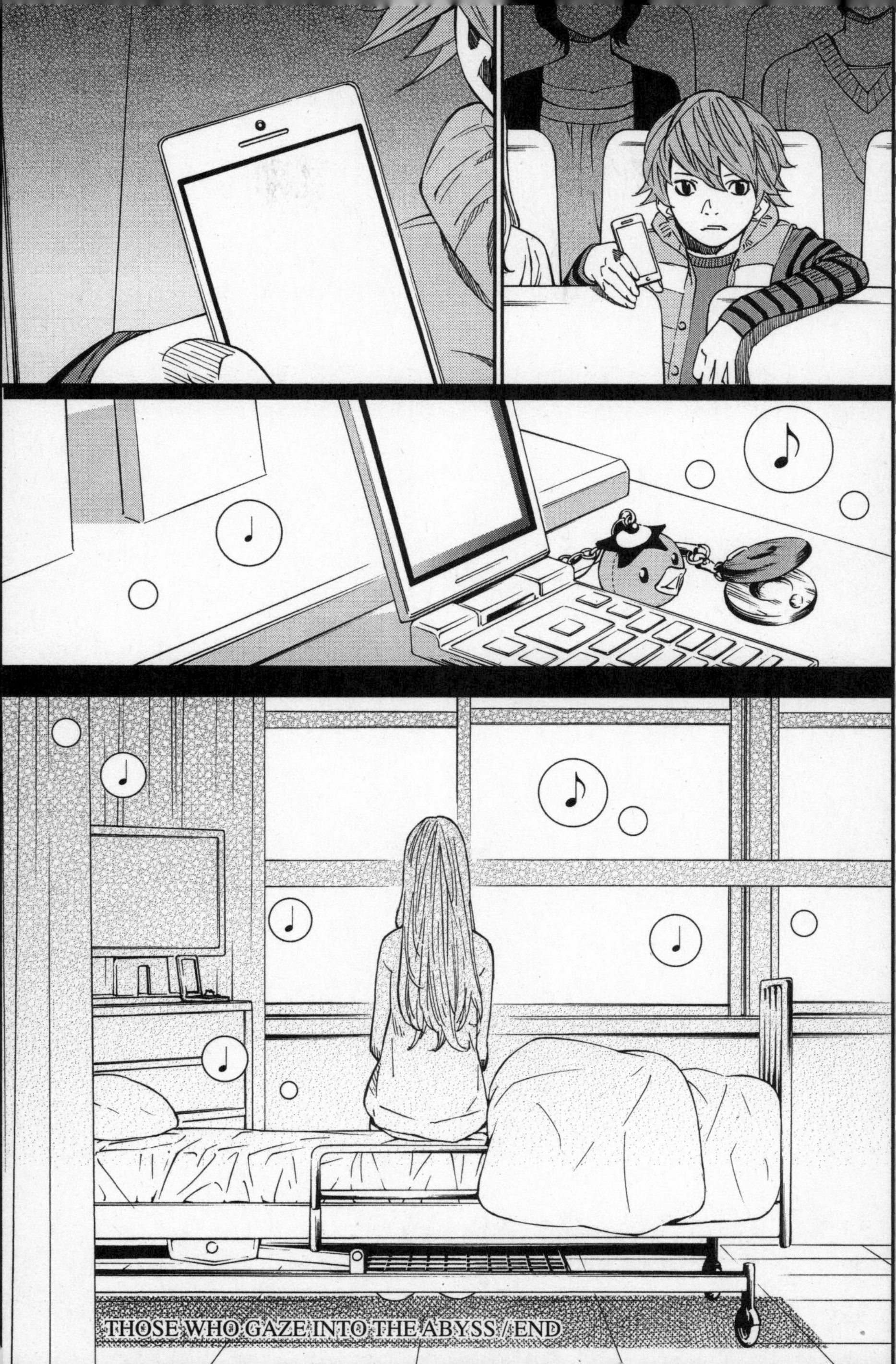
THOSE WHO GAZE INTO THE ABYSS / END

Your Lie in April

I met the girl under full-bloomed cherry blossoms, and my fate has begun to change.

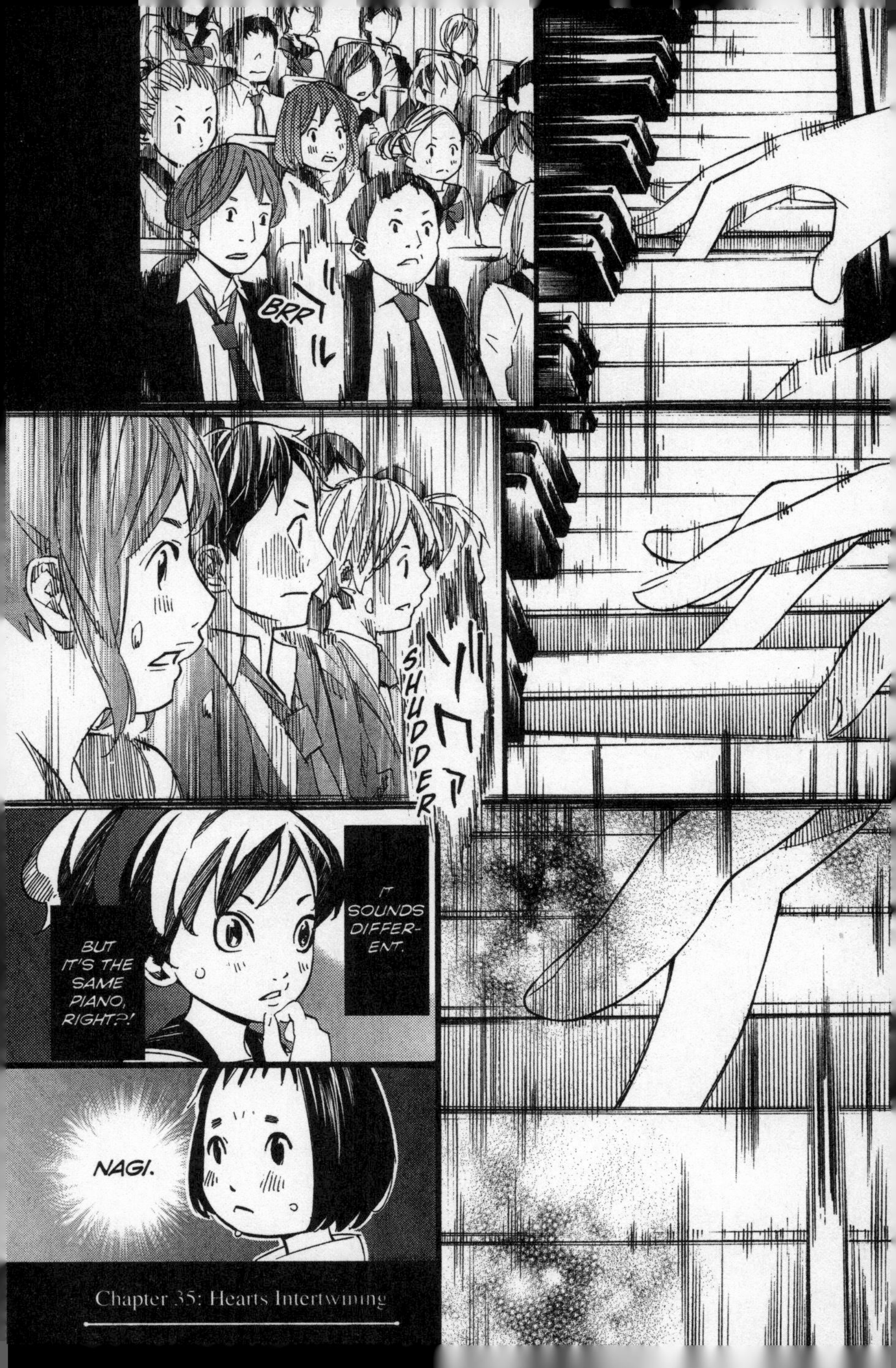
BRR
SHUDDER
IT SOUNDS DIFFERENT.
BUT IT'S THE SAME PIANO, RIGHT?!
NAGI.
Chapter 35: Hearts Intertwining

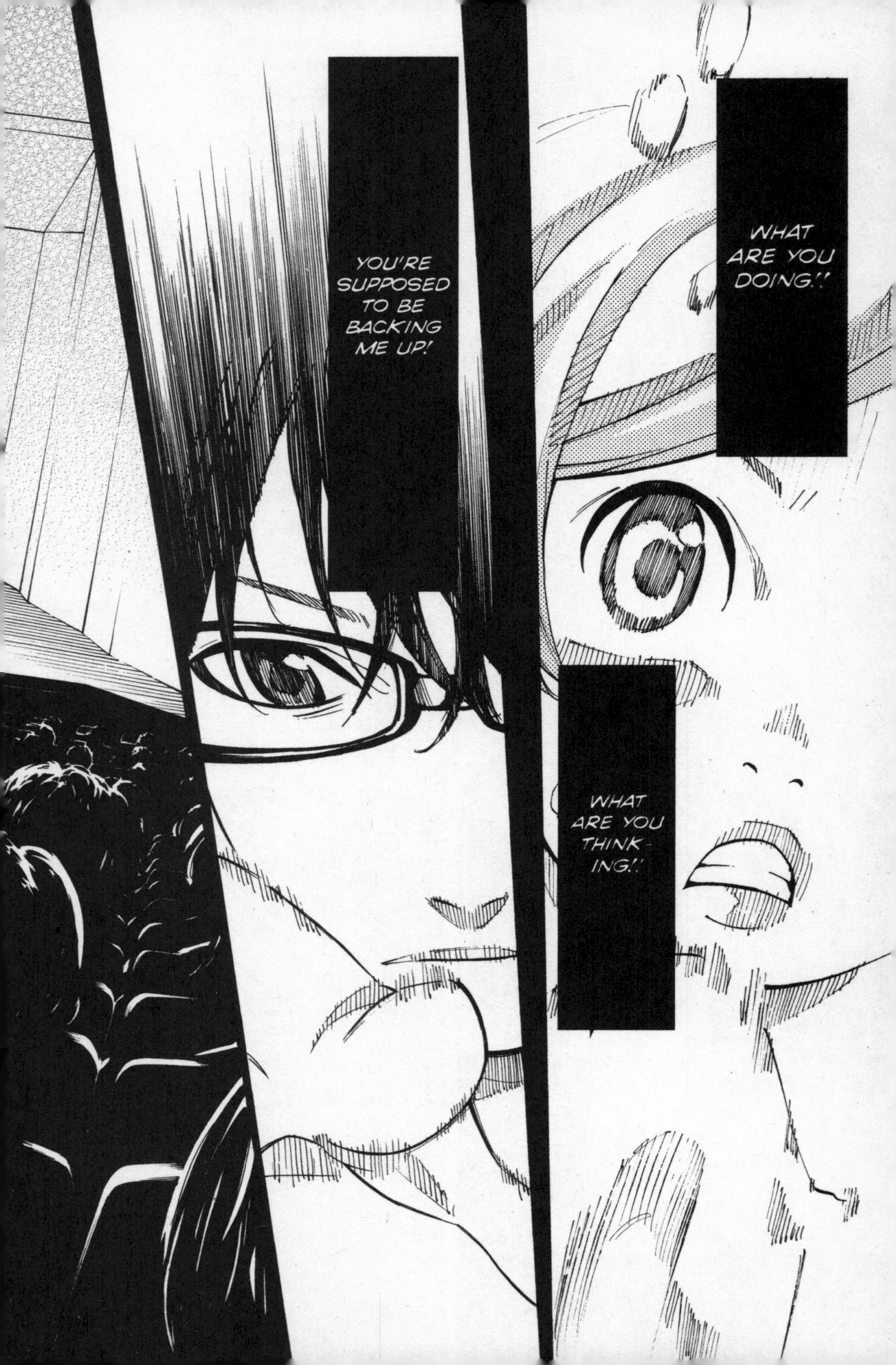
WHAT ARE YOU DOING!!
WHAT ARE YOU THINKING!!
YOU'RE SUPPOSED TO BE BACKING ME UP!

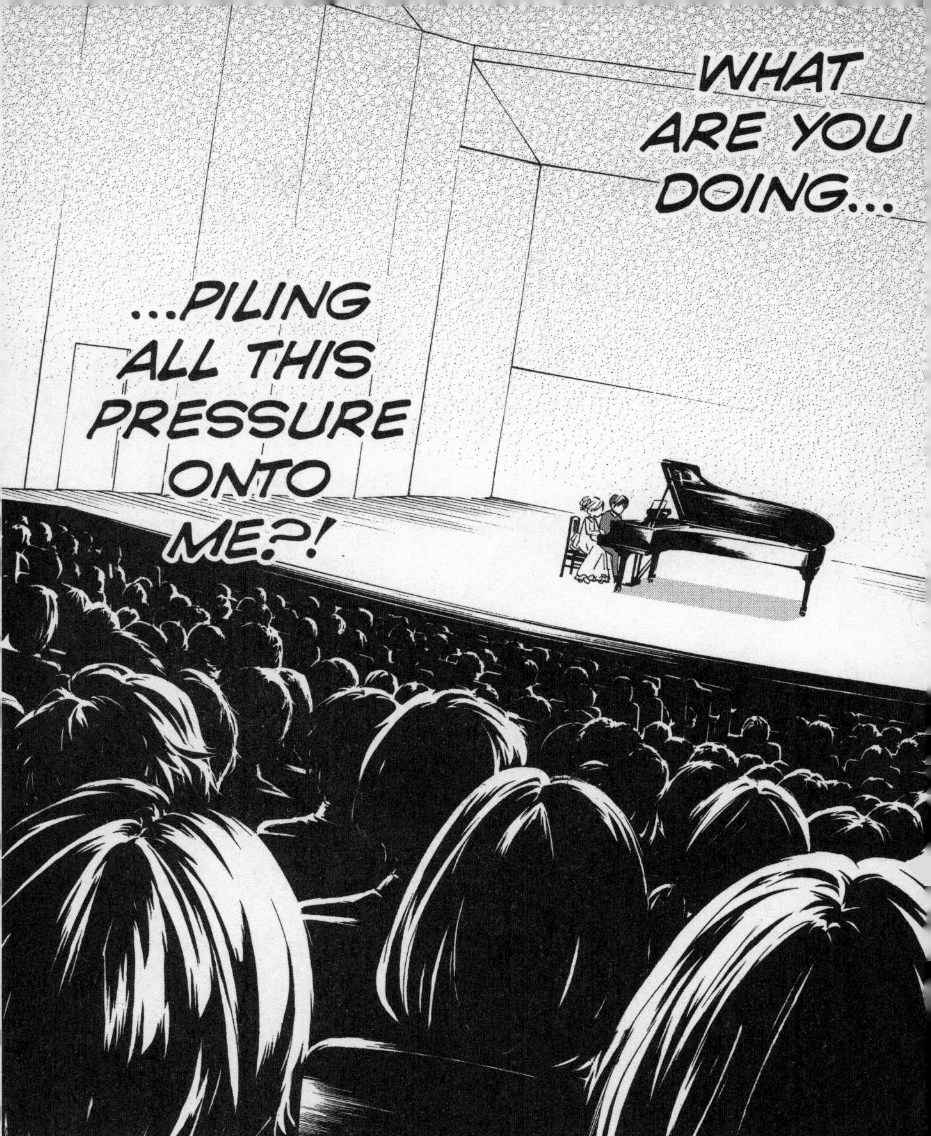
WHAT ARE YOU DOING...
...PILING ALL THIS PRESSURE ONTO ME?!
"THE GARLAND WALTZ" FROM *THE SLEEPING BEAUTY*

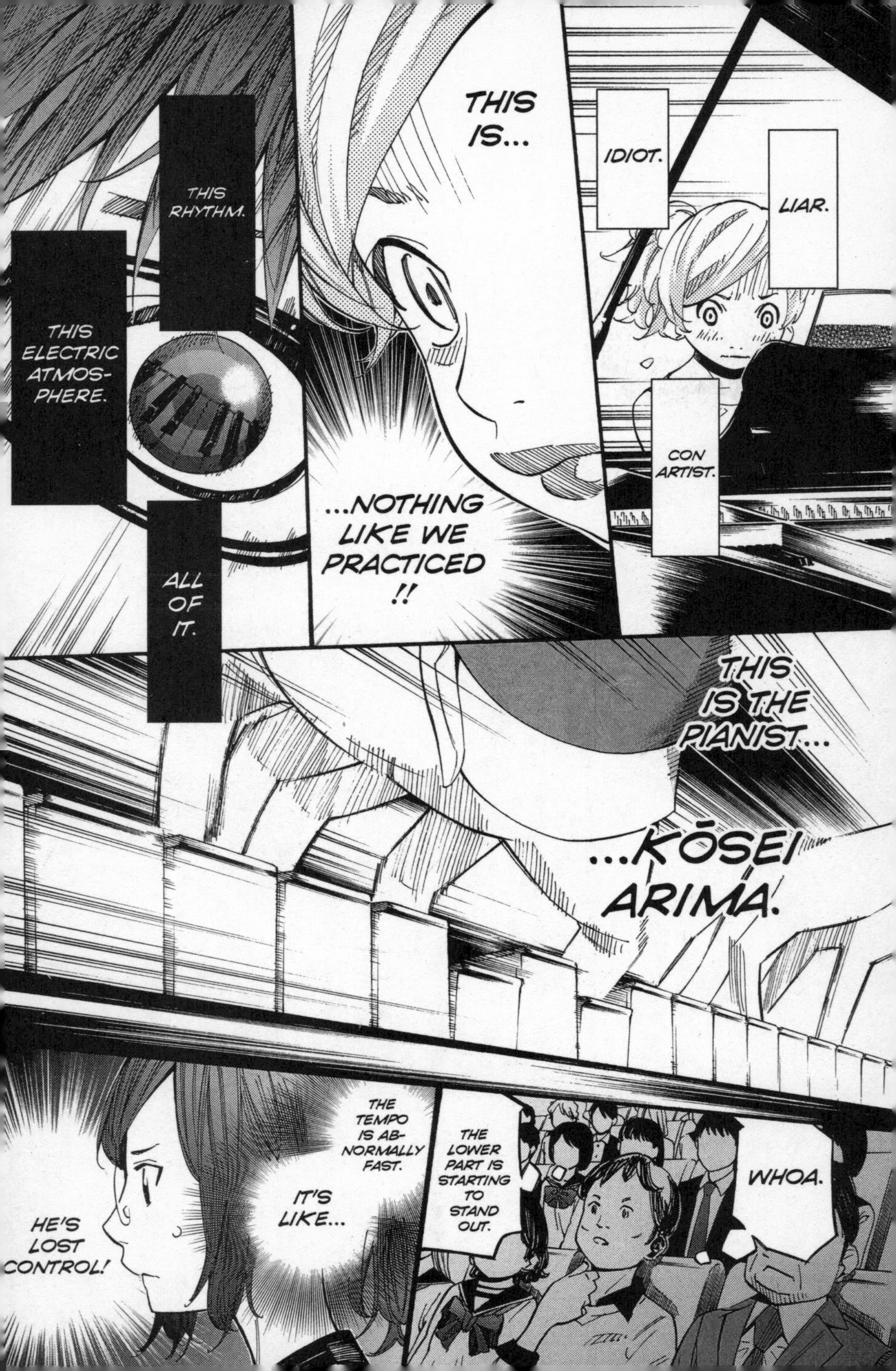
IDIOT.
LIAR.
CON ARTIST.
THIS IS...
...NOTHING LIKE WE PRACTICED !!
THIS RHYTHM.
THIS ELECTRIC ATMOS-PHERE.
ALL OF IT.
THIS IS THE PIANIST...
...KŌSEI ARIMA.
WHOA.
THE LOWER PART IS STARTING TO STAND OUT.
THE TEMPO IS AB-NORMALLY FAST.
IT'S LIKE...
HE'S LOST CONTROL!

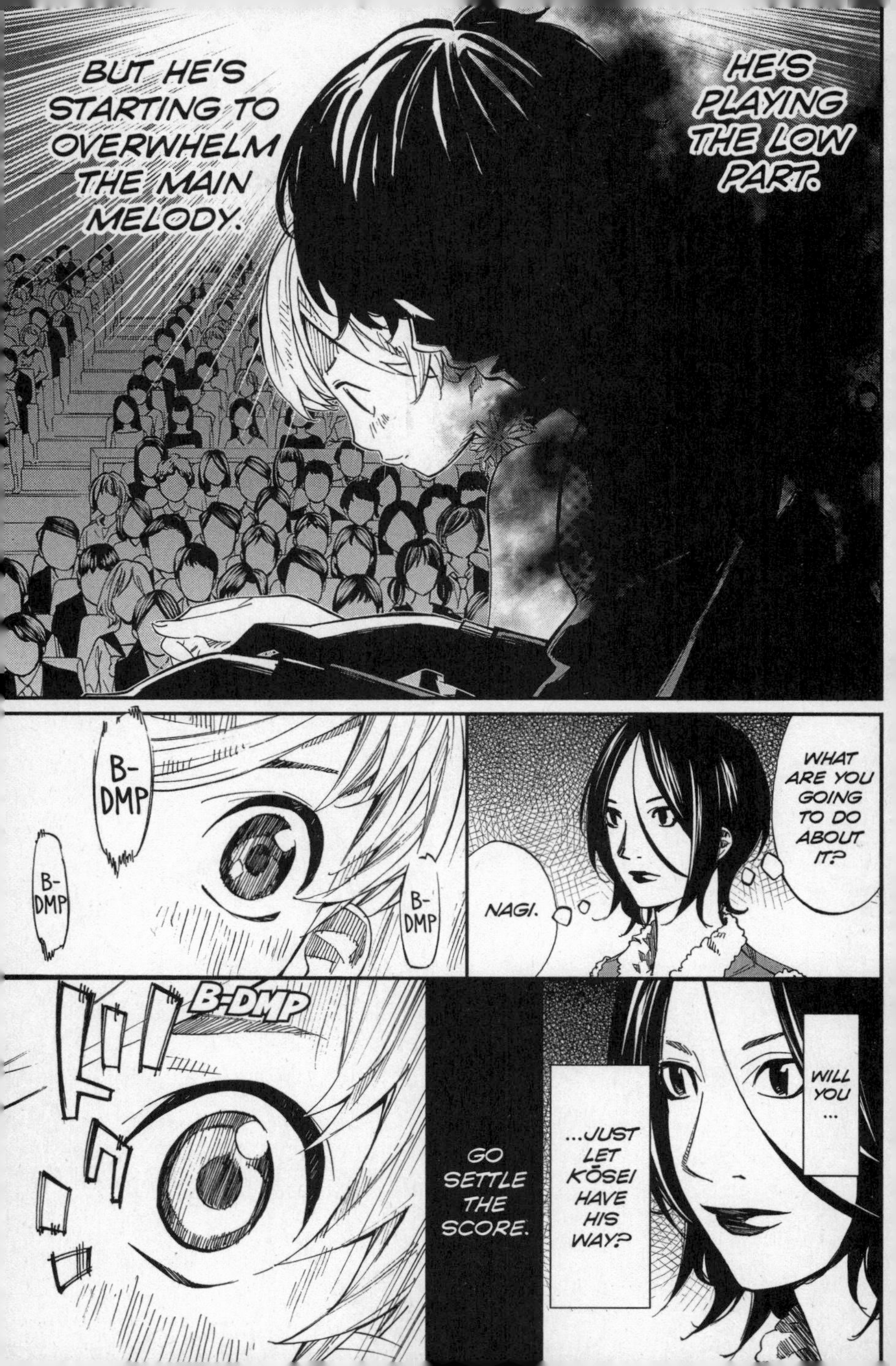
HE'S PLAYING THE LOW PART.
BUT HE'S STARTING TO OVERWHELM THE MAIN MELODY.
WHAT ARE YOU GOING TO DO ABOUT IT?
NAGI.
B-DMP
B-DMP
B-DMP
WILL YOU ...
...JUST LET KŌSEI HAVE HIS WAY?
GO SETTLE THE SCORE.
B-DMP

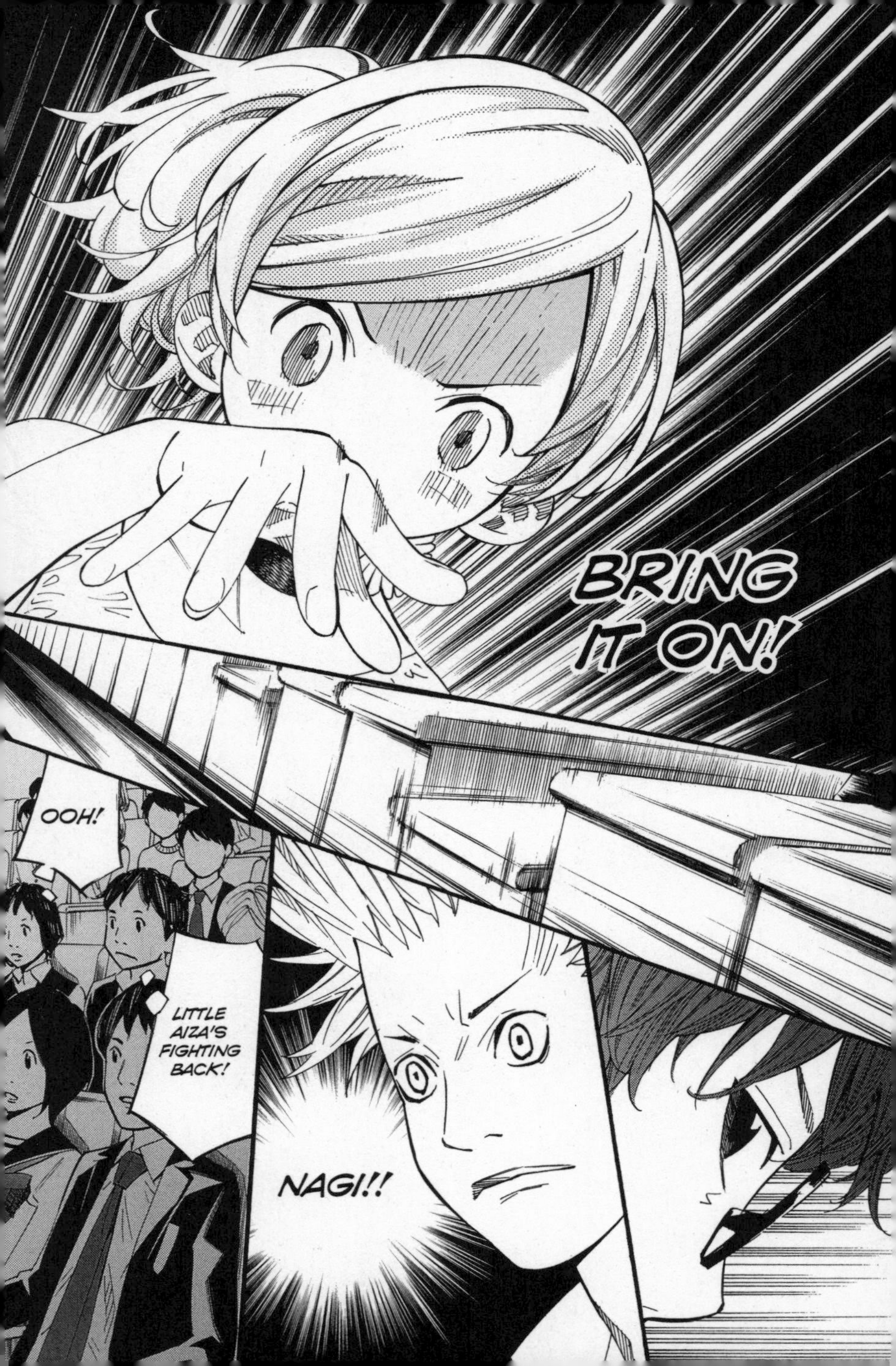
BRING IT ON!
NAGI!!
OOH!
LITTLE AIZA'S FIGHTING BACK!

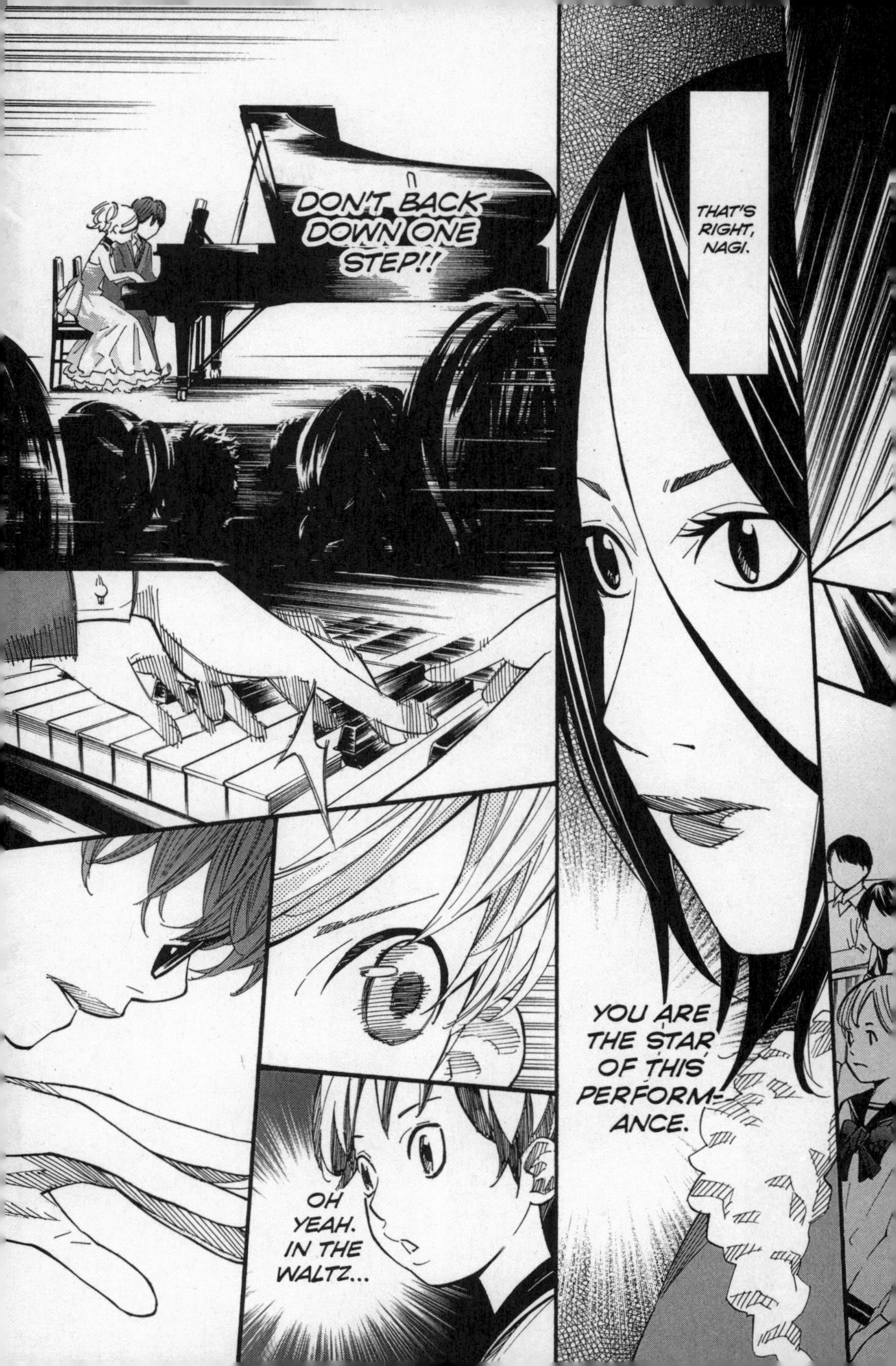
THAT'S RIGHT, NAGI.
YOU ARE THE STAR OF THIS PERFORMANCE.
DON'T BACK DOWN ONE STEP!!
OH YEAH. IN THE WALTZ...

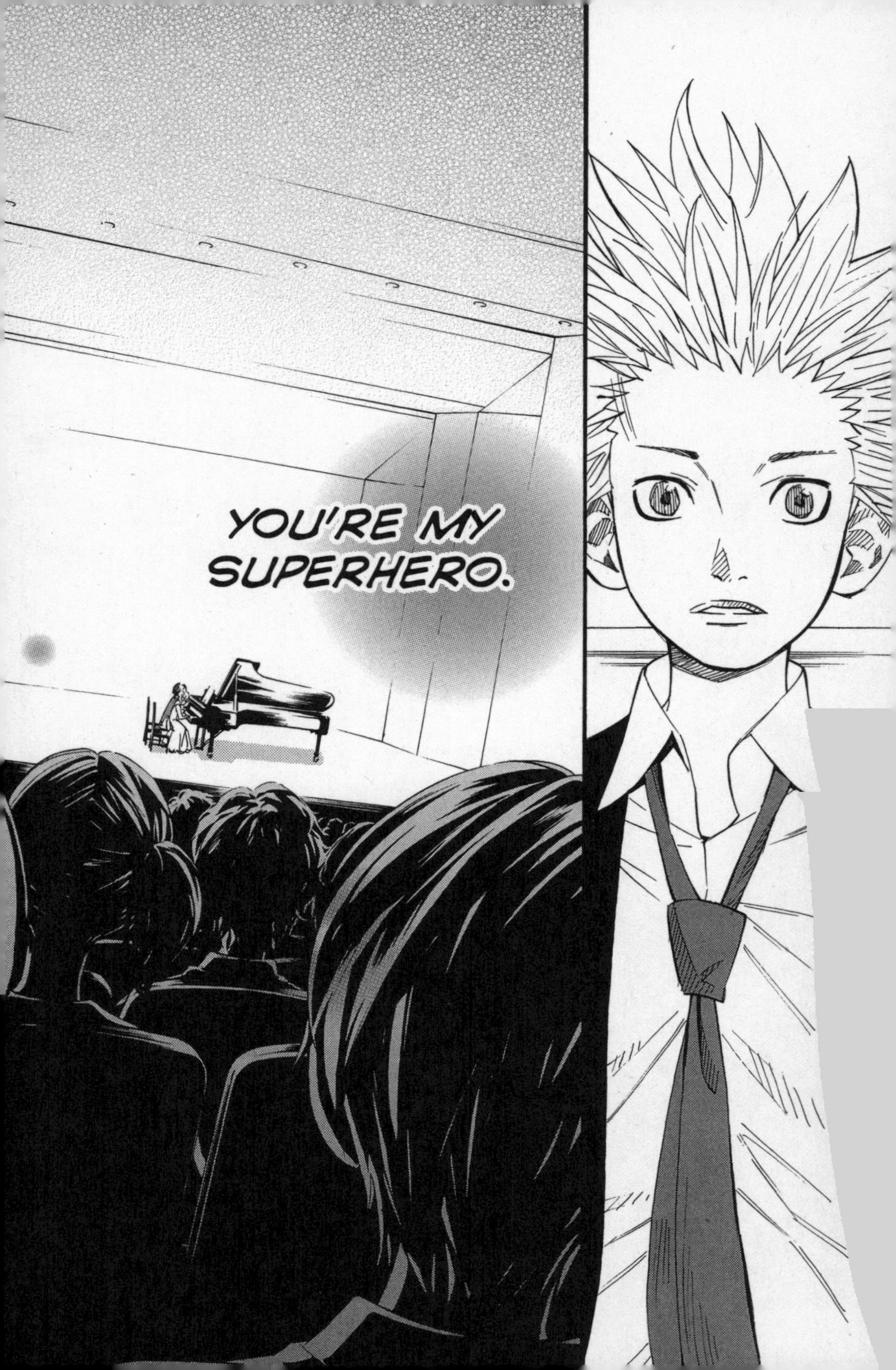
YOU'RE MY SUPERHERO.

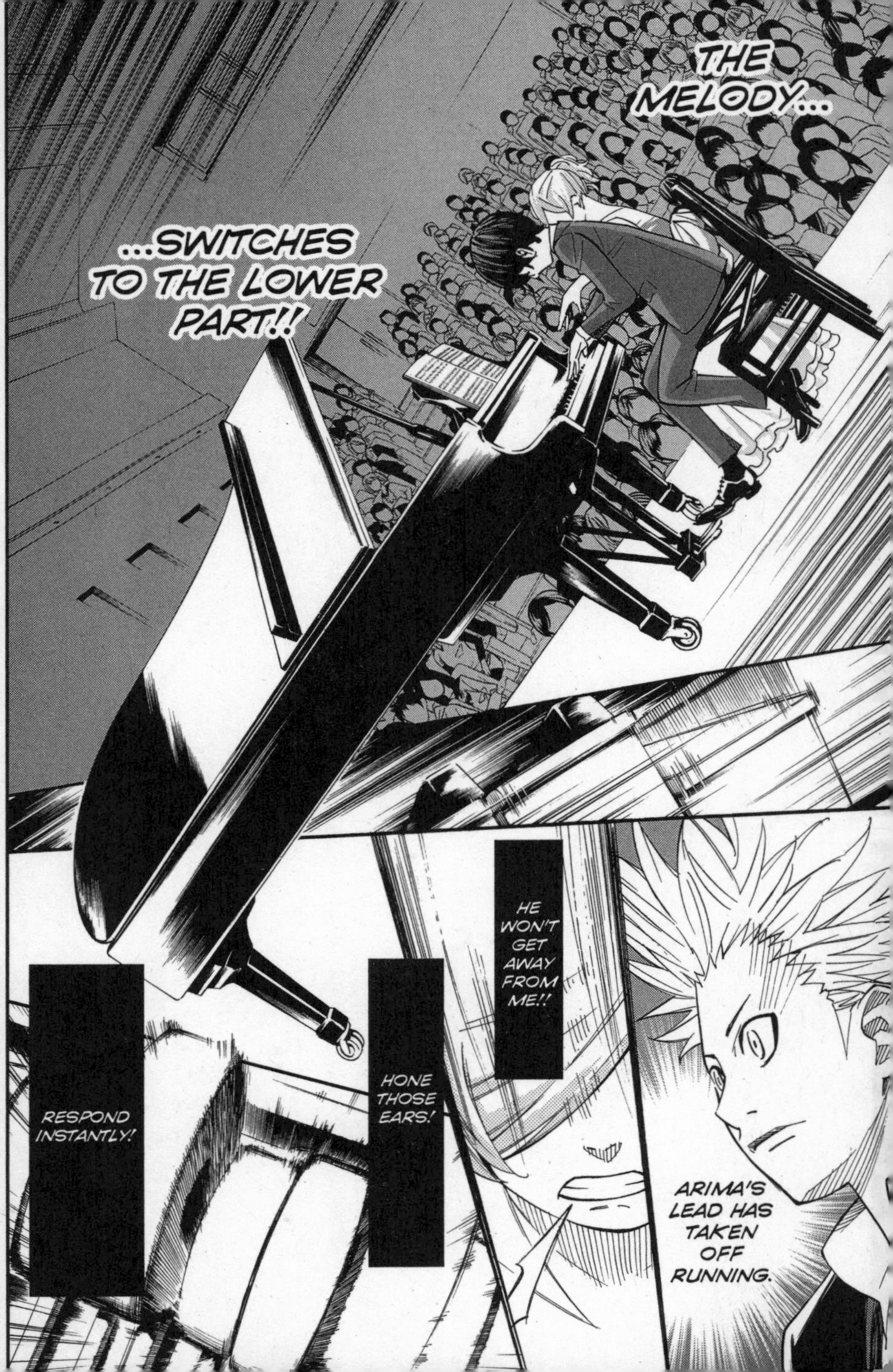
THE MELODY...
...SWITCHES TO THE LOWER PART!!
ARIMA'S LEAD HAS TAKEN OFF RUNNING.
HE WON'T GET AWAY FROM ME!!
HONE THOSE EARS!
RESPOND INSTANTLY!

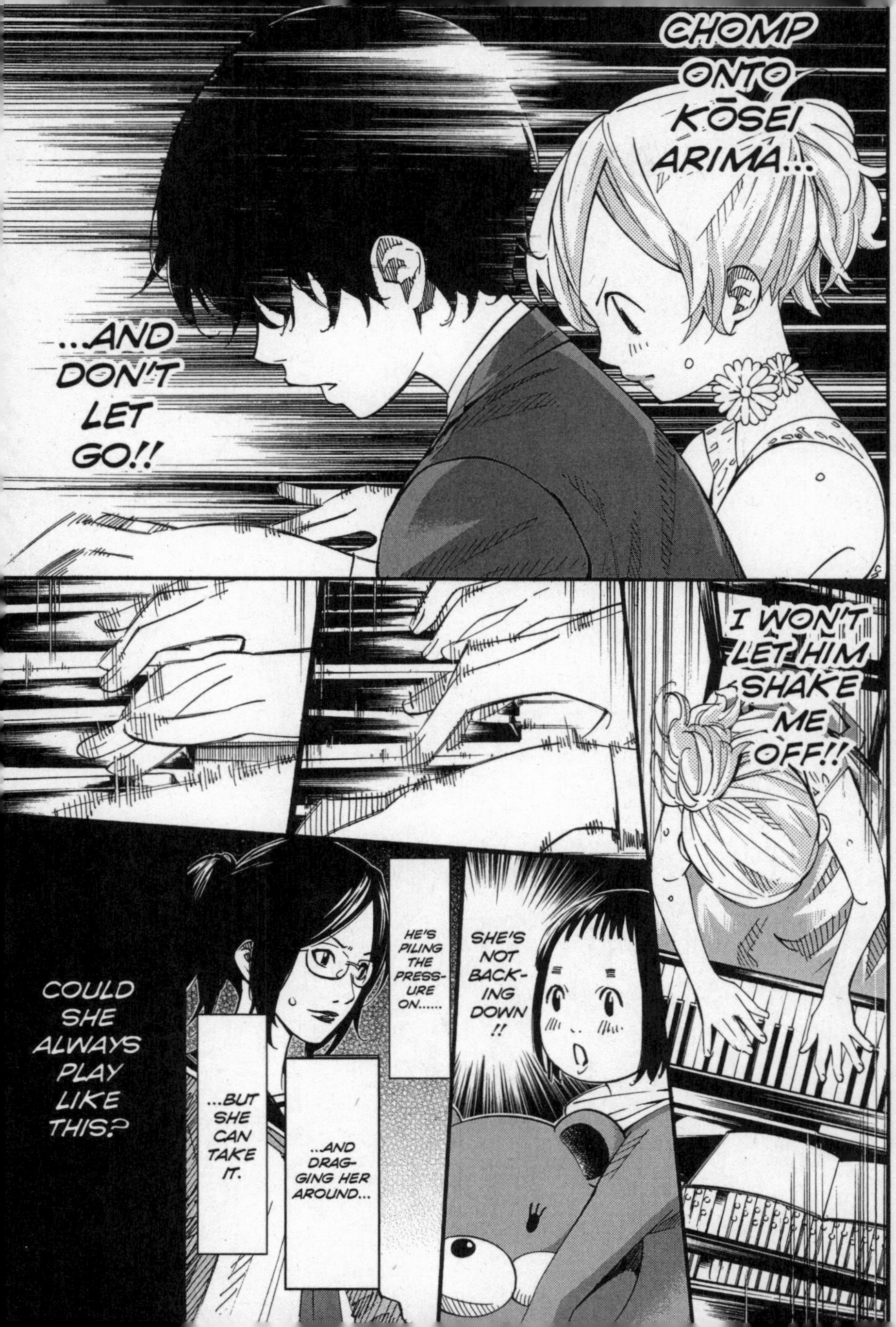
CHOMP ONTO KŌSEI ARIMA...
...AND DON'T LET GO!!
I WON'T LET HIM SHAKE ME OFF!!
SHE'S NOT BACKING DOWN!!
HE'S PILING THE PRESSURE ON......
...AND DRAGGING HER AROUND...
...BUT SHE CAN TAKE IT.
COULD SHE ALWAYS PLAY LIKE THIS?

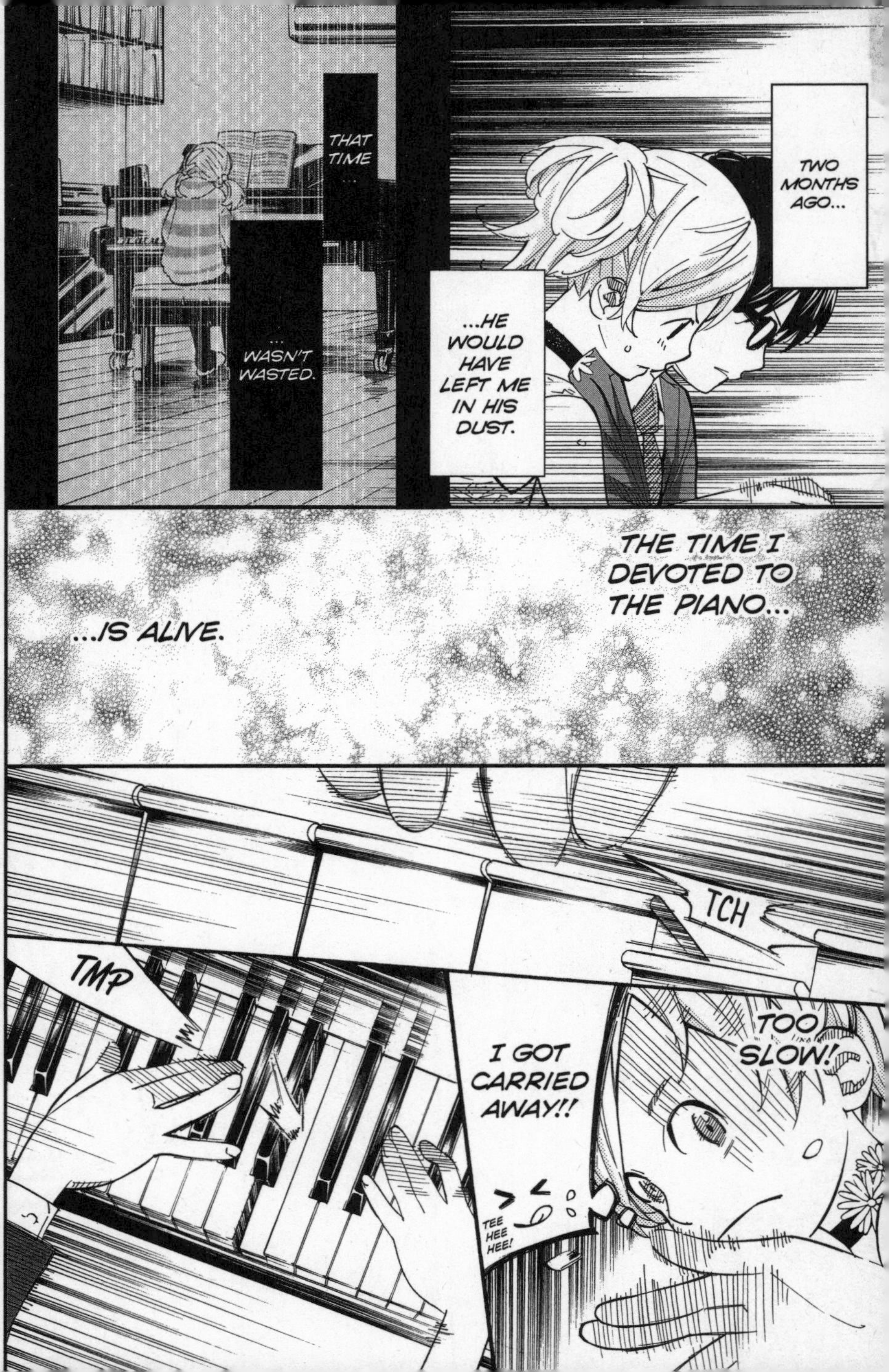
TWO MONTHS AGO...
...HE WOULD HAVE LEFT ME IN HIS DUST.
THAT TIME ...
... WASN'T WASTED.
THE TIME I DEVOTED TO THE PIANO...
...IS ALIVE.
TCH
TOO SLOW!
I GOT CARRIED AWAY!!
TEE HEE HEE!
TMP

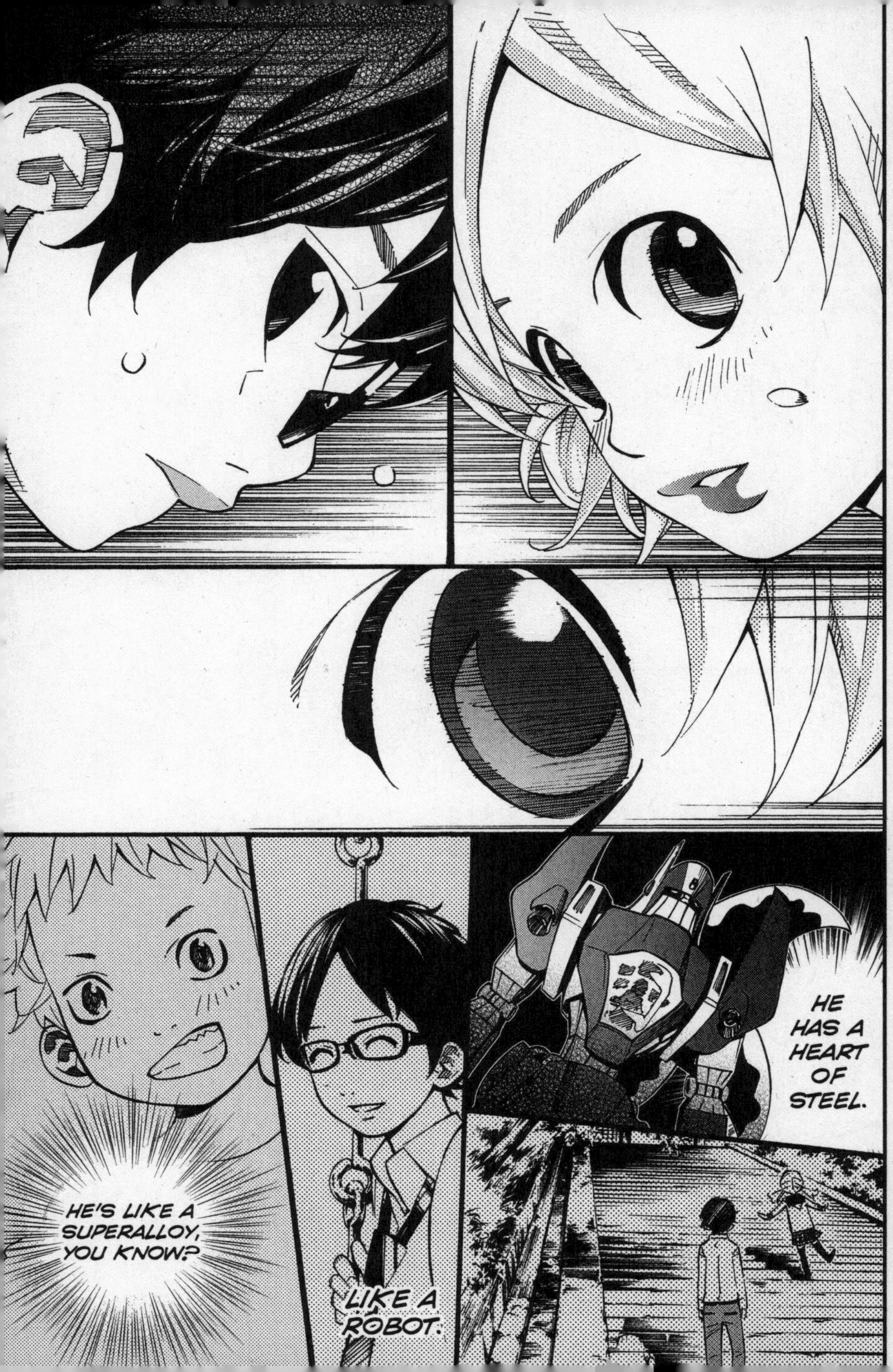
HE HAS A HEART OF STEEL.
LIKE A ROBOT.
HE'S LIKE A SUPERALLOY, YOU KNOW?

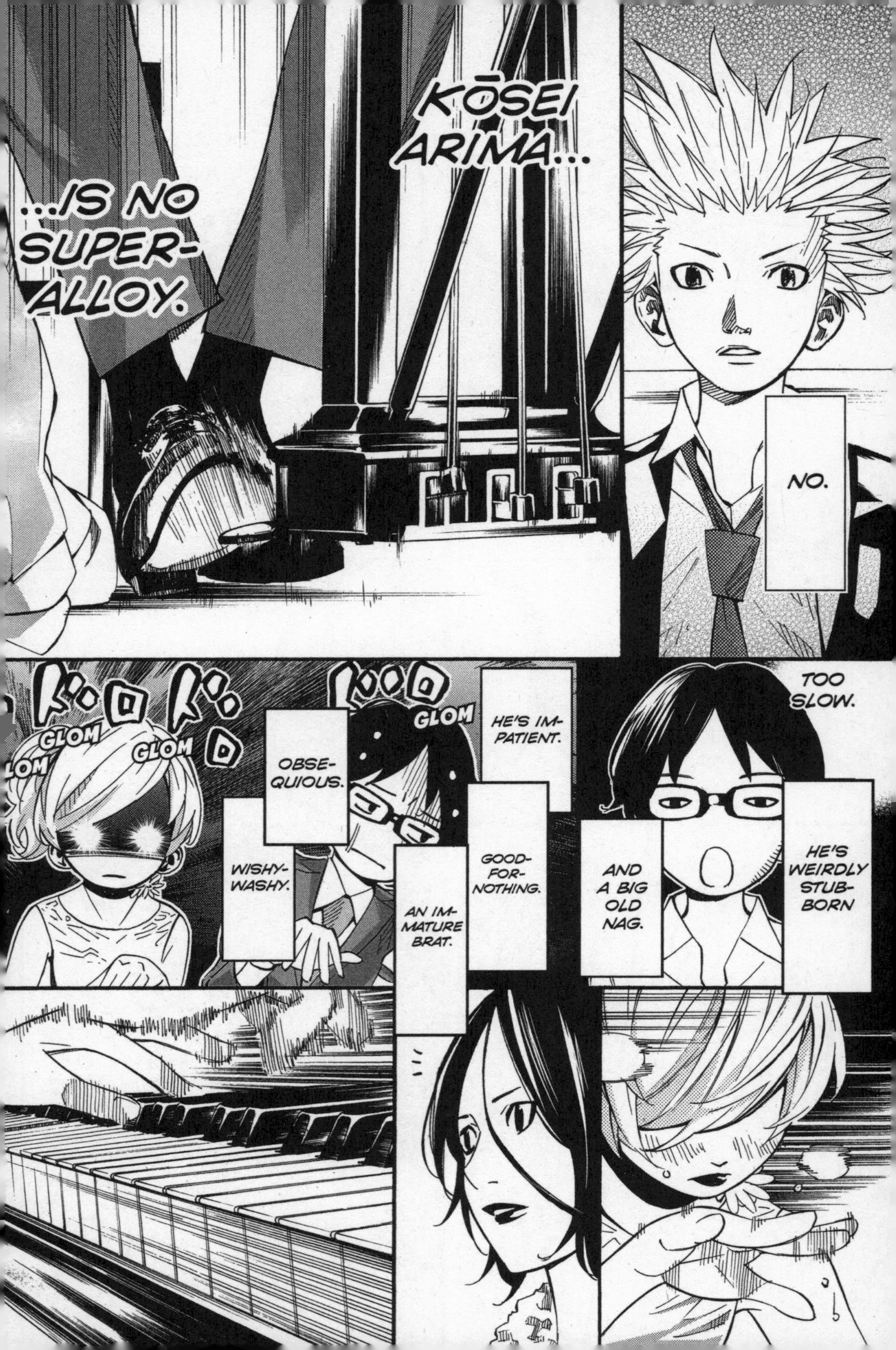
NO.
KŌSEI ARIMA...
...IS NO SUPER-ALLOY.
TOO SLOW.
HE'S WEIRDLY STUB-BORN
AND A BIG OLD NAG.
HE'S IM-PATIENT.
GOOD-FOR-NOTHING.
AN IM-MATURE BRAT.
GLOM
OBSE-QUIOUS.
WISHY-WASHY.
GLOM
GLOM
LOM

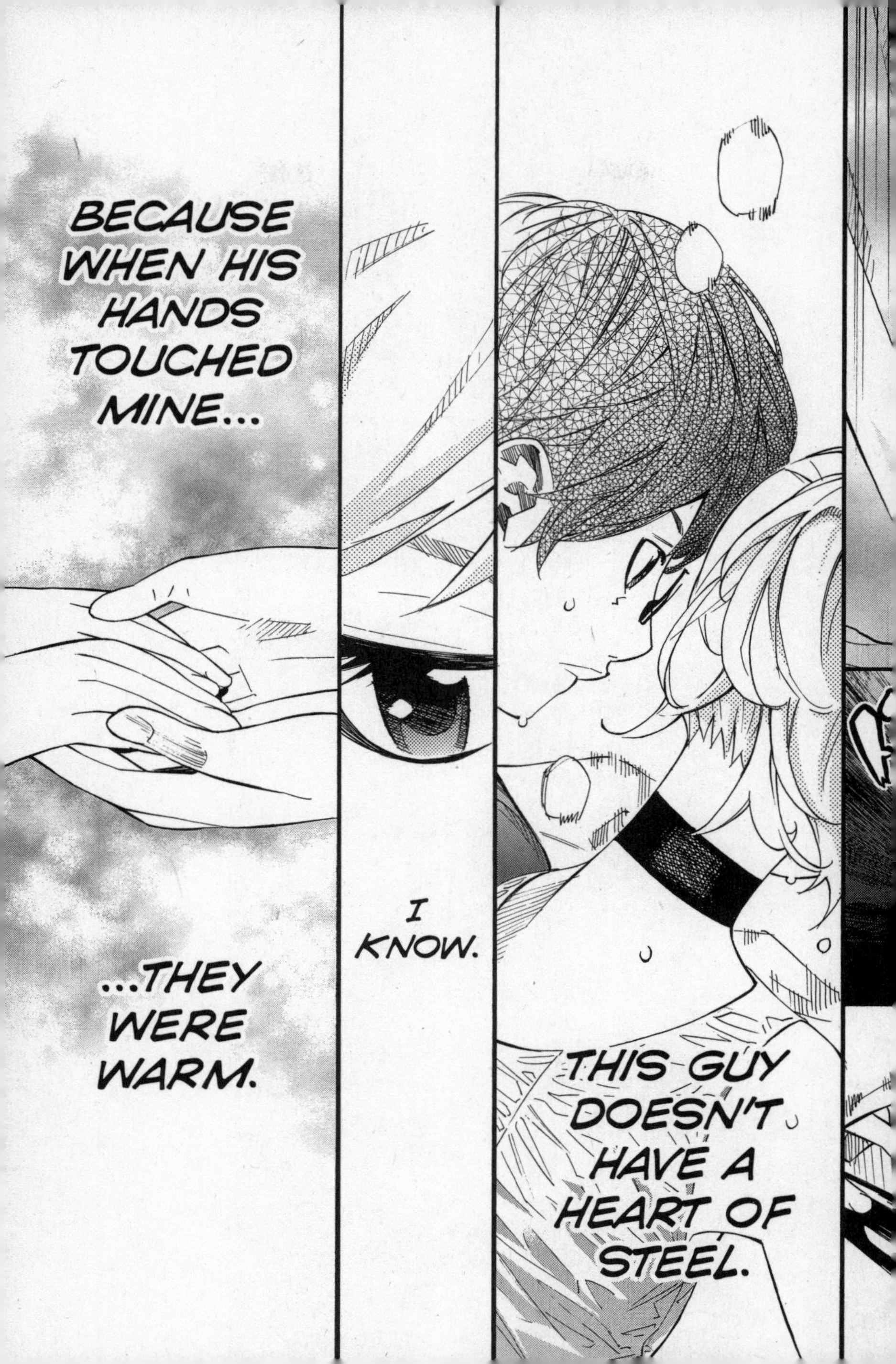
THIS GUY DOESN'T HAVE A HEART OF STEEL.
I KNOW.
BECAUSE WHEN HIS HANDS TOUCHED MINE...
...THEY WERE WARM.

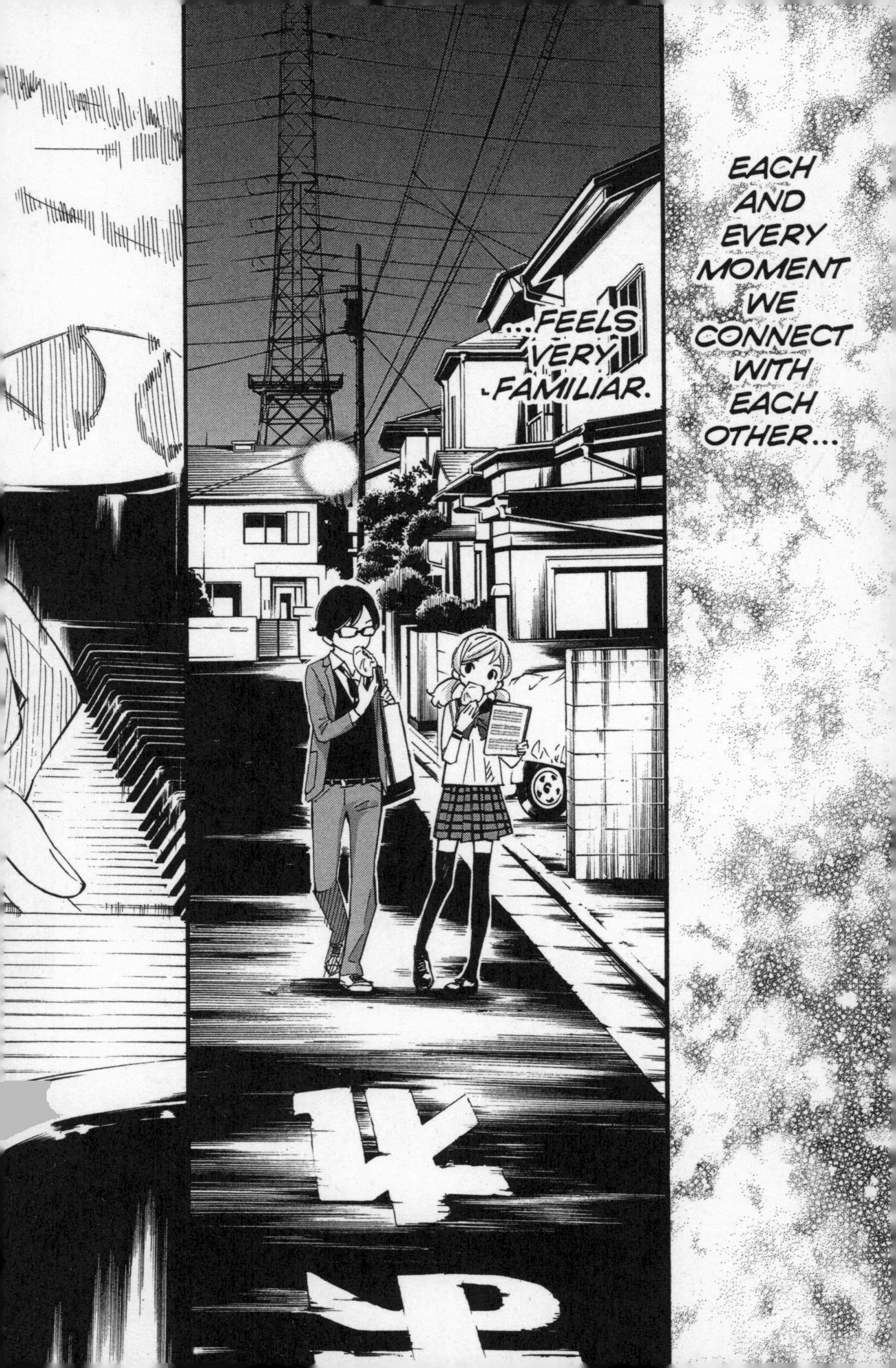
EACH AND EVERY MOMENT WE CONNECT WITH EACH OTHER...
...FEELS VERY FAMILIAR.

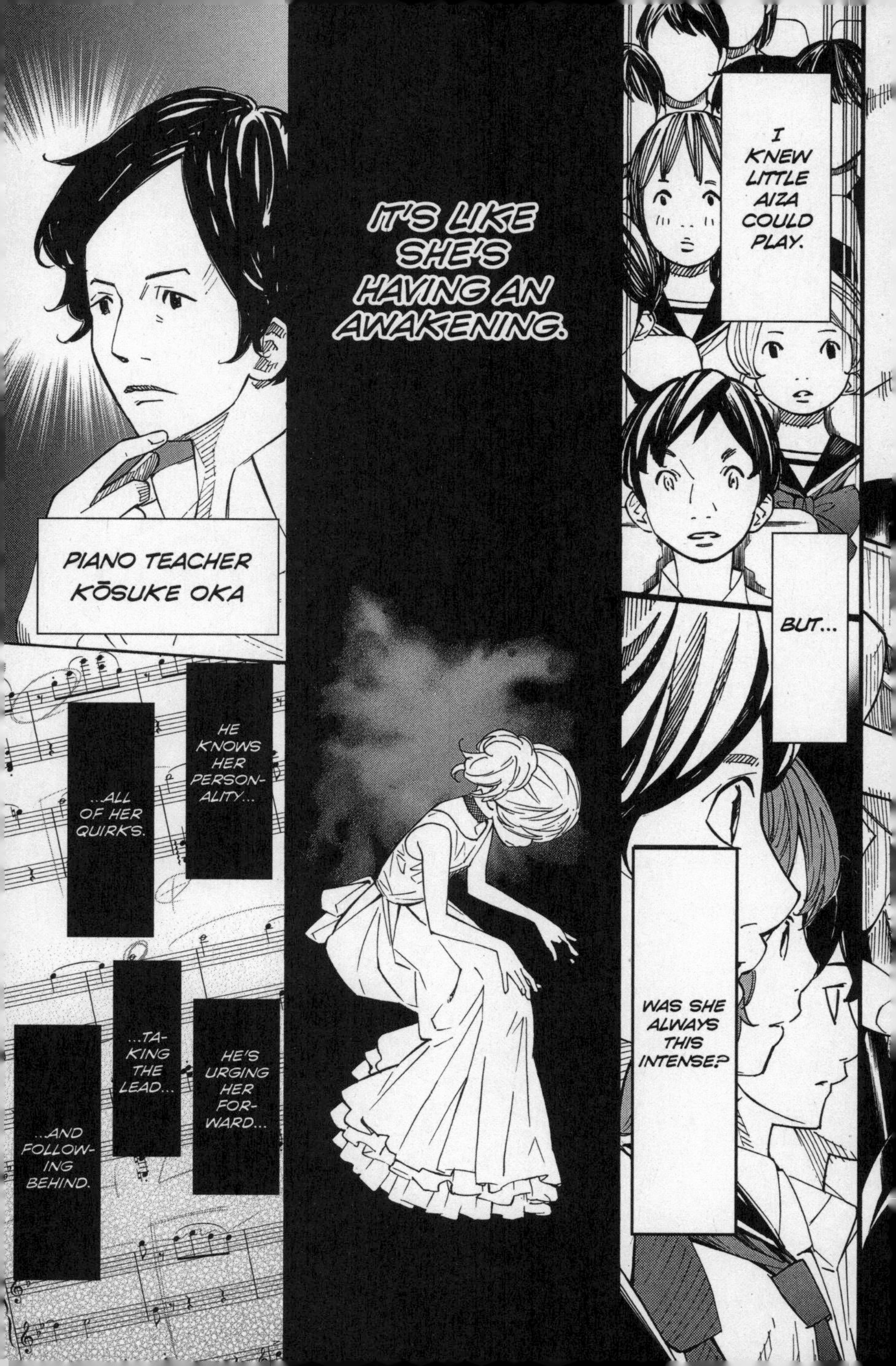
I KNEW LITTLE AIZA COULD PLAY.
BUT...
WAS SHE ALWAYS THIS INTENSE?
IT'S LIKE SHE'S HAVING AN AWAKENING.
PIANO TEACHER KŌSUKE OKA
HE KNOWS HER PERSONALITY...
...ALL OF HER QUIRKS.
HE'S URGING HER FORWARD...
...TAKING THE LEAD...
...AND FOLLOWING BEHIND.

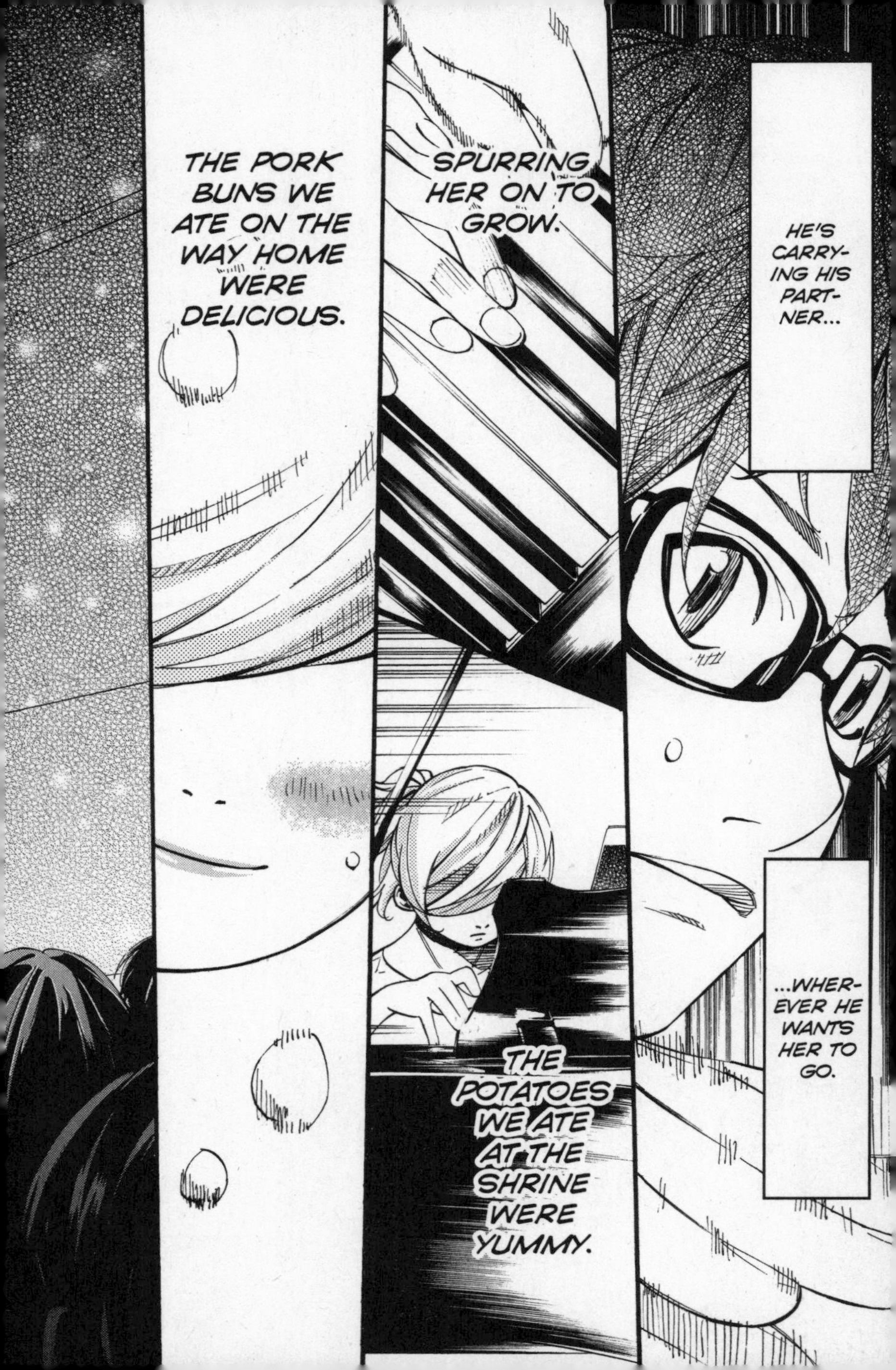
HE'S CARRYING HIS PARTNER...
...WHEREVER HE WANTS HER TO GO.
SPURRING HER ON TO GROW.
THE POTATOES WE ATE AT THE SHRINE WERE YUMMY.
THE PORK BUNS WE ATE ON THE WAY HOME WERE DELICIOUS.

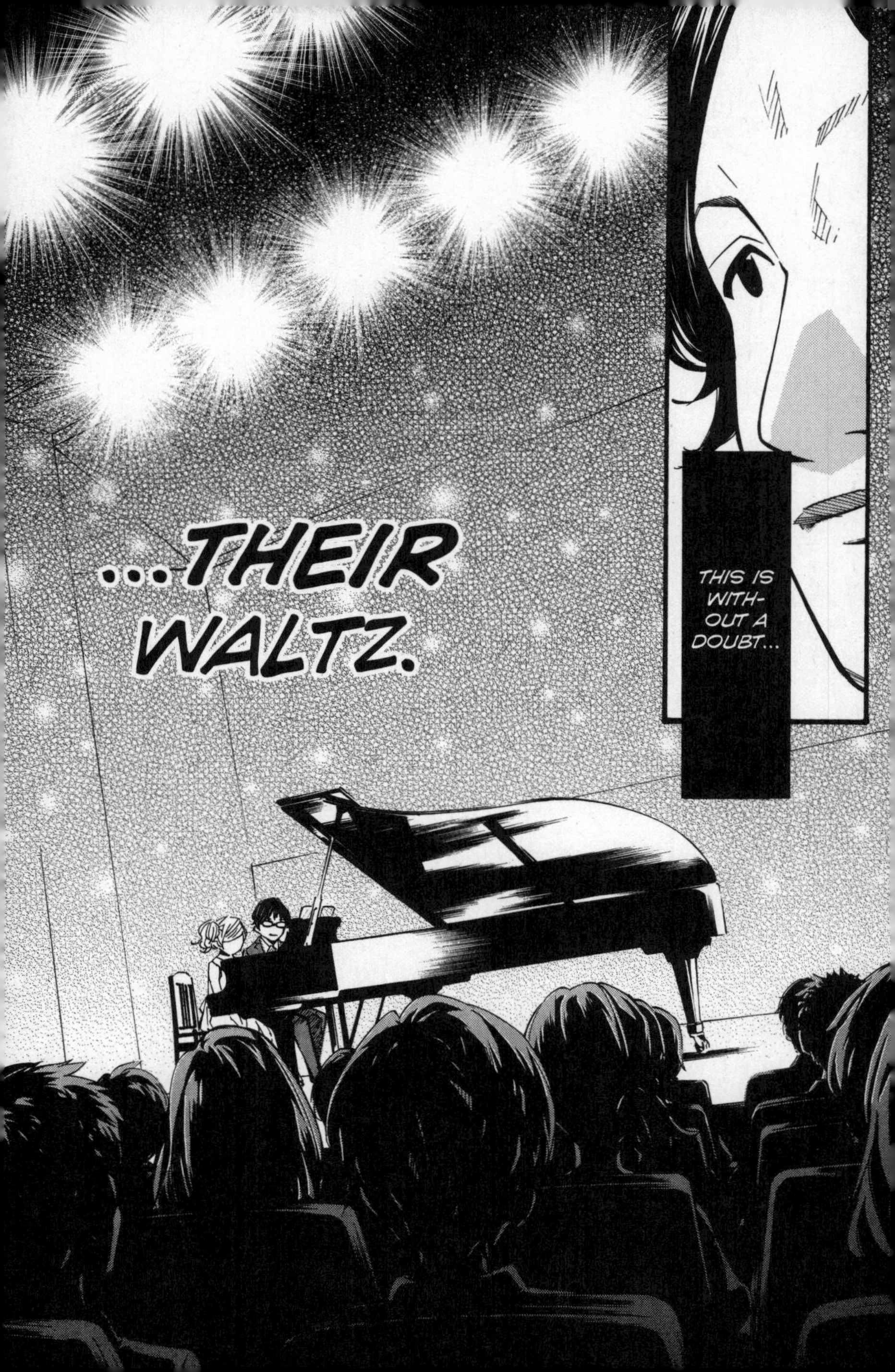
THIS IS WITH-OUT A DOUBT...
...THEIR WALTZ.

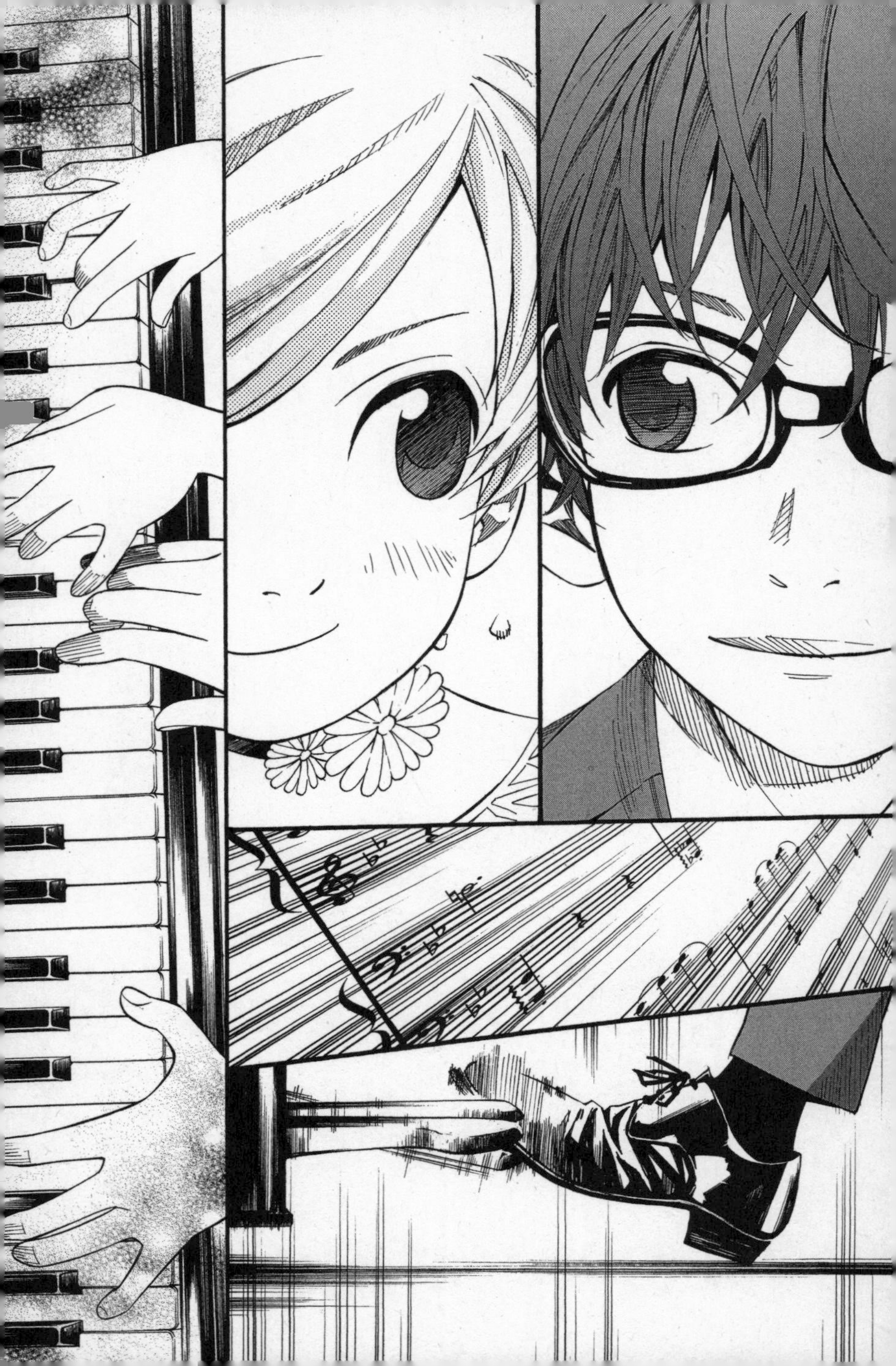

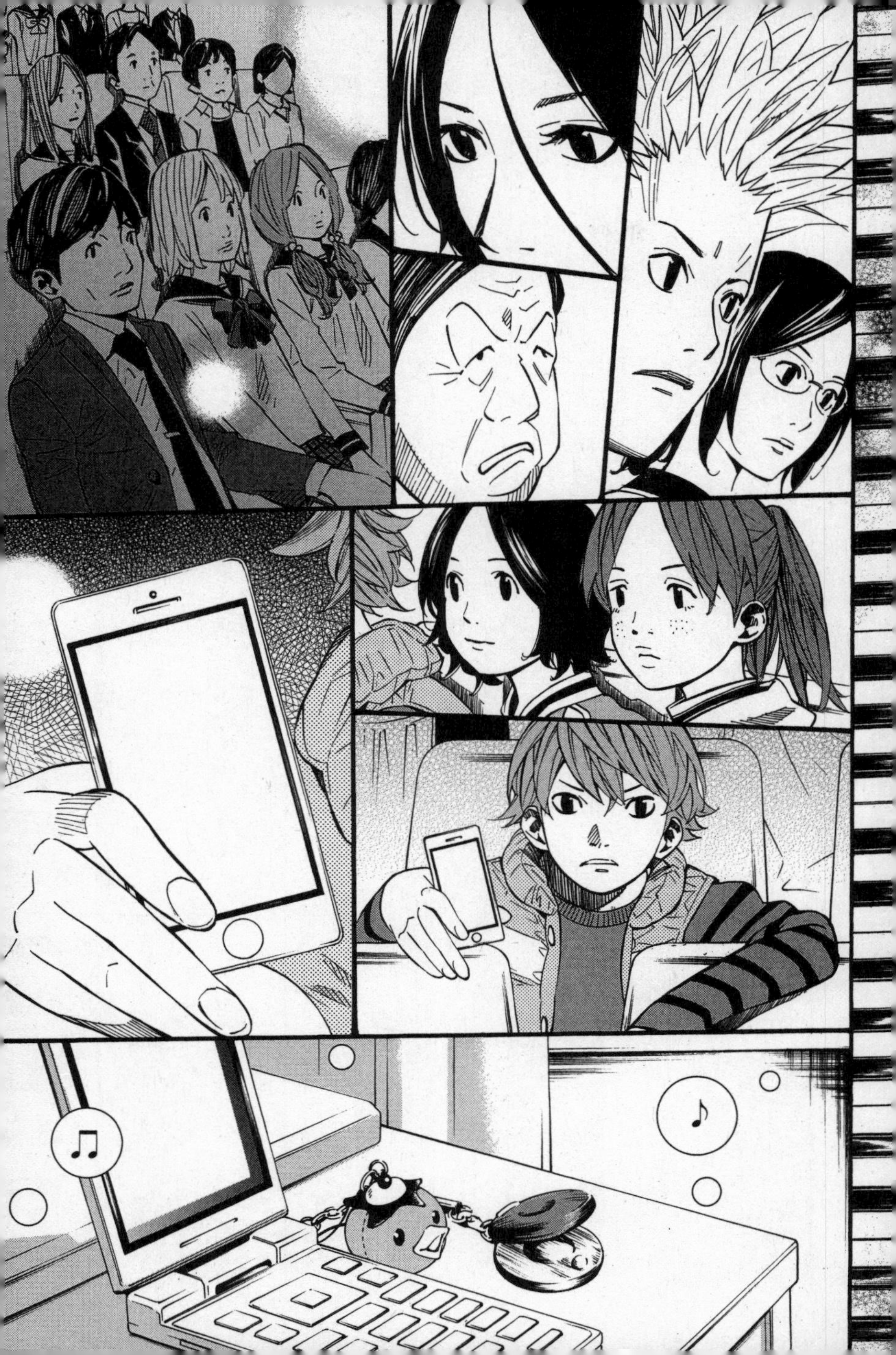

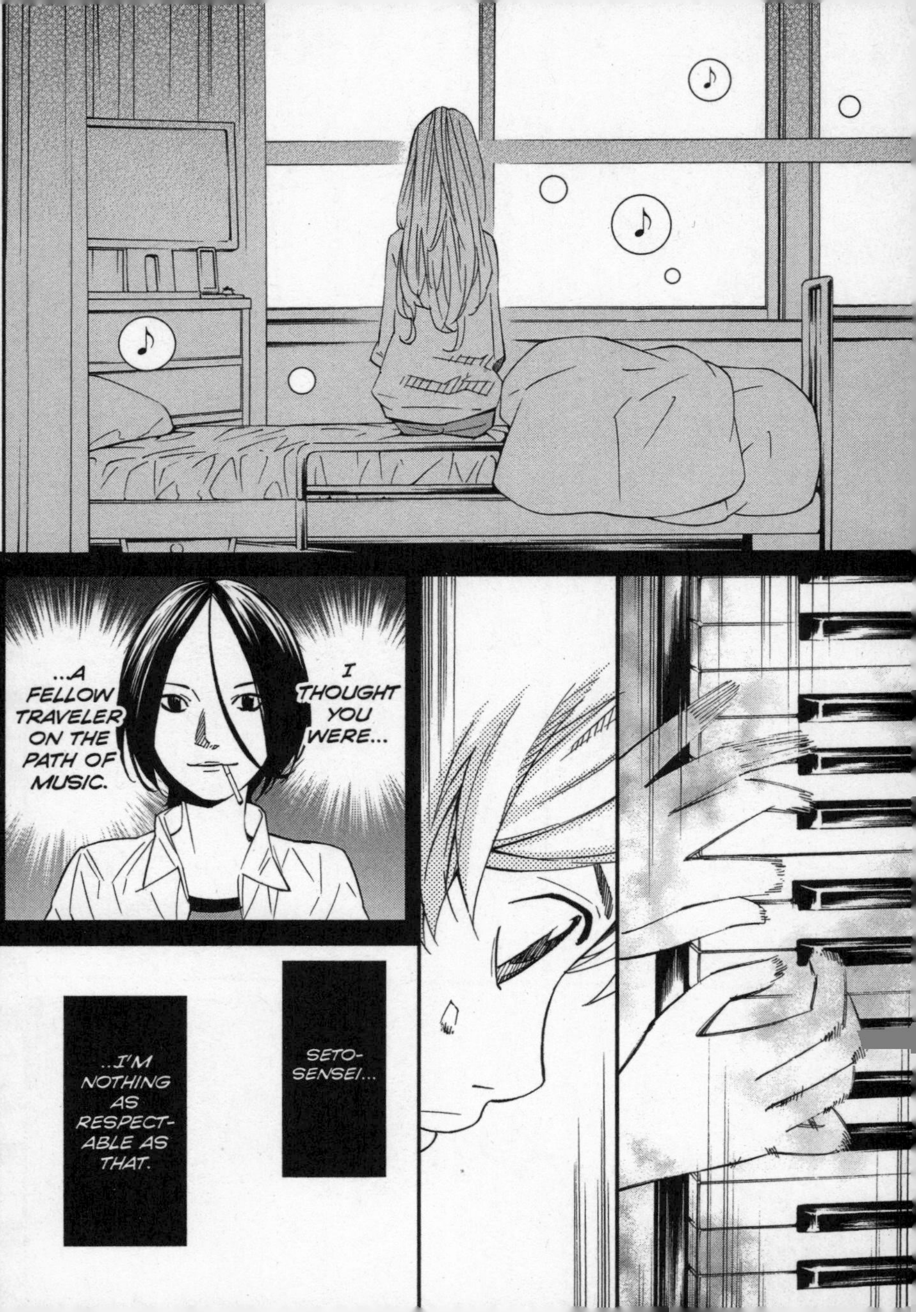
I THOUGHT YOU WERE...
...A FELLOW TRAVELER ON THE PATH OF MUSIC.
SETO-SENSEI...
..I'M NOTHING AS RESPECT-ABLE AS THAT.

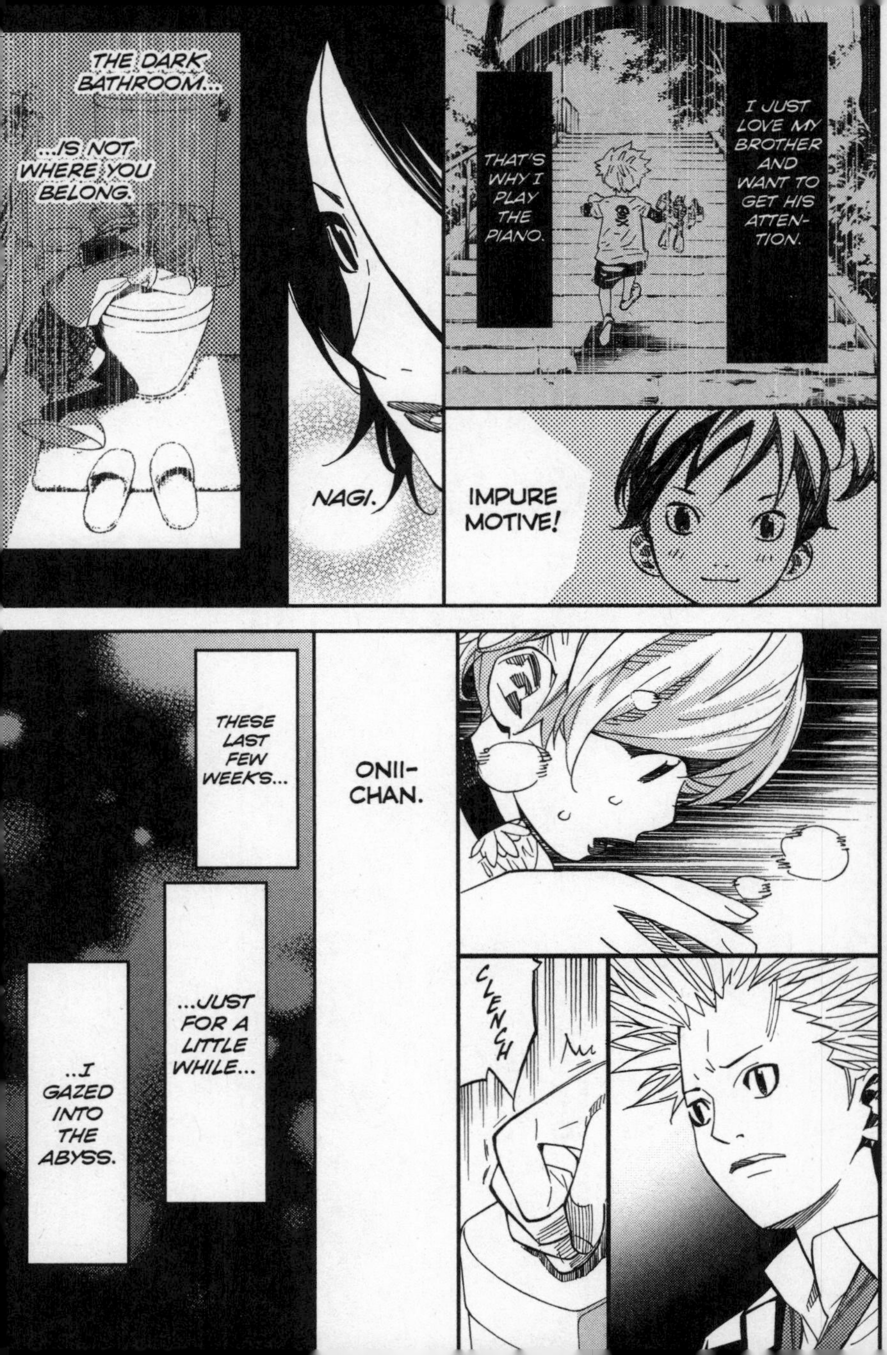
I JUST LOVE MY BROTHER AND WANT TO GET HIS ATTENTION.
THAT'S WHY I PLAY THE PIANO.
IMPURE MOTIVE!
NAGI.
THE DARK BATHROOM...
...IS NOT WHERE YOU BELONG.
CLENCH
ONII-CHAN.
THESE LAST FEW WEEKS...
...JUST FOR A LITTLE WHILE...
...I GAZED INTO THE ABYSS.

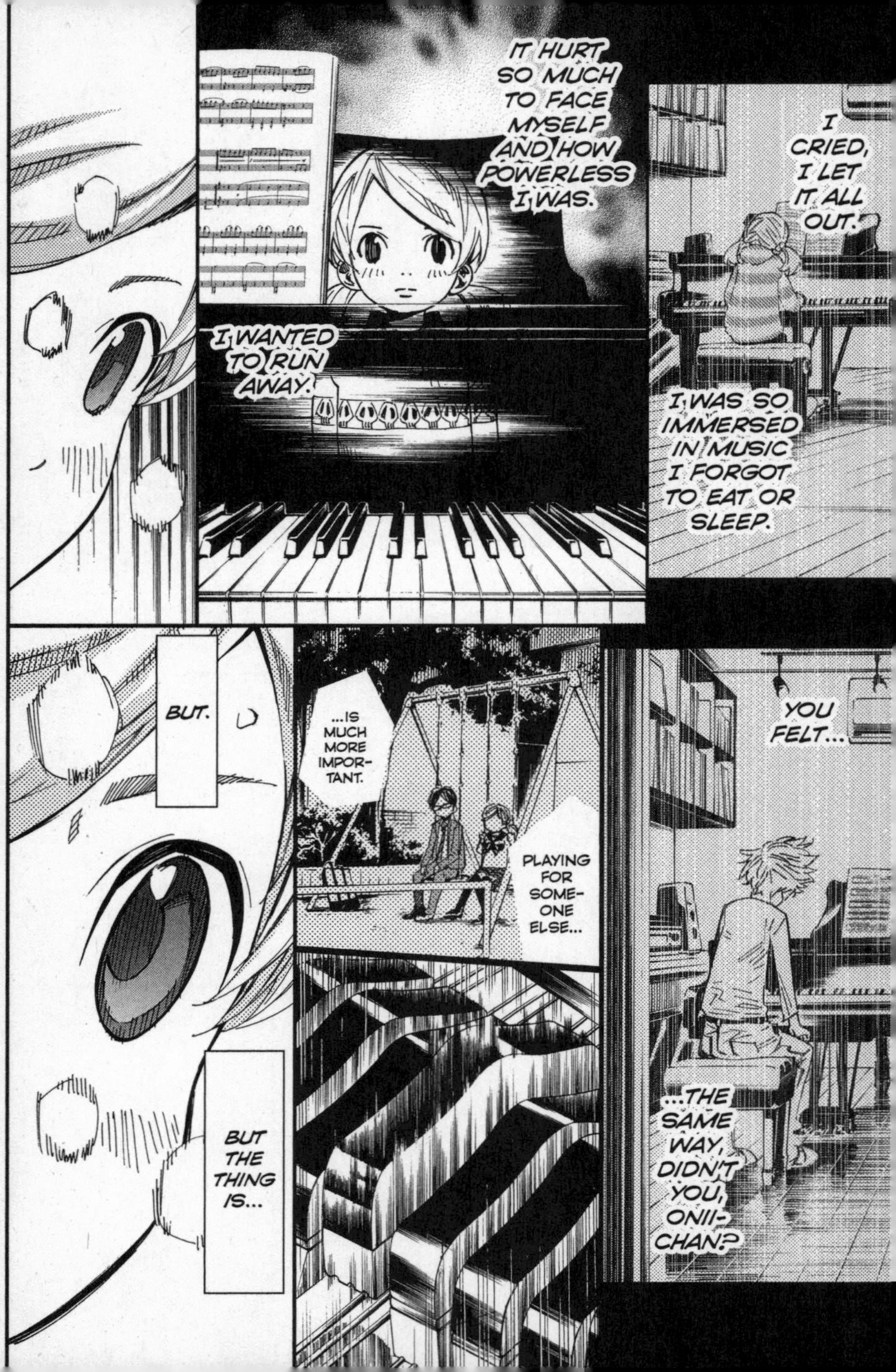
I CRIED, I LET IT ALL OUT.
I WAS SO IMMERSED IN MUSIC I FORGOT TO EAT OR SLEEP.
IT HURT SO MUCH TO FACE MYSELF AND HOW POWERLESS I WAS.
I WANTED TO RUN AWAY.
YOU FELT...
...THE SAME WAY, DIDN'T YOU, ONII-CHAN?
PLAYING FOR SOMEONE ELSE...
...IS MUCH MORE IMPORTANT.
BUT.
BUT THE THING IS...

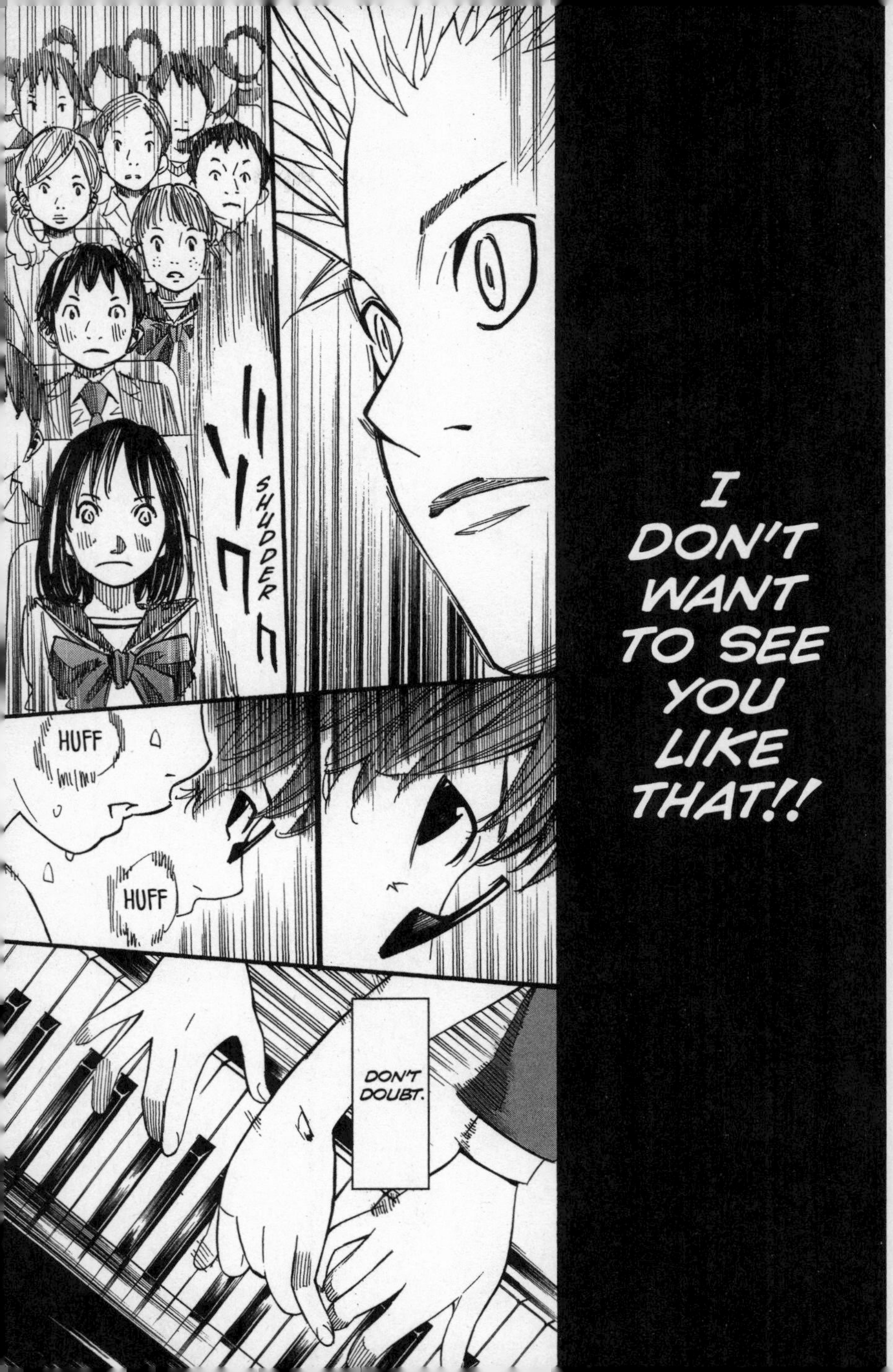
I DON'T WANT TO SEE YOU LIKE THAT!!
SHUDDER
HUFF
HUFF
DON'T DOUBT.

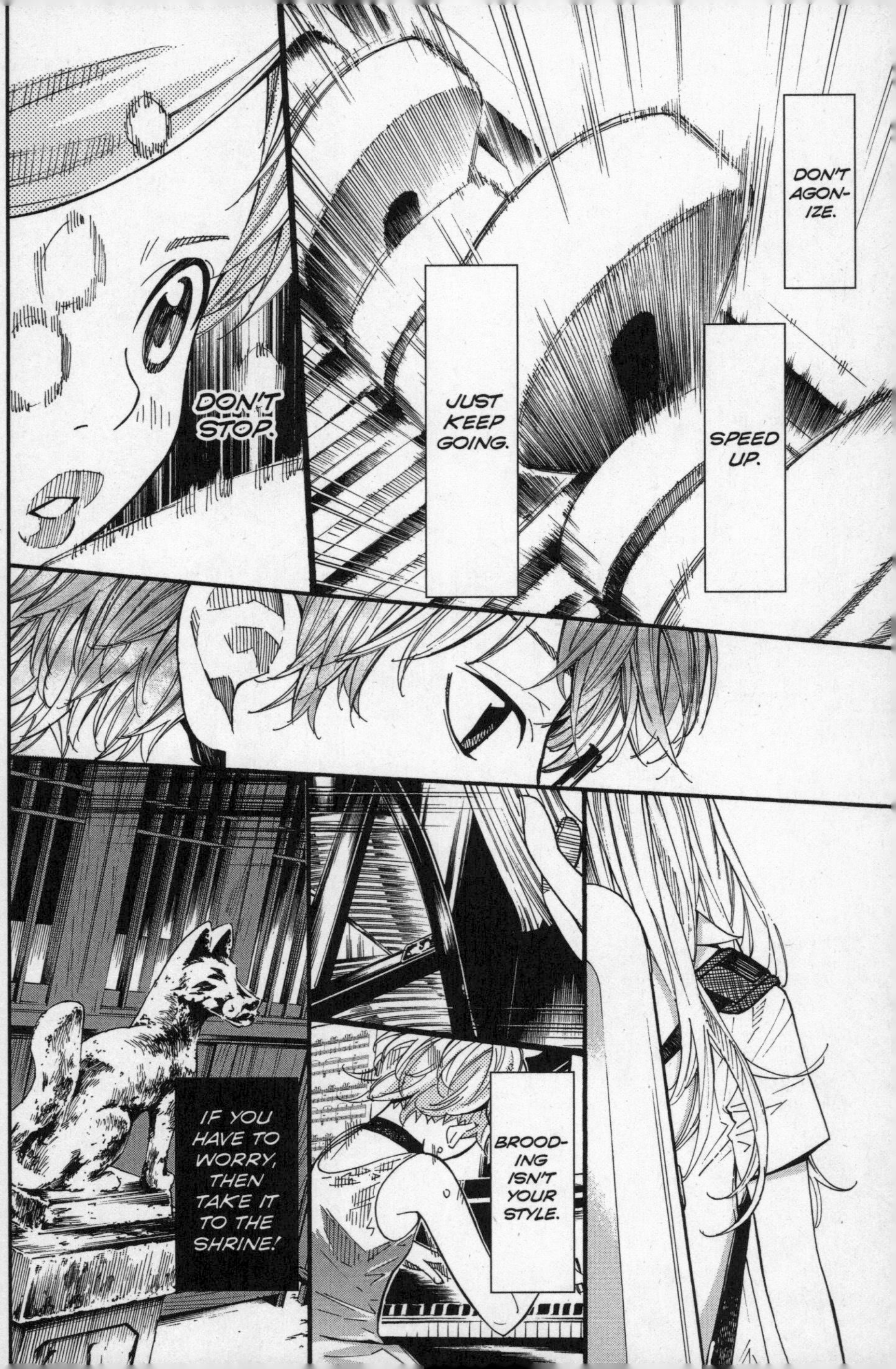
DON'T AGON-IZE.
SPEED UP.
JUST KEEP GOING.
DON'T STOP.
BROOD-ING ISN'T YOUR STYLE.
IF YOU HAVE TO WORRY, THEN TAKE IT TO THE SHRINE!

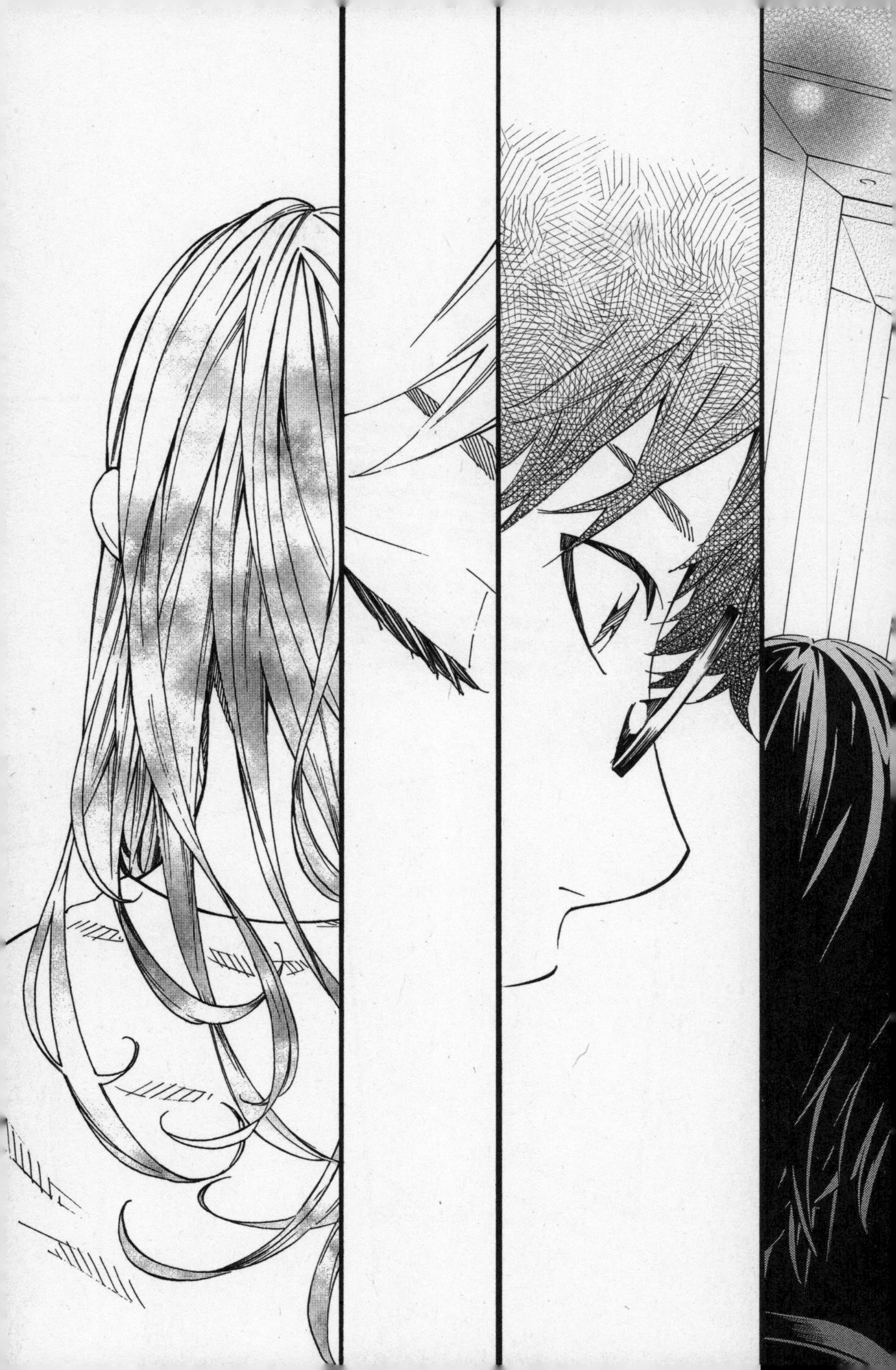

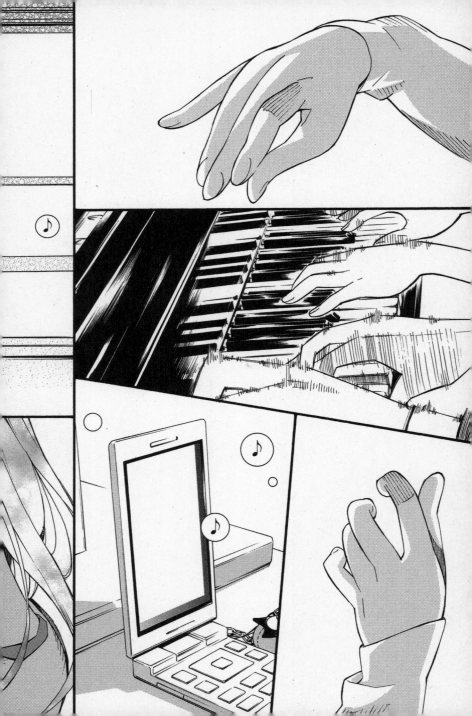

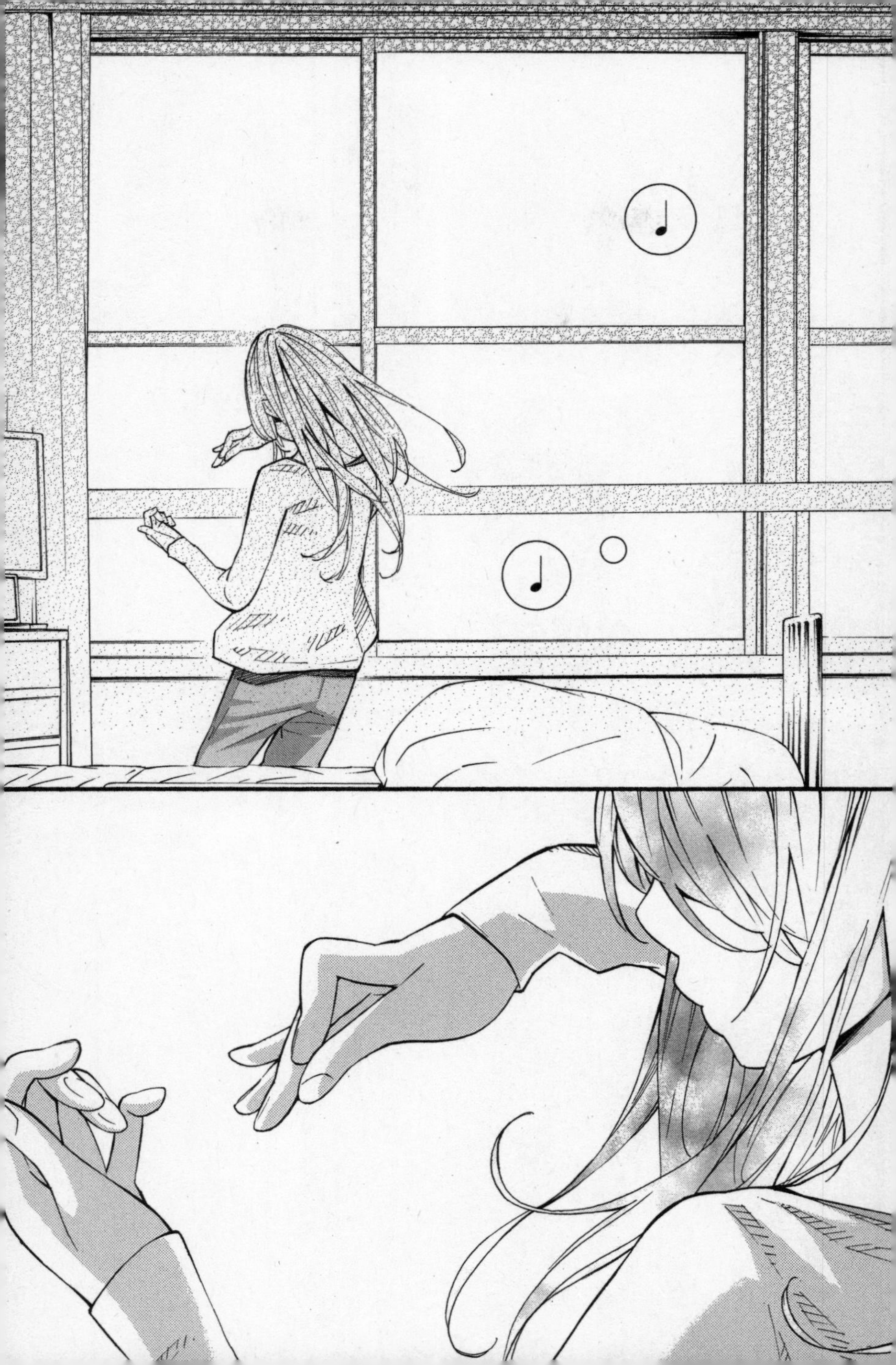

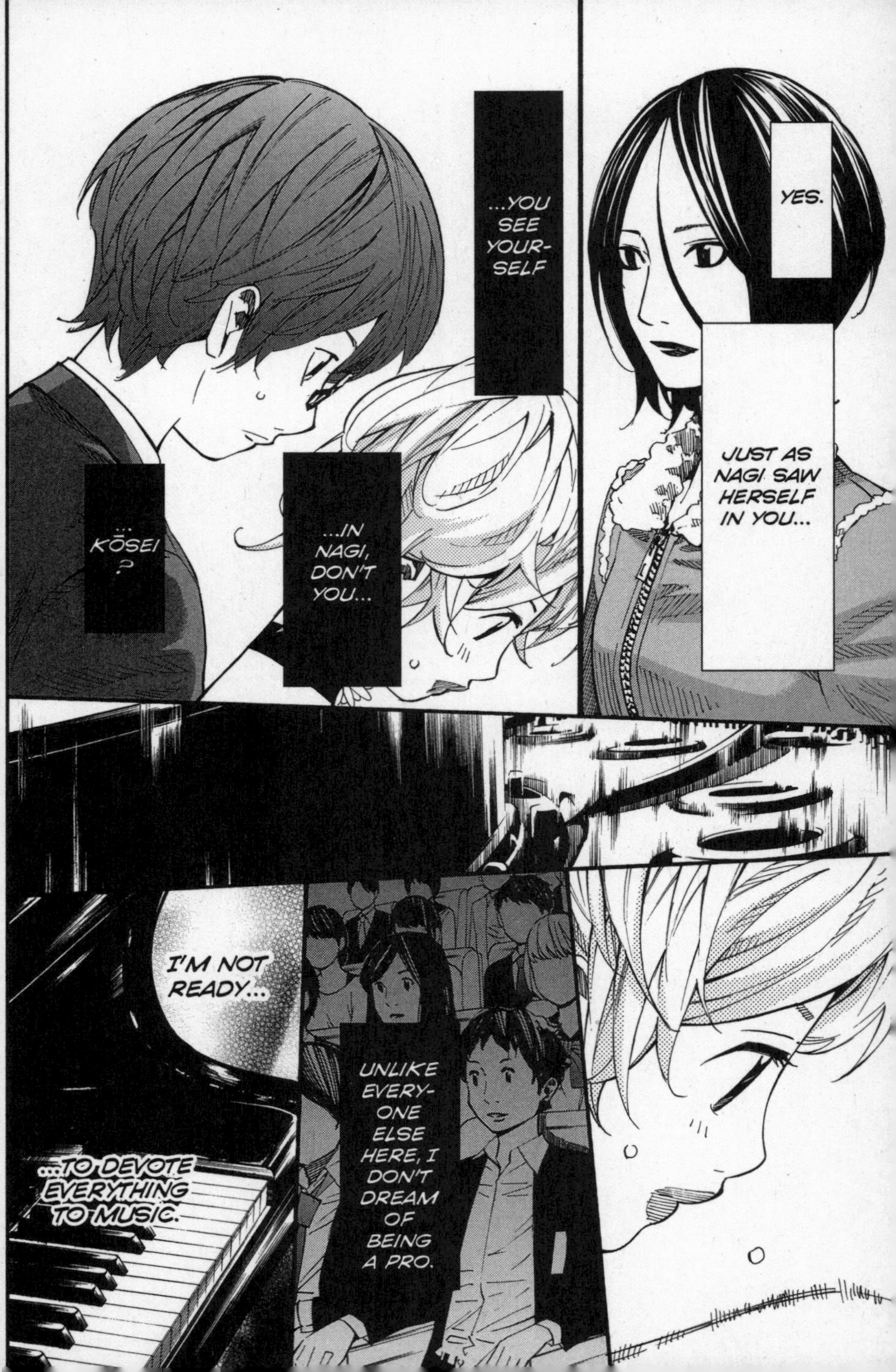
YES.
JUST AS NAGI SAW HERSELF IN YOU...
...YOU SEE YOURSELF
...IN NAGI, DON'T YOU...
...KŌSEI?
UNLIKE EVERYONE ELSE HERE, I DON'T DREAM OF BEING A PRO.
I'M NOT READY...
...TO DEVOTE EVERYTHING TO MUSIC.

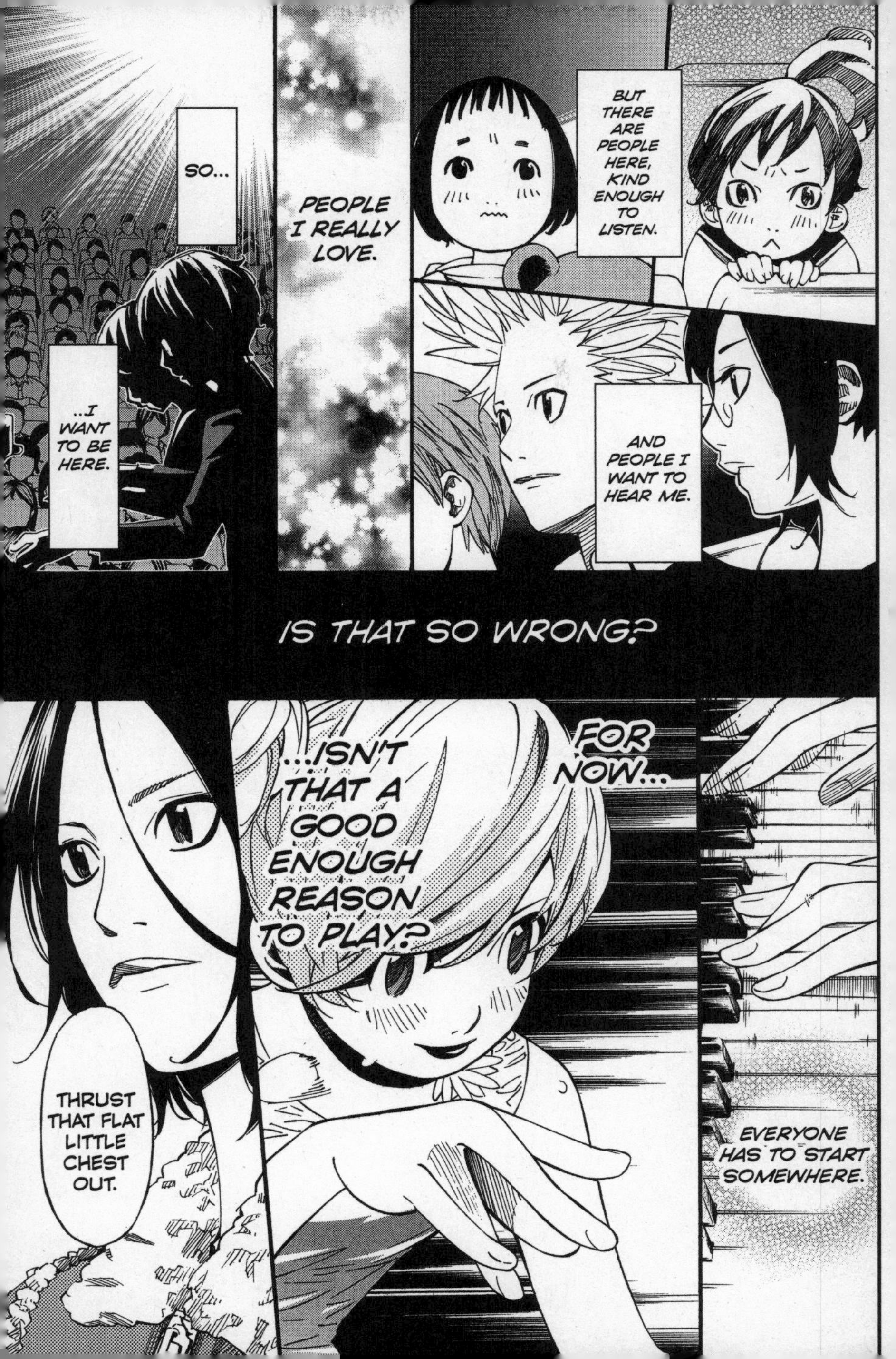
BUT THERE ARE PEOPLE HERE, KIND ENOUGH TO LISTEN.
AND PEOPLE I WANT TO HEAR ME.
PEOPLE I REALLY LOVE.
SO...
...I WANT TO BE HERE.
IS THAT SO WRONG?
EVERYONE HAS TO START SOMEWHERE.
FOR NOW...
...ISN'T THAT A GOOD ENOUGH REASON TO PLAY?
THRUST THAT FLAT LITTLE CHEST OUT.

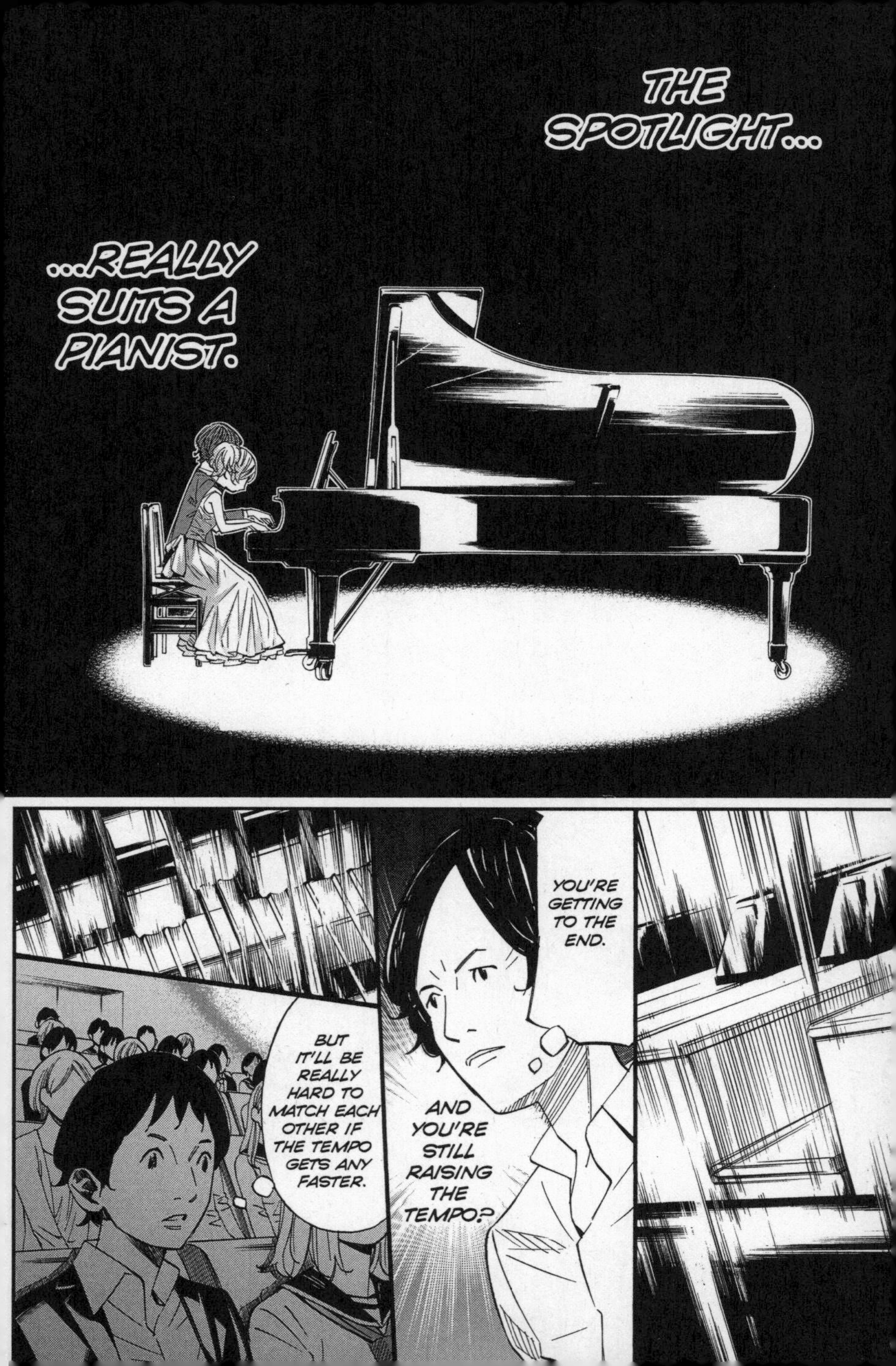
THE SPOTLIGHT...
...REALLY SUITS A PIANIST.
YOU'RE GETTING TO THE END.
AND YOU'RE STILL RAISING THE TEMPO?
BUT IT'LL BE REALLY HARD TO MATCH EACH OTHER IF THE TEMPO GETS ANY FASTER.

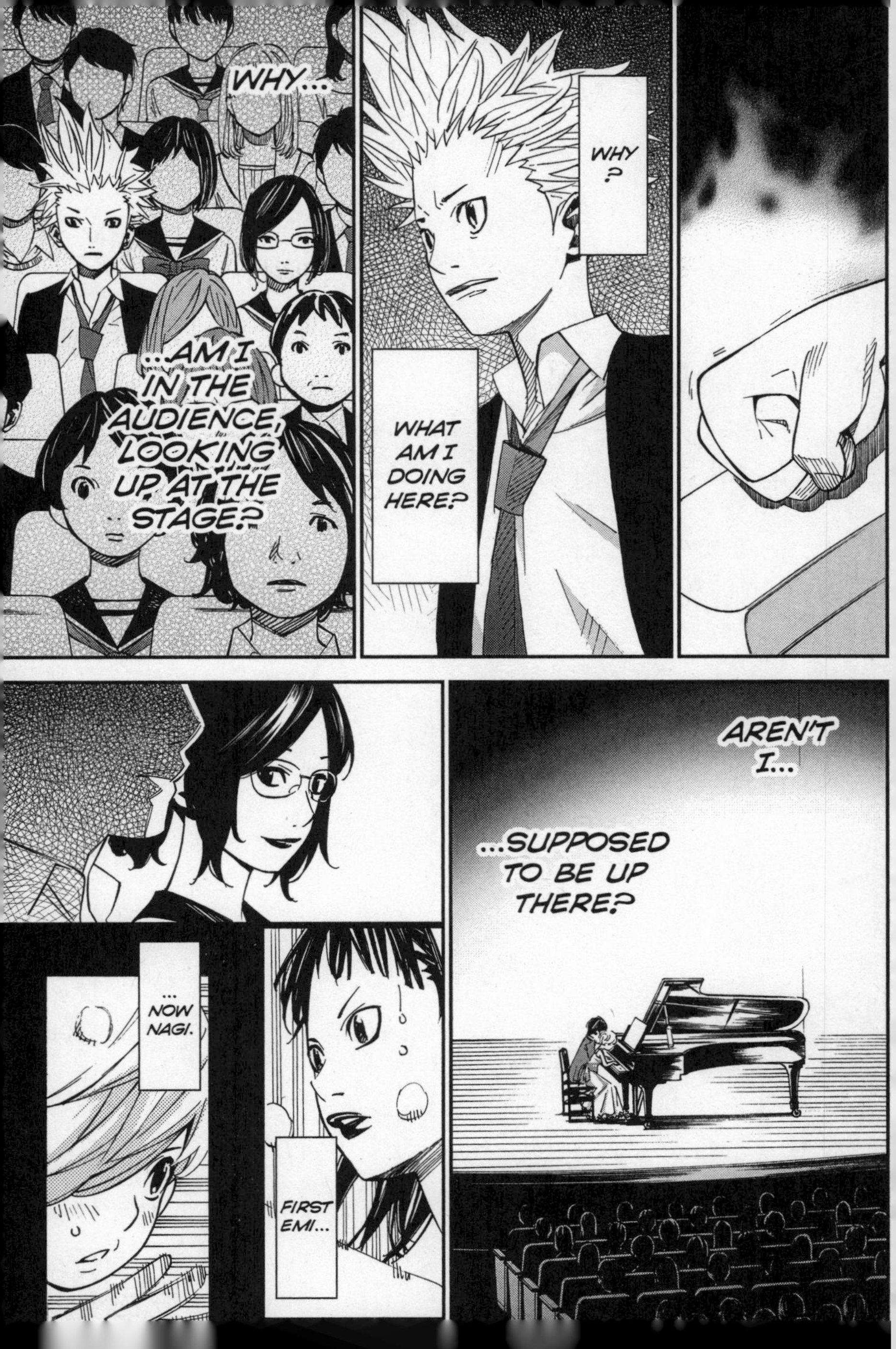
WHY?
WHAT AM I DOING HERE?
WHY...
...AM I IN THE AUDIENCE, LOOKING UP AT THE STAGE?
AREN'T I...
...SUPPOSED TO BE UP THERE?
FIRST EMI...
...NOW NAGI.

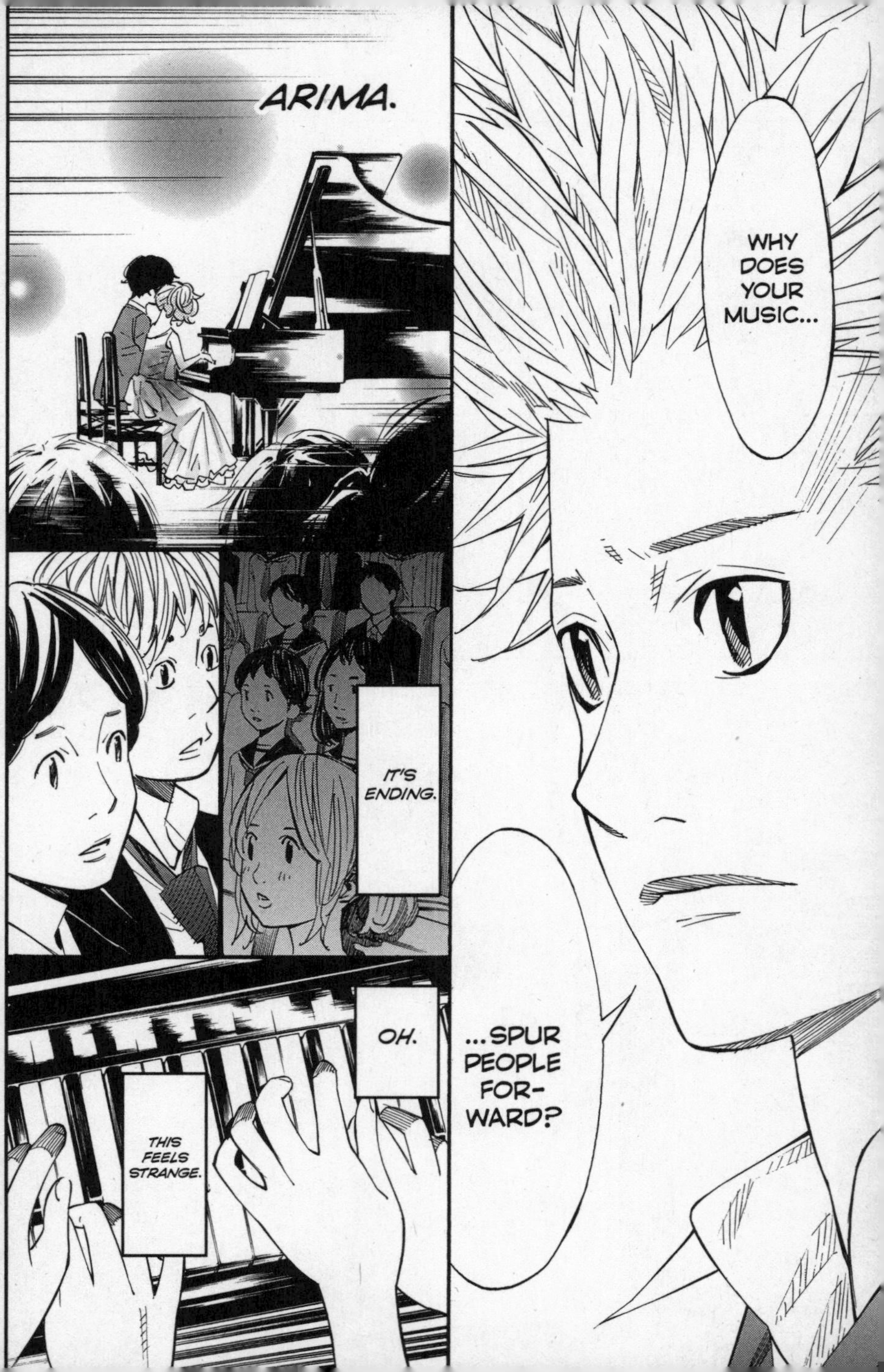
WHY DOES YOUR MUSIC...
...SPUR PEOPLE FOR-WARD?
ARIMA.
IT'S ENDING.
OH.
THIS FEELS STRANGE.

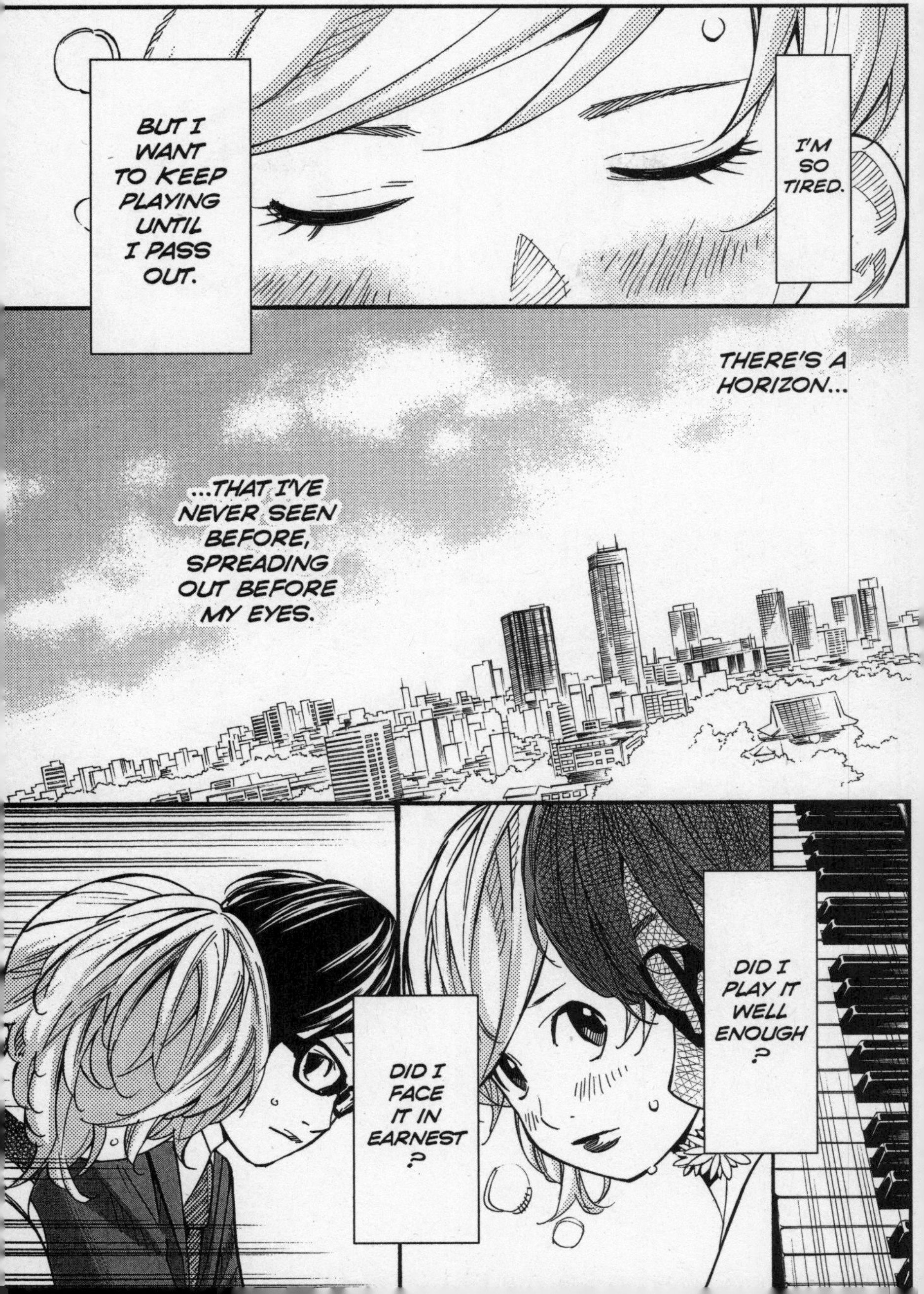
I'M SO TIRED.
BUT I WANT TO KEEP PLAYING UNTIL I PASS OUT.
THERE'S A HORIZON...
...THAT I'VE NEVER SEEN BEFORE, SPREADING OUT BEFORE MY EYES.
DID I PLAY IT WELL ENOUGH?
DID I FACE IT IN EARNEST?

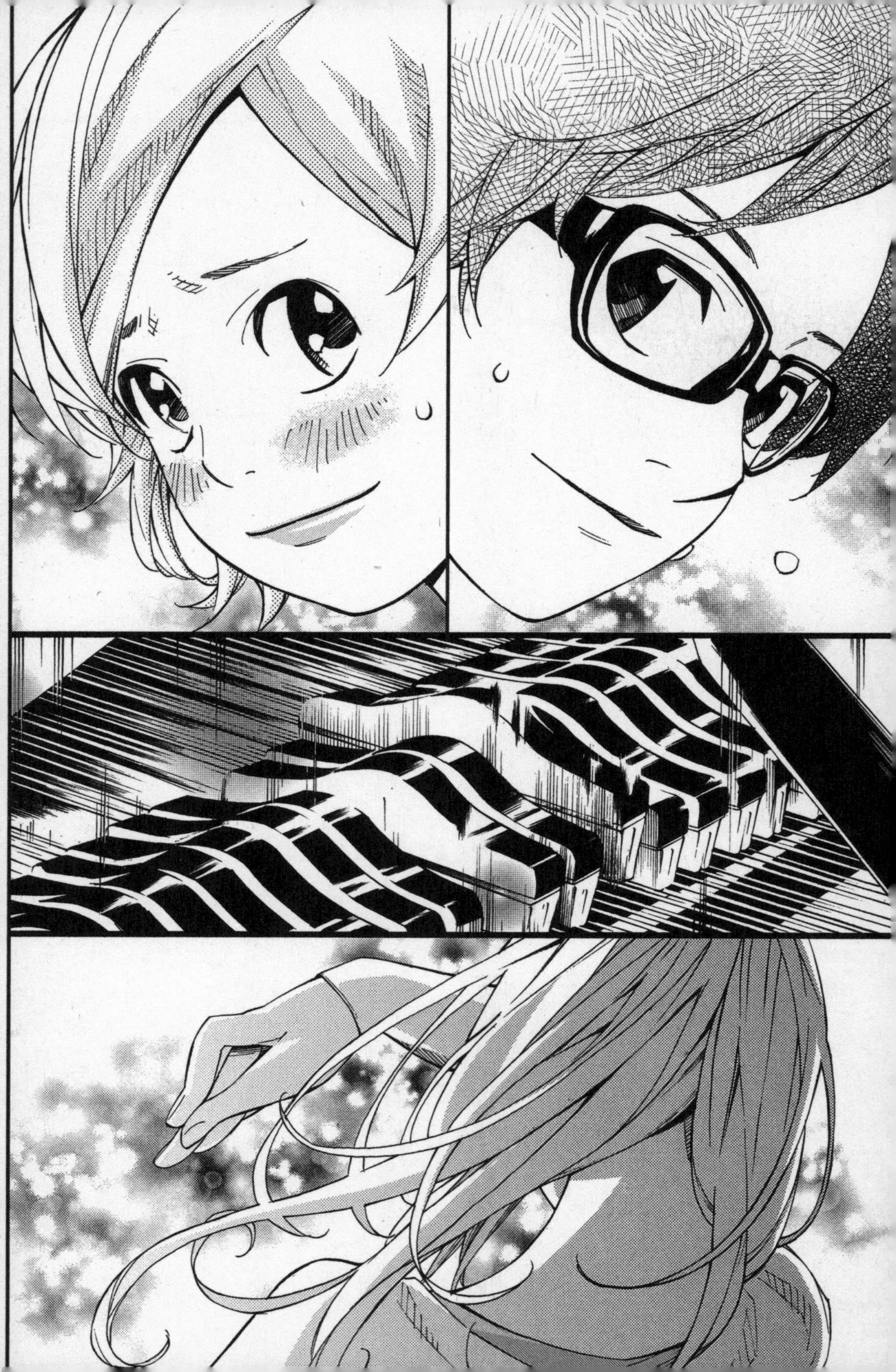

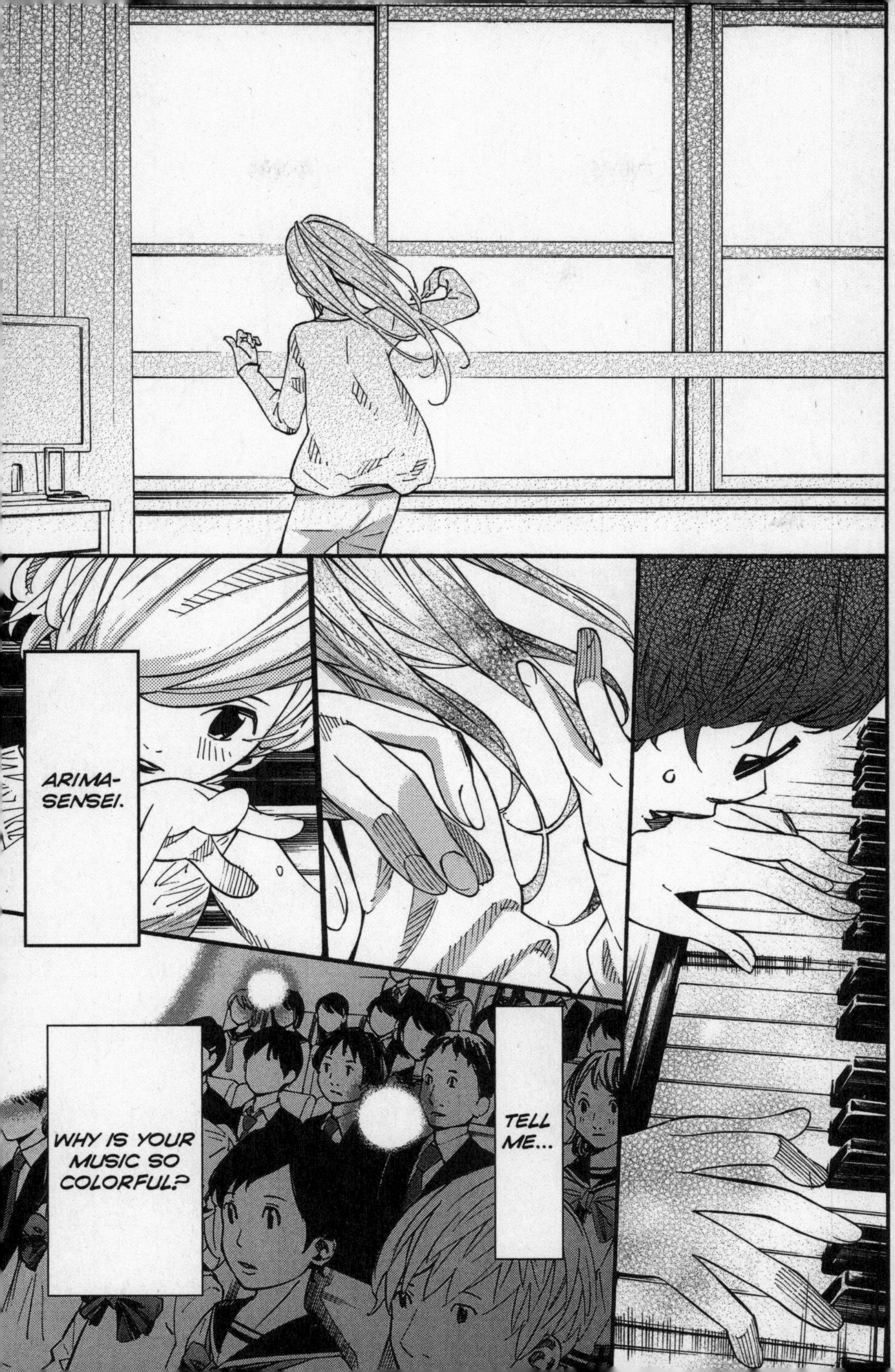
ARIMA-
SENSEI.
TELL
ME...
WHY IS YOUR
MUSIC SO
COLORFUL?

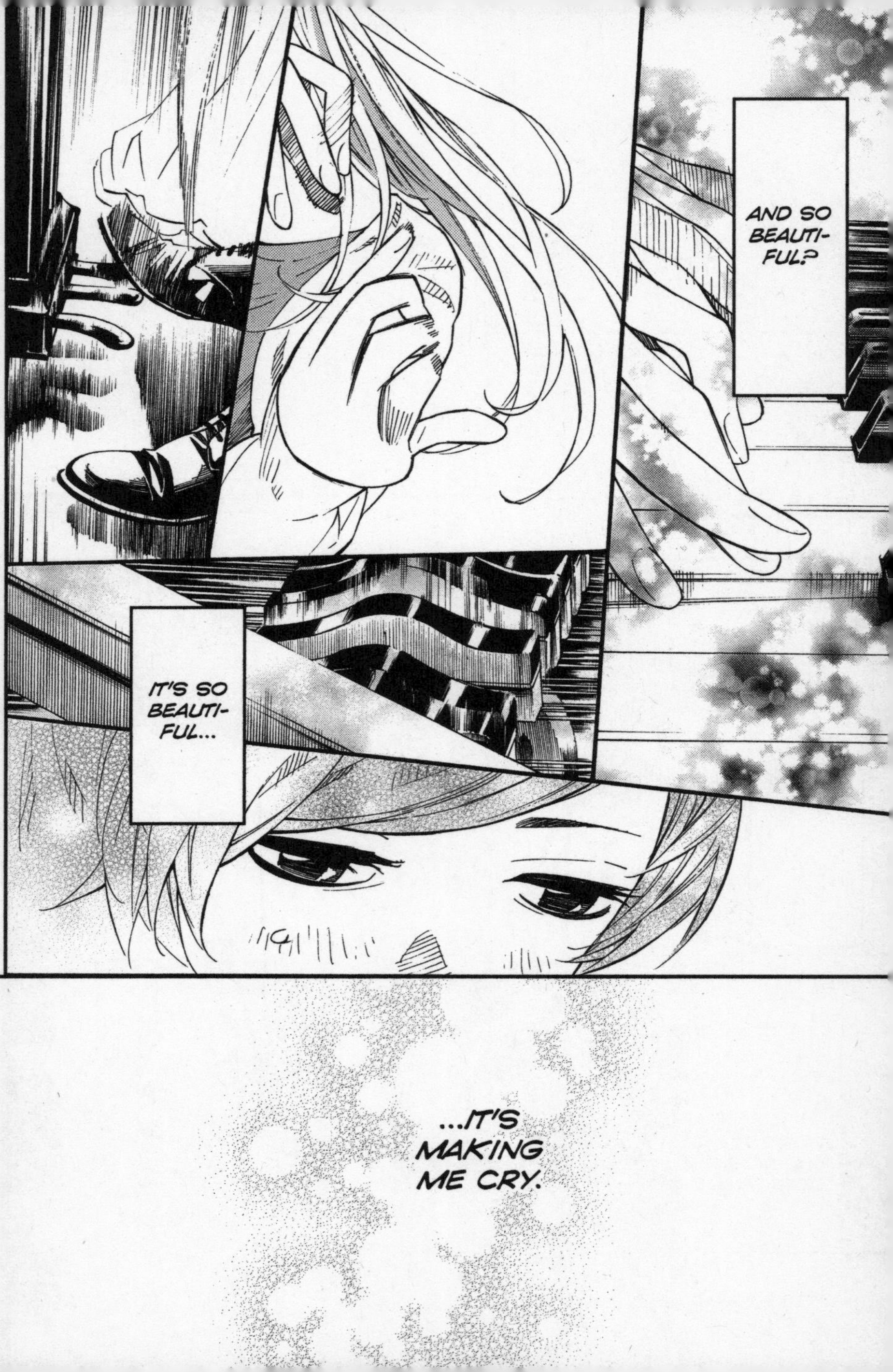
AND SO BEAUTI-FUL?
IT'S SO BEAUTI-FUL...
...IT'S MAKING ME CRY.

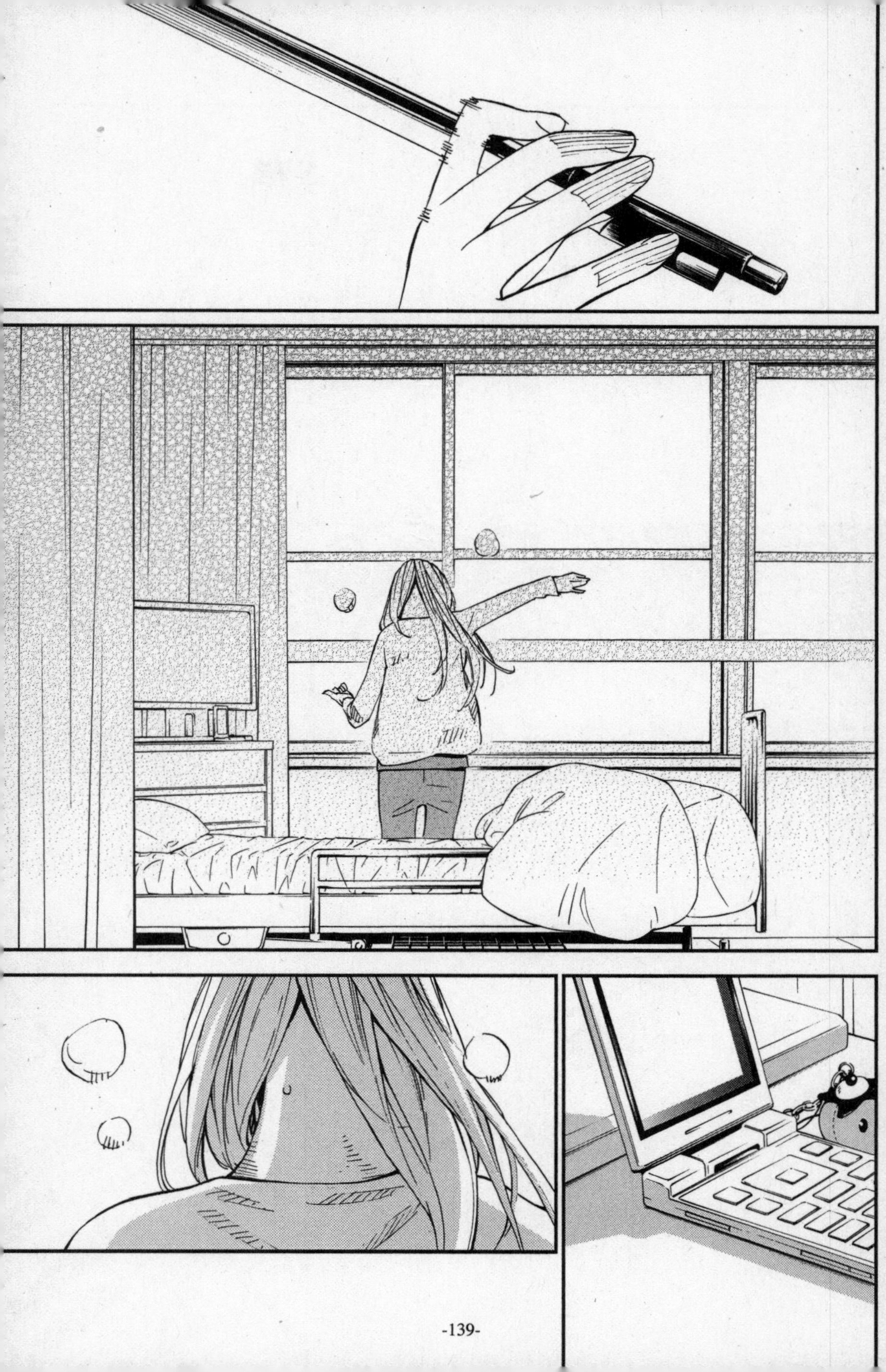

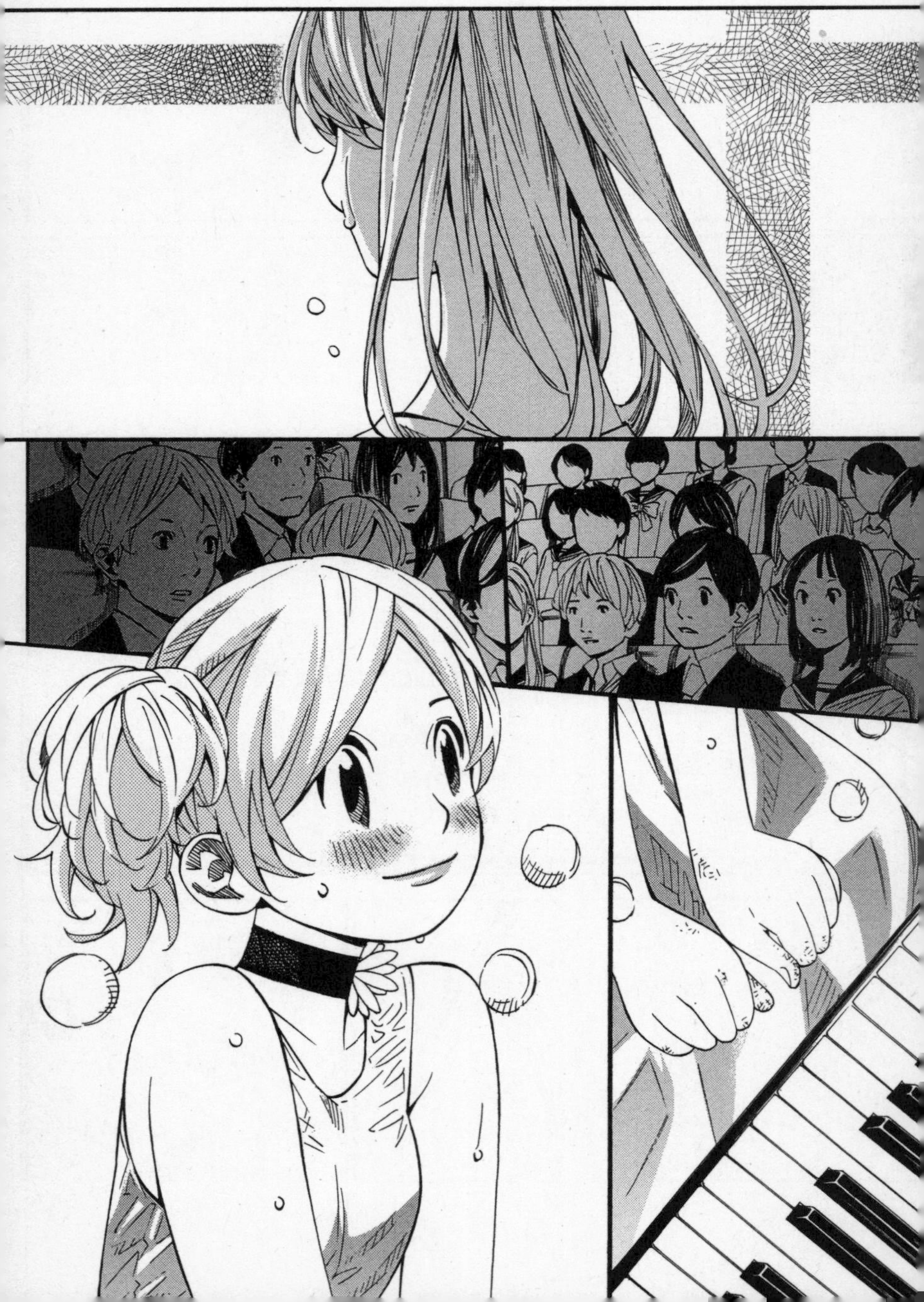

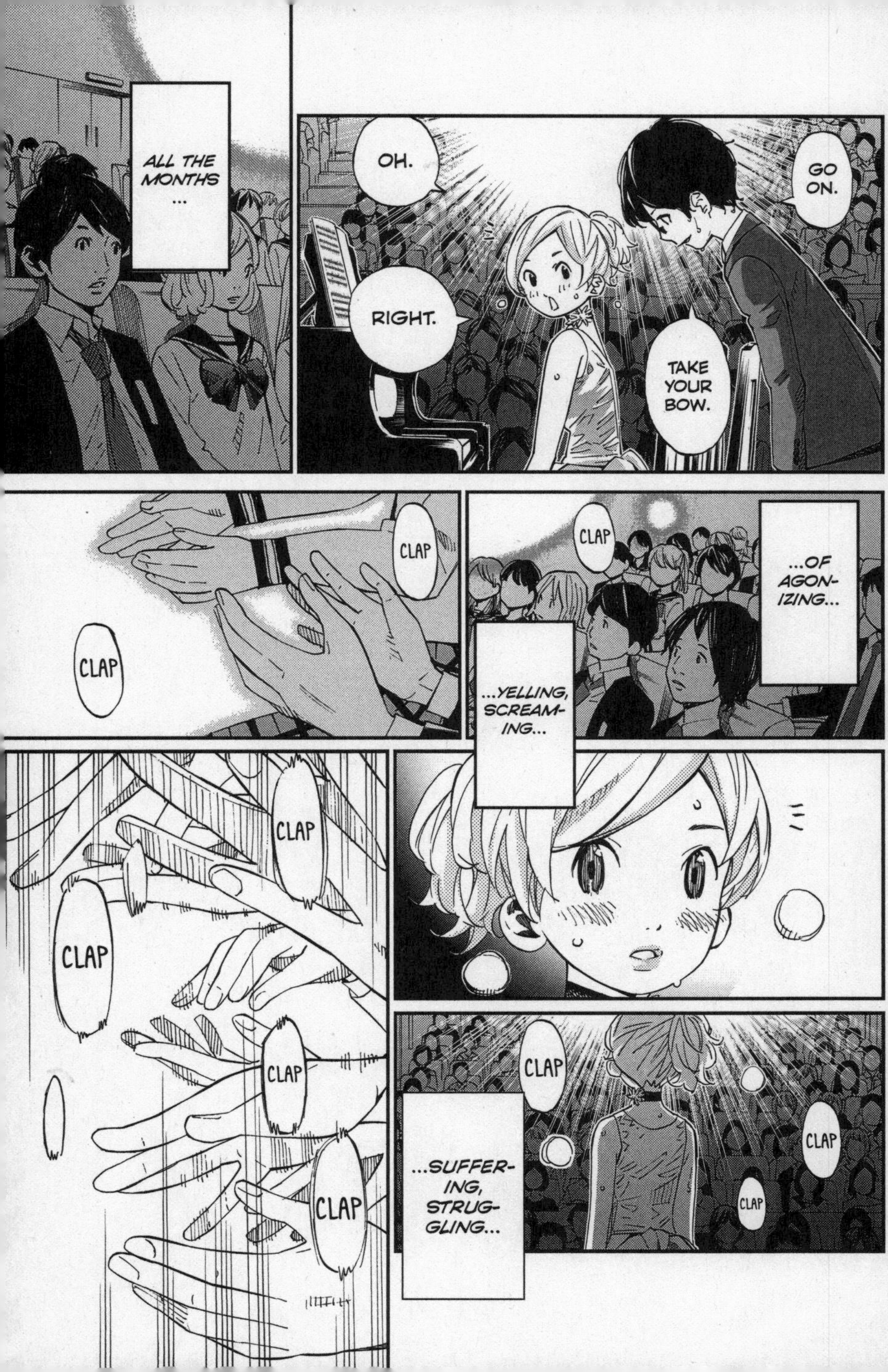
GO ON.
OH.
TAKE YOUR BOW.
RIGHT.
ALL THE MONTHS ...
...OF AGONIZING...
CLAP
...YELLING, SCREAMING...
CLAP
CLAP
CLAP
CLAP
CLAP
...SUFFERING, STRUGGLING...
CLAP
CLAP
CLAP
CLAP
CLAP

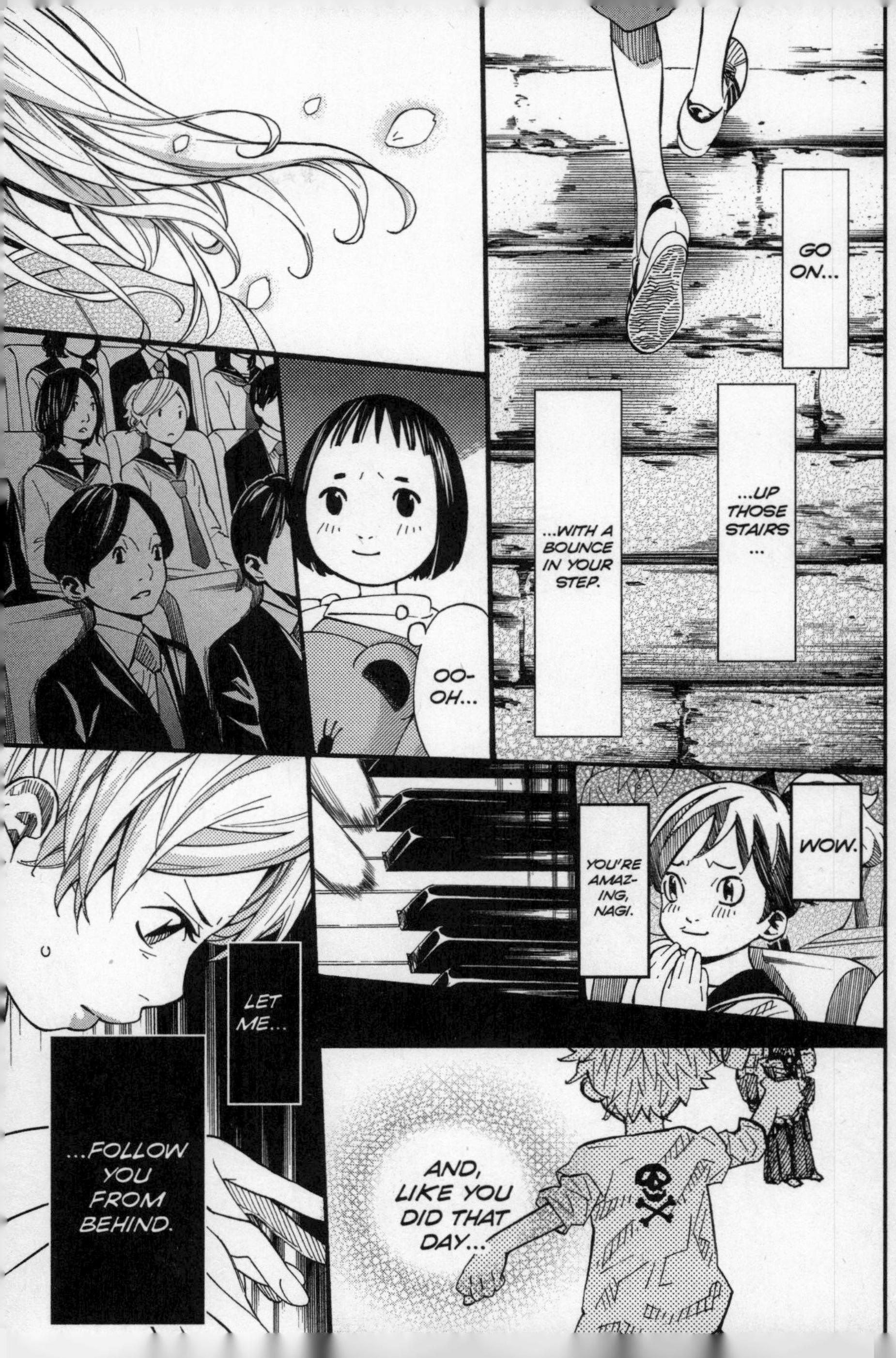
GO ON...
...UP THOSE STAIRS ...
...WITH A BOUNCE IN YOUR STEP.
OO-OH...
WOW.
YOU'RE AMAZ-ING, NAGI.
AND, LIKE YOU DID THAT DAY...
LET ME...
...FOLLOW YOU FROM BEHIND.

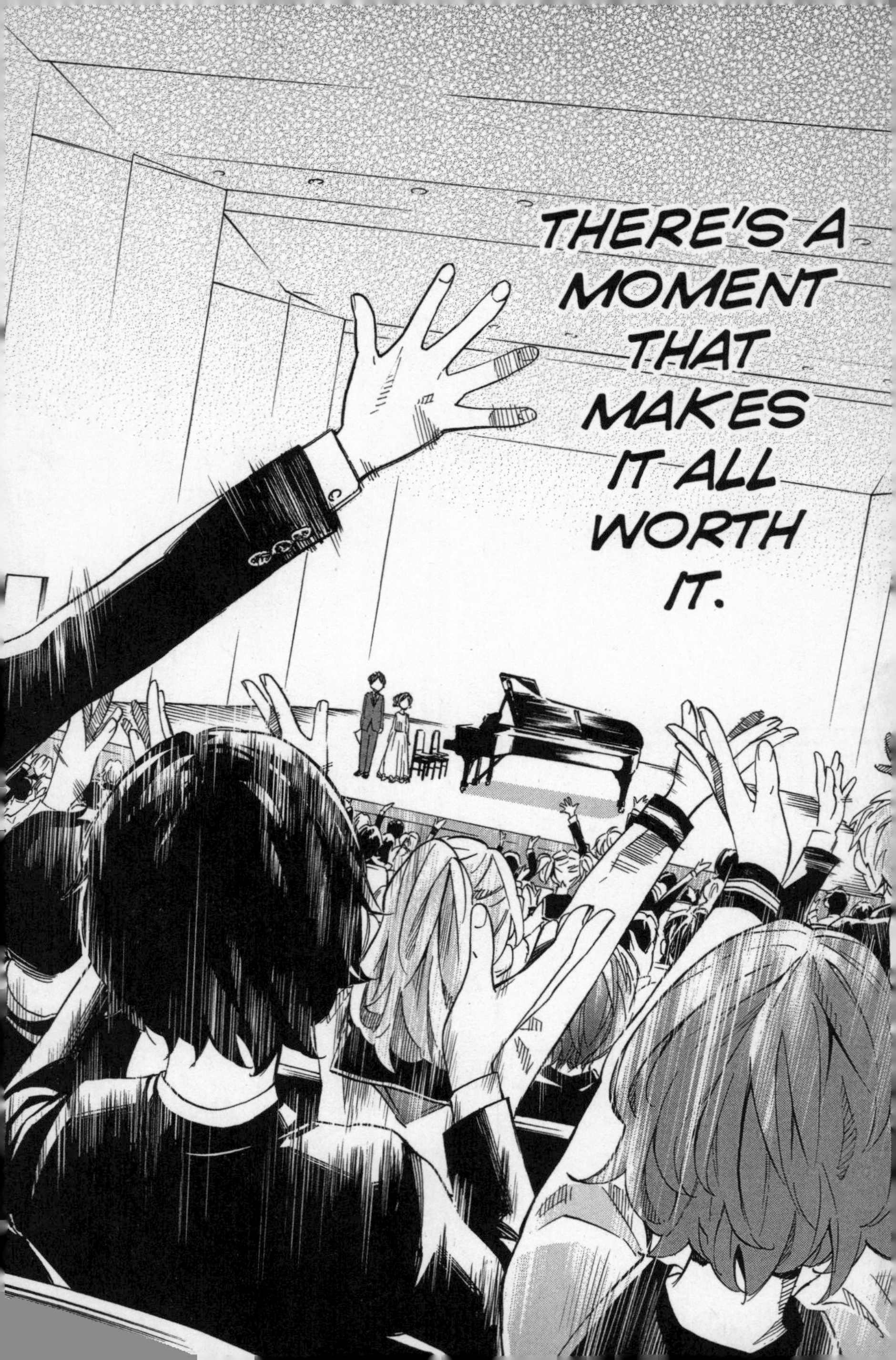
THERE'S A MOMENT THAT MAKES IT ALL WORTH IT.

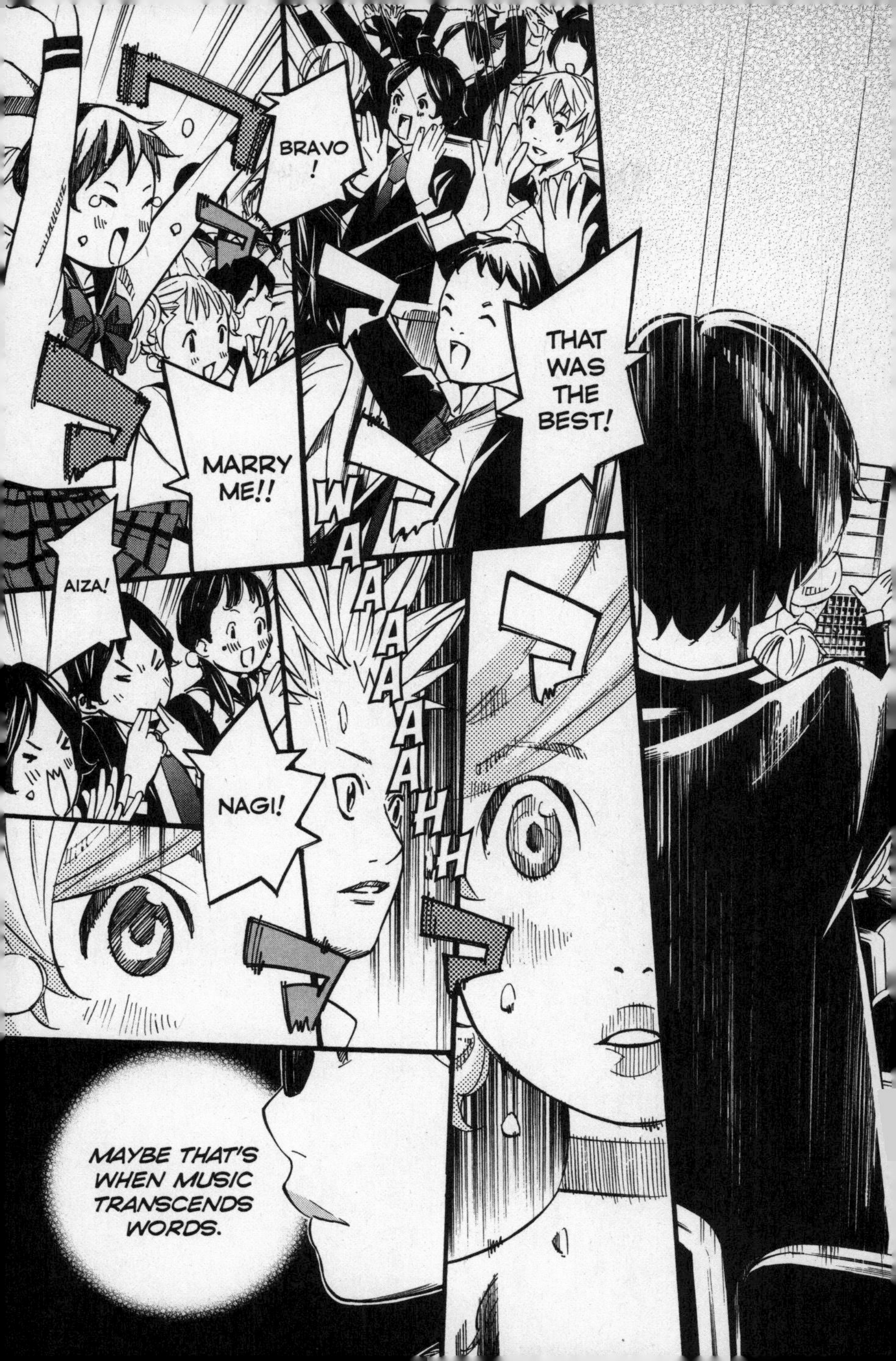
THAT WAS THE BEST!
BRAVO!
MARRY ME!!
WAAAAAAAAAHH
AIZA!
NAGI!
MAYBE THAT'S WHEN MUSIC TRANSCENDS WORDS.

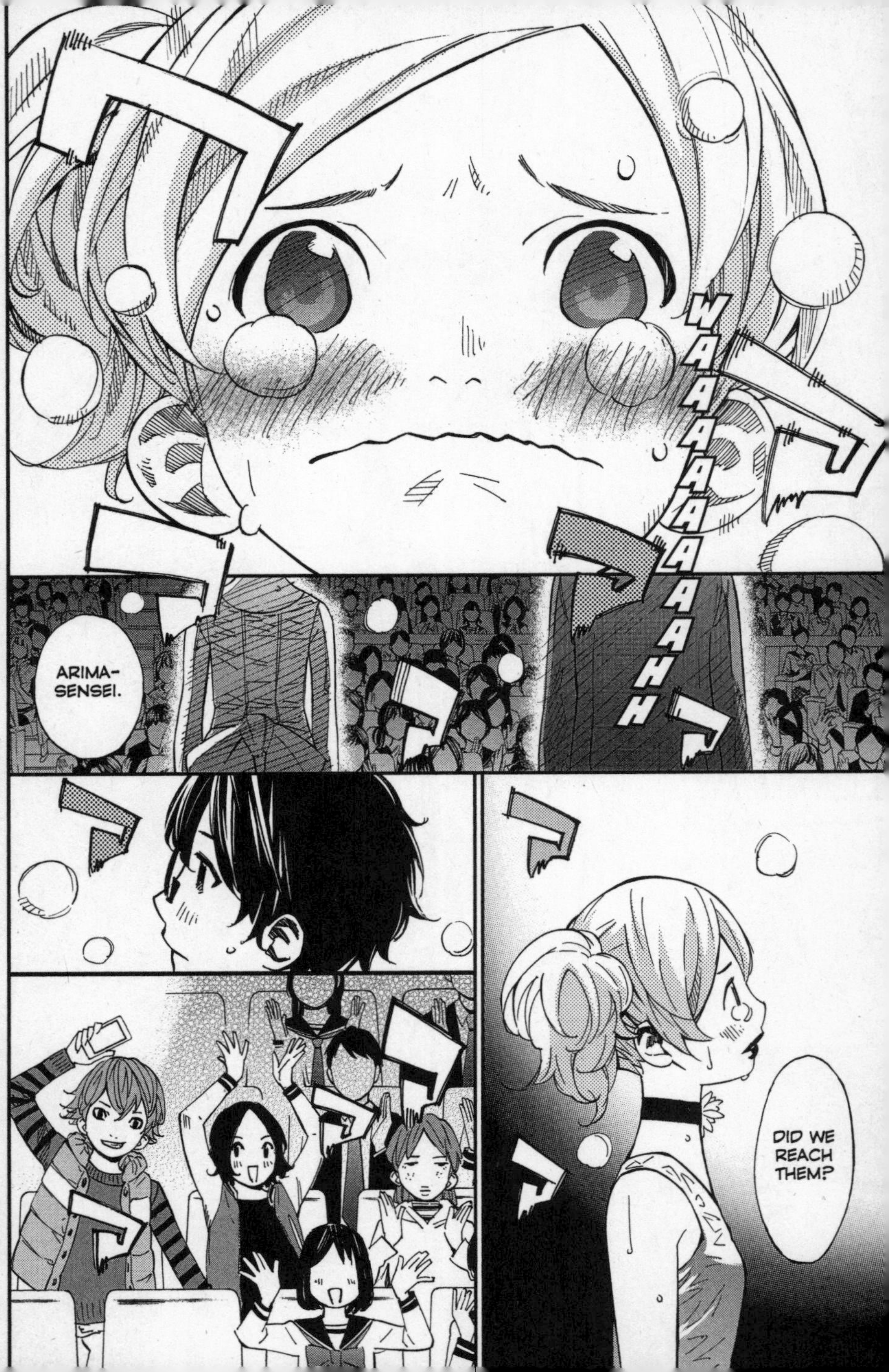
WAAAAAAAAHH
ARIMA-SENSEI.
DID WE REACH THEM?

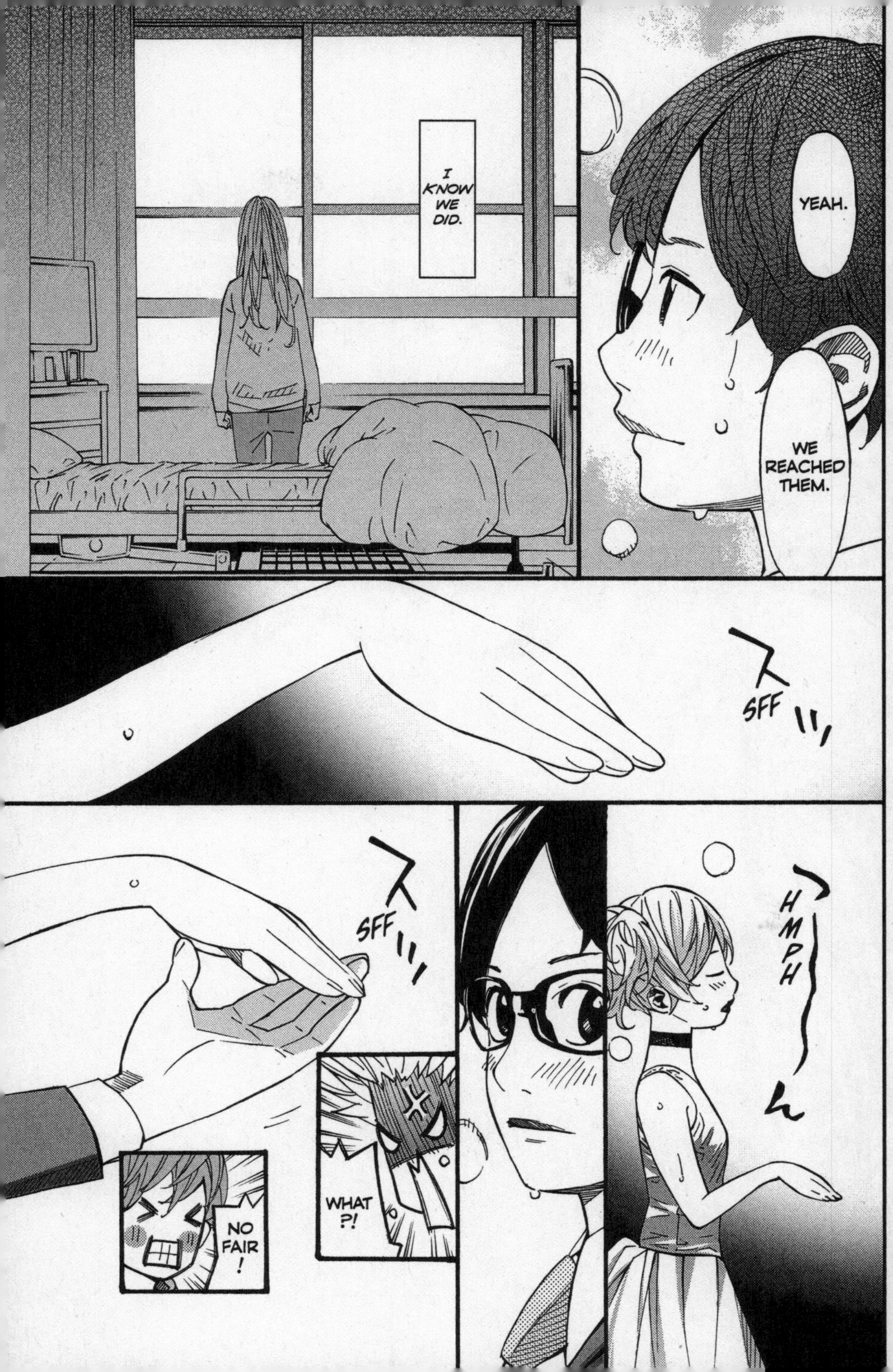
YEAH.
WE REACHED THEM.
I KNOW WE DID.
ス
SFF
HMPH
ス
SFF
WHAT ?!
NO FAIR !

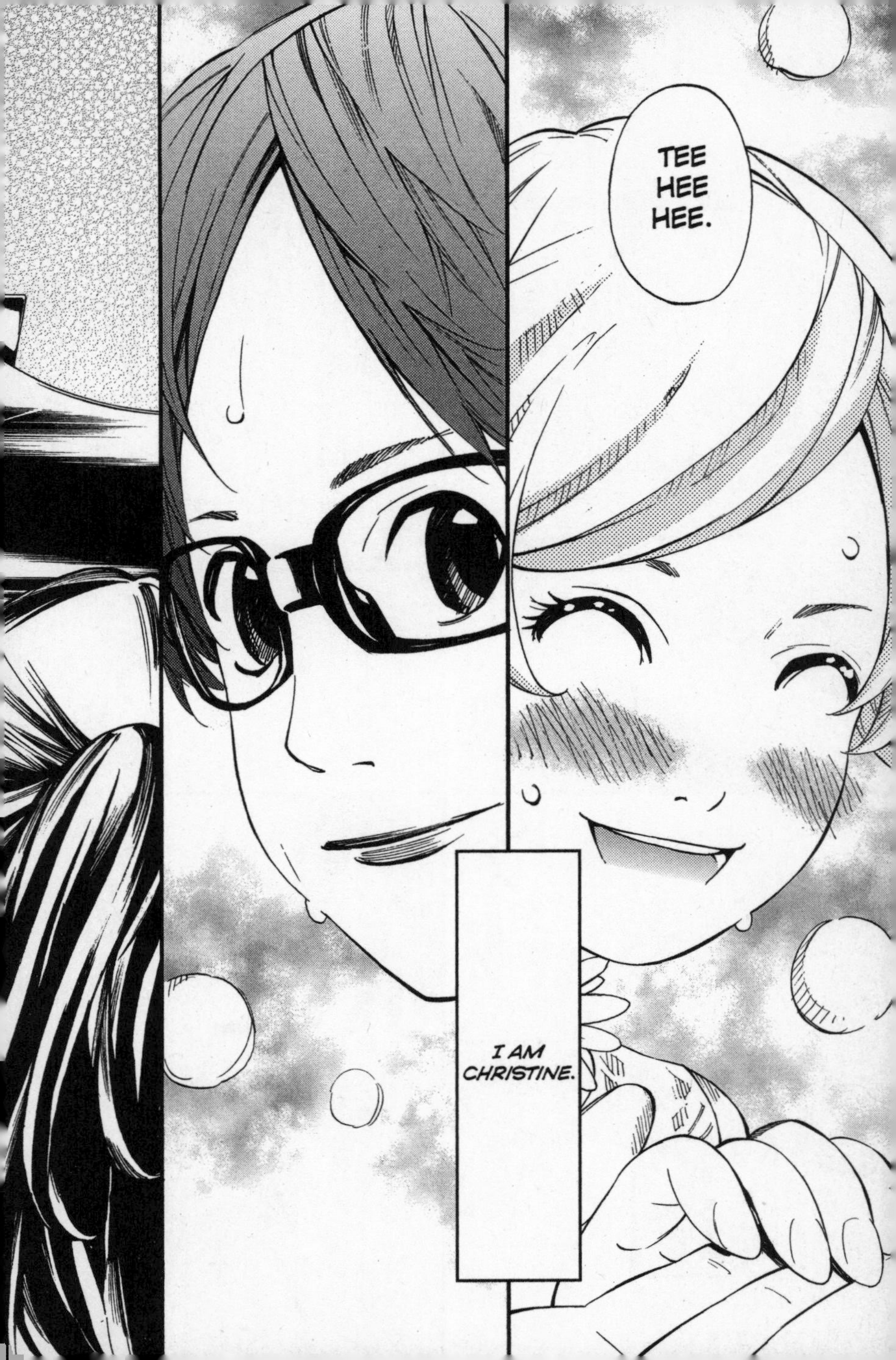
TEE HEE HEE.
I AM CHRISTINE.

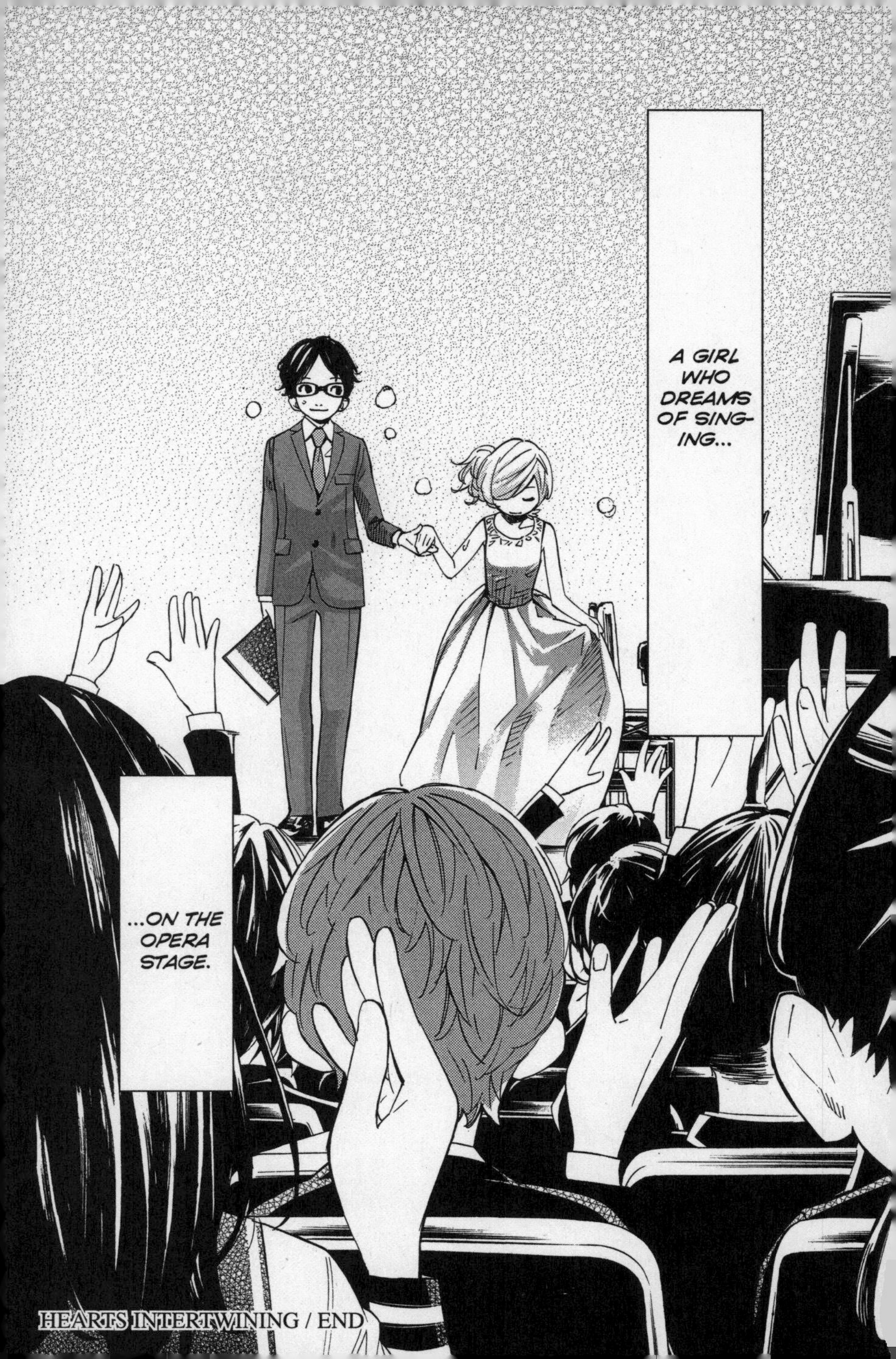
A GIRL WHO DREAMS OF SING-ING...
...ON THE OPERA STAGE.
HEARTS INTERTWINING / END

Your Lie in April

I met the girl under full-bloomed cherry blossoms, and my fate has begun to change.

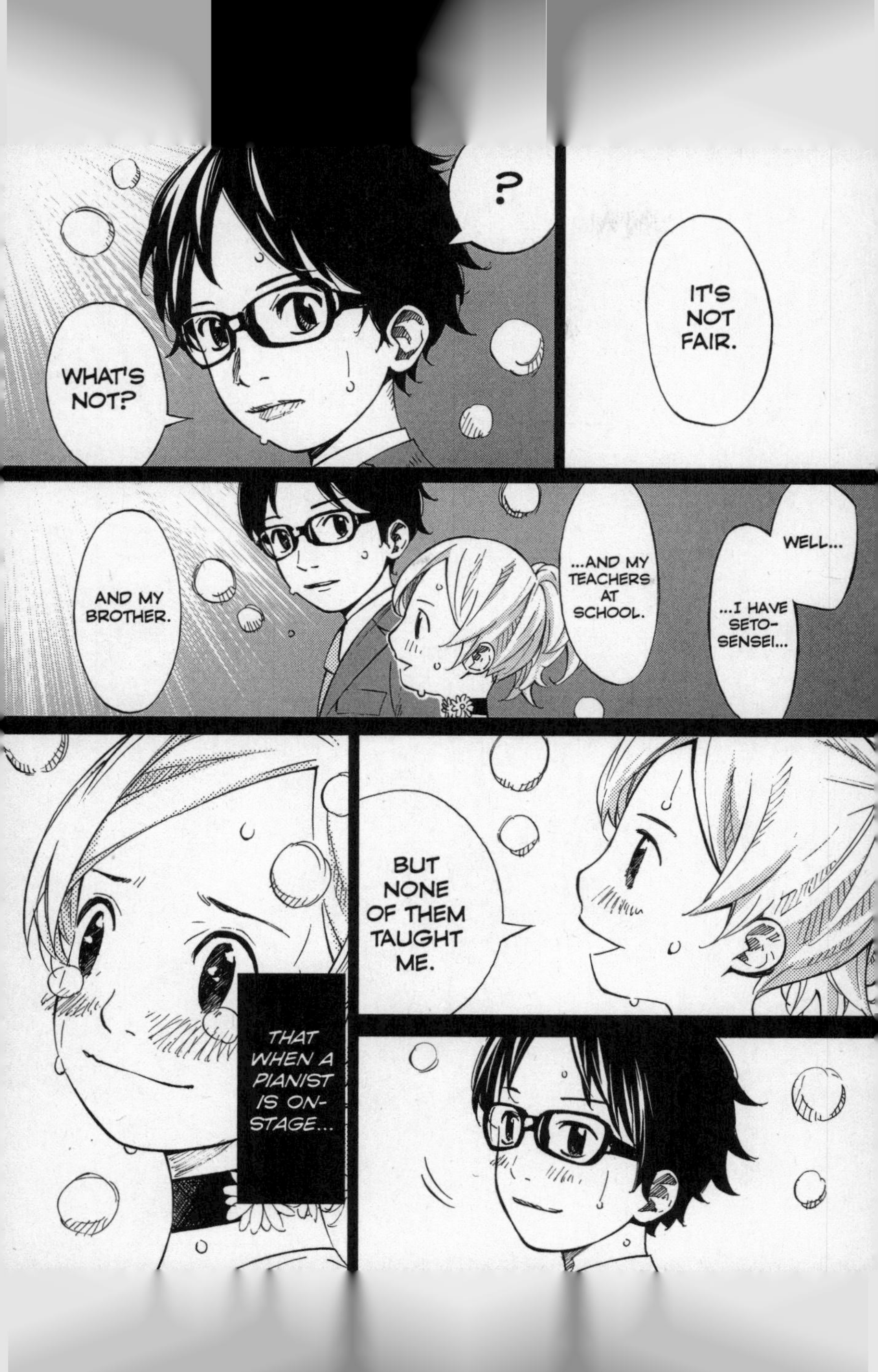
IT'S NOT FAIR.
?
WHAT'S NOT?
WELL...
...I HAVE SETO-SENSEI...
...AND MY TEACHERS AT SCHOOL.
AND MY BROTHER.
BUT NONE OF THEM TAUGHT ME.
THAT WHEN A PIANIST IS ON-STAGE...

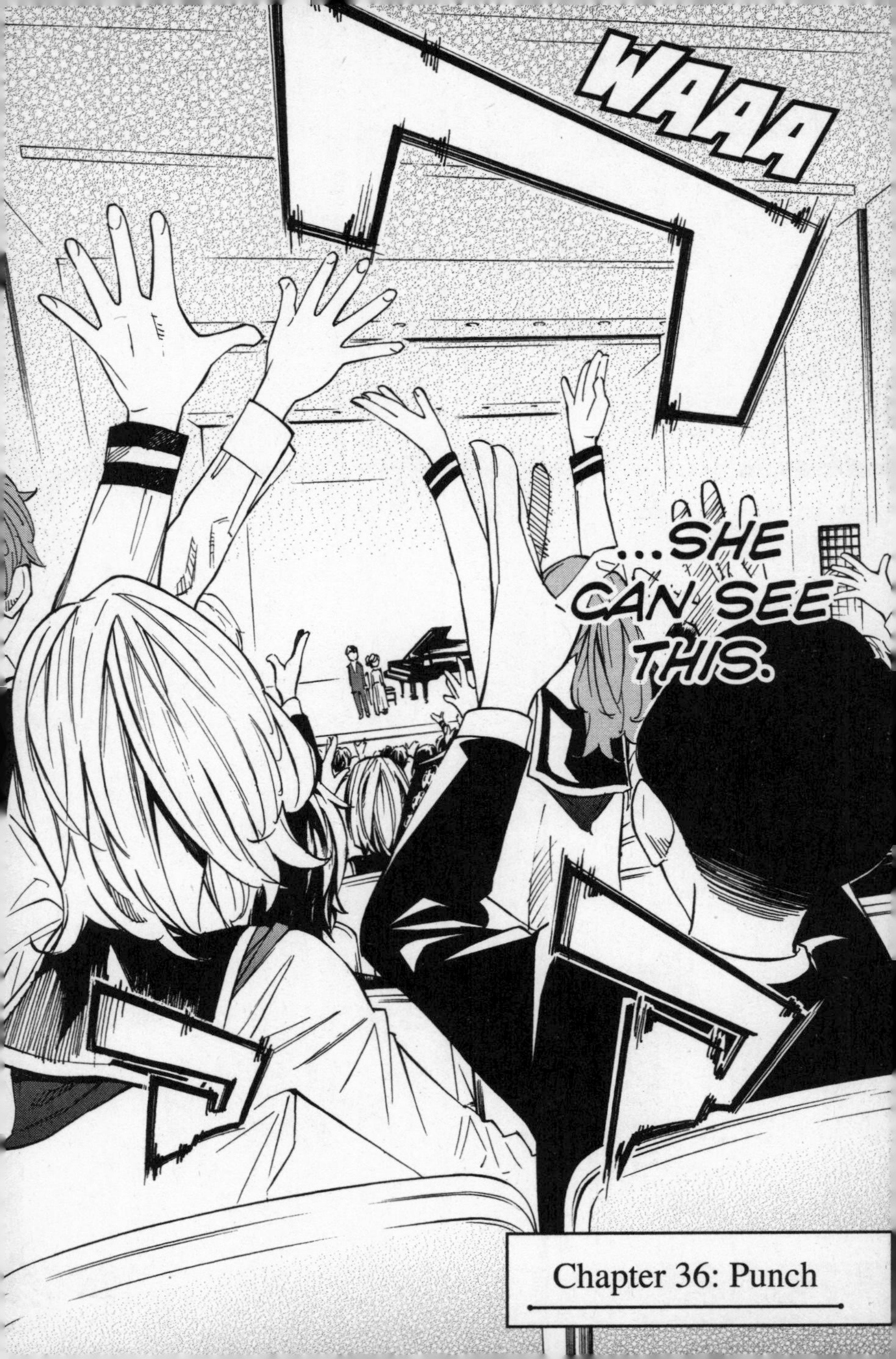
WAAA
...SHE CAN SEE THIS.

Chapter 36: Punch

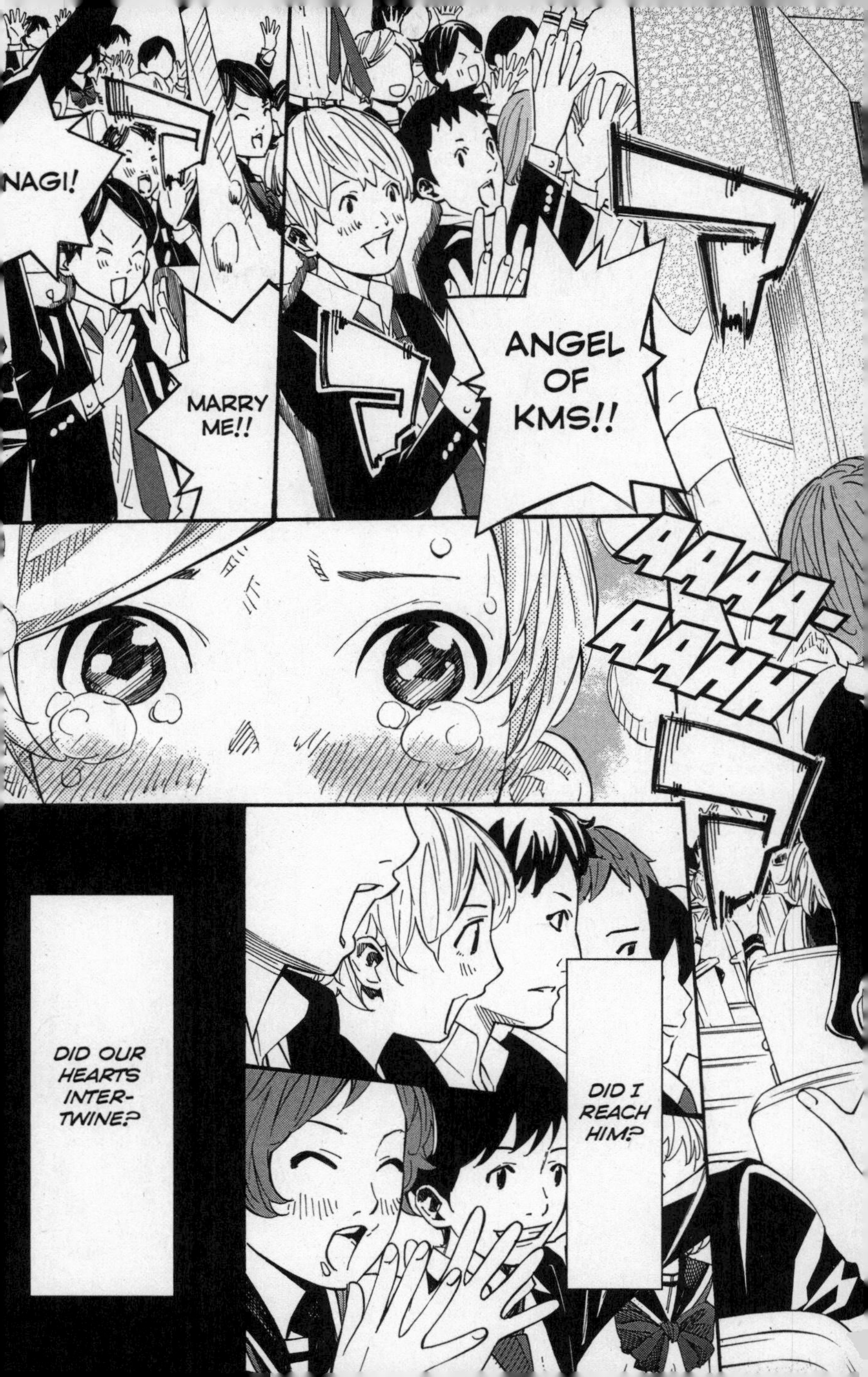
ANGEL OF KMS!!
MARRY ME!!
NAGI!
AAAA-AAHH
DID I REACH HIM?
DID OUR HEARTS INTER-TWINE?

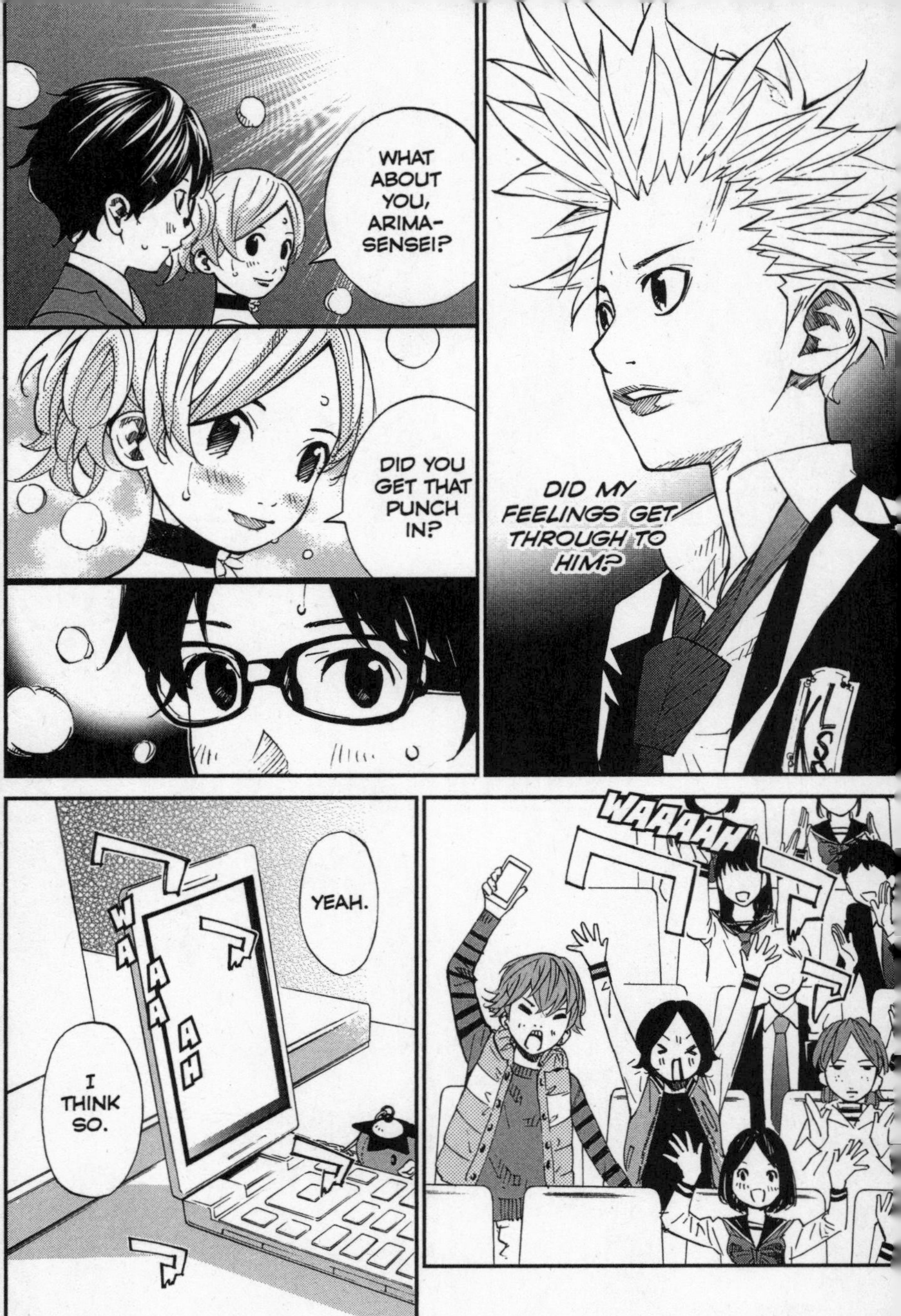
DID MY FEELINGS GET THROUGH TO HIM?
WHAT ABOUT YOU, ARIMA-SENSEI?
DID YOU GET THAT PUNCH IN?
WAAAAAH
YEAH.
WAAAAAH
I THINK SO.

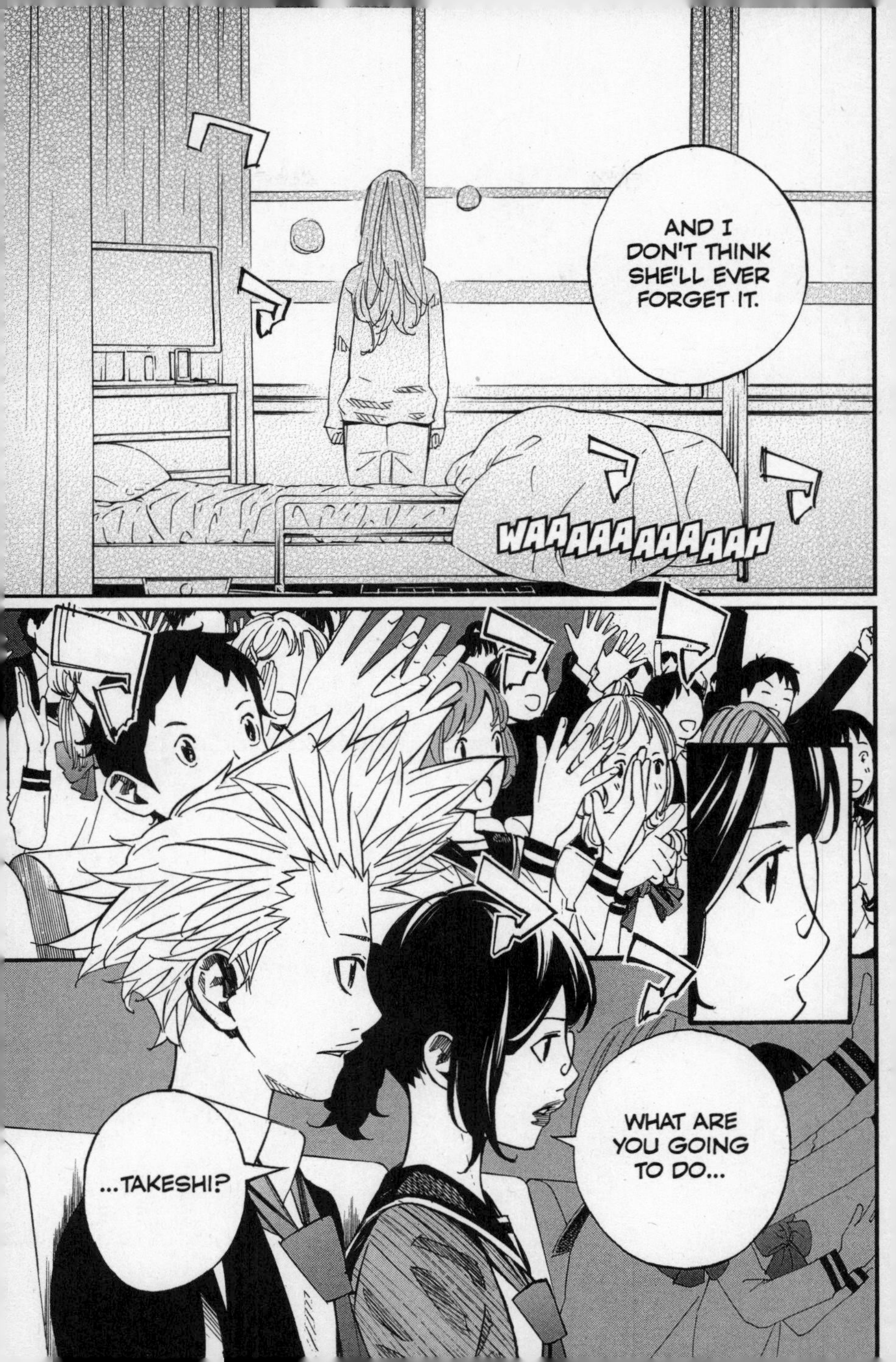
AND I DON'T THINK SHE'LL EVER FORGET IT.
WAAAAAAAAAAH
WHAT ARE YOU GOING TO DO...
...TAKESHI?

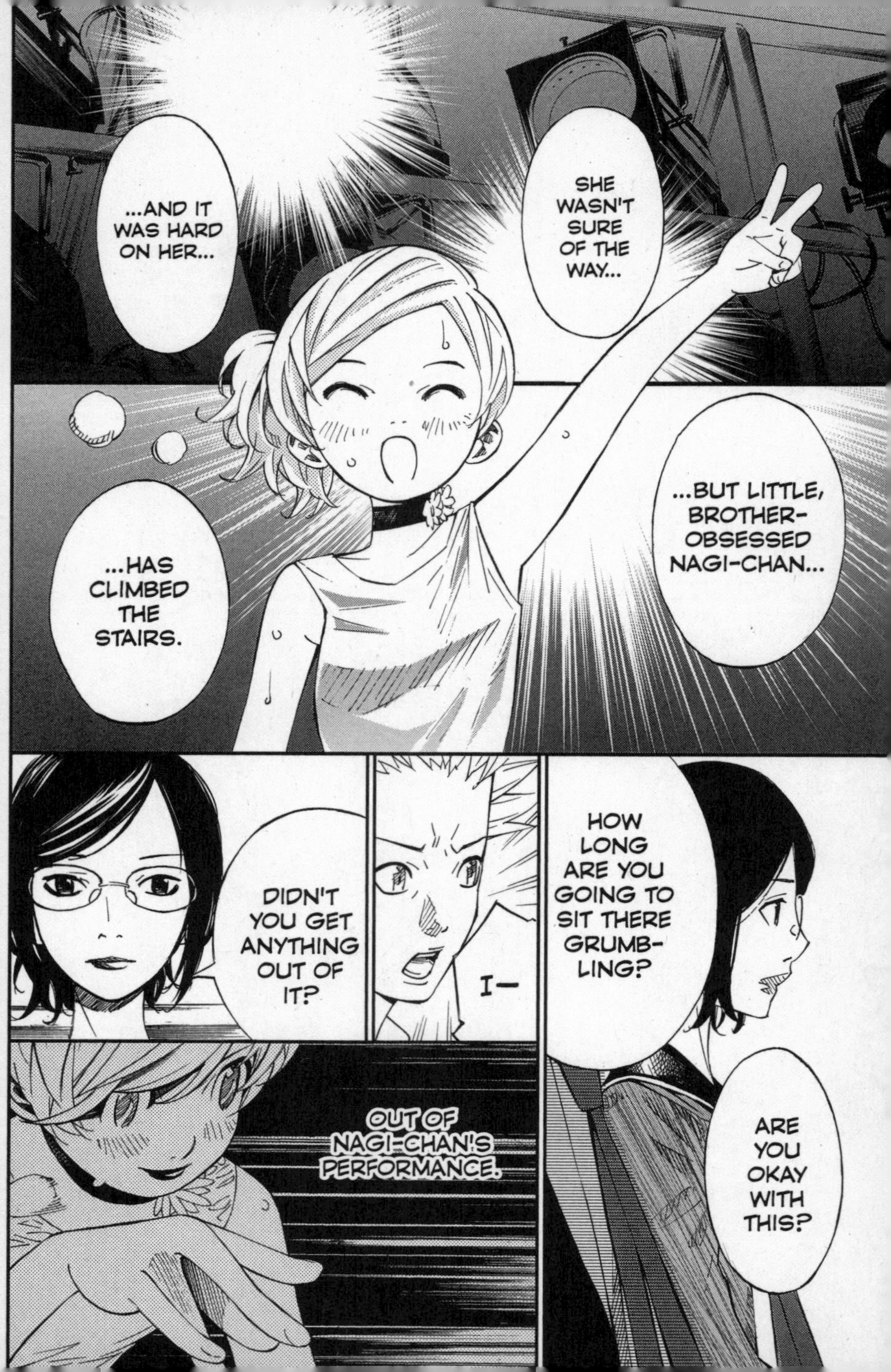
SHE WASN'T SURE OF THE WAY...
...AND IT WAS HARD ON HER...
...BUT LITTLE, BROTHER-OBSESSED NAGI-CHAN...
...HAS CLIMBED THE STAIRS.
HOW LONG ARE YOU GOING TO SIT THERE GRUMB-LING?
I—
DIDN'T YOU GET ANYTHING OUT OF IT?
ARE YOU OKAY WITH THIS?
OUT OF NAGI-CHAN'S PERFORMANCE.

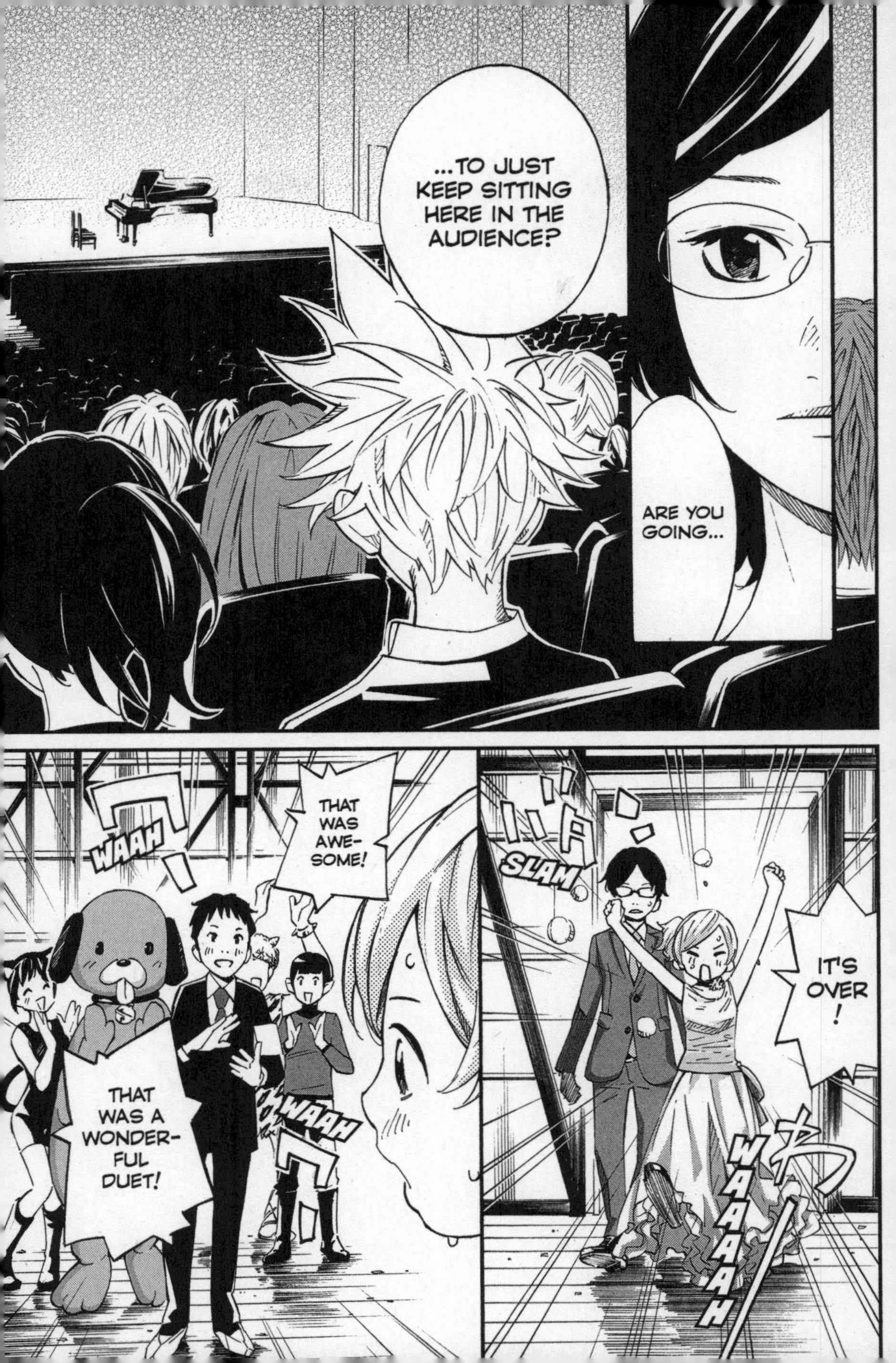
ARE YOU GOING...
...TO JUST KEEP SITTING HERE IN THE AUDIENCE?
SLAM
IT'S OVER!
WAAAAAH
WAAH
THAT WAS AWESOME!
WAAH
THAT WAS A WONDERFUL DUET!

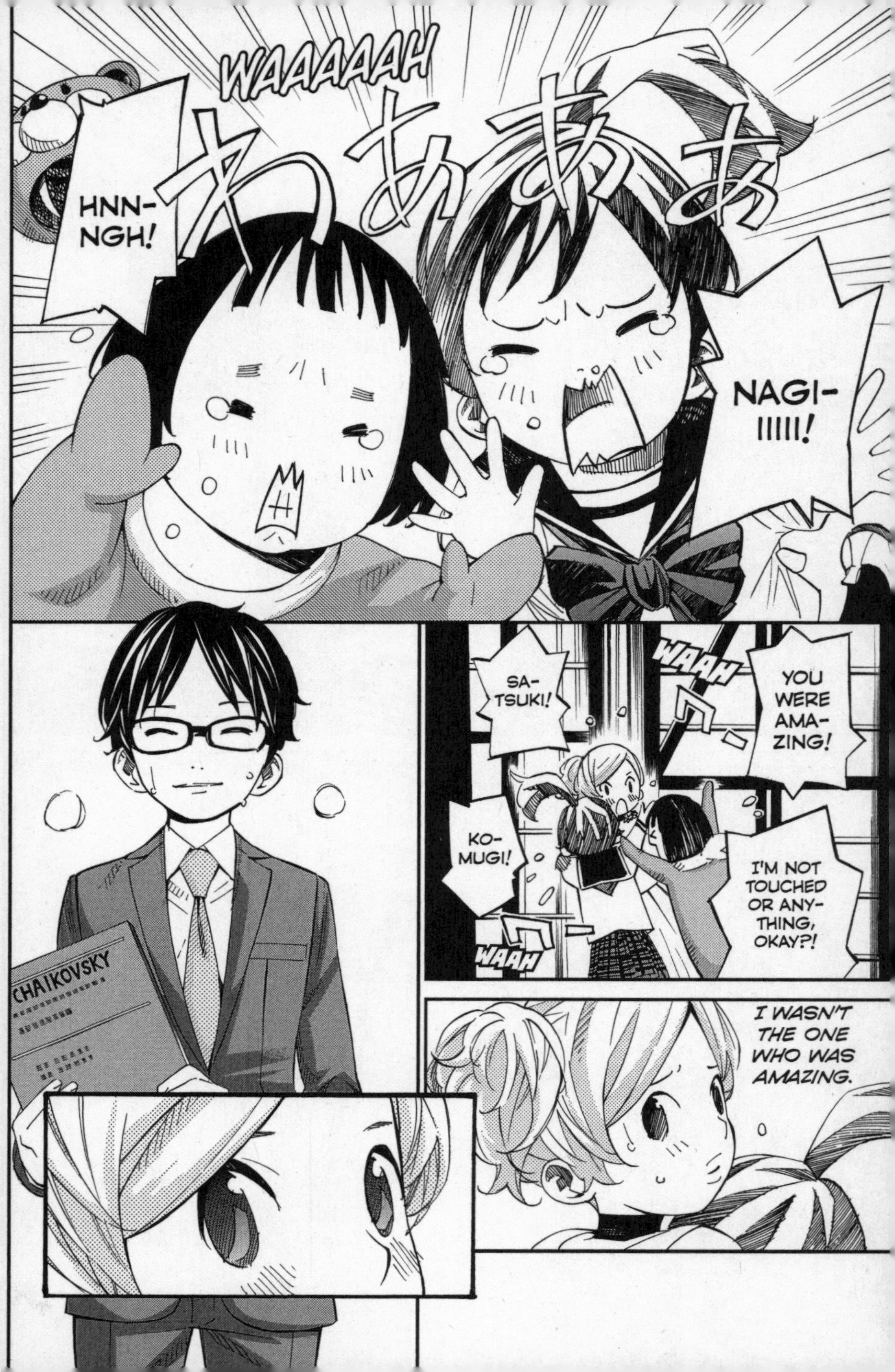
WAAAAAH
わあああ
NAGI-IIIIII!
HNN-NGH!
YOU WERE AMAZING!
WAAH
SA-TSUKI!
I'M NOT TOUCHED OR ANY-THING, OKAY?!
KO-MUGI!
WAAH
I WASN'T THE ONE WHO WAS AMAZING.
CHAIKOVSKY

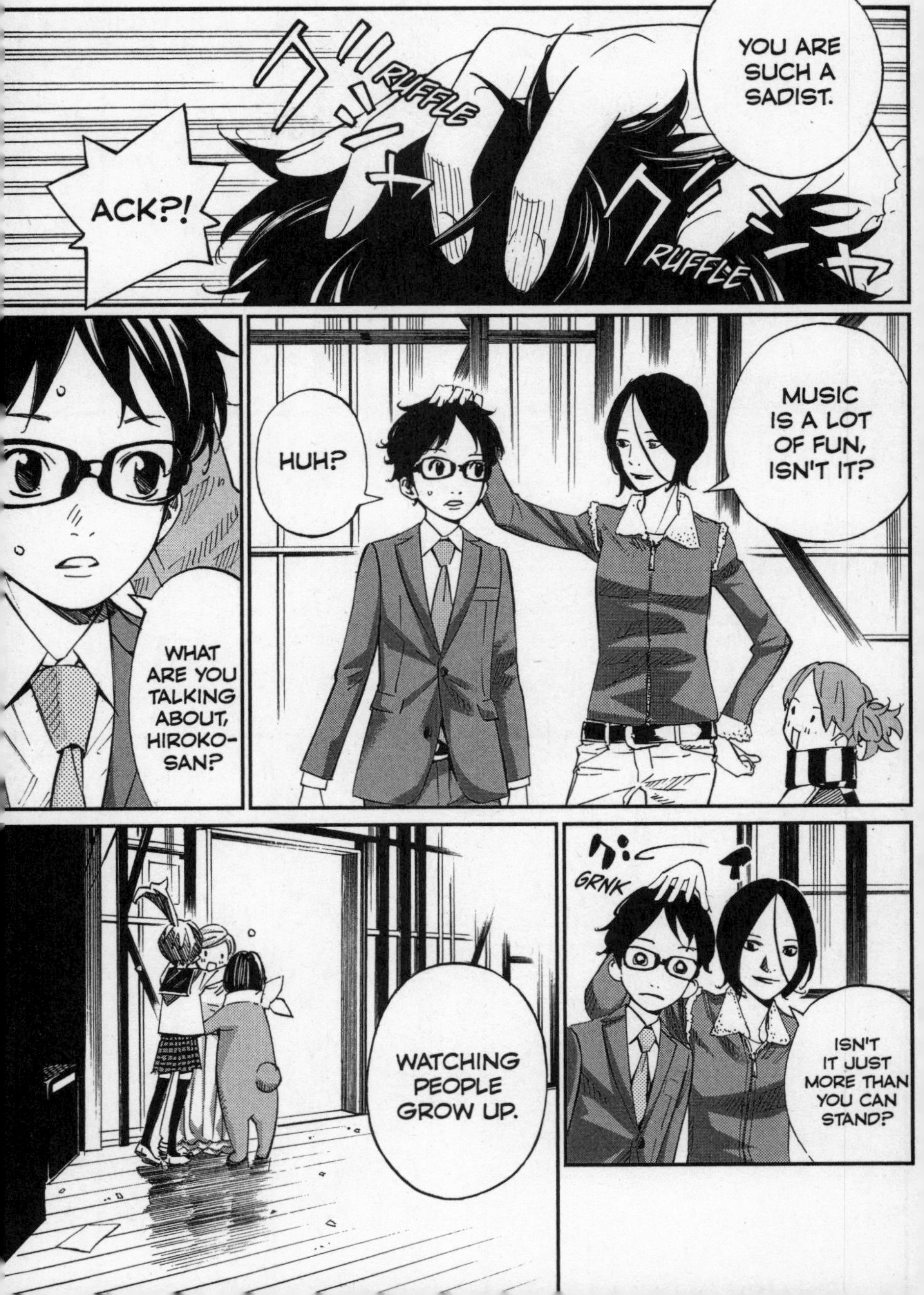
YOU ARE SUCH A SADIST.
RUFFLE
RUFFLE
ACK?!
MUSIC IS A LOT OF FUN, ISN'T IT?
HUH?
WHAT ARE YOU TALKING ABOUT, HIROKO-SAN?
GRNK
ISN'T IT JUST MORE THAN YOU CAN STAND?
WATCHING PEOPLE GROW UP.

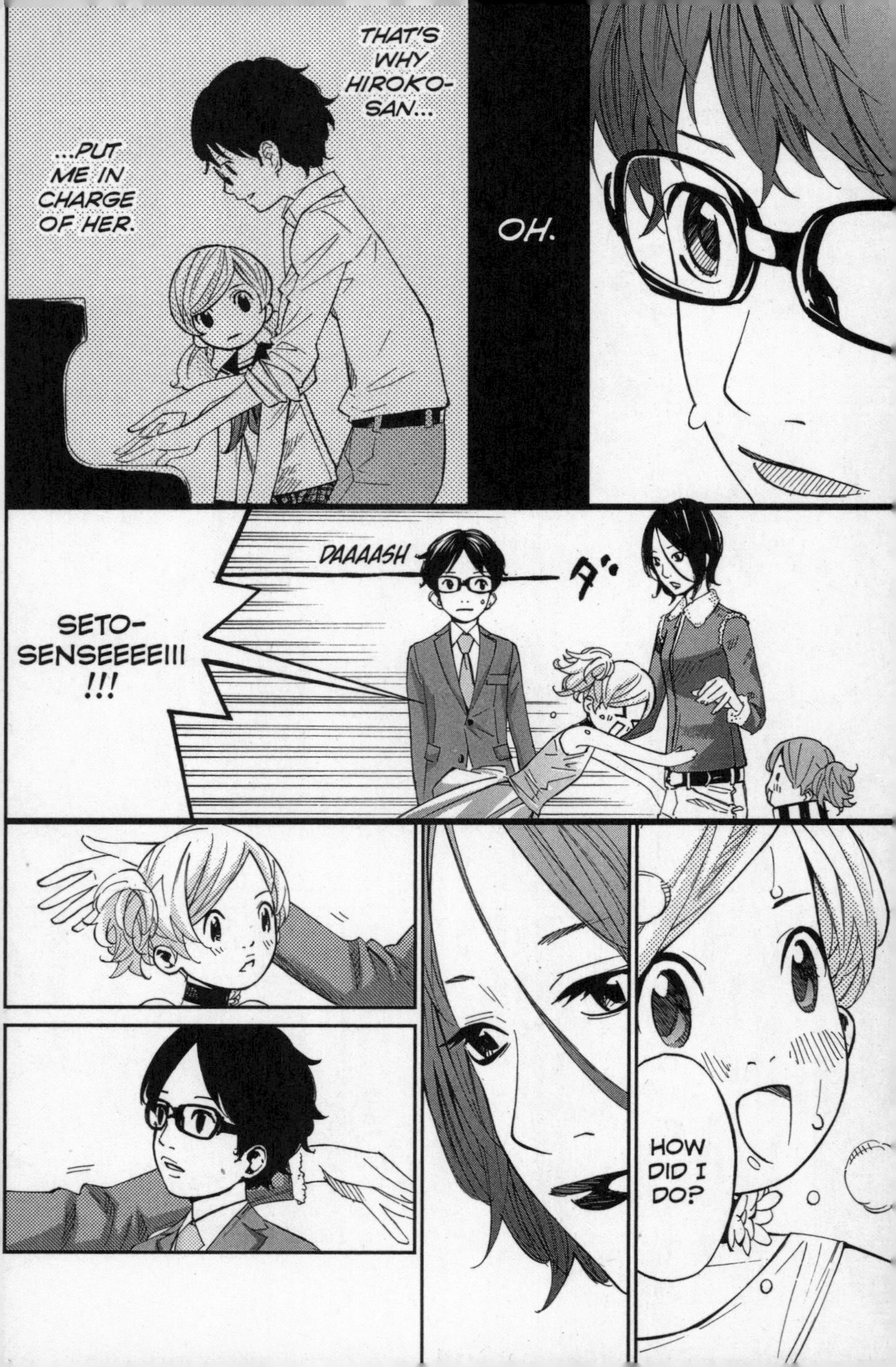
OH.
THAT'S WHY HIROKO-SAN...
...PUT ME IN CHARGE OF HER.
ダ
DAAAASH
SETO-SENSEEEIII!!!
HOW DID I DO?

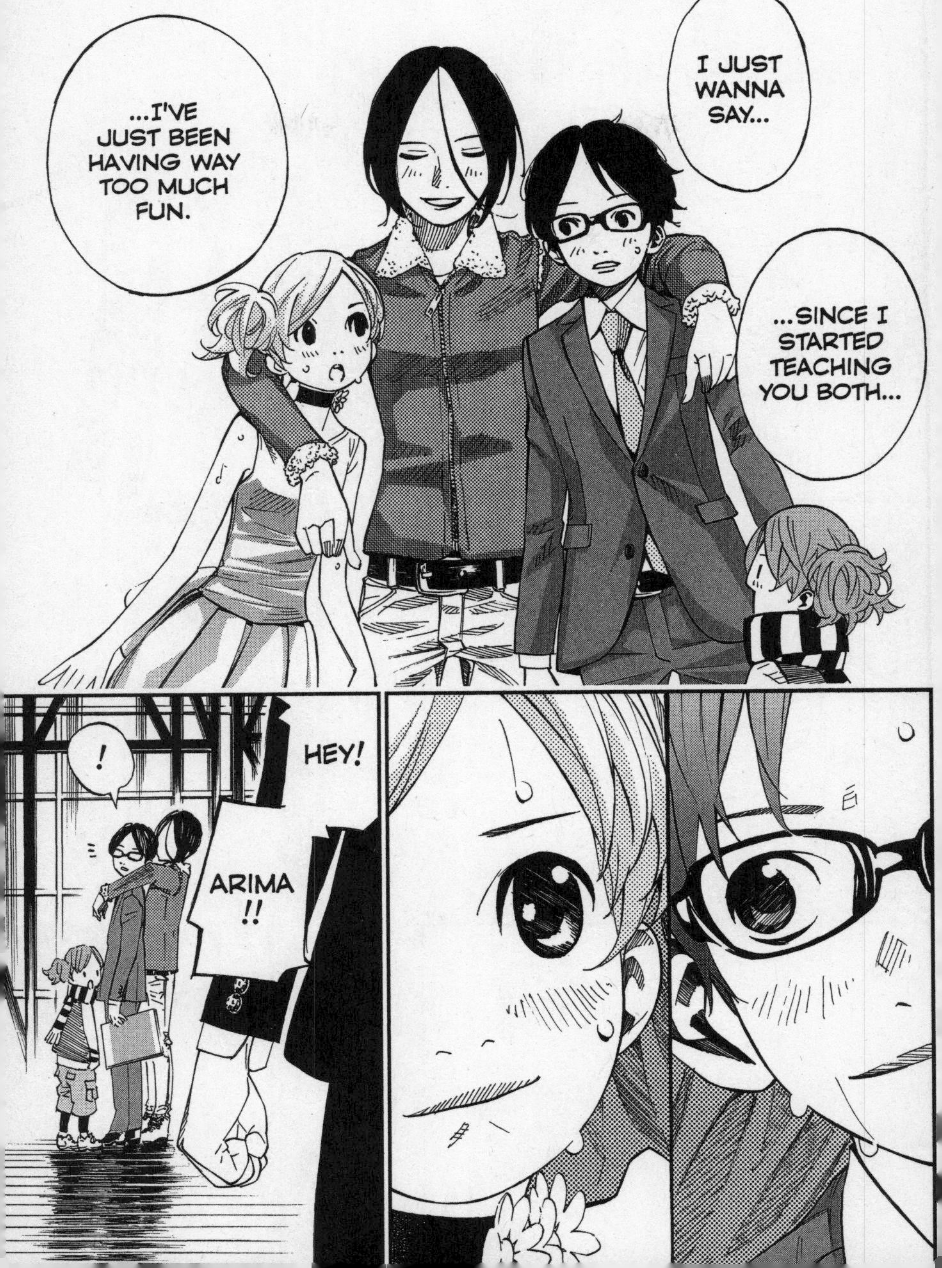
I JUST WANNA SAY...
...SINCE I STARTED TEACHING YOU BOTH...
...I'VE JUST BEEN HAVING WAY TOO MUCH FUN.
HEY!
ARIMA!!
!

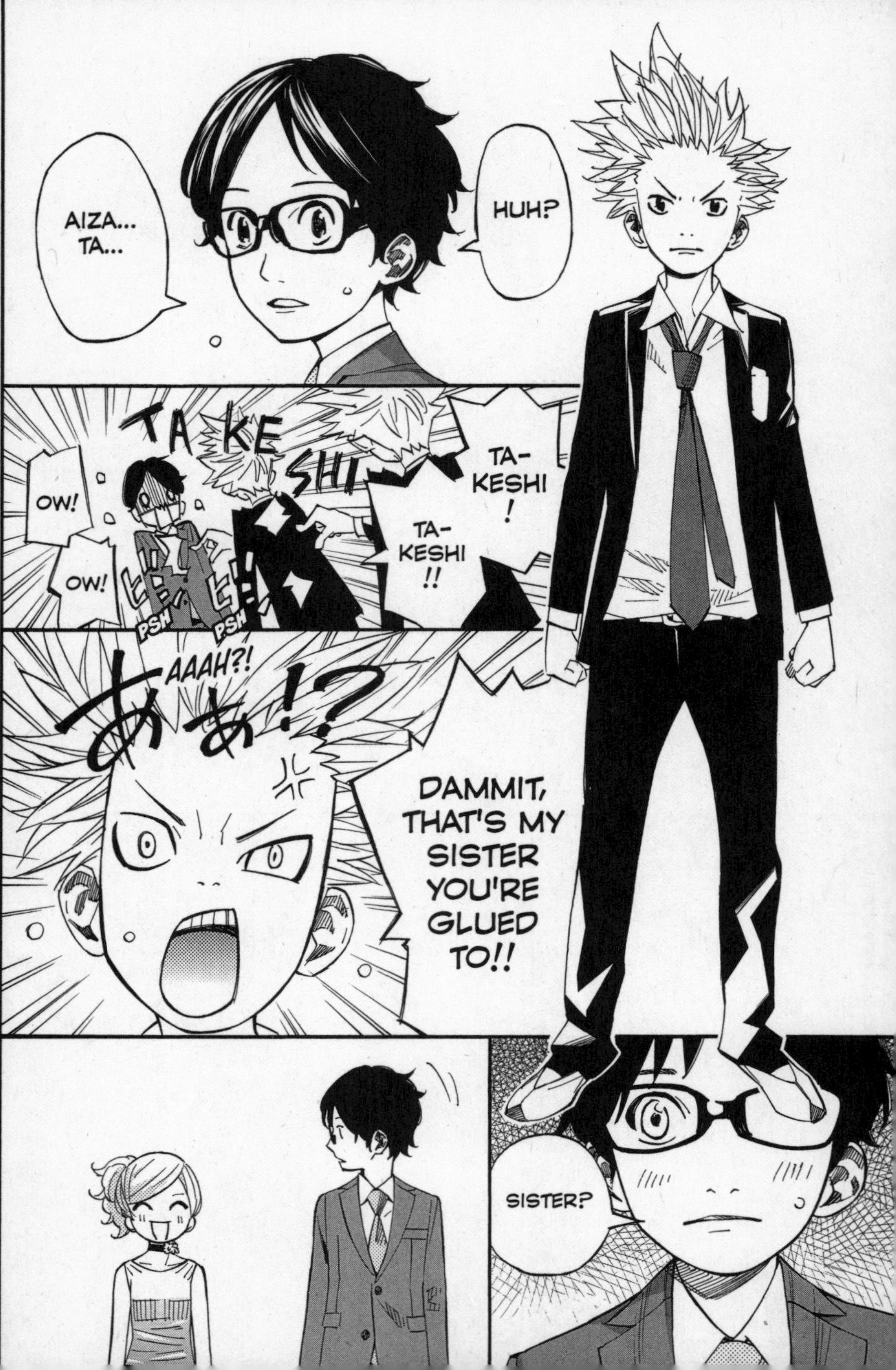
HUH?
AIZA... TA...
TA-KESHI!
TA-KESHI!!
TAKESHI
OW!
OW!
PSH
PSH
AAAH?!
DAMMIT, THAT'S MY SISTER YOU'RE GLUED TO!!
SISTER?

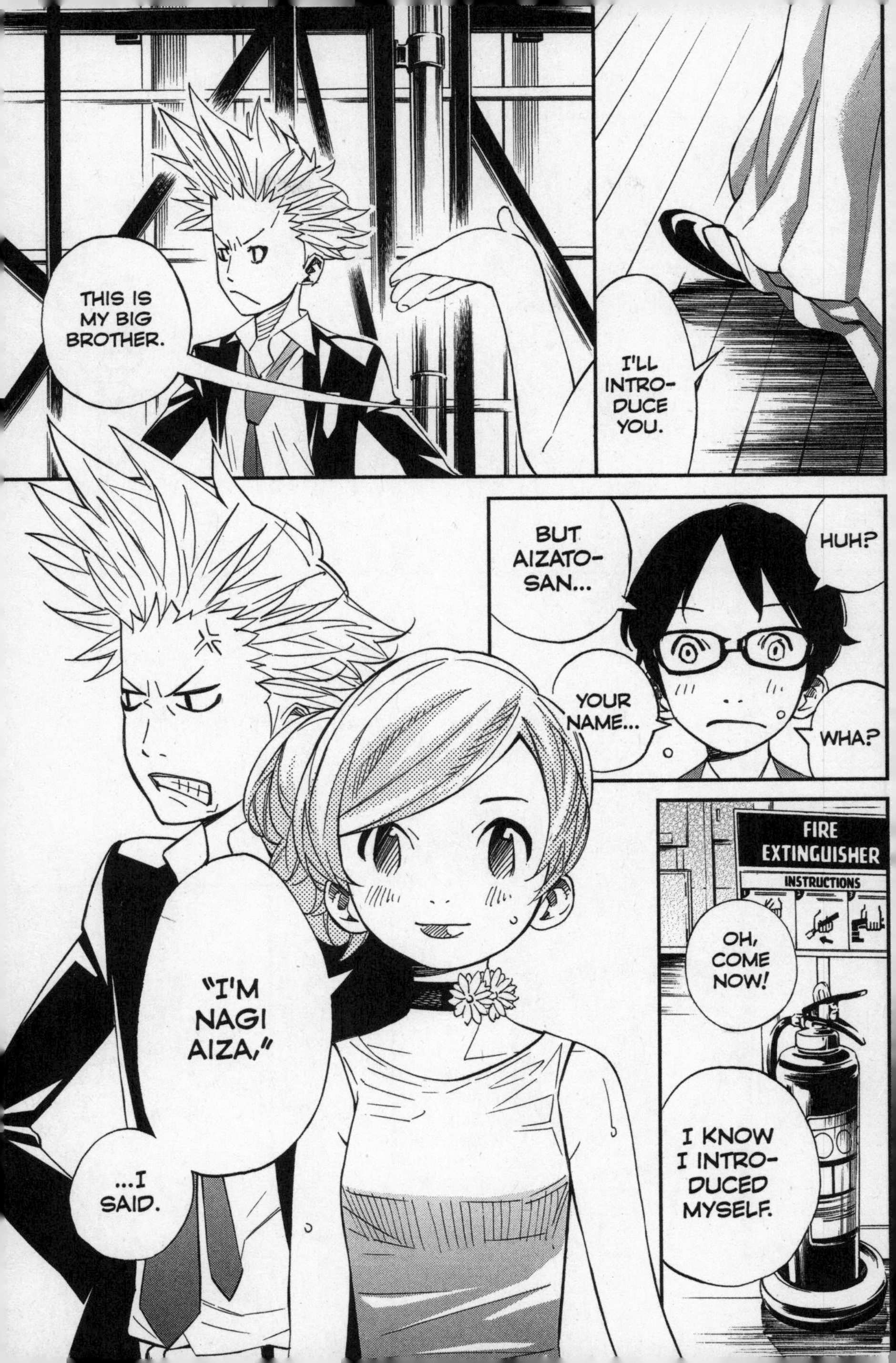
I'LL INTRO-DUCE YOU.
THIS IS MY BIG BROTHER.
HUH?
BUT AIZATO-SAN...
WHA?
YOUR NAME...
FIRE EXTINGUISHER
INSTRUCTIONS
OH, COME NOW!
I KNOW I INTRO-DUCED MYSELF.
"I'M NAGI AIZA,"
...I SAID.

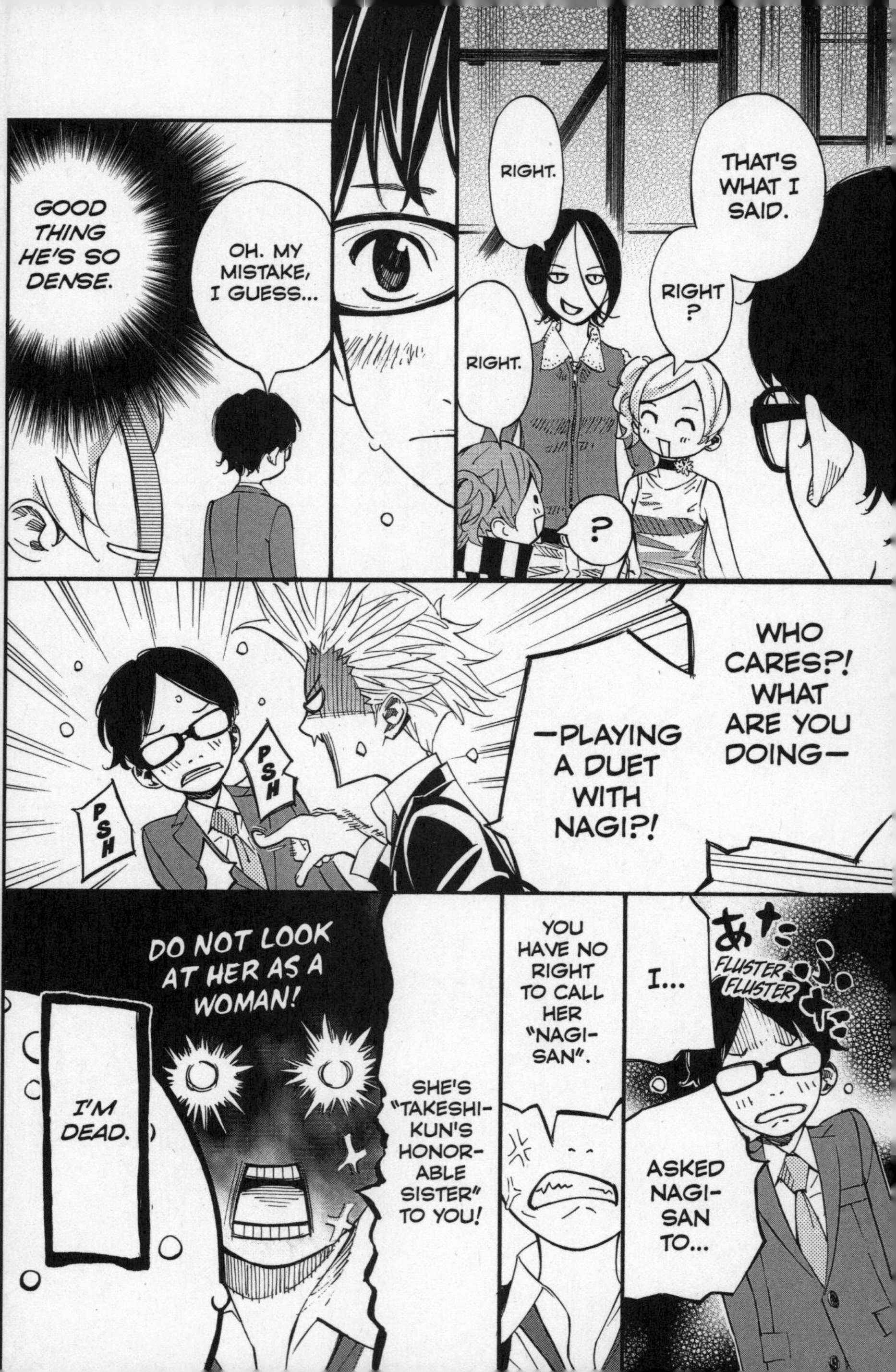

THAT'S WHAT I SAID.
RIGHT.
RIGHT?
RIGHT.
?
OH. MY MISTAKE, I GUESS...
GOOD THING HE'S SO DENSE.
WHO CARES?! WHAT ARE YOU DOING—
—PLAYING A DUET WITH NAGI?!
PSH
PSH
FLUSTER FLUSTER
I...
ASKED NAGI-SAN TO...
YOU HAVE NO RIGHT TO CALL HER "NAGI-SAN".
SHE'S "TAKESHI-KUN'S HONORABLE SISTER" TO YOU!
DO NOT LOOK AT HER AS A WOMAN!
I'M DEAD.

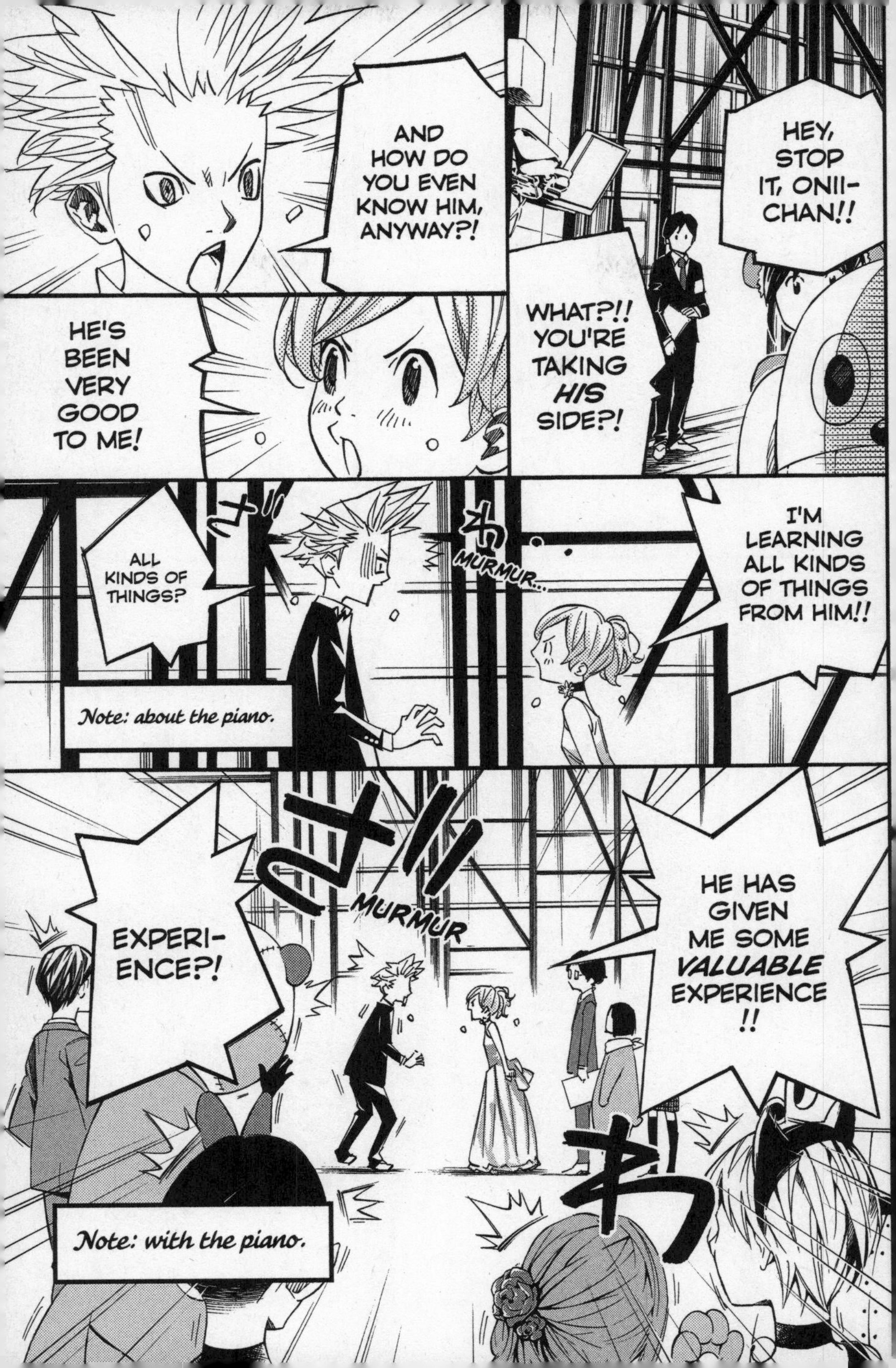
HEY, STOP IT, ONII-CHAN!!
WHAT?!! YOU'RE TAKING *HIS* SIDE?!
AND HOW DO YOU EVEN KNOW HIM, ANYWAY?!
HE'S BEEN VERY GOOD TO ME!
I'M LEARNING ALL KINDS OF THINGS FROM HIM!!
MURMUR...
ALL KINDS OF THINGS?
Note: about the piano.
HE HAS GIVEN ME SOME *VALUABLE* EXPERIENCE!!
MURMUR
EXPERI-ENCE?!
Note: with the piano.

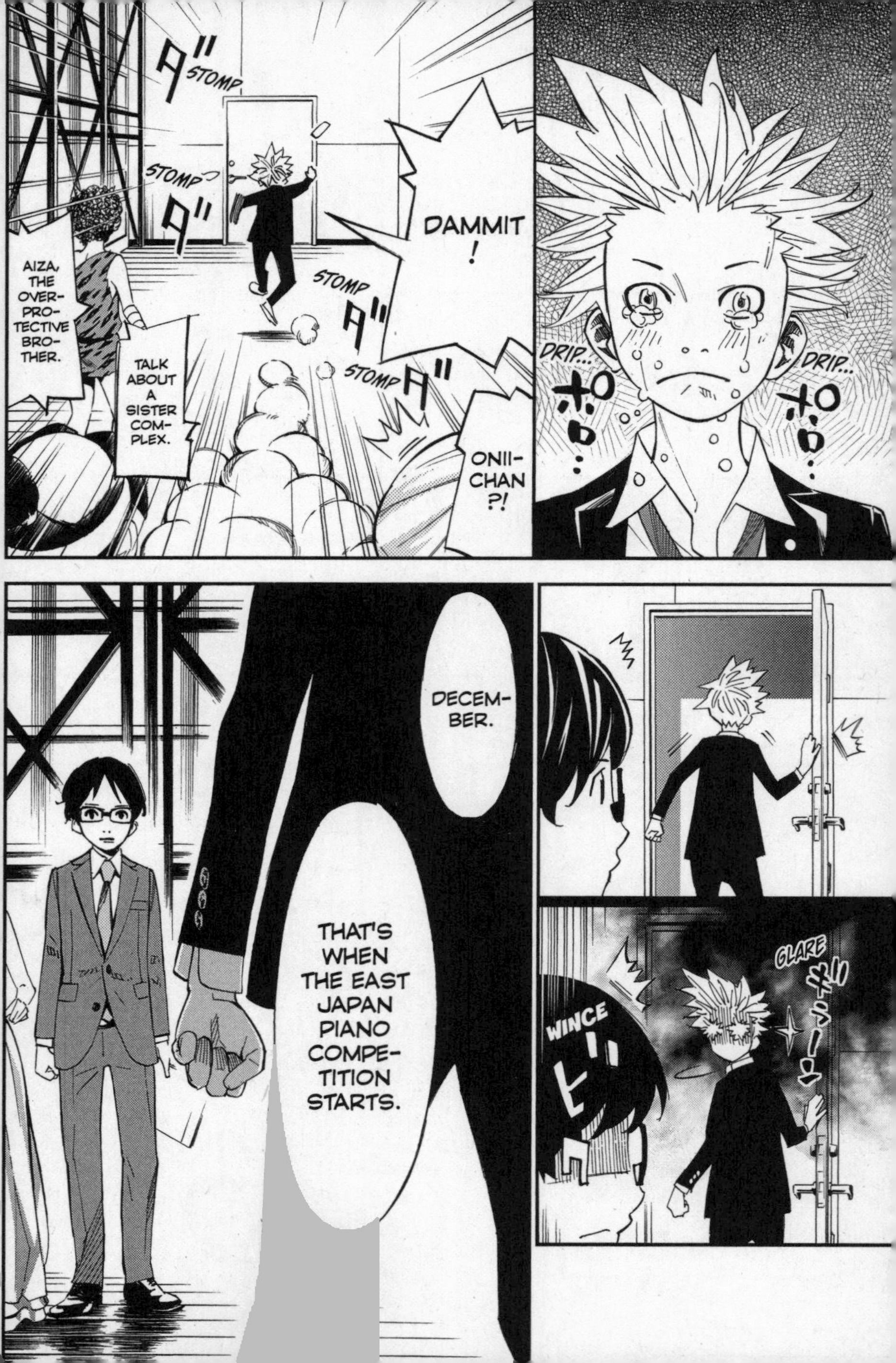
DRIP...
DRIP...
DAMMIT!
ONII-CHAN?!
STOMP
STOMP
STOMP
STOMP
AIZA, THE OVER-PROTECTIVE BRO-THER.
TALK ABOUT A SISTER COM-PLEX.
GLARE
WINCE
DECEM-BER.
THAT'S WHEN THE EAST JAPAN PIANO COMPE-TITION STARTS.

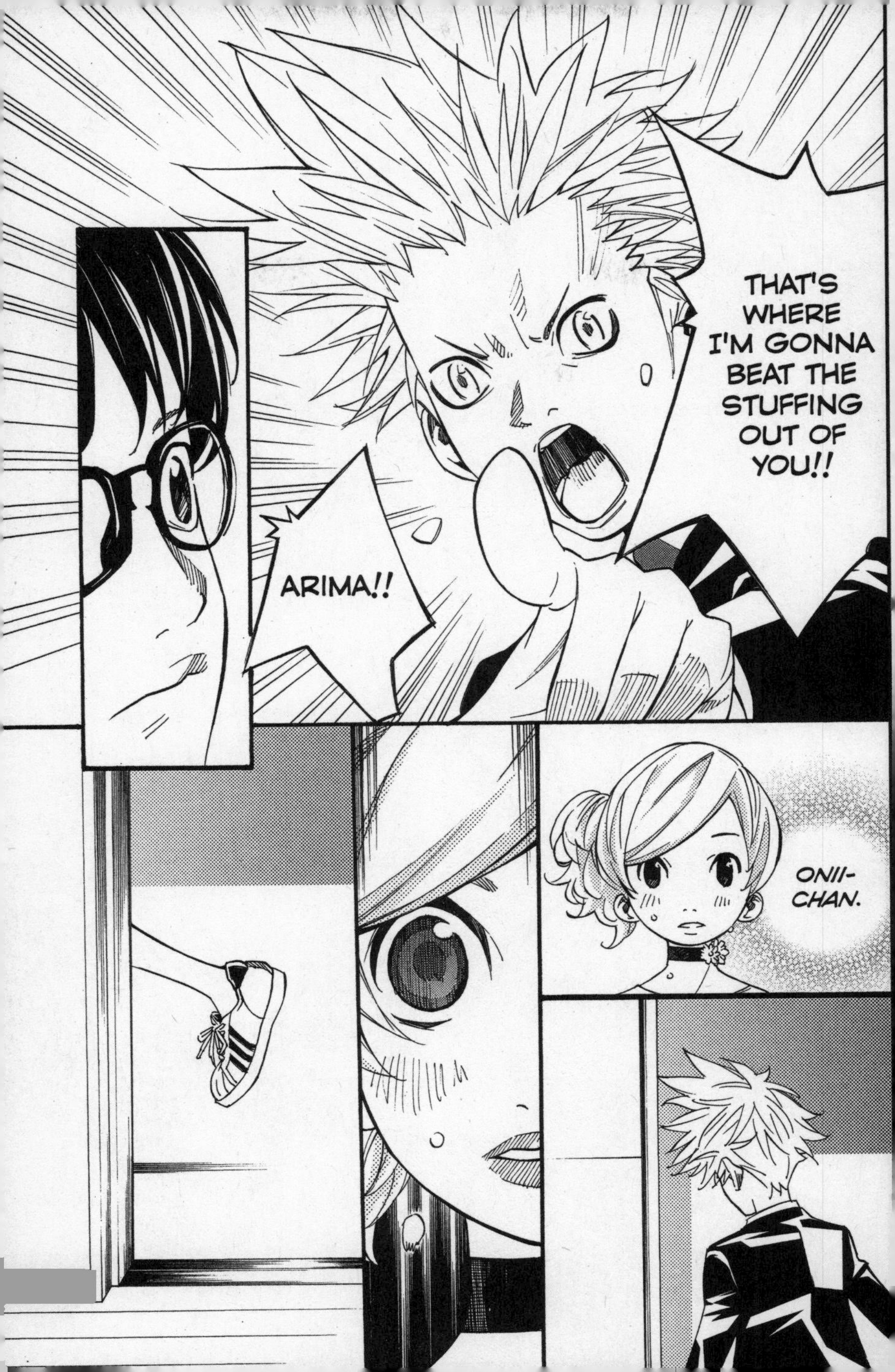
THAT'S WHERE I'M GONNA BEAT THE STUFFING OUT OF YOU!!
ARIMA!!
ONII-CHAN.

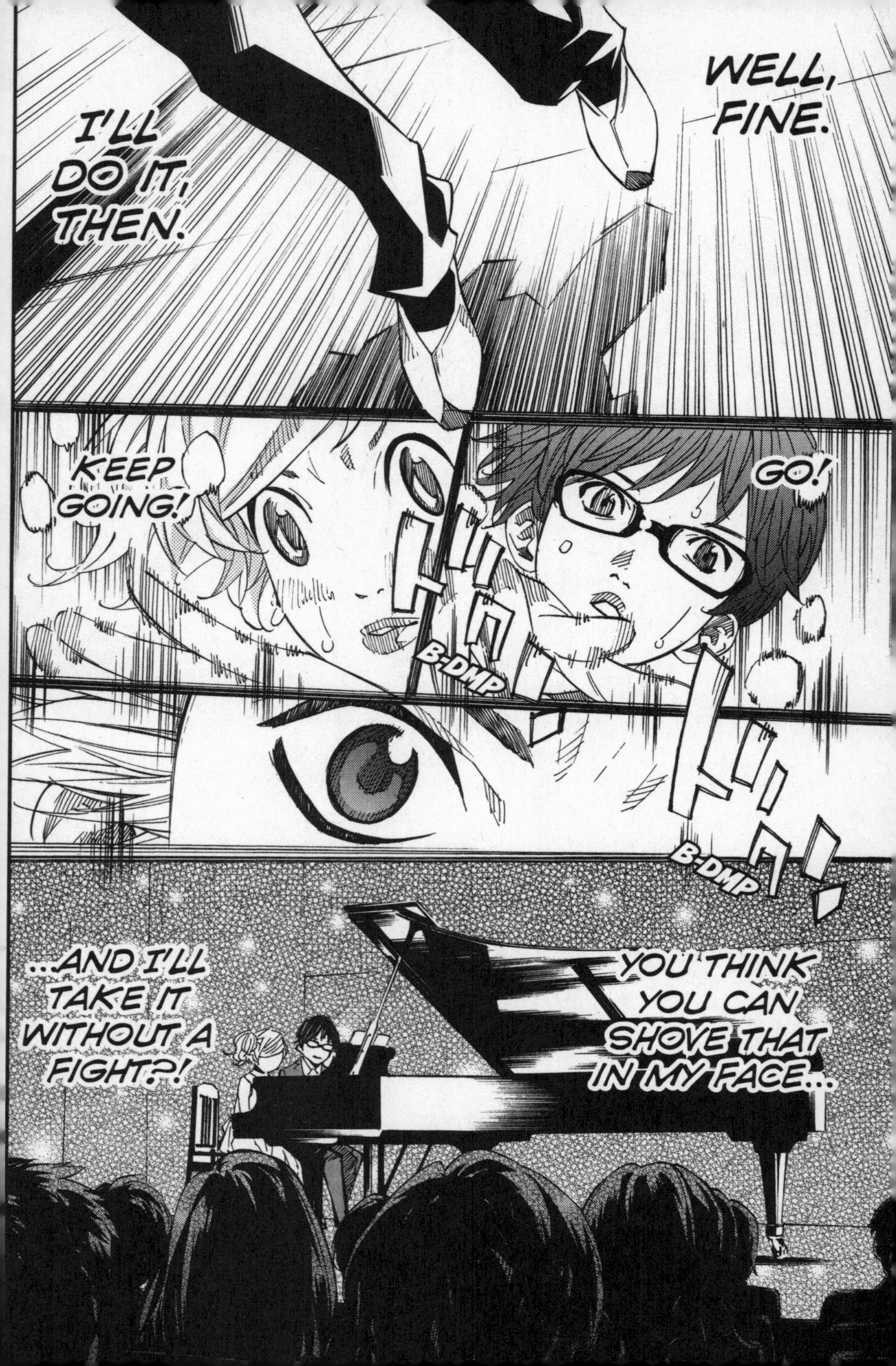
WELL, FINE.
I'LL DO IT, THEN.
GO!
B-DMP
KEEP GOING!
B-DMP
YOU THINK YOU CAN SHOVE THAT IN MY FACE...
...AND I'LL TAKE IT WITHOUT A FIGHT?!

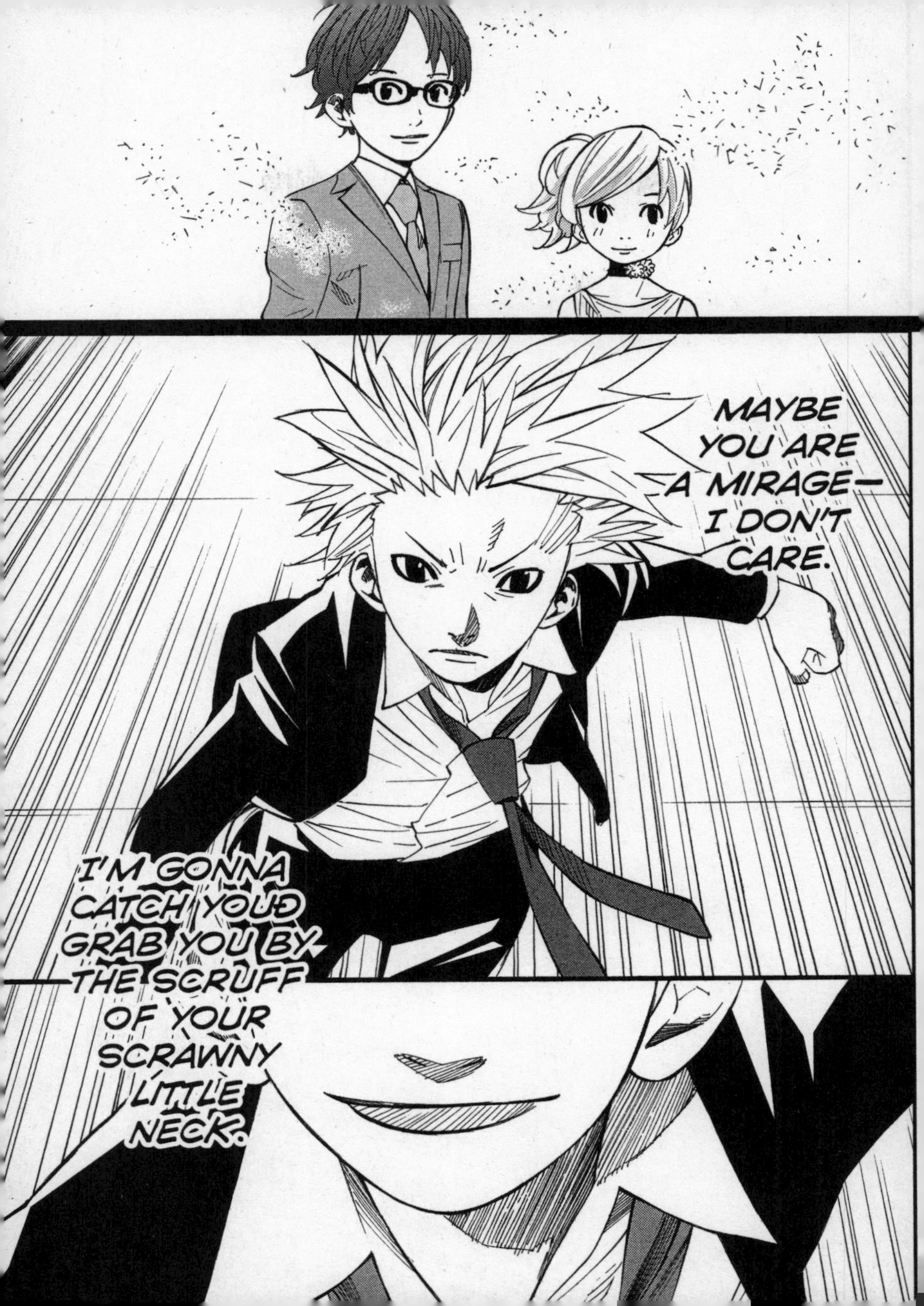
MAYBE YOU ARE A MIRAGE— I DON'T CARE.
I'M GONNA CATCH YOU & GRAB YOU BY THE SCRUFF OF YOUR SCRAWNY LITTLE NECK.

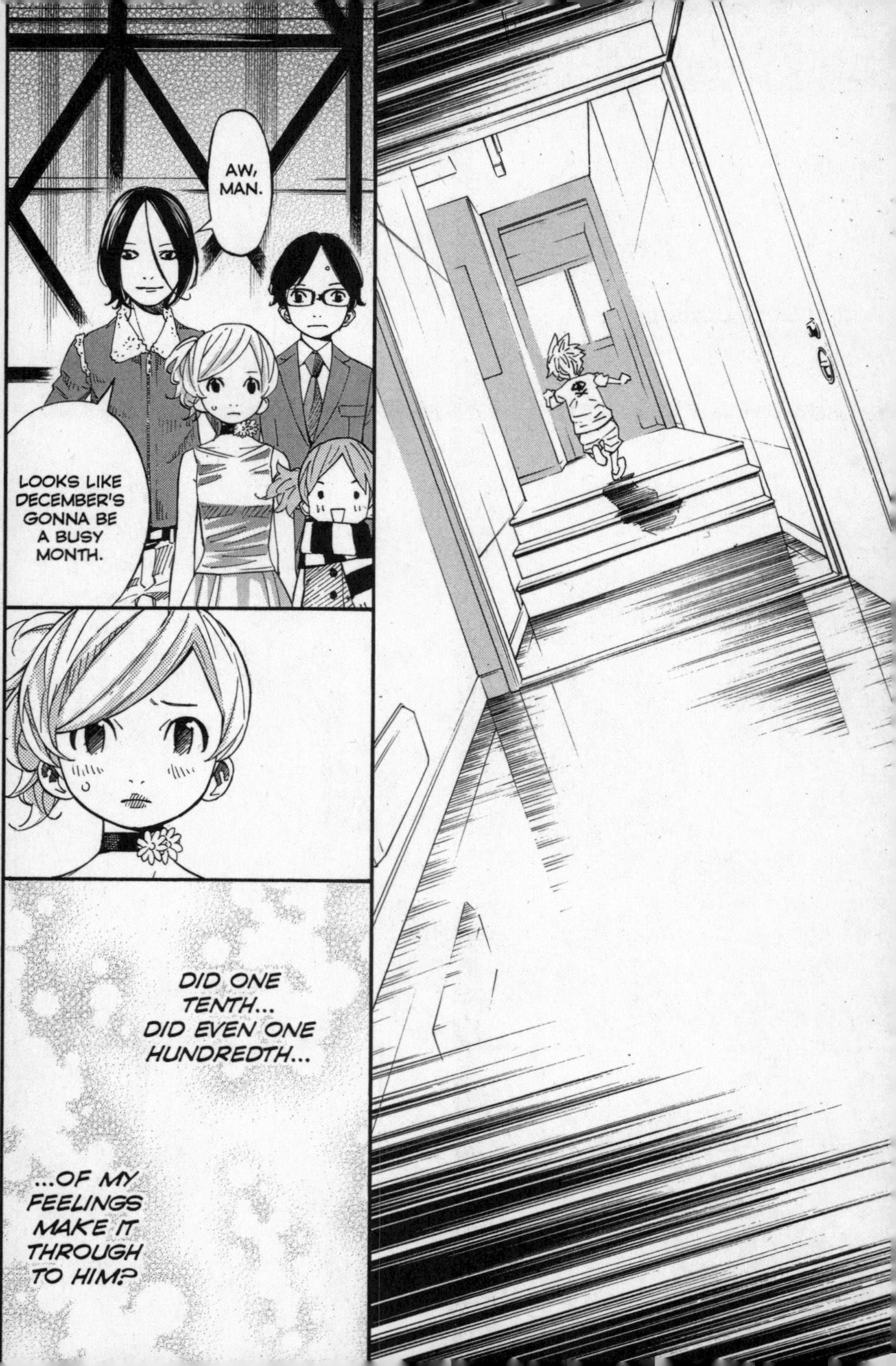
AW, MAN.
LOOKS LIKE DECEMBER'S GONNA BE A BUSY MONTH.
DID ONE TENTH... DID EVEN ONE HUNDREDTH...
...OF MY FEELINGS MAKE IT THROUGH TO HIM?

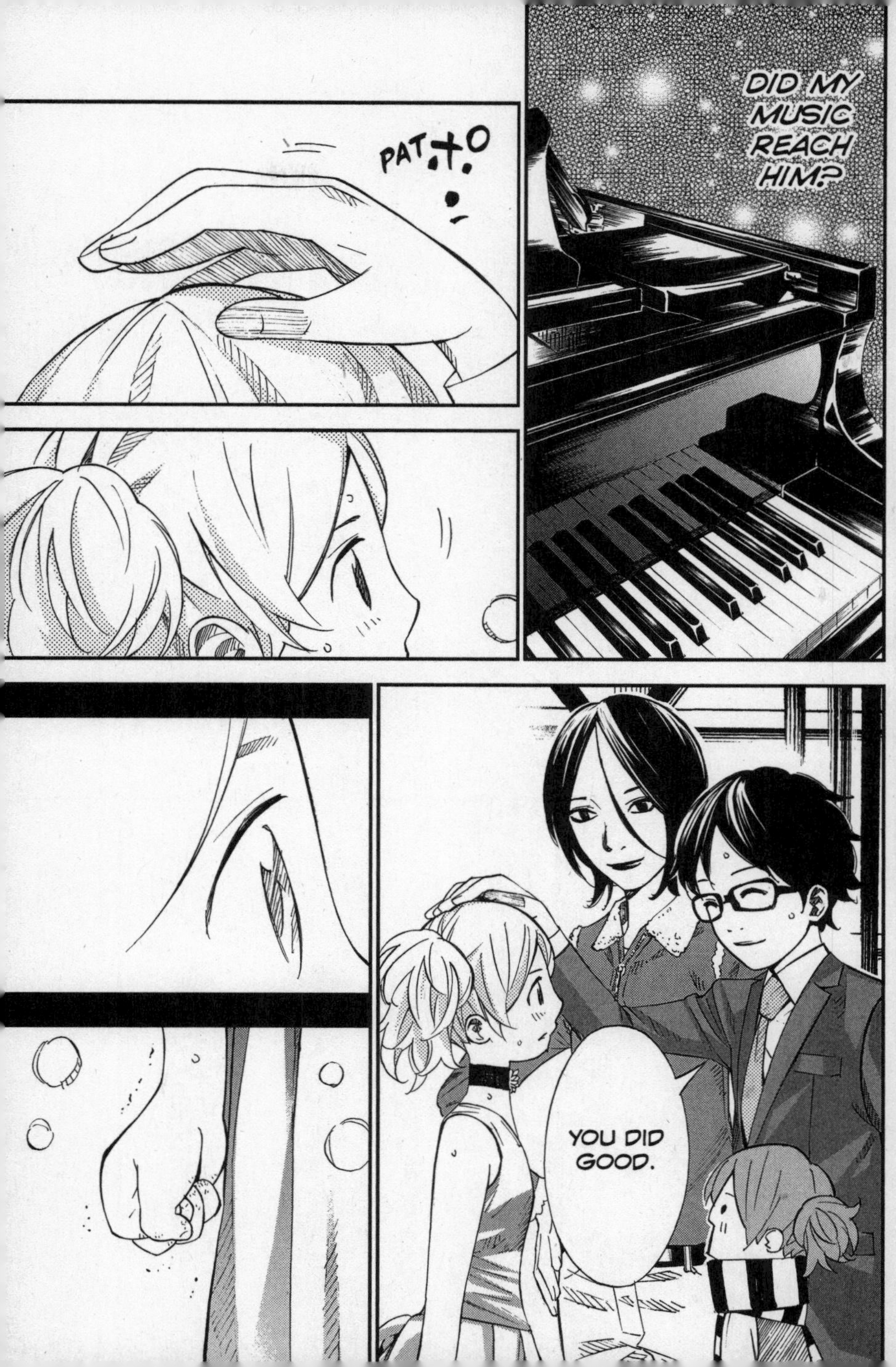

DID MY MUSIC REACH HIM?
PAT
YOU DID GOOD.

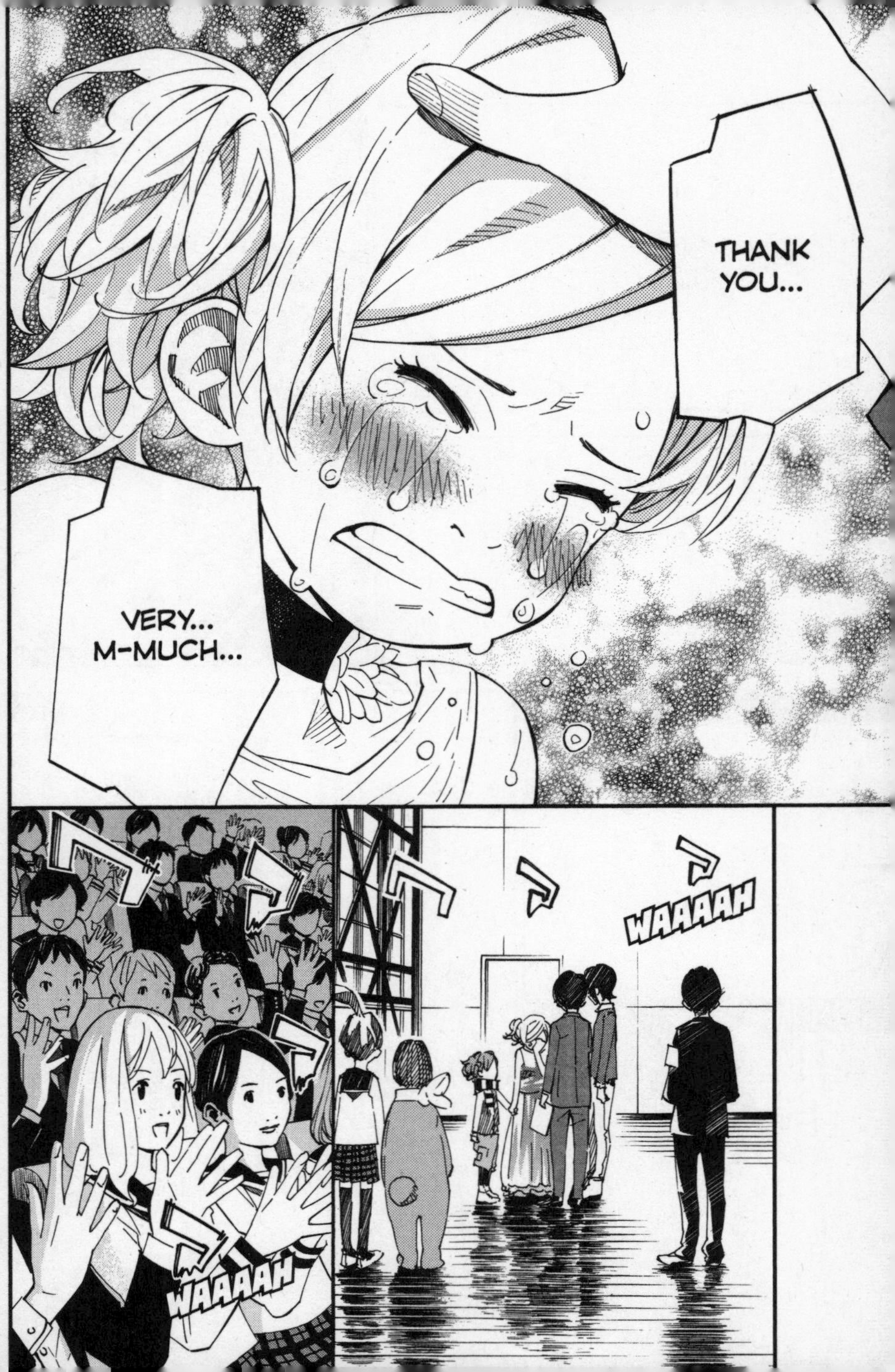
THANK YOU...
VERY... M-MUCH...
WAAAAH
WAAAAH

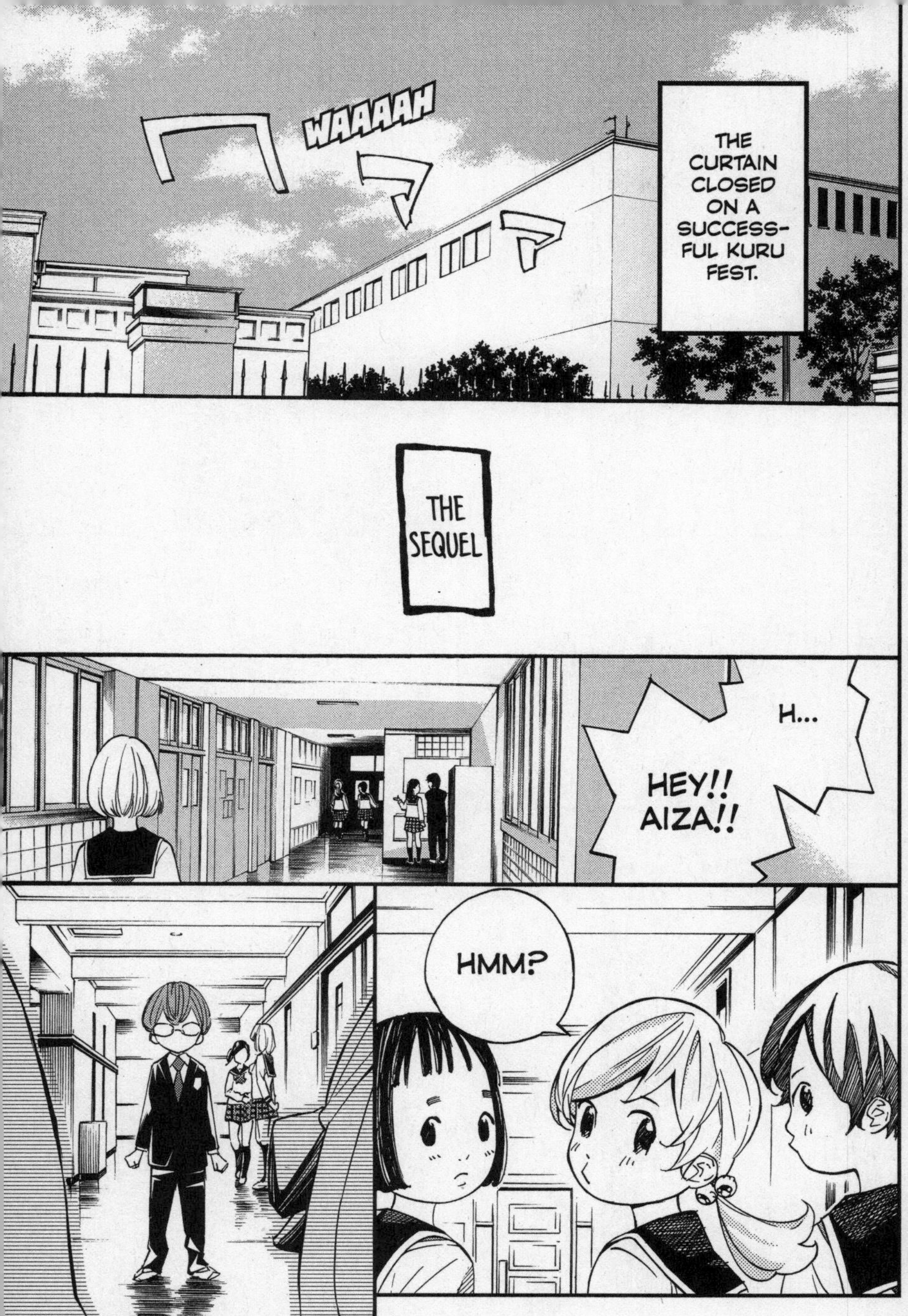
THE CURTAIN CLOSED ON A SUCCESS-FUL KURU FEST.
WAAAAH
THE SEQUEL
H...
HEY!! AIZA!!
HMM?

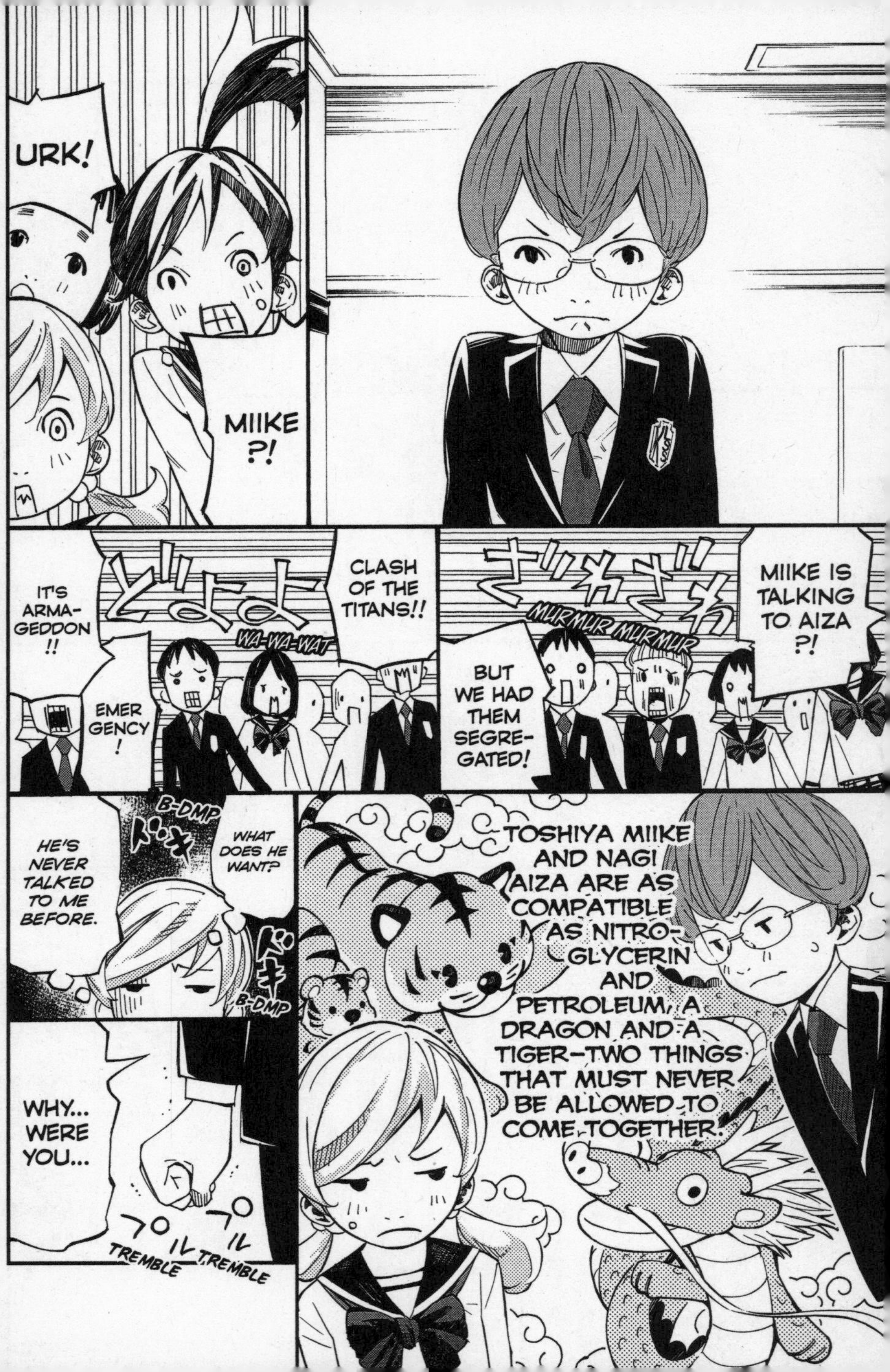
URK!
MIIKE ?!
MIIKE IS TALKING TO AIZA ?!
ざわざわ
MURMUR MURMUR
BUT WE HAD THEM SEGREGATED!
CLASH OF THE TITANS!!
どよよ
WA-WA-WAT
IT'S ARMAGEDDON !!
EMERGENCY !
TOSHIYA MIIKE AND NAGI AIZA ARE AS COMPATIBLE AS NITRO-GLYCERIN AND PETROLEUM, A DRAGON AND A TIGER—TWO THINGS THAT MUST NEVER BE ALLOWED TO COME TOGETHER.
WHAT DOES HE WANT?
ドキ
B-DMP
HE'S NEVER TALKED TO ME BEFORE.
ドキ
B-DMP
WHY... WERE YOU...
プル プル
TREMBLE TREMBLE

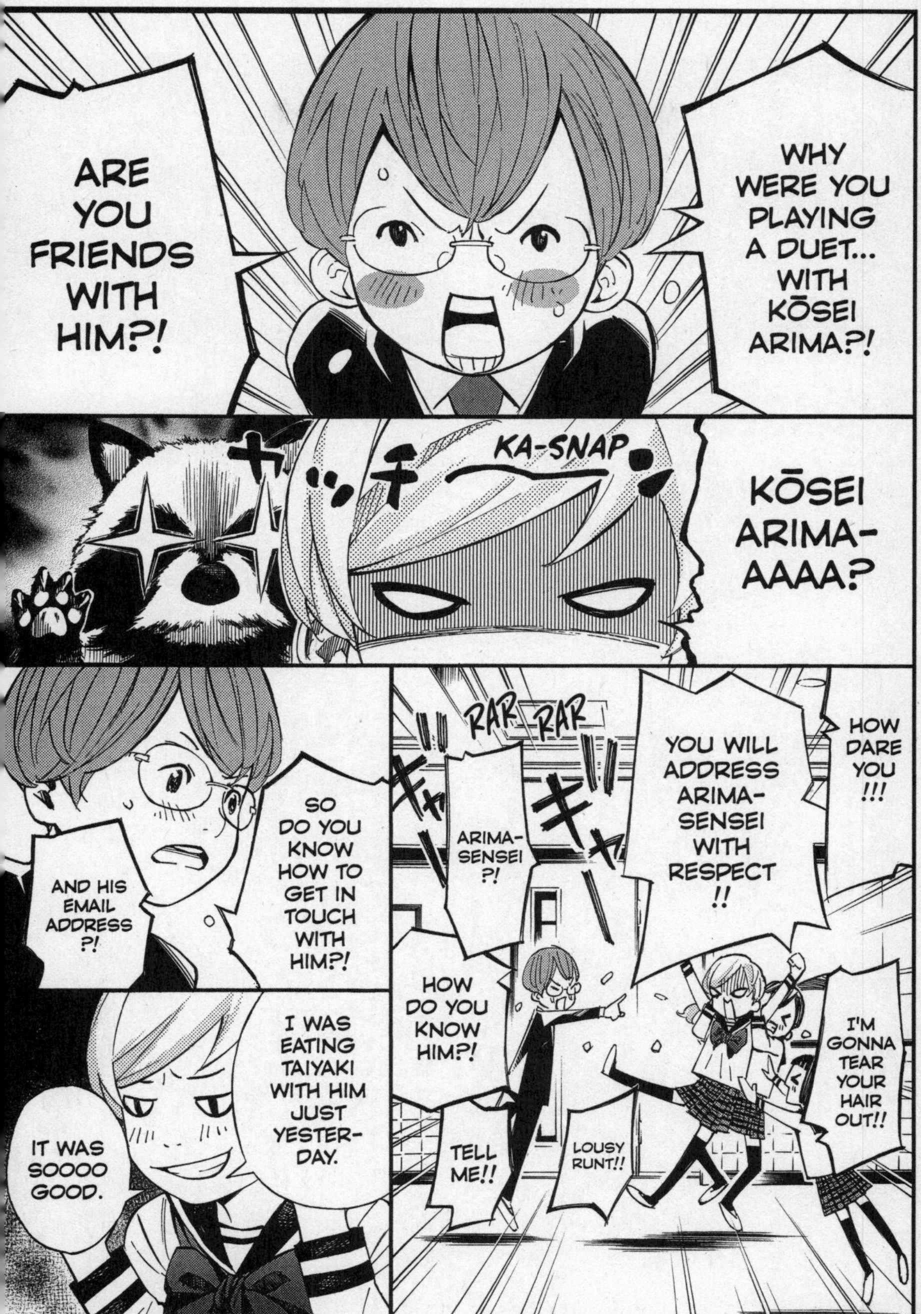
WHY WERE YOU PLAYING A DUET... WITH KŌSEI ARIMA?!
ARE YOU FRIENDS WITH HIM?!
KŌSEI ARIMA-AAAA?
KA-SNAP
HOW DARE YOU!!!
YOU WILL ADDRESS ARIMA-SENSEI WITH RESPECT!!
RAR RAR
ARIMA-SENSEI?!
HOW DO YOU KNOW HIM?!
I'M GONNA TEAR YOUR HAIR OUT!!
LOUSY RUNT!!
TELL ME!!
SO DO YOU KNOW HOW TO GET IN TOUCH WITH HIM?!
AND HIS EMAIL ADDRESS?!
I WAS EATING TAIYAKI WITH HIM JUST YESTER-DAY.
IT WAS SOOOO GOOD.

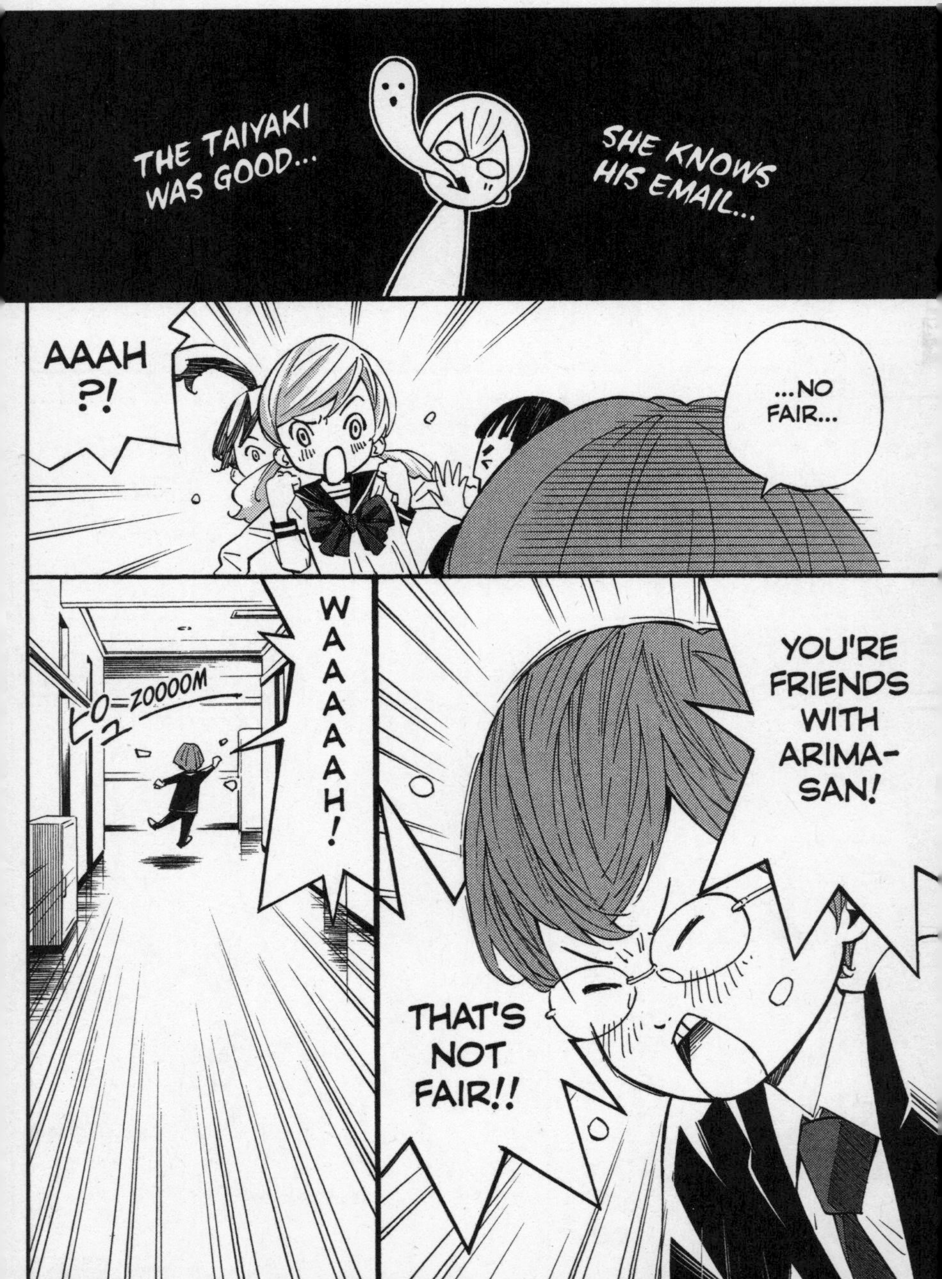
SHE KNOWS HIS EMAIL...
THE TAIYAKI WAS GOOD...
...NO FAIR...
AAAH ?!
YOU'RE FRIENDS WITH ARIMA-SAN!
THAT'S NOT FAIR!!
WAAAAAAH!
ZOOOOM

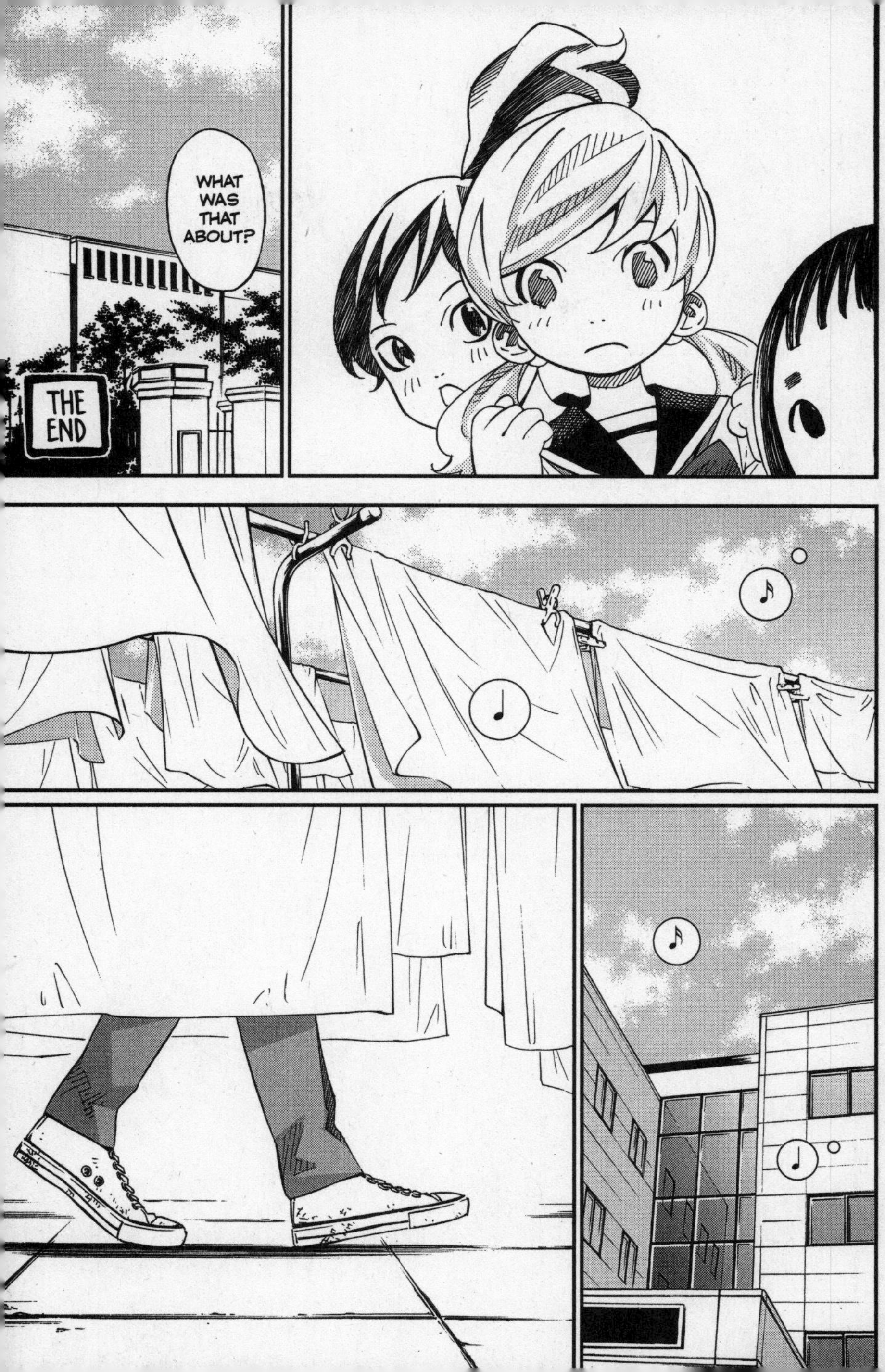
WHAT WAS THAT ABOUT?
THE END

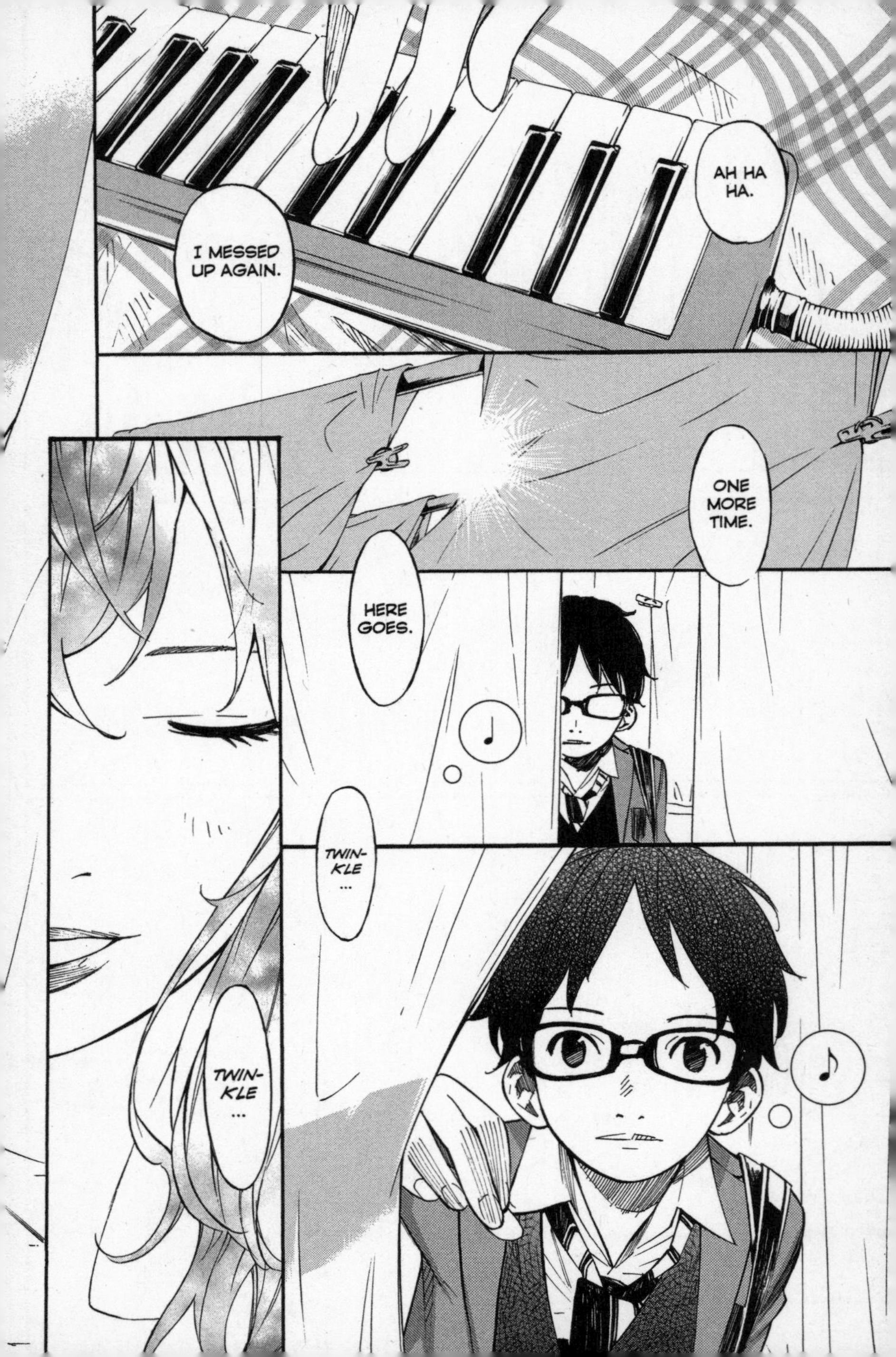
AH HA HA.
I MESSED UP AGAIN.
ONE MORE TIME.
HERE GOES.
TWIN-KLE ...
TWIN-KLE ...

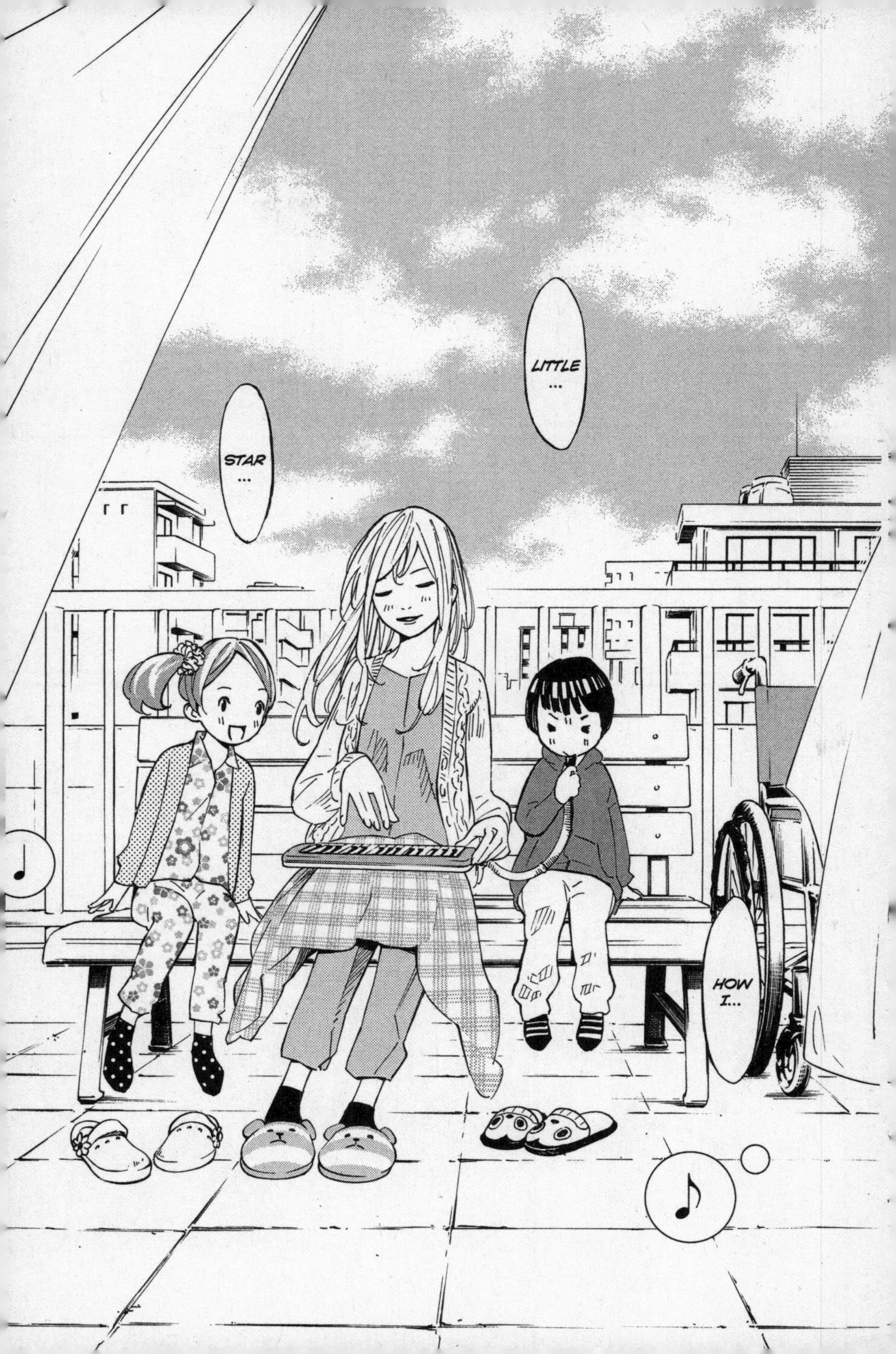
LITTLE ...
STAR ...
HOW I...

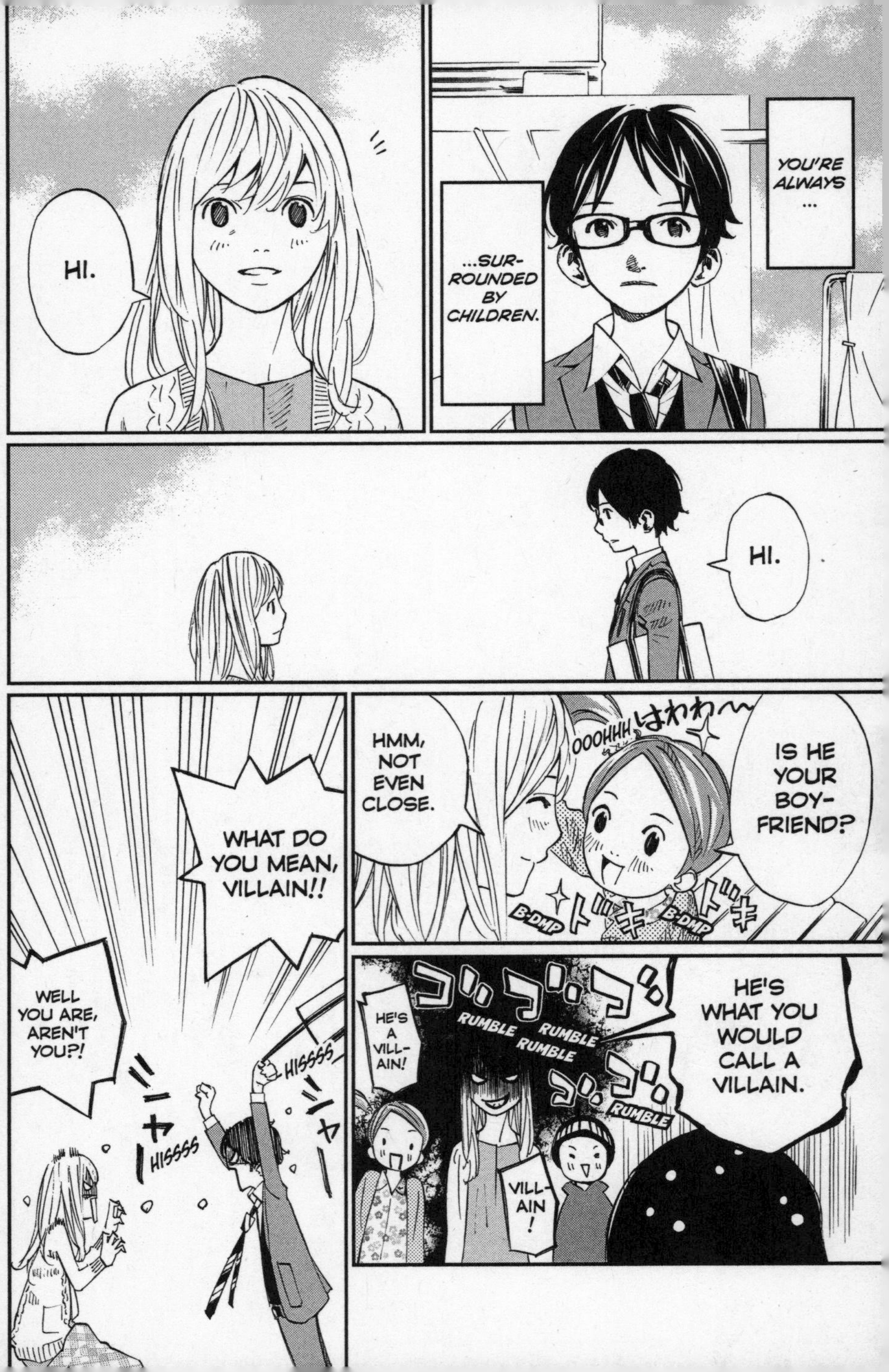
YOU'RE ALWAYS ...
...SUR-ROUNDED BY CHILDREN.
HI.
HI.
IS HE YOUR BOY-FRIEND?
OOOHHH はわわ〜
HMM, NOT EVEN CLOSE.
B-DMP ドキ B-DMP ドキ
HE'S WHAT YOU WOULD CALL A VILLAIN.
ゴゴゴ RUMBLE RUMBLE RUMBLE
ゴゴ RUMBLE
HE'S A VILL-AIN!
VILL-AIN!
WHAT DO YOU MEAN, VILLAIN!!
WELL YOU ARE, AREN'T YOU?!
シャー HISSSS
シャー HISSSS

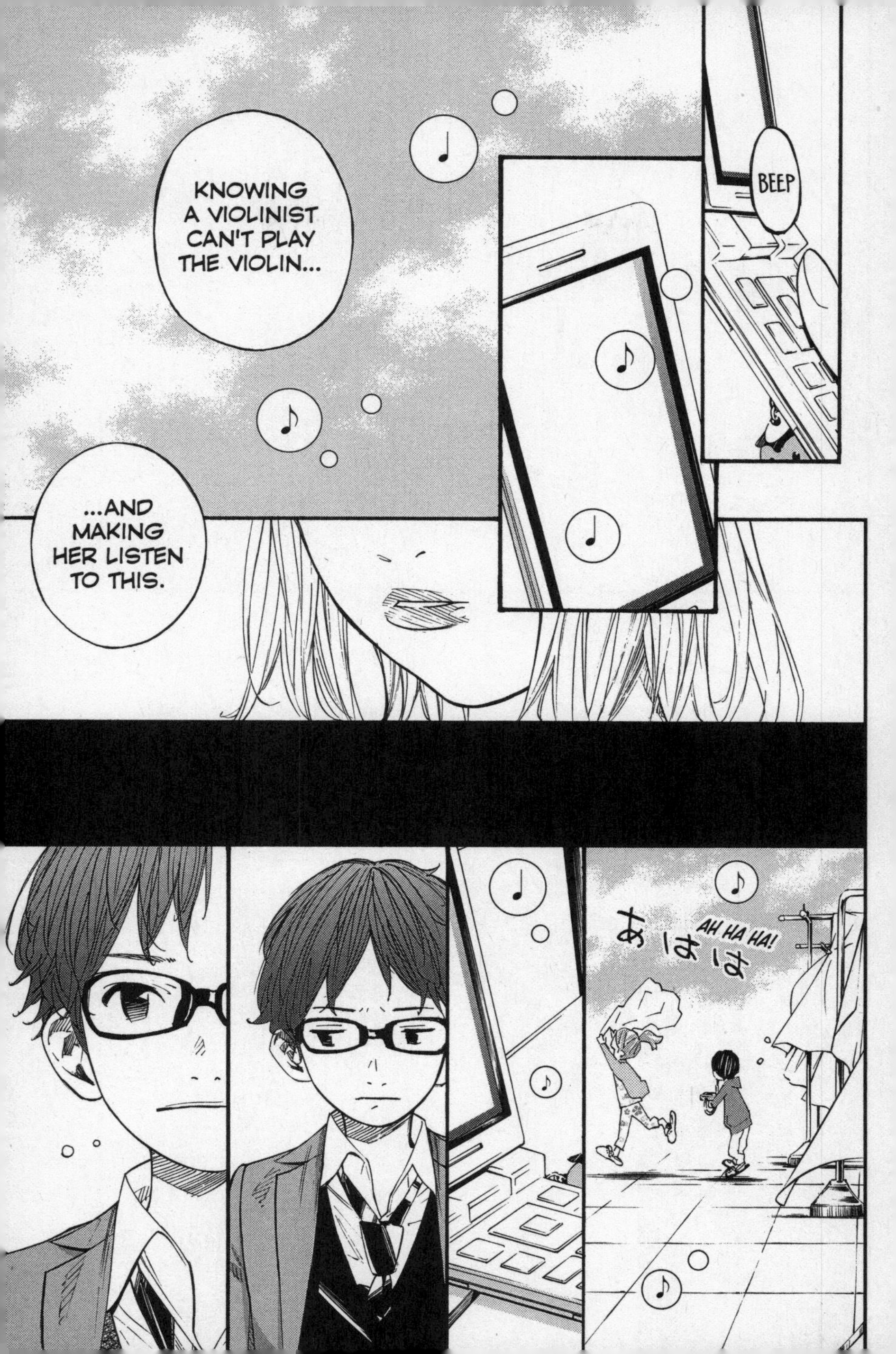
BEEP
KNOWING A VIOLINIST CAN'T PLAY THE VIOLIN...
...AND MAKING HER LISTEN TO THIS.
あはは
AH HA HA!

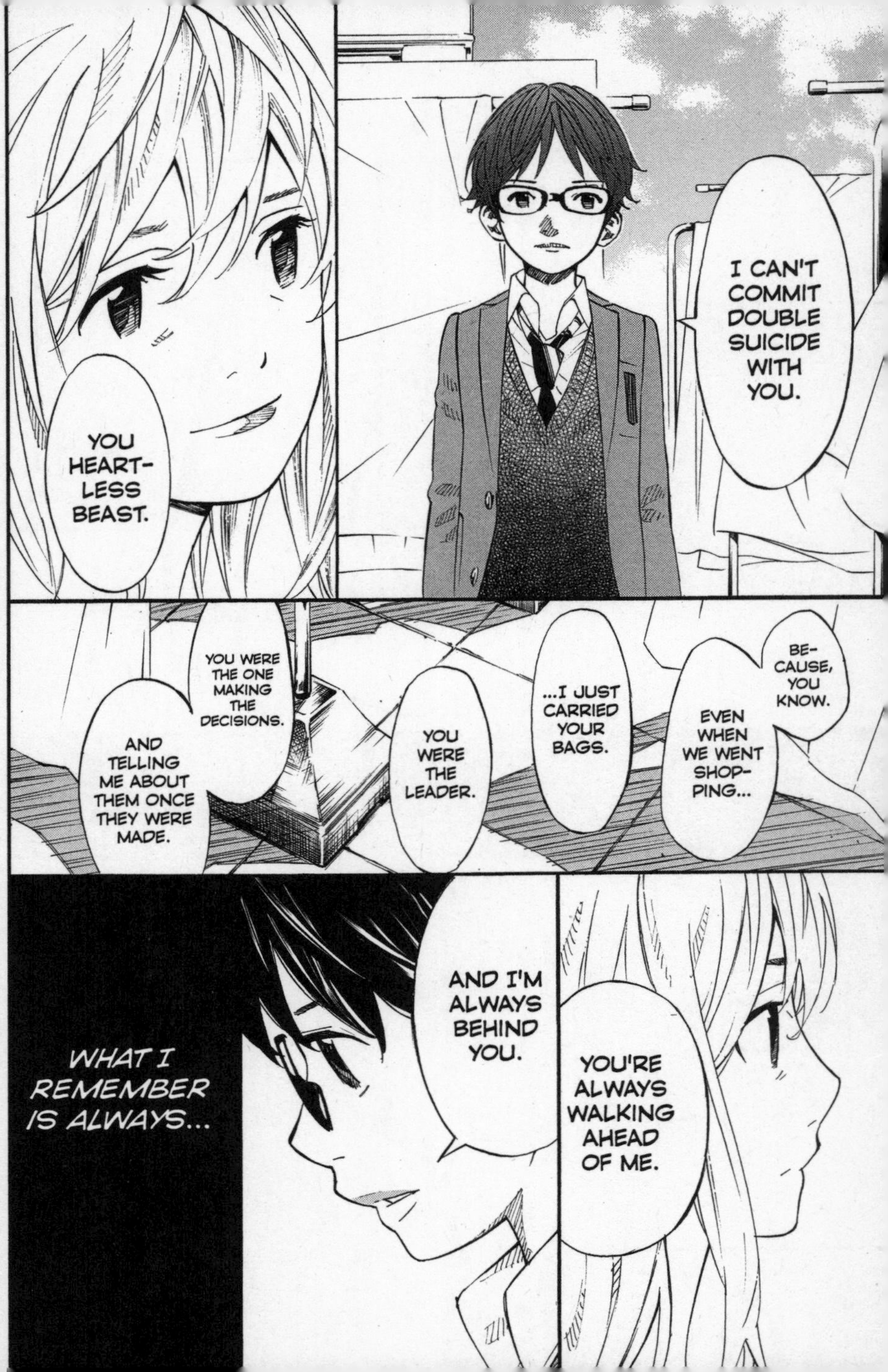
I CAN'T COMMIT DOUBLE SUICIDE WITH YOU.
YOU HEART-LESS BEAST.
BE-CAUSE, YOU KNOW.
EVEN WHEN WE WENT SHOP-PING...
...I JUST CARRIED YOUR BAGS.
YOU WERE THE LEADER.
YOU WERE THE ONE MAKING THE DECISIONS.
AND TELLING ME ABOUT THEM ONCE THEY WERE MADE.
YOU'RE ALWAYS WALKING AHEAD OF ME.
AND I'M ALWAYS BEHIND YOU.
WHAT I REMEMBER IS ALWAYS...

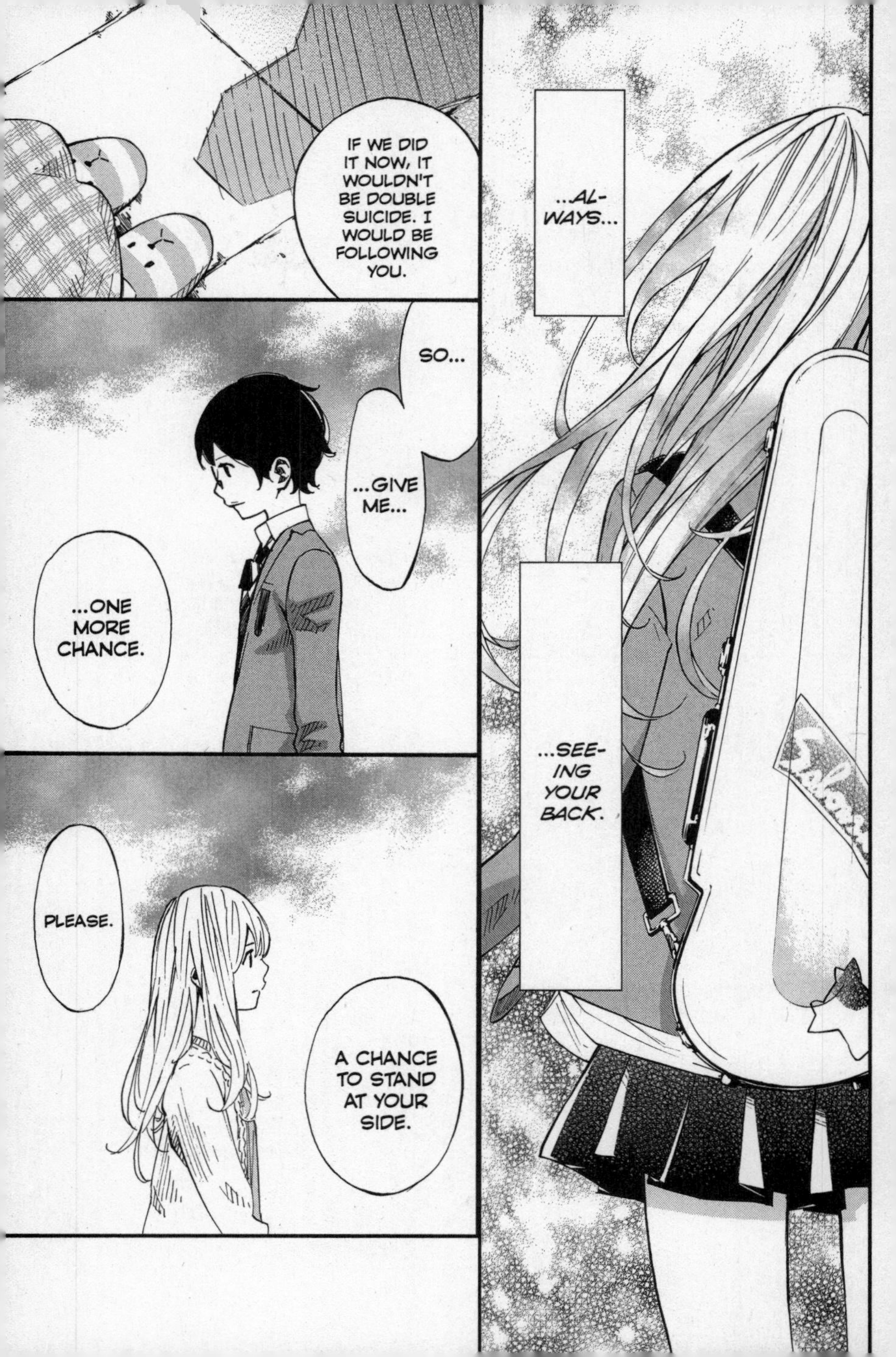
...AL-
WAYS...
...SEE-
ING
YOUR
BACK.
IF WE DID IT NOW, IT WOULDN'T BE DOUBLE SUICIDE. I WOULD BE FOLLOWING YOU.
SO...
...GIVE ME...
...ONE MORE CHANCE.
PLEASE.
A CHANCE TO STAND AT YOUR SIDE.

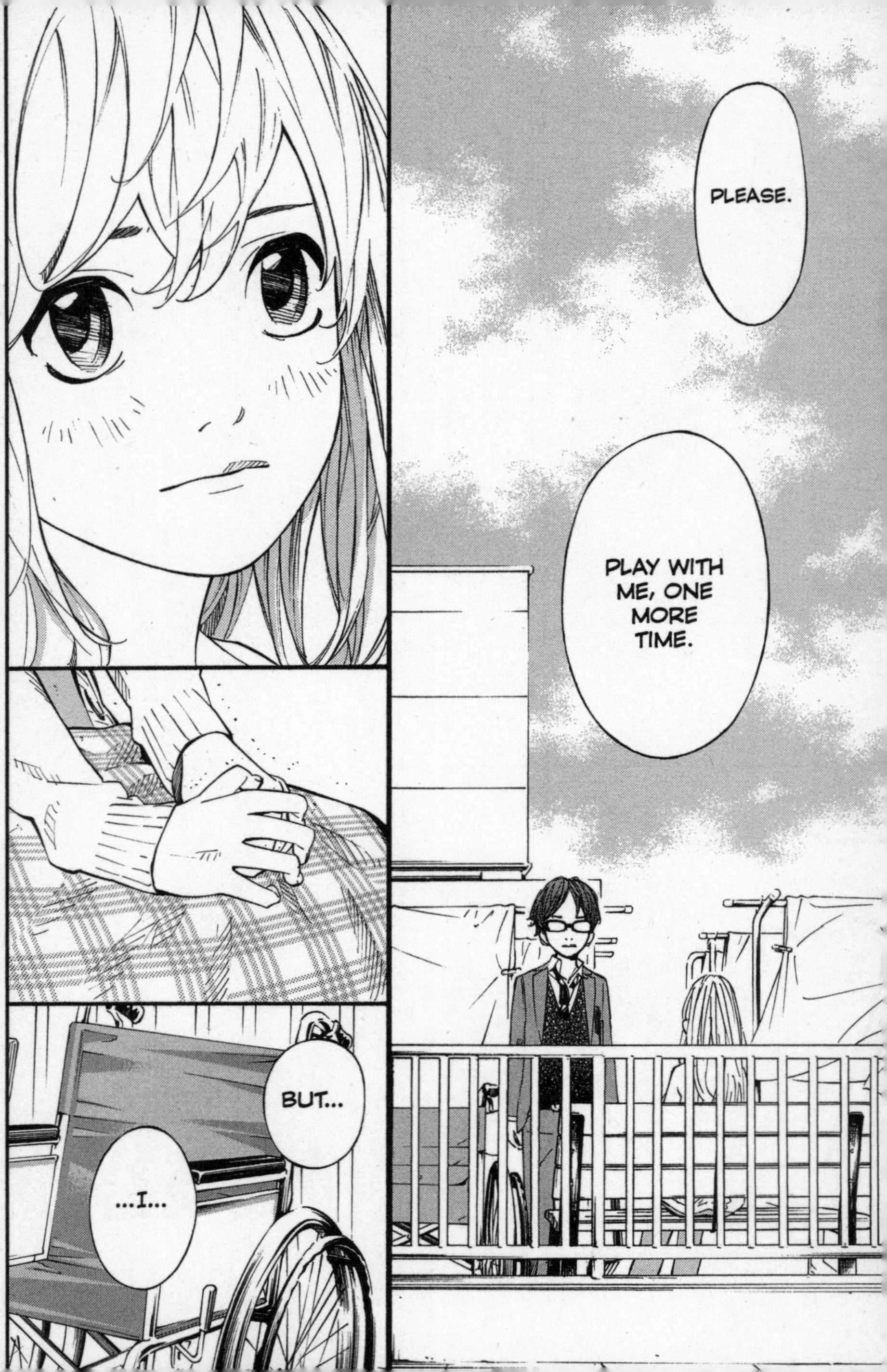
PLEASE.
PLAY WITH ME, ONE MORE TIME.
BUT...
...I...

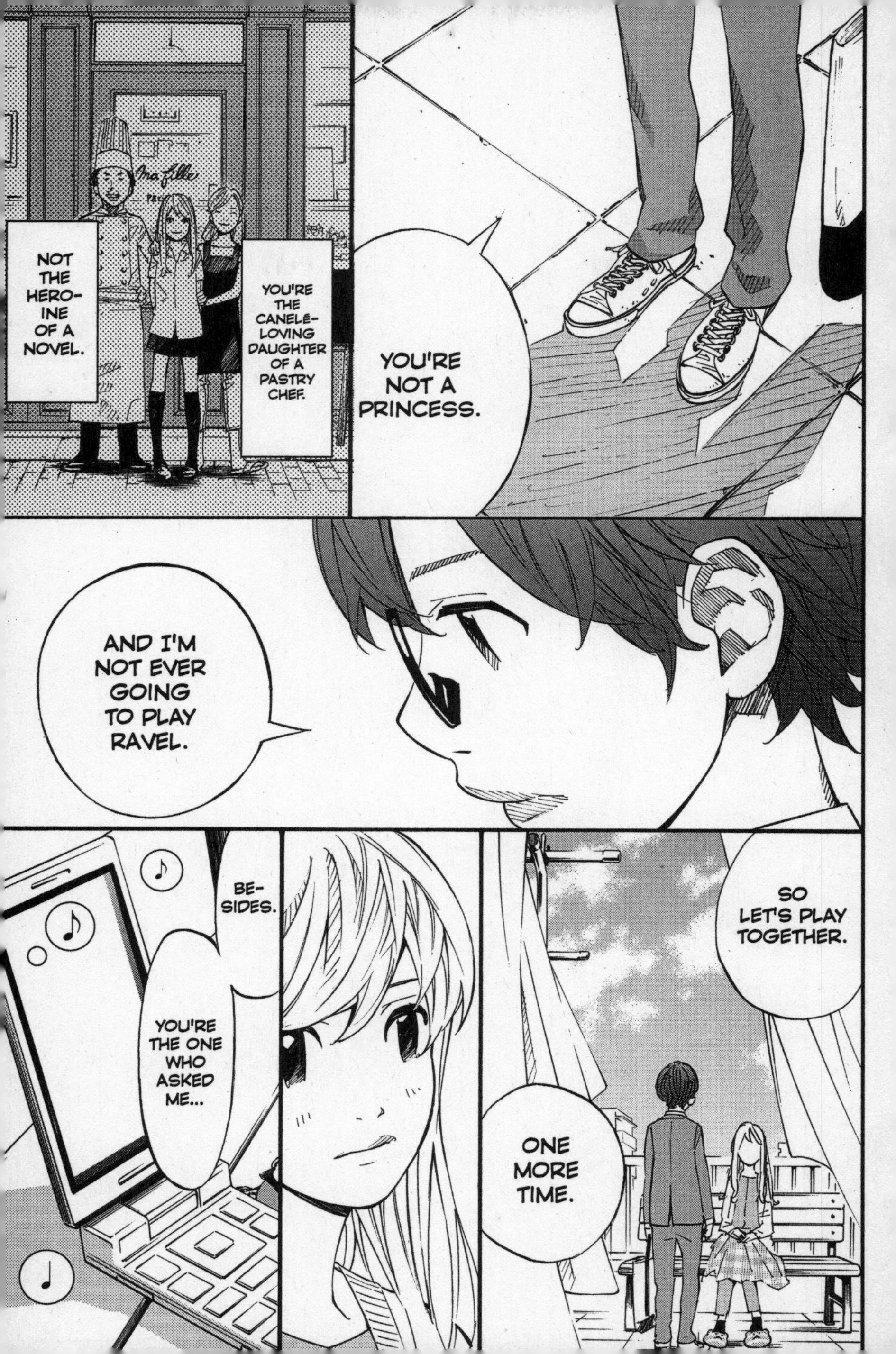

YOU'RE NOT A PRINCESS.
YOU'RE THE CANELÉ-LOVING DAUGHTER OF A PASTRY CHEF.
NOT THE HERO-INE OF A NOVEL.
AND I'M NOT EVER GOING TO PLAY RAVEL.
SO LET'S PLAY TOGETHER.
ONE MORE TIME.
BE-SIDES.
YOU'RE THE ONE WHO ASKED ME...

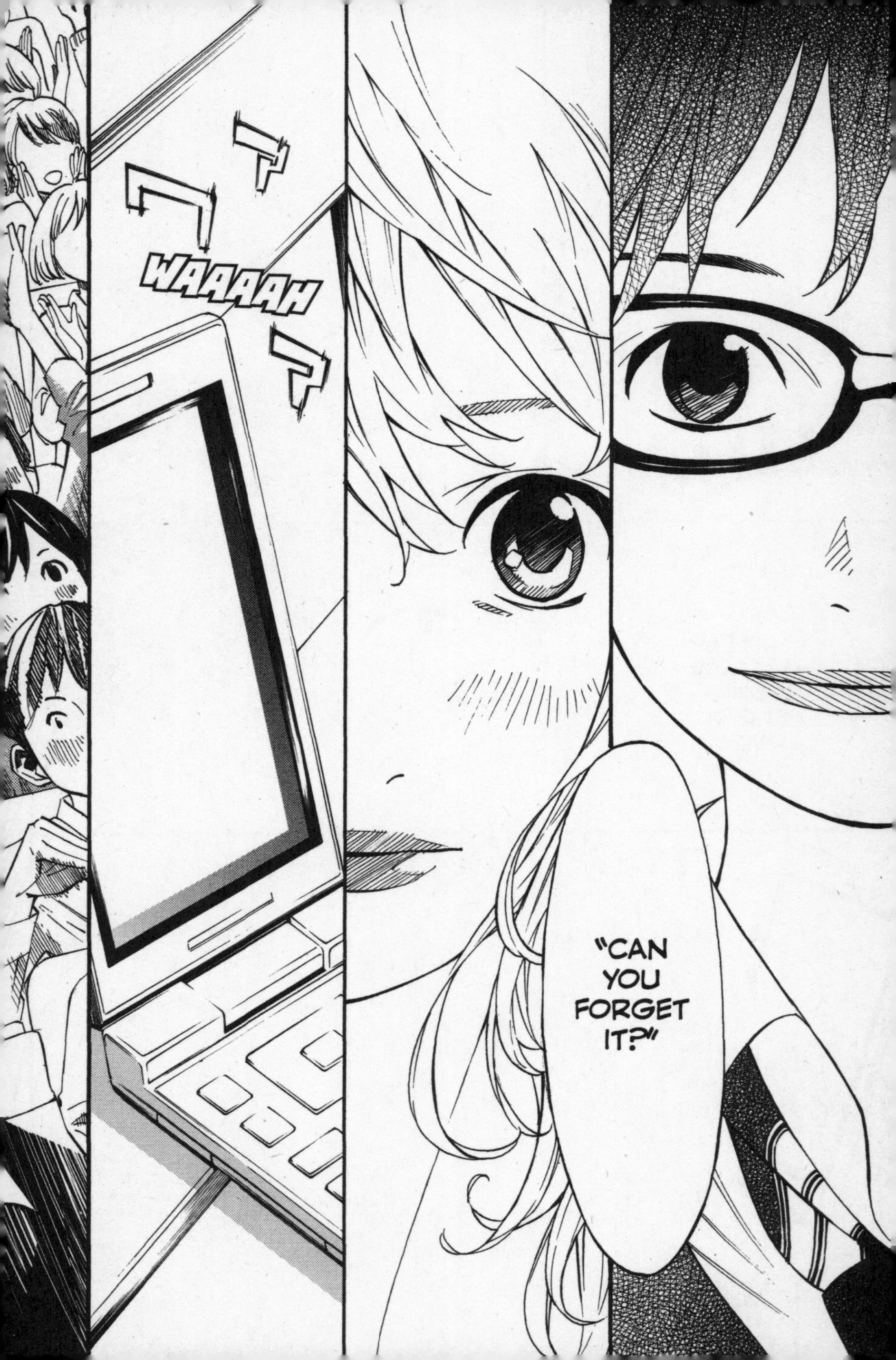
"CAN YOU FORGET IT?"
WAAAAH

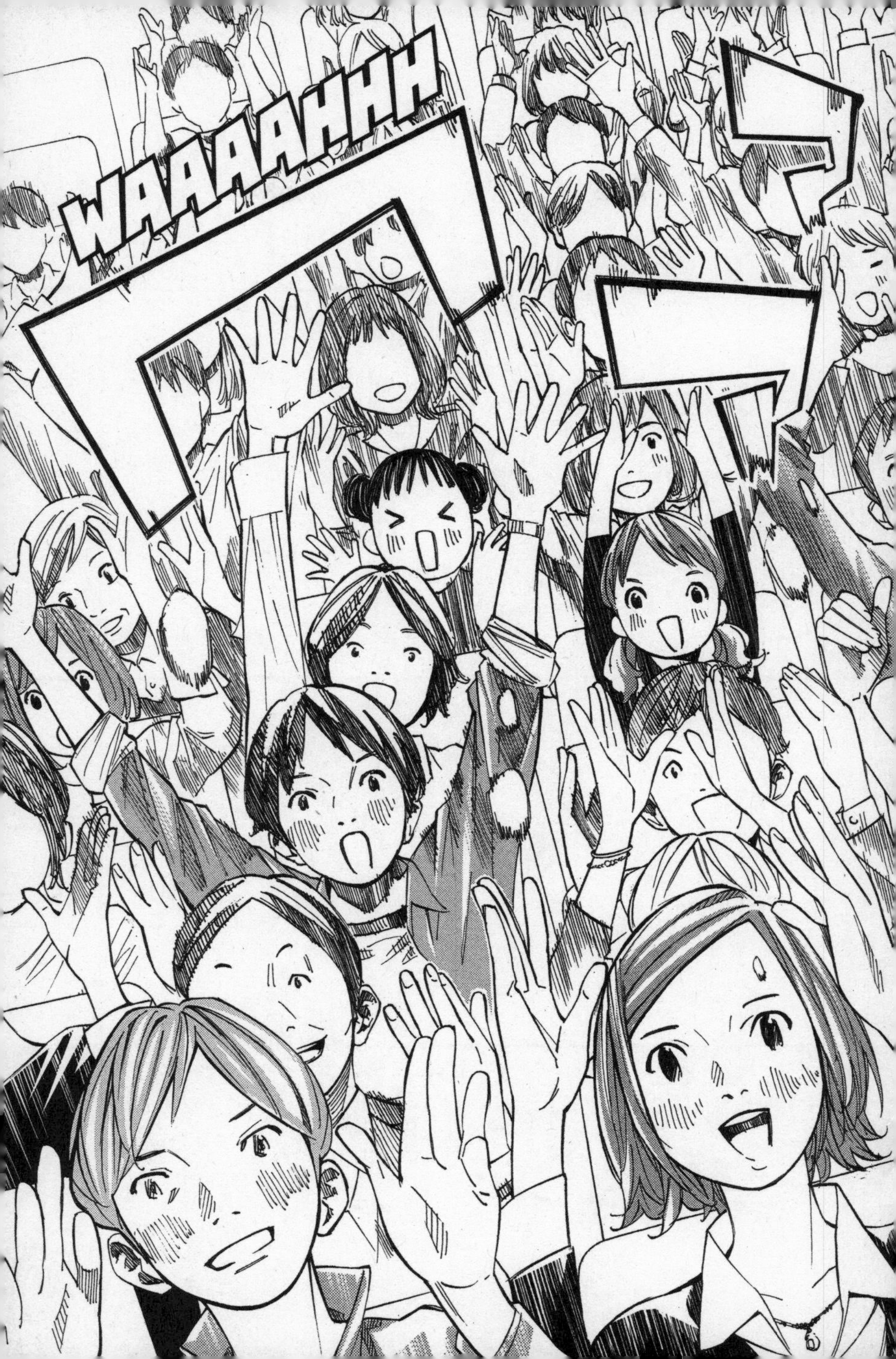
WAAAAHHH

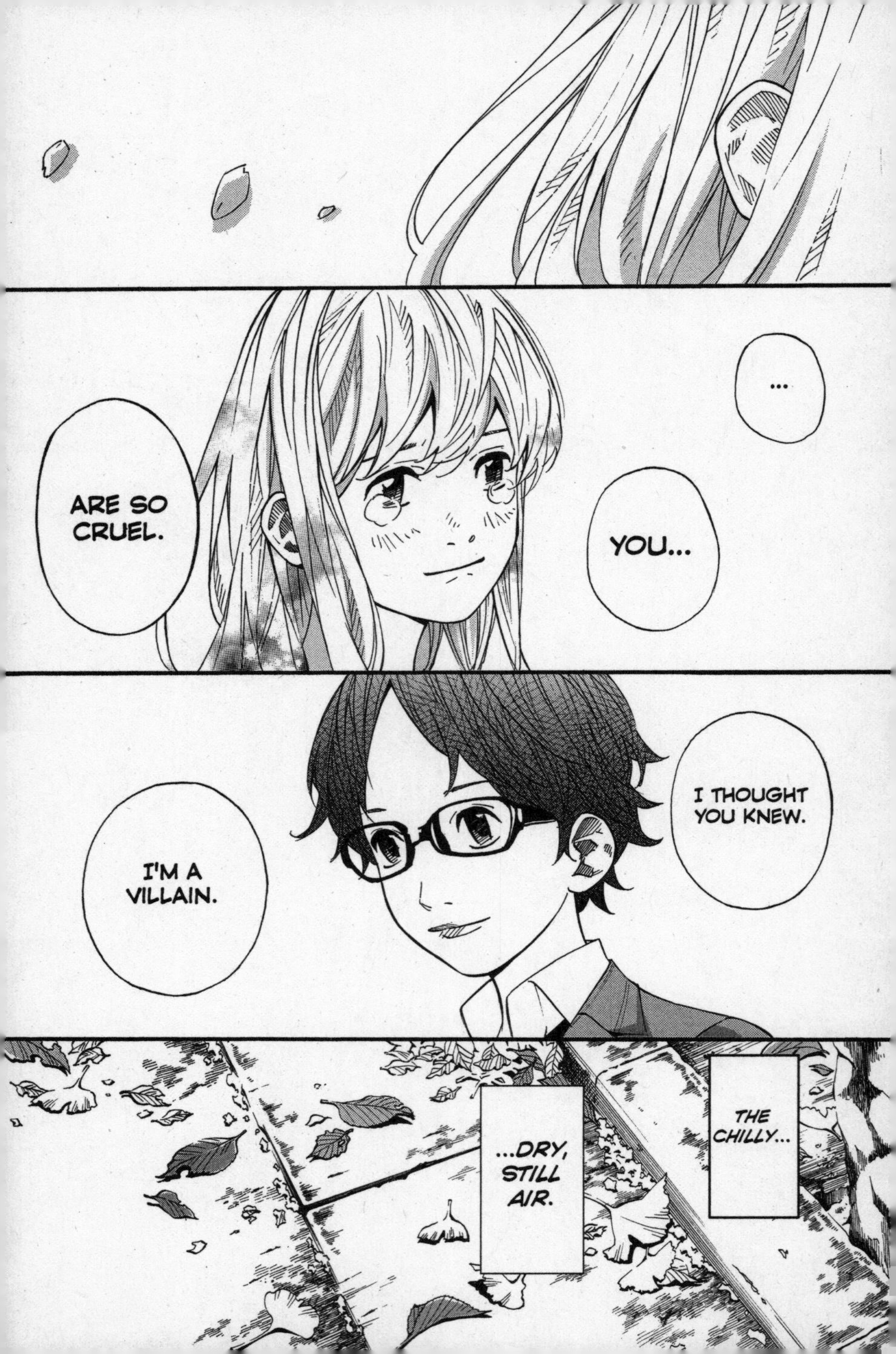
...
YOU...
ARE SO CRUEL.
I THOUGHT YOU KNEW.
I'M A VILLAIN.
THE CHILLY...
...DRY, STILL AIR.

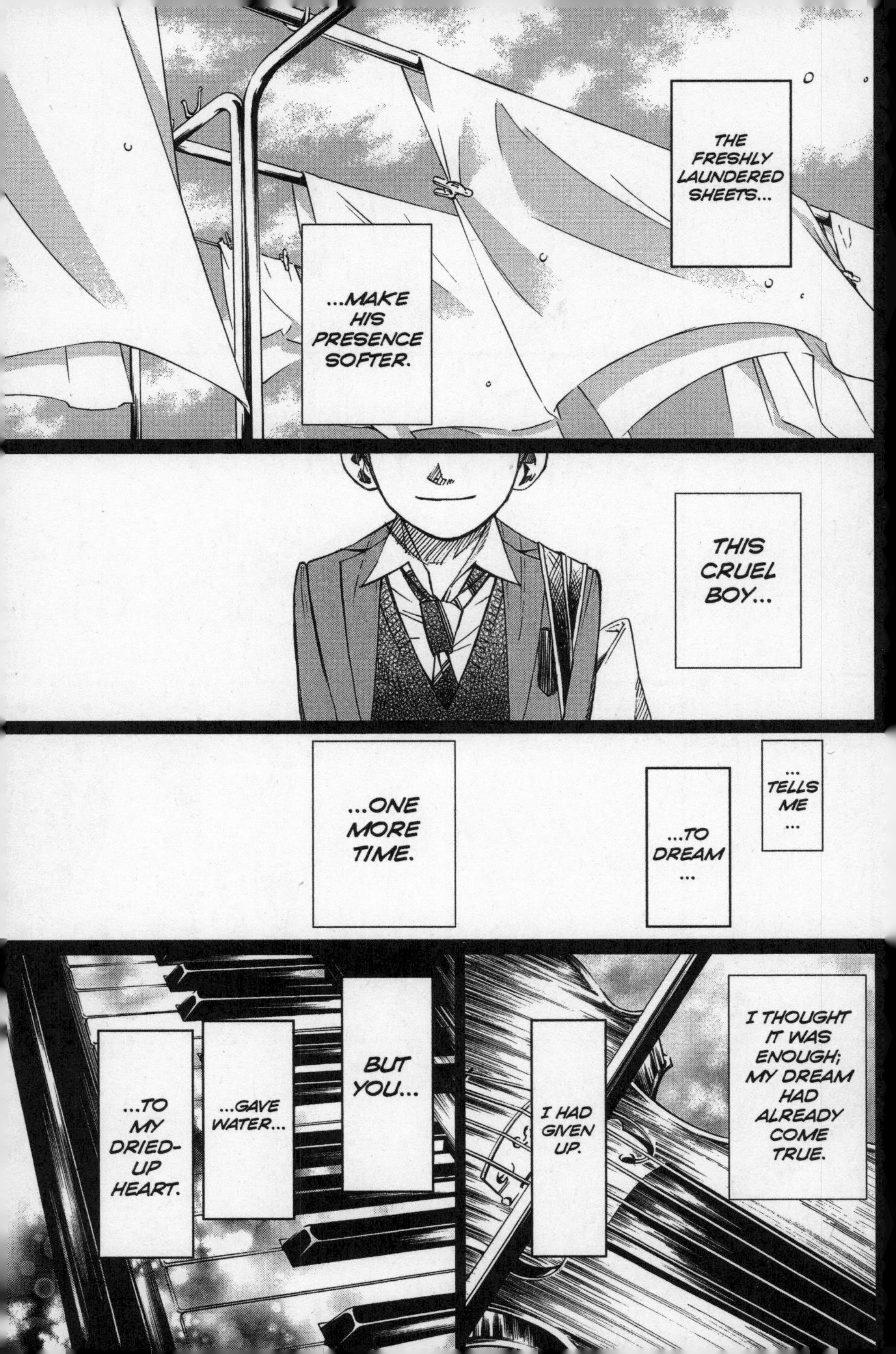
THE FRESHLY LAUNDERED SHEETS...
...MAKE HIS PRESENCE SOFTER.
THIS CRUEL BOY...
... TELLS ME ...
...TO DREAM ...
...ONE MORE TIME.
I THOUGHT IT WAS ENOUGH; MY DREAM HAD ALREADY COME TRUE.
I HAD GIVEN UP.
BUT YOU...
...GAVE WATER...
...TO MY DRIED-UP HEART.

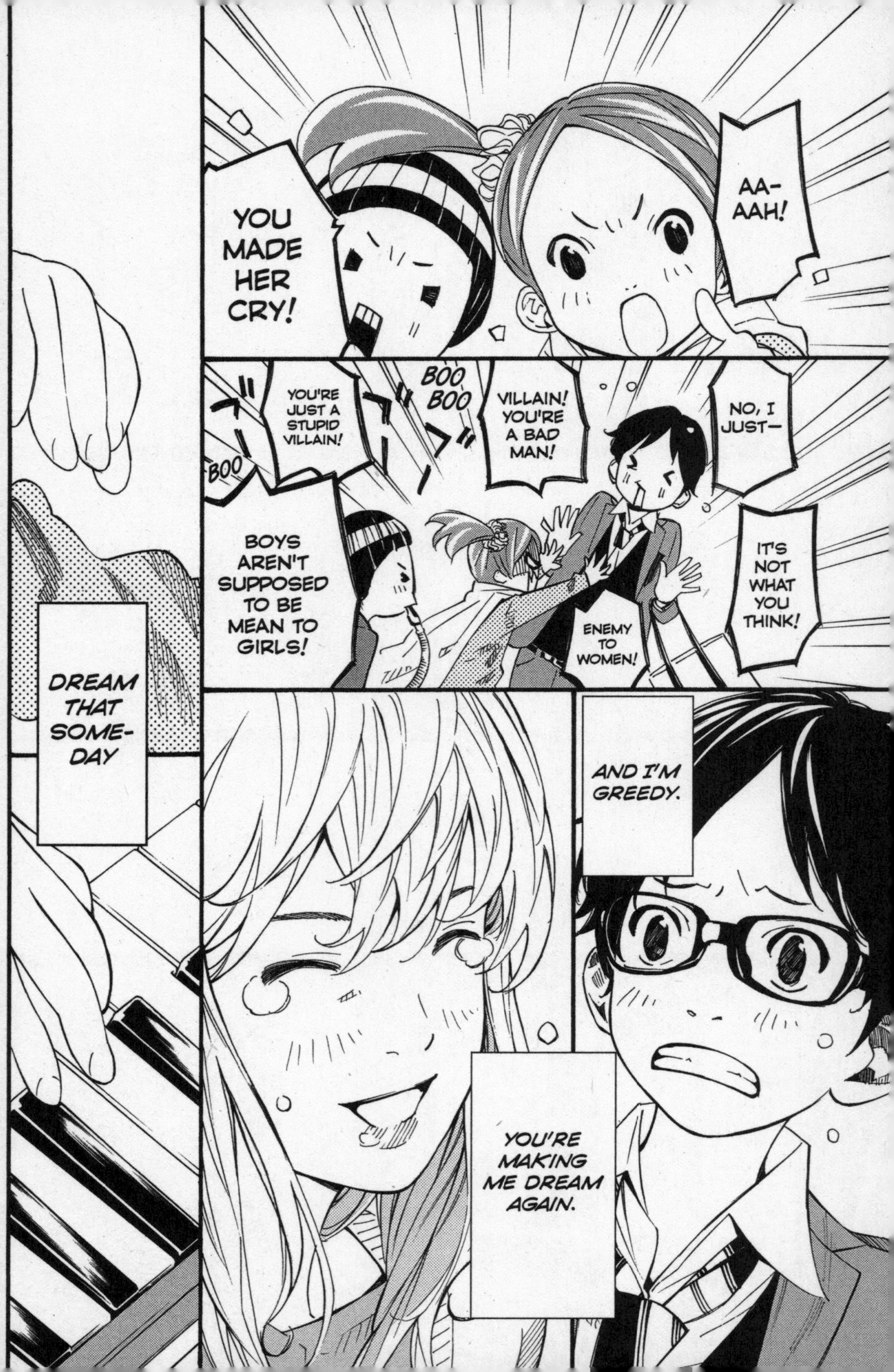
AA-AAH!
YOU MADE HER CRY!
NO, I JUST—
IT'S NOT WHAT YOU THINK!
VILLAIN! YOU'RE A BAD MAN!
ENEMY TO WOMEN!
BOO BOO
YOU'RE JUST A STUPID VILLAIN!
BOO
BOYS AREN'T SUPPOSED TO BE MEAN TO GIRLS!
AND I'M GREEDY.
YOU'RE MAKING ME DREAM AGAIN.
DREAM THAT SOME-DAY

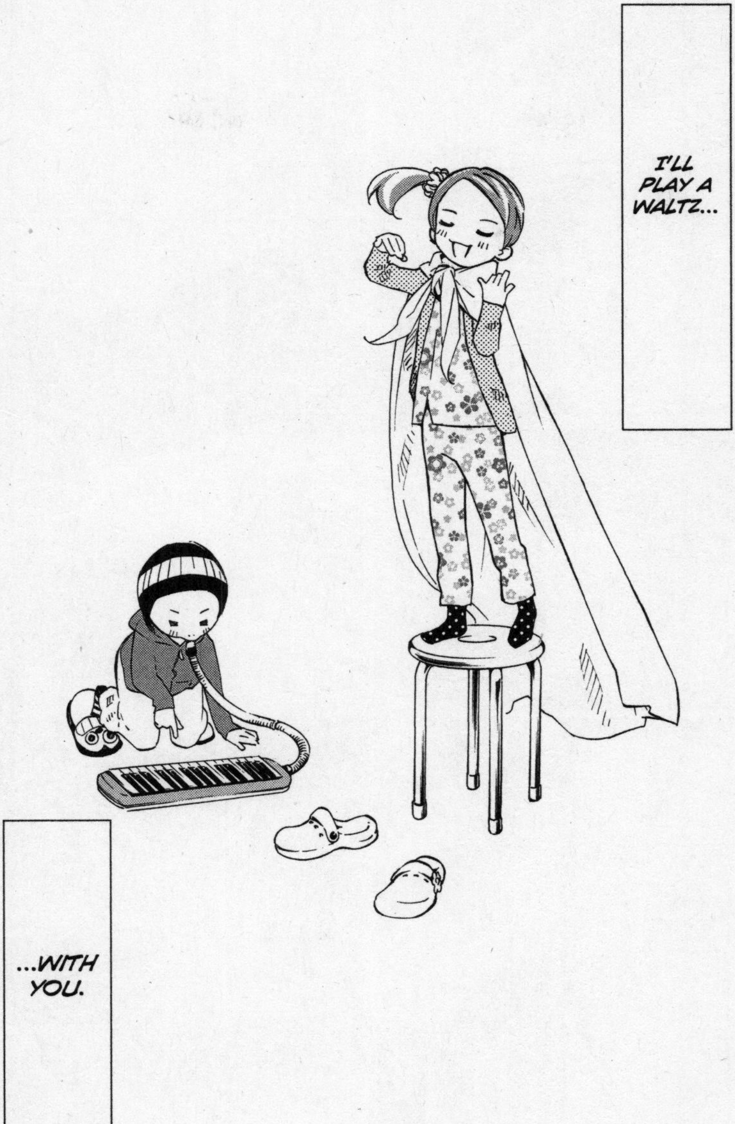
I'LL PLAY A WALTZ...
...WITH YOU.

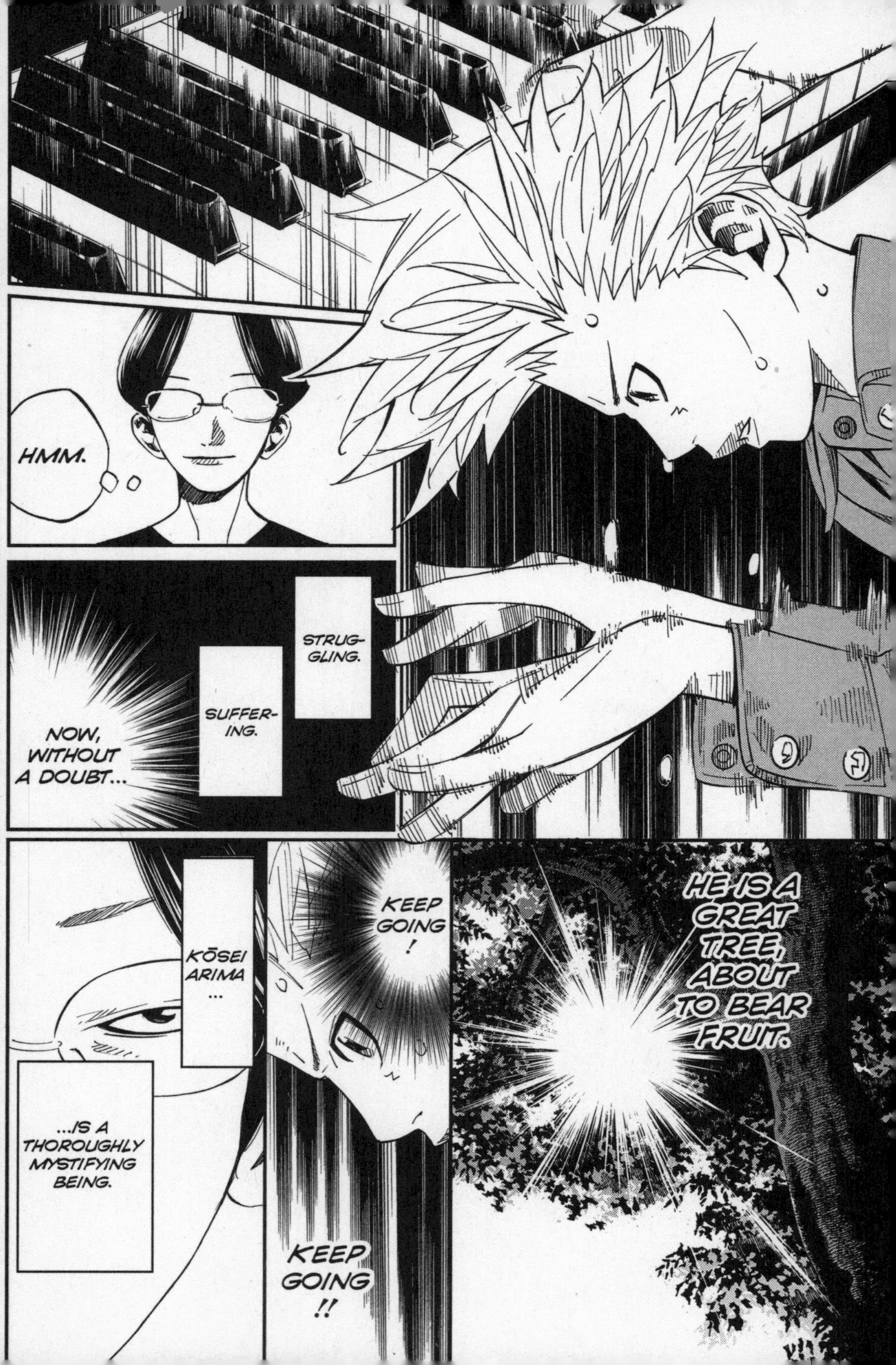
HMM.
STRUG-GLING.
SUFFER-ING.
NOW, WITHOUT A DOUBT...
HE IS A GREAT TREE, ABOUT TO BEAR FRUIT.
KEEP GOING!
KEEP GOING!!
KŌSEI ARIMA...
...IS A THOROUGHLY MYSTIFYING BEING.

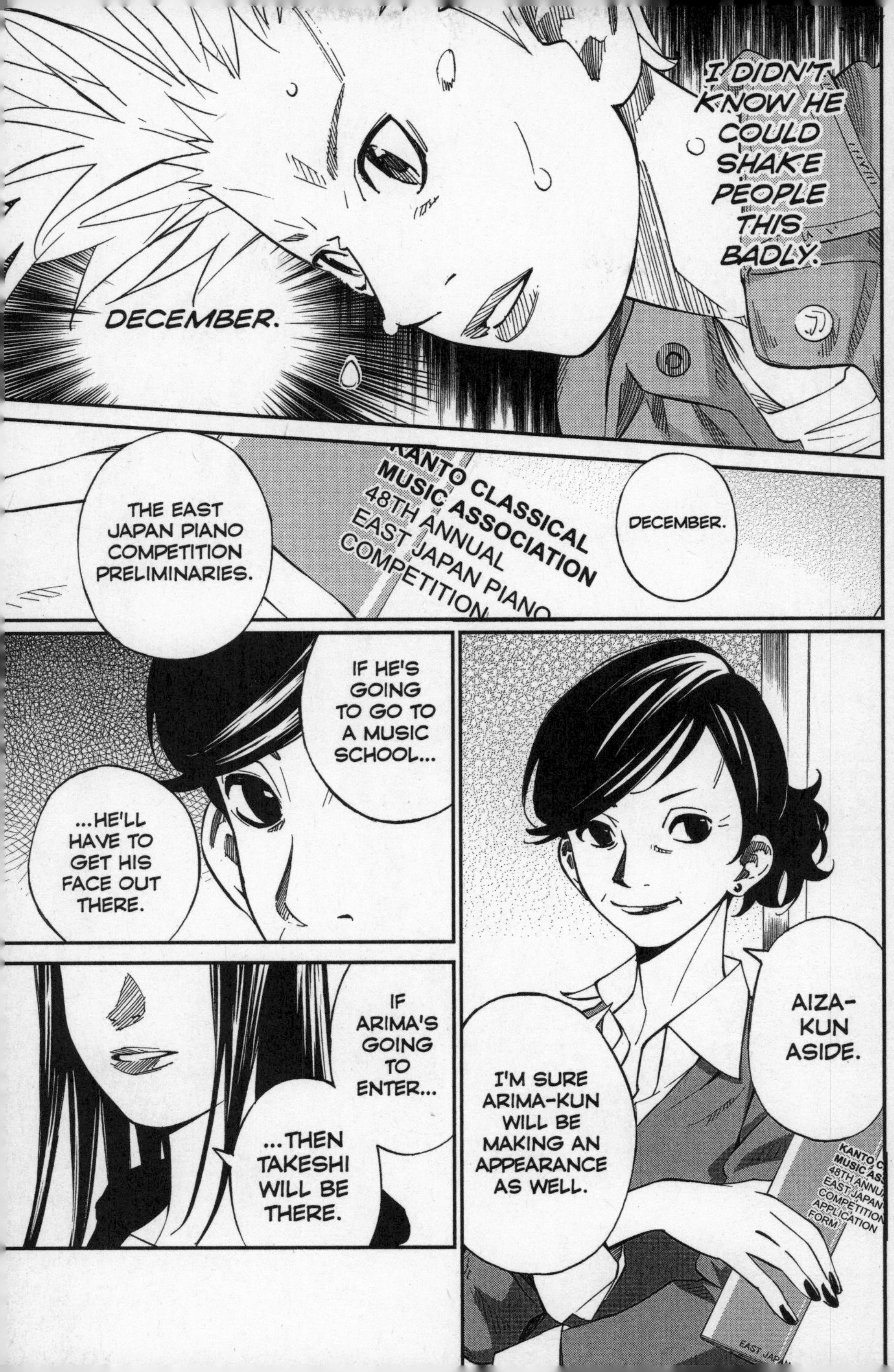
I DIDN'T KNOW HE COULD SHAKE PEOPLE THIS BADLY.
DECEMBER.
DECEMBER.
KANTO CLASSICAL MUSIC ASSOCIATION 48TH ANNUAL EAST JAPAN PIANO COMPETITION
THE EAST JAPAN PIANO COMPETITION PRELIMINARIES.
AIZA-KUN ASIDE.
I'M SURE ARIMA-KUN WILL BE MAKING AN APPEARANCE AS WELL.
APPLICATION FORM
IF HE'S GOING TO GO TO A MUSIC SCHOOL...
...HE'LL HAVE TO GET HIS FACE OUT THERE.
IF ARIMA'S GOING TO ENTER...
...THEN TAKESHI WILL BE THERE.

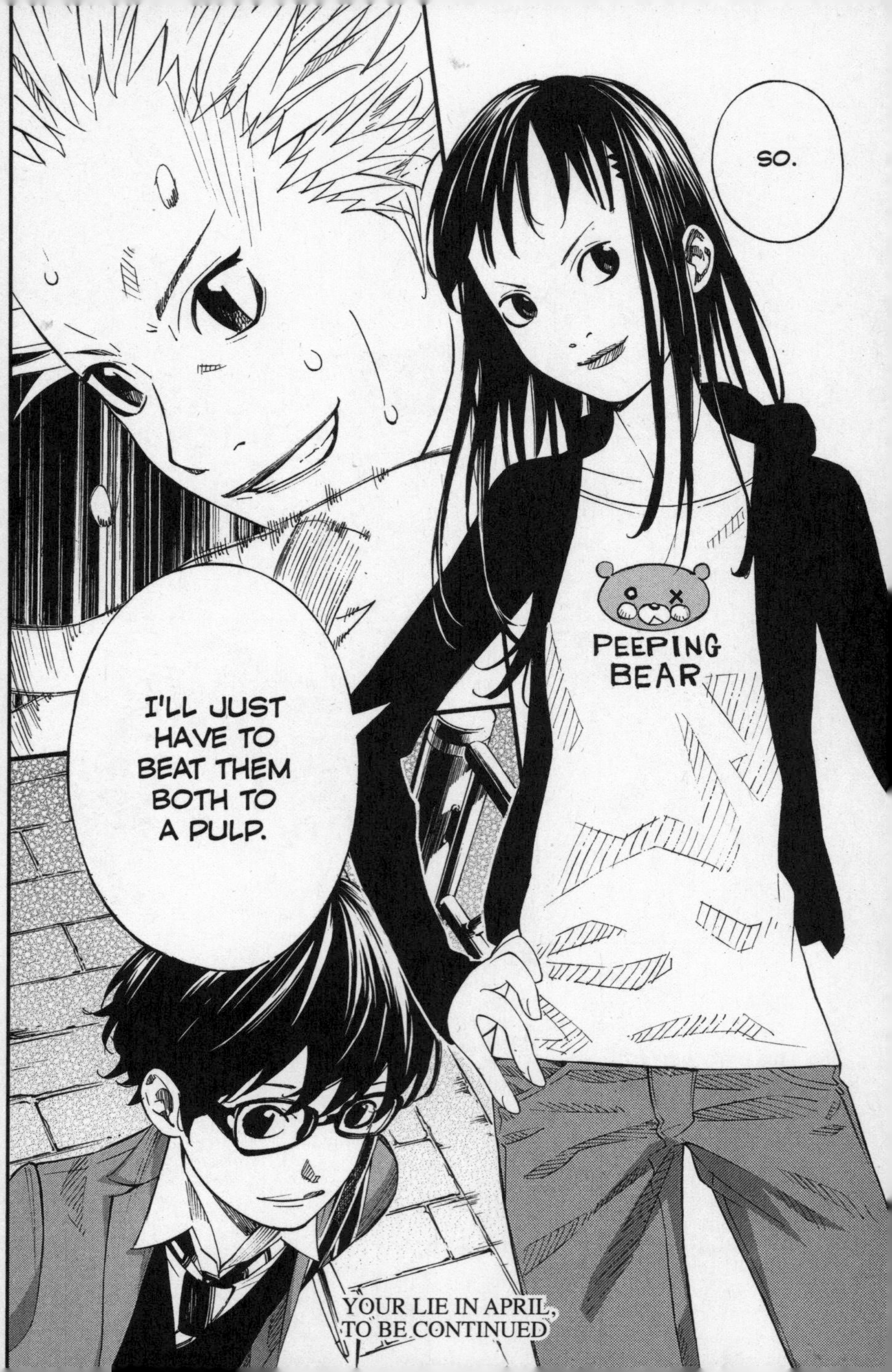
SO.
PEEPING BEAR
I'LL JUST HAVE TO BEAT THEM BOTH TO A PULP.
YOUR LIE IN APRIL, TO BE CONTINUED

Your Lie in April Featured Music

Sergei Rachmaninoff's arrangement of Pyotr Tchaikovsky's "Rose Adagio" and "Garland Waltz" from The Sleeping Beauty

A melody full of melancholic beauty and the echoes of a magnificent orchestra. *Swan Lake, Sleeping Beauty,* and *The Nutcracker*—the ballet scores of Tchaikovsky, the most well-known Russian composer—are known as "the Three Great Ballets" and have won persistent popularity as the standard ballet repertory. One tune from *The Sleeping Beauty* is also well-known from the Disney animated movie of the fairytale about a beautiful princess who is placed under a curse. Tchaikovsky's melody is used in the opening sequence of the film, and is loved by people the world over.

Another Russian composer, the brilliant pianist Rachmaninoff, arranged the Sleeping Beauty concert suite for piano. From its lowest note to its highest, the piano has 88 keys. While a human has only ten fingers, the expressive potential of the piano can expand when two pianists play with twenty fingers. To get closer to the grand expressive power of an orchestra, Rachmaninoff arranged the piece as a piano duet.

The two pianists try to match their breathing in order to match their timing. Their hands get closer and farther away from each other's, sometimes even crossing over during a few thrilling sections of the piece. The pianist playing the lower part is also responsible for pedaling, so sometimes he must move his feet with precision even when he isn't moving his hands. Because it is performed as an ensemble, each player must understand the other's part, and it is good manners to play with the score on the piano's music stand.

(Pianist Masanori Sugano, lecturer at Tokyo University of the Arts and Musashino Academia Musicae)

Watch them on YouTube. Search "Your Lie in April Sleeping Beauty Waltz" and "Your Lie In April Rose Adagio"

Special Thanks:

AKINORI ŌSAWA

MASANORI SUGANO

RIEKO IKEDA

KAORI YAMAZAKI

Your Lie in April 09 Translation Notes

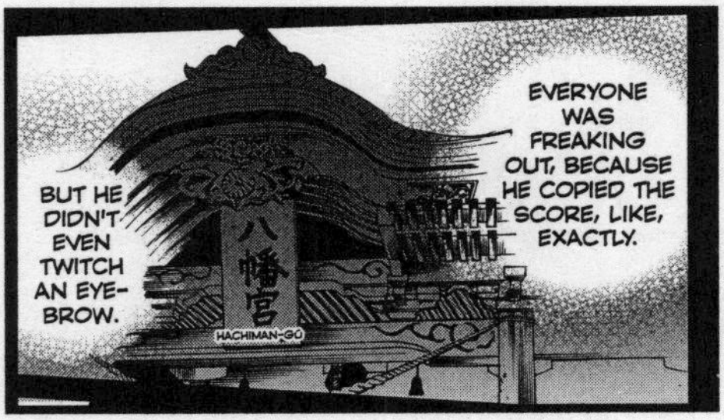
EVERYONE WAS FREAKING OUT, BECAUSE HE COPIED THE SCORE, LIKE, EXACTLY.
BUT HE DIDN'T EVEN TWITCH AN EYE-BROW.
八幡宮
HACHIMAN-GU

Hachiman-gū, page 5

A Hachiman-gū, or Hachiman shrine, is a shrine dedicated to Hachiman, who is one of the most popular deities in Japan. He is a patron of warriors, and the first Shinto deity to be adopted into Japanese Buddhism. There are shrines to him all over Japan.

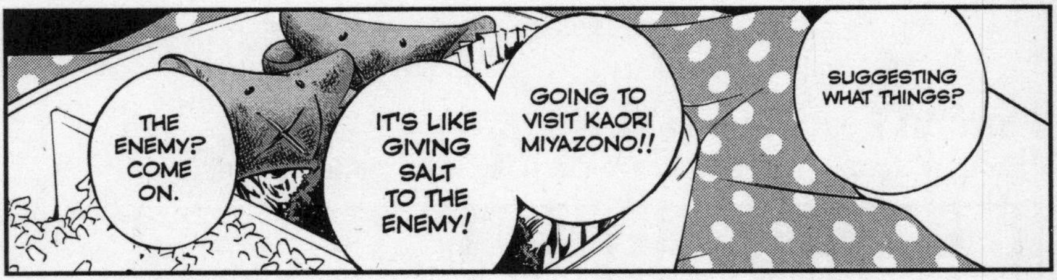
SUGGESTING WHAT THINGS?
GOING TO VISIT KAORI MIYAZONO!!
IT'S LIKE GIVING SALT TO THE ENEMY!
THE ENEMY? COME ON.

Salt to the enemy, page 12

This is an idiom that refers to helping one's enemy. It comes from a story about two rival lords from the Warring States Era of Japan's history, Uesugi Kenshin and Takeda Shingen. There was a time when other feudal lords refused to send rice and salt, which was very important in preserving food, to Shingen's province. Although Shingen was his bitter rival, Kenshin sent him salt anyway, saying that "wars are to be won with swords and spears, not with rice and salt."

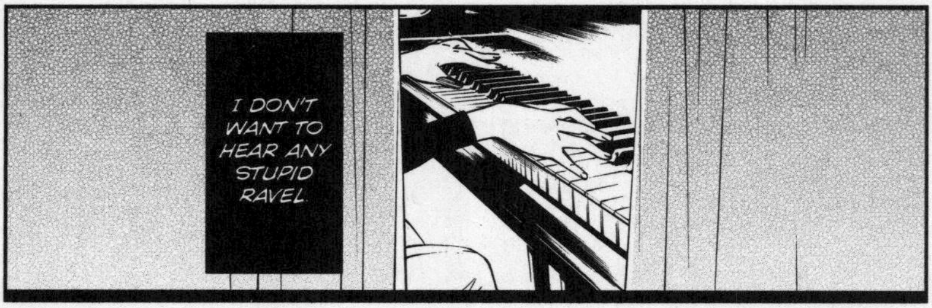
I DON'T WANT TO HEAR ANY STUPID RAVEL.

Don't want to hear Ravel, page 28

The reason Kōsei seems to have such an aversion to Ravel is that it reminds him of the book that Kaori has been quoting to him. In this book, the main character Ichigo Dōmei is in the music room when he meets the heroine, Naomi. He is playing Ravel's *Pavane for a Dead Princess*. The heroine of the book dies of cancer, and so when thoughts of this book are so fresh in Kōsei's mind, hearing Ravel reminds him that Kaori has been quoting Naomi, who has accepted her death, and makes him fear that Kaori has done the same.

Kurumi Festival, page 49

"Kurumi" means "walnut," hence the walnuts on the festival sign.

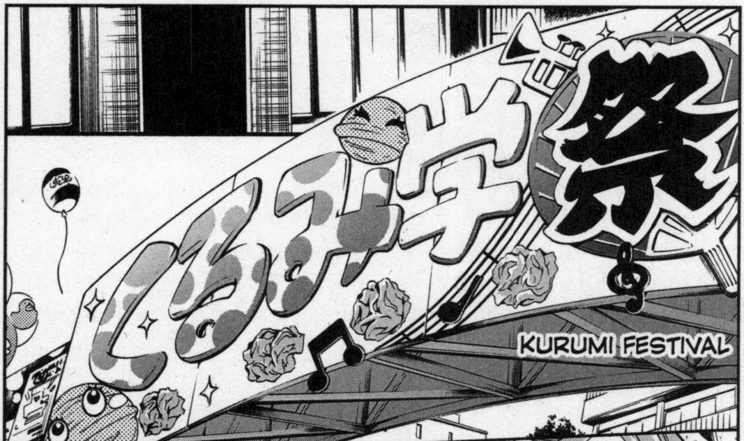
KURUMI FESTIVAL

STORY & CHARACTERS

The autumn of his 12th year, Kōsei Arima's mother died, causing him to lose the ability to play the piano. He lost his purpose and his days lost their color, continuing on in a drab monotone. But the spring he was 14… He met the exceptionally quirky violinist Kaori Miyazono.

As Kosei accompanied Kaori and played solo in the Maiho piano competition, color gradually returned to Kosei's days. But when Kaori failed to appear at the gala concert, he took the stage alone. As the boy played Love's Sorrow, he was filled with thoughts of the days his mother loved him, and the memories that still connected him to her.

Released from his mother's curse, Kosei began to walk the path of a pianist. When he mentioned going far away for high school, Tsubaki's heart was shaken up and she realized how she truly felt about him. Meanwhile, oblivious to Tsubaki's feelings, Kosei found himself at the mercy of Nagi Aizato, a girl who appeared out of nowhere and demanded piano instruction.

Kōsei Arima

An ex-piano prodigy who lost his ability to play when his mother died. After meeting Kaori, he returns to the path of music.

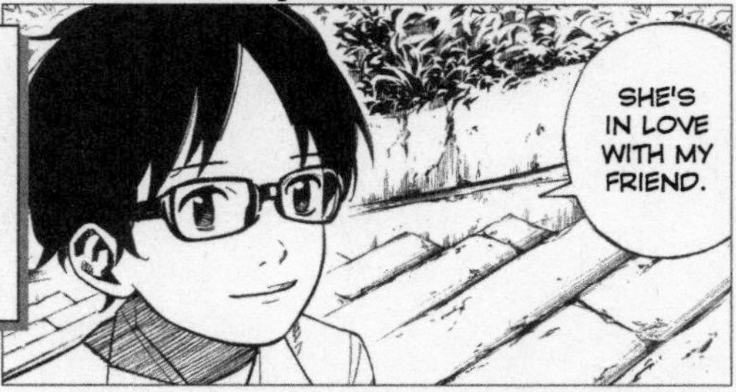
SHE'S IN LOVE WITH MY FRIEND.

Nagi Aizato

A girl who unexpectedly appeared before Hiroko Seto and Kōsei and demanded training. In reality, she is Nagi Aiza, the younger sister of Takeshi Aiza.

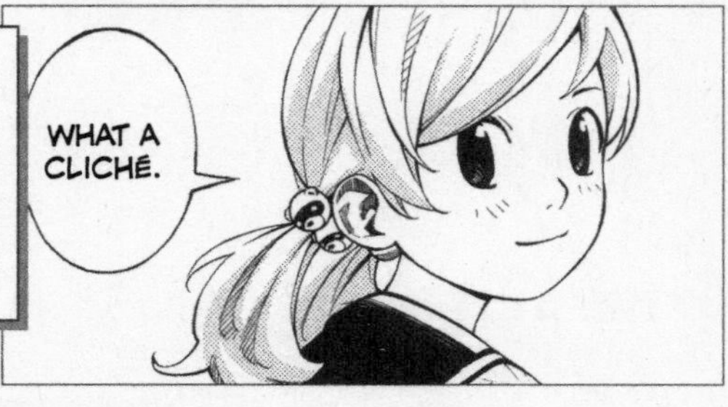
WHAT A CLICHÉ.

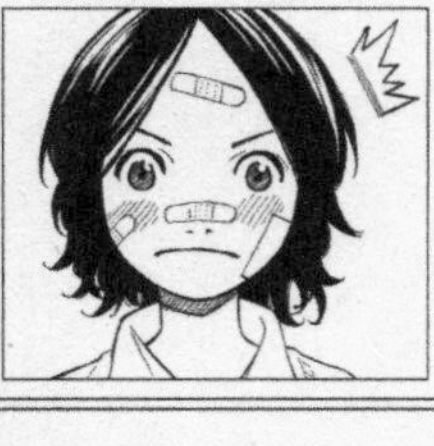

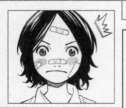

Tsubaki Sawabe

A longtime friend of Kōsei's. She realizes how she truly feels about Kōsei when she learns that the boy who has been with her all her life will be moving far away.

Your Lie in April

*I met the girl
under full-bloomed cherry blossoms,
and my fate has begun to change.*

9

Naoshi Arakawa